The Power Lovers

AN INTIMATE LOOK AT POLITICS AND MARRIAGE

MYRA MACPHERSON is a feature writer for the Washington *Post* and previously worked for the New York *Times*. Her interviews and profiles of leading political figures have been praised for their insight and professional quality. During the height of the Watergate investigations, her story on Charles Colson received particular notice. She has been called one of the best political profile writers in the country, and has written on a broad range of topics, including the arts and women's rights movement.

Myra
MacPherson

FOUNDED 1838

GPPS

THE POWER LOVERS

AN INTIMATE LOOK
AT POLITICS AND MARRIAGE

G. P. PUTNAM'S SONS, NEW YORK

COPYRIGHT © 1975 BY MYRA MACPHERSON

SBN: 399-11495-5

Library of Congress Catalog
Card Number: 75-18581

PRINTED IN THE UNITED STATES OF AMERICA

To my children, Michael and Leah,
and to my parents

Acknowledgments

I am grateful to many who gave time, talent, support and encouragement to me during the research and writing of this book. The Eagleton Institute of Politics at Rutgers University provided needed funds through a Policy Research Associate Award grant, as well as invaluable guidance from Alan Rosenthal, director of the Eagleton Institute, and Ida Schmertz, then director of development at the Center for the American Woman and Politics.

A long list of friends and colleagues got me through what often seemed an endless project—among them my editor at Putnam's, Bill Targ; Ann Buchwald, Denise Scali, Fred Dutton, Jules Witcover, Dick Cohen, Bill Greider, Roz Targ, Jean and Pete Hendry, Bill Mattson, Warren Weaver, Mark Shields, Bill Dickinson, Roger Wilkins, B. J. Phillips, Jamie and Charles Murphy, Lucille Larkin, John Saar, Madeline Amgott.

I am especially grateful to the Washington *Post*, not only for my sabbatical but for assistance readily given; among those who gave enthusiastic support are Kay Graham, Howard Simons, Ben Bradlee, Shelby Coffey, Tom Kendrick, Harry Rosenfeld, Post Librarian William Hifner and the library staff, and Donna Crouch and those who assisted her in typing the manuscript.

Above all, I am indebted to two people. Without the expert editing and guidance of Haynes Johnson this book would never have been completed. Nor would it have been without the support and understanding of another writer and close friend, Morrie Siegel.

Contents

8   Contents

Foreword

IN recent times, a handful of political families influenced the course of American politics. In a sad way, Joan Kennedy with her emotional problems and Teddy, Jr., with the cancer he bore bravely, did what no political opponent could have done—took Senator Edward M. Kennedy out of the 1976 Presidential race in the Fall of 1974. It left a scramble among the Democrats. Some rushed in, even as others dropped out. Senator Walter Mondale had made little headway in his recognition quest, but he found he didn't want the presidency enough for the grueling pursuit of it. He had not seen his family in a year. And at that same time Gerald Ford, a shaken man who came to an economic conference from his wife's side following her radical operation for breast cancer in 1974, looked unlike a man who would run for President. His wife's recovery brought about his announcement to run a few months later. Happy Rockefeller insisted that her husband continue his confirmation hearings for the vice presidency during her second operation for breast cancer.

These, of course, are the more prominent political families, whose private decisions have obvious public meaning. And although some political families do profess to like the life, no one knows for sure how many others wish for another life. Or, more important, how many dedicated people never entered politics in the first place because of family considerations. A record number of Congressmen quit in 1974. Some Republicans knew they were doomed by Watergate and used their private lives as an excuse. Still, a large percentage said they were quitting to be with their families more. Most seemed weary of the legislative grind in Congress, where members scurry to answer an average of four roll calls a day when the House is in session.

I decided to examine political families because I was intrigued, as a reporter, with those families I saw appearing summarily frozen on platform after campaign platform—in victory or defeat. I wondered if it was possible to get behind the masks and find the effect of politics on their private lives. I interviewed more than 200 people—politicians, spouses, children, aides, journalists, political scientists and analysts, pollsters, psychologists and psychiatrists.

There is a 1970's phenomenon: the intense interaction between the media and a politician's public—and ultimately, his private—life. The attitude of the family toward the press as a force for discontent and the exploitation on both sides have more than surface bearing on their lives. This book also looks at this.

What politics does to a politician's marriage and family and how his private life can effect his public actions have been of little importance to the "serious" reporters in Washington, where issues and amorphous political intrigue were regarded as the only valid subjects. In print that is. But gossip is one of the great byproducts of Washington, and inside stories forever abound: which politician is drinking too much or which presidential hopeful didn't have a chance because of an alcoholic wife; how perfectly awful a candidate was to his wife or what less-than-bright Senator was being pushed by his ambitious wife; who engaged in what various romantic liaisons. These topics cropped up as often at dinner parties as any current political crisis. But for years the myth of the lockstepping political family was preserved by the woman's pages. At the risk of being called the Rona Barrett of Washington, every thoughtful journalist still struggles with whether perhaps it is more just to keep the covers on—and wait for a biographer or psycho-social historian some 20 or 200 years after a politician's death to reveal what he was "really" like. But there has been a shift in attitude of the male-dominated press in this area. It could shape the private members of a political family.

Many question the ability and qualifications of the press to wander into the sociological probing of public lives.

But people, such as James David Barber, professor of political science at Duke University, argue that to avoid another Nixon, it is imperative to examine character. "We need data on the overt habits of the man, his continuously expressed beliefs, his visible pattern of character response. . . . The fact that Mr. Ford played football tells us virtually nothing; discovering what that meant to him might cast helpful light on his beliefs about sportsmanship in politics. The task is thus biographical. If that means journalists must make judgments about human responses—even psychological judgments—so be it. For the best are and long have been in that business." To make sense of Presidents, Barber said, we must look past the events of the day to the "experience of the life, and try to gauge the pattern and rhythm of it."

To what degree this means examining, by extension, the politician's interaction with his family is an area with which the press will have to wrestle.

Just where the family and wife should come into play is difficult. In order to present a new post-Watergate "morality" image, some politicians will probably more than ever "use" the family to corroborate that image. Is the press to go along with this act?

How much privacy can a politician reasonably expect to maintain for himself and his family? If, as public men have often said, they have no private lives, then where does the curtain reasonably come down? Should we have different regulations for different types of political wives? Should a wife who acts as a lieutenant or auxiliary politician for her husband and has untold private influence in his decision making be as liable to criticism as the officeholder? Can a wife and family of a political leader skip back and forth between a public figure one day and a private citizen the next? The instinct of many good-thinking people, including those in the press, is that we should allow as much privacy as possible and that the emotional or physical illnesses or divorce or any such conditions should remain in the private world of the family. However, as I have pointed out, these private situations can significantly influence politics, and therefore no absolute rule can be made.

The right of privacy is often poorly defined, and it is sometimes in conflict with the right of the public to know. But the *need* for privacy is a social and biological factor; it is a balance needed for personal survival. In public office that balance is easily tipped.

Recently some progress has been made regarding analysis of the political family. As political divorces escalated and some families spoke more candidly about their problems, there has been a growing trend, at least superficially, to look at the grueling life of the political family, to try to gauge the effect of politics on their lives. At the end of such examination, no one seemed further along in suggesting how the conditions surrounding that consuming quest for public office and power might somehow be altered to create a more rewarding family life.

One beginning is to examine in detail political families and to hear what they have to say. I am grateful for the countless public people who cooperated in this book. I hope it will be of some value in presenting political people as reality and lead to a better understanding of their lives. Through an understanding of the conflict between their public and private lives and confrontation of the problem, perhaps our public priorities and the private needs of political families might be more satisfactorily united in the future.

Part I

Till Power Do Us Part

1

"I Don't Think Much About Washington, It's Just Where You Have to Be"

NEARLY everyone in official Washington has a small town in his past.

The nation's capital was surely the place to realize those dreams of glory and power that propelled one out of Ocilla, Georgia; Okmulgee, Oklahoma; Sylacauga, Alabama; Grand Rapids, Michigan; Tuscaloosa, Alabama; Paris, Tennessee; Carbon County, Utah; Ida Grove, Iowa.

"I don't think much about Washington," a politician once told me, "it's just where you have to be."

The trouble is many people have never realized that Washington is also a place in which you change. If you're a politician, it takes a lot of effort to change for the better. The odds are against it.

In a city where public title and power speak, a Supreme Court Justice could pick his teeth in public and still be lionized because he's a Supreme Court Justice, it was once noted. Mark Twain wrote of the low-life political parvenus who populated Washington in his day. It is ever thus. Money and old family name count for little, and even the lowliest politician can convince himself that in Washington, while he may not have power and fame today, it can be his tomorrow.

Politicians, those people who have power or lust after it, are among the last in modern society who live with their courts around them. True, if the politician is new or unimportant, his kingdom may be only a niche in one of those House of Representatives marble mausoleums where he surrounds himself with a mimeograph machine, a secretary and aide, and all those pictures of himself with as many important people as he can collect. Still, it beats city hall back home, he tells himself.

And yet politicians who have been in Washington long enough will, in rare moments of solitude, sometimes wonder if it's worth it all. Senator Frank Church says that after eighteen years there is a loneliness about living in Washington. Hubert Humphrey nearly cried himself to sleep when he first came

15

here, until Russell Long took him in tow. In the evening hours they walked up and down a highway near their home, with Long telling Humphrey he had to get to know all those influential Southern Senators who thought of Hubert as just a pop-off kid with queer populist notions. So Humphrey sat at their exclusive table in the Senators' dining room and fawned a little, and they got to like him in spite of his ideological bent. Only as a member of the establishment did he find himself really liking Washington.

For the mavericks who choose not to play the establishment game it is a lonelier route. One Senator, a deviant in that crowd, who shows rare introspection, called a former Senator one day and said, "Hell, I am so goddamn depressed, you gotta come down." So they went out drinking and talked about the hollowness that comes in the pit of your stomach after you've done all the driving to get there and find it doesn't always match the dream.

Fred Harris, an ex-Senator by the time he was forty, said, "If I'm reincarnated I'd like to come back as Jim Abourezk [Senator from South Dakota]. There I was, up there on that Hill, kissin' ass for five years, and the sixth year I realized it didn't make a goddamn bit of difference. All you do is become a member of the establishment—a group of old farts—and you *still* don't get all that much accomplished. Abourezk figured that out the first two weeks he was up there."

Some are willing to take the sprints of friendships or acquaintances that pass for friendships, the fleeting contacts that militate against intimacy, even though it must dawn on them that they just go with the office. Others say that their best friends are back home. Still others have put "back home" behind them forever.

Most inhabitants of political Washington who ever stopped for an instant's reflection would express ambivalence about living in the transient world where it hardly pays to get deeply involved with people. There is a numbing coldness about this town—no matter the surface warmth and excitement. There's the knowledge that you may not be liked just for yourself. Or even hated just for yourself. One Senator said, "It's a town of phonies who like you for all the wrong reasons." Nicholas Johnson, a former Federal Communications Commissioner who ran unsuccessfully for Congress from Iowa in 1974, said, "You know you're being invited somewhere only because of your title, not because of you, so you fight your own insecurities. And your wife knows she's being invited only because she's an appendage to that title." (The Johnsons are now divorced.)

One ex-Senator said there was no going home again for him. "Shit, one thing I don't miss is church every Sunday. When I was a lawyer back there—and because I was thinking about running for office and having to be the pillar of the community and all—I *had* to go to church. If I didn't, someone would check up on me."

One of Capitol Hill's important aides, who has worked for two famous Senators, one maverick Senator, and a Congresswoman, said, "Even the best ones get a little swept up by the emoluments. As for their private lives, most are disasters."

I might add that the same can be said of many of the aides and journalists who are caught up in the political world. Most of those I know are separated or divorced or into another marriage. Washington can be a viper town; the atmosphere makes it so easy to believe that the events of today and the sense of adventure in being part of them are more important than the problems, the caring, and the time for what is at home.

Some people object to my concentration on the family wreckage that is caused by the fantasy, pursuit, illusion—and sometimes the *actual* possession—of power that compels politicians to neglect their families.

One former Congressman's wife said the common denominator was not politics but success; the success-oriented man is geared to achieve his goal at any cost. If a woman wants "togetherness," she ought to marry a nine-to-five man who will never move beyond GS-9, wrote Mrs. Andy Biemiller, whose husband was a member of Congress for many years and is now the chief lobbyist for the AFL-CIO.

I once wrote that I found politicians feared intimacy, preferred the roar of the crowd to one-to-one relationships, were unable to cope with the personal demands of a family, and used politics as a noble escape hatch. The wife of a psychiatrist sent me a poignant letter saying it was the same with psychiatrists: "I don't know of one single male counselor who hasn't left his family and in very sad circumstances. They seem to be able to feel pain for other families which they cannot face in their own," she wrote. "There seems to be a certain fear of the intimacy you mention, and maybe for this reason they go into counseling because they can lose themselves in someone else's problems and not have to face their own."

The American struggle for success has stamped its sorrows on many families, but politics is the quintessence of that struggle. In many cases public office and esteem are gained through enormous sacrifice and deprivation—of one's family and one's humanity. For politicians and their families there is an intensifying of all the problems that overachievers face in this country.

And their problems are compounded by the rosy portrayal of political life. That there was a complex real life, with all its sorrows and joys and human frailties, behind that public mask of the "happy political couple" was for years hardly ever questioned. And yet, politicians and their families have lived with incredible pain and sorrow. I have interviewed politicians and their families who have known violent deaths and suicides and emotionally disturbed children and alcoholic spouses and infidelity and financial defeats and private failures. But coping is of the essence; the public face must always be smooth, and if it shows concern, it must be for others.

The strain of upholding the myth at times becomes unbearable. For some, marriages and families are there in name only. There are weeks and hours and days of loneliness and apartness—ended only for the "togetherness" of the campaign photo. There have been incredible masquerades. One ex-wife of a prominent politician said they had not made love in ten years but kept the marriage together for his image. Only now are some political couples beginning to rebel against this unreal and stressful system.

It is heartening that some of those who have spoken out have managed to find fulfilling private lives even given the public stress and strain; perhaps they can afford to be more open and less defensive than those who still keep the pretense but cannot admit, even to themselves, that it is not a happy life.

The famous, recognized everywhere, struggle for personal identity and a glimmer of a normal life for themselves and their children, despite the abnormal, constant following of Secret Service agents, the press, public worshipers and vilifiers. The seering publicness of such a political life allows for no private illness and no private recuperation. Betty Ford, Joan Kennedy,

Margaret Trudeau, and Happy Rockefeller found this true in 1974. Bulletins relayed the details of Mrs. Ford's operation and her chances for recovery. She was photographed throwing a football with her right arm, to prove that her recuperation from a radical mastectomy was more than satisfactory. There was no shred of privacy about a very personal sorrow, but Mrs. Ford, long used to a public life, said she minded none of it because her experience might aid other women in early detection of breast cancer.

There are, of course, pluses to a life of political fame: the place in history, the attention, the irreplaceable and unique experiences. Lady Bird Johnson said of her White House years, "I knew those days were measured and were going right through the hourglass, and I wanted to live it up. Anybody who doesn't enjoy living in the White House is unfeeling. It's great!" She also said, however, "A politician ought to be born a foundling and remain a bachelor—have as few pressing personal requirements as possible."

Countless more typical political families live relatively obscure lives and put up with the emotional and physical stresses of prolonged and frequent absences without the anesthetizing whirl of glamor or the cushion of money. When she returned to her district, one such congressional wife was eagerly asked how often she went to the White House. She watched her questioner's face fall as she said she had never been there and then recounted her activities in suburbia—Girl-Scout-cookie, bake-sale mother and actress in church plays. These women scrub their own floors because they cannot afford help. Private money goes into the required obligations their political husbands feel important—membership in the Elks or Kiwanis or Rotarians or other clubs back home, presents or at least graduation cards for children of constituents, lunches for visiting constituents, extra trips back home over and above the government allowance. During election year, these women pile the children into cars and drive across country to save the cost of flying.

While there is much to loathe about politics, many of these women concede that the lives that would otherwise have been theirs, as the wives of small-town lawyers or hardware store owners, are less appealing than even the most peripheral place in Washington. One such wife put her children to work addressing seven thousand Christmas cards that adorned constituents' mantels one year. The next year her husband was voted out of office. With amazing good cheer she accepted this as part of the political process, even though it meant uprooting their seven children again.

There are major differences that magnify the problems of political families and set politicians farther apart from those who pursue success in other fields: (1) the psyches and motivations of men who not only willingly but compulsively seek public office, a way of life that is often ridiculed and fraught with insecurity, a profession where defeat and victory are sudden and absolute and public, depending on the roulette wheel of election night and larger forces and trends beyond control; (2) the star syndrome of the political world; (3) the overriding and constant demands of constituents—or at least what politicians perceive to be such demands; (4) the anti-wife, in particular, and anti-female, in general, tone of politics—as women running for office find out when seeking votes and campaign funds; (5) the additional political duties of the wife; (6) the traditional expectations and myths of the public regarding politicians and the American Political Family; (7) the fact that politics claims almost all the evenings and weekends and energy of those who pursue it, leaving little for a family except shameless exploitation.

It is important to examine the kind of men who vie for elected public office. The curbstone Freuds who populate Washington expound theories. There are some psychoanalytical studies about the mind of the politician, and psychohistorical analyses of prominent political figures. Unfortunately there are few studies on the politician's role and its interaction with his private life.

It is as impossible to name one simple reason that motivates politicians as it is to ascribe the same characteristics to all politicians. There are countless variables. Politicians are no more monolithic or less paradoxical than the rest of society. The study of human beings is by nature contradictory, conflicting, and untidy. However, there are some patterns. The most popular concept is that these men need constant nourishment and reinforcement from without; that they are overcompensating for deep-rooted insecurities; that they seek constant external approval; that they translate the roar of the crowd and votes into "love."

For many this is, indeed, true. No less a bully than Congressman Wayne Hays of Ohio, who is feared for his vitriol and his meanness, told me that he was "overcompensating" when he went into politics. He turned into the Wizard of Oz, just a little man hiding behind a curtain, when he said, "I always felt inadequate. I had an inferiority complex and I stammered and I was shy. As a kid I used to walk across the street to avoid having to say hello to people I knew."

The psyches of some politicians are so damaged that they are egotistical beyond belief, preoccupied and absorbed with themselves in an attempt to prove that their inner fears can be eclipsed by public acclaim and achievement. The very nature of the role breeds narcissism. Just like an actor, the politician is selling only one product: himself. "How many votes can I get?" "What can I get in the press to make me look good?" "How am I going to look best in this speech?"

There is a story that Senator Walter F. Mondale, in an attempt to be a "regular guy" with his staff, wandered through the office to talk to them. Talking to one secretary, and feeling awkward at it, he absentmindedly shuffled through some letters in the out basket. He saw one that was in reply to a constituent's request of six weeks before. He stared at the date, realized how long it was in reply, and yelled, "Doesn't anyone here care about Fritz Mondale?"

"It is a terrible burden, the constant need of assurance from outside," the actor James Cagney once said. "I see it in other people, this screaming need for approbation. You see it in politicians, constantly pushing, pushing, pushing. 'Please, please like me.' And this is one helluva burden."

Harold Lasswell writes in *Psychopathology and Politics* about one particular category of politician, the "political agitator." "The essential mark of the agitator is the high value he places on the emotional response of the public. The agitator is willing to subordinate personal considerations to the superior claims of principle. Children may suffer while father and mother battle for the 'cause.' . . . Ever on the alert for the pernicious intrusions of private interest from public affairs, the agitator sees 'unworthy' motives where others see the just claims of friendship. Believing in direct, emotional responses from the public, the agitator trusts in mass appeals and general principles. Agitators are, as a class, strongly narcissistic types. Narcissism is encouraged by obstacles in the early love relationships, or by over-indulgence and admiration in the family circle. Sexual objects like the self are preferred." There is a "yearning for emotional response," which is "displaced upon generalized objects. High value is placed on arousing emotional responses from the community at large." Lasswell continues that the narcissistic reactions prevent the developing individual from entering into full and warm emotional relationships during puberty, and sexual adjustments show varying degrees of rigidity or impotence and other forms of maladjustment.

Will Rogers once commented about politicians and issues, "It's like a baby with a hammer. You hope you can get it away before he'll do too much damage. Politicians are just little boys who never growed up anyway."

Or, put even more succinctly by Nadine Eckhardt, wife of Texas Representative Robert Eckhardt, "Most politicians are just little men who couldn't get it up in high school. They all manifest some form of being emotional cripples."

Fawn Brodie, who studied Thomas Jefferson's private life, said, "A passion for politics stems usually from an insatiable need, either for power or for friendship and adulation or a combination of both." She notes that historian James Flexner propounded that George Washington had a similar passion, and "sought power not for its own sake but in order to earn love and praise."

It is this *quest* for power that sets them apart from other achievement-oriented people. One man who has been a top aide in national presidential campaigns and considered running for office himself, said, "Politics has always been the lure of the fellow with what I call an 'extra gland.' Many don't know it, but they're still looking for fulfillment long after they succeed in other ways. They get the big house, the fine law practice, chairman of this and that, prominent in the community, and it's still not enough. So they run for office."

Politicians can deceive, not only the country, but themselves, about what they need to do and what they can use that power for: "What I need to do is get into office by hook or crook, then become the greatest Senator or President this country has ever had," can be a convenient excuse. I am sure that many politicians *start out* with altruistic goals, but the ratio of personal aggrandizement and altruism varies enormously. It could be 90–10 in one politician, and just the opposite in another. Some may be 50–50 mix. And even altruism can be blurred by the complexity of what triggers that desire to help others. The messianic sense of omnipotence, for example. Not unlike the surgeon who plays God with people's bodies, politicians also have the desire to play God with people's lives. It takes supreme gall to stand up and tell people, "Vote for me, I'm the best man for the job," and yet a few possess genuine humbleness in equal proportion.

There is a Senator who walks those cool halls of marble on Capitol Hill, lonely and disillusioned. He remembers a dream he used to have. It would repeat itself in those nights before he was ever in office. In his dream he would fly, his arms out, above the world, high up, like some great and powerful eagle. When he got elected to office, the dream stopped. He interprets the dream as his own fantasy search for power, his need to soar above everyone else—even as he tried to tell himself that the *only* reason he was entering politics was to do good, to help. Not only has that dream stopped, so has the other dream—for in this man they were truly intertwined—the hunger for power and the hope he could effect enough change to help "the little man" and the abused masses. "Hell, if you've got a good idea, it gets stolen by others around here with seniority and changed or maybe held back by those who oppose it. And if it's a good idea—and the time is not right—they're perfectly willing to let you keep it. And then make sure it never goes anywhere."

He sat on the grass, shoes off, with a beer, on a warm day in the summer of 1974 and said his staff and friends try to buck him up about running for office again on the grounds that if nothing else, he's plugging the hole, preventing some business-oriented junior-grade Nixon from taking his place. But he wonders if it's worth it, particularly the time away from his wife and kids. We talked of the politicians who left town every Thursday, not to return until Monday, campaigning every weekend of the year. "What in hell do they do it for? They're fools." Then he looked sad. He was no stranger to it himself. "I remember during my campaign. My teenage son came out with me one weekend. Well, there was an aide on the plane; and then in the hotel, there was some local party guy and then this reporter, and then, uh, another aide and the telephone ringing off the wall, and well, my son and I never did get a chance to talk. . . ."

The compromisers on Capitol Hill feel that men like former Senator Harold Hughes, who quit a long political career to be a professional preacher, were naïve and downright kooky about expending time reflecting on what it all means. In the Senate club of one hundred they are, after all, convinced daily of their importance by scurrying staffs and schedules that never give them time to stop to ponder who they really are.

Which brings us to the "escape hatch" theory of politics. Many observers and some politicians who've been at the game a long time feel that much of their absence from home is make-work subterfuge. "I have seen more politicians go into politics as a means of escape. They can't handle their own private problems," said one political consultant. A politician can fill his hours with a dazzling array of duties, all under the guise of being terribly important, either to the country or to the goal of keeping himself in office.

One may ask, "Is that so different from the corporate executive who is gone all the time? If his wife complains, *he* has a noble excuse—'I am doing this all for you.'" I think there is an important distinction. In that case the wife can say, "I've had enough of all this goodness on your part for me and the family. What I want is you home." If the executive still disappears from her life, his wife can often live a quite elegant separate life of her own, anonymous and unrecognized. The wife of a politician, however, can appear not only petty, but downright unpatriotic if she complains about a husband who is under the lofty illusion that he is saving the country. It is more like the dilemma faced by wives of men who immerse themselves in such professions as the ministry, science, or medicine; it is tough to ask for equal time with noble endeavors as your competition.

Politicians themselves note a distinction between the amount of time they give to politics compared to other endeavors. Politicians I interviewed who were previously in other professions, or those no longer in politics and now in other professions, *universally* say that—while there is always a full-speed-ahead drive to *achieve*—they can and do tamp down their time away from home more easily in professions other than politics.

Within political men is a strong gambling instinct that draws admiration, if not from the family that must struggle with an insecure livelihood based on the roll-of-the-dice election night, at least from other men who observe them.

"They're willing to put their ego on the line; in no other profession does defeat and victory come so hard and quick. You get a thousand votes, your opponent gets a thousand and one, and you're out. I have to admire them," said a political aide. "I couldn't do it." Fred Dutton, a lawyer and a top adviser in the Kennedy administration, who has been in and out of presidential campaigns, said, "I stumbled into politics in part out of boredom with the law. It is close to what I perceive as the realities of life. Greed, passions, loves, hates, intense causes, friendships, are all there. Take corporate executives; I don't think most of them know what humanness is all about. Just as writers and artists live existentially, on the edge of life, so do politicians. I'm not saying a lot of 'em aren't half-formed humans. They are, with all their neuroses and idiosyncrasies and need to strut, but that's what makes them fascinating."

Fascinating to some, perhaps, but while writers and artists may be flawed with the need to immerse themselves in too much introspection, emotion and personal involvement, politicians are flawed in other ways.

One always has to face the fact that politicians are on guard, thinking more of presenting themselves in a good light than in giving honest reactions. Still, beyond a natural reluctance shared by many to detail their private lives, politicians—unlike people in other professions I have interviewed—often seem *unable* to unlock their lives. With many it is no doubt pure defense. If you got involved in introspection and examination of the day's activities, it would give you little peace of mind to pull some strings yourself. A tendency to hide or obliterate feelings can come from the desensitizing necessary to function in the political arena. It can also stem from experiences deeply rooted in childhood that pushed them in a political direction in the first place. In any event, by the time politicians reach office much of their lives is a performance. They have a smokescreen of automatic responses for nearly everyone—the public, the interviewer, the psychiatrist, even the family.

Politicians are actors. It is difficult not to be cynical as you observe them over the years, as you watch their artful "sincerity"—the quick and constant handshake, and all-purpose smile.

(Millionaire Senator Lloyd Bentsen, for example, looks as if he stands in front of the mirror, practicing humbleness.) With the politician at times is the wife/robot, programmed to smile—or listen intently—through his every speech as if hearing it for the first time.

Some of the best actors are those who couldn't make it any-place else. The biggest crooks are able to stand before a crowd and march to victory on the phrases of law and order and integrity. The politician can be a machine hack who accepts corruptness and venality as the natural order of things; he can go into politics simply because he's failing at everything else and can be dangerous beyond belief if he ever succeeds in politics. The greatest example in history was a man who couldn't make it as a paperhanger, Hitler.

Texas Congressman Robert Eckhardt said, "A perfect example of this kind of politician is Nixon. He couldn't do anything else. He talks about how he made money as a lawyer—but he forgets that was *after* he was a politician and had that reputation going for him." In the superb book on fallen Agnew, *A Heartbeat Away,* Jules Witcover and Richard Cohen write, "As a lawyer who had not succeeded in private practice, bouncing in and out of a series of jobs and small law firms, teaching in law school at night, he [Agnew] had seized upon politics as a vehicle to lift him out of mediocrity and obscurity."

It also helps if a politician is schizophrenic. The role playing we all go through daily is of considerable variety. But the politician has enough sides to his character to be octagonal. Almost all politicians carry "idiot cards" in their breast pockets, with the day's appointments, to indicate what face to put on for what crowd. There he is, being an "okay guy" with the press for good coverage. He is being a "leader among men" in his 4-H address, a noble foe of corrupters who will lead us into a bright and Watergateless society in his college commencement speech. Then he shifts to his King Farouk moment: he is a potentate who can give an order—without a please or a thank you—and know that an underling, who serves only at his pleasure, will rush to carry it out. He can immediately switch to the patient patriarch who has time to have his picture taken, smiling, with the Girl Scouts who descend on his office for a few giggling moments. He is minutes later performing as a wary member of one of the most competitive, cutthroat "clubs"—where ill-disguised insults are cloaked in such venerable phrases as "my distinguished colleague." Then he is on a plane, ever mindful, often hopeful, that someone might recognize him. If that is the case, it is of course time for a leisurely chat about this or that issue. You never know if that person might be a vote or even a potential contributer.

A California Congressman who dropped out from higher ambitions and deliberately chose to be with his family said, "On top of all that, most of us have such massive egos that there is nothing left over for the family." One complaint of political families is that the politician is not psychically available to his wife or children. This is doubly onerous to a family often called on to bolster his "happy family man" image.

Such exploitation of the family is an integral part of politics. Politicians often cite family pressures or a newfound interest in the family as grounds for leaving office. The real reason can be mainly political. Nixon's cynical use of the family was refined to an art.

One such callous exploitation came in the summer of 1972 when Nixon was the machiavellian architect of John Mitchell's "Martha-induced" resignation as director of Nixon's reelection campaign. Nixon sounded his most solicitous when he accepted Mitchell's resignation so that Mitchell could "meet the one obligation that came first—the happiness and welfare of my wife and family." As we all now know, the family excuse was just one of Nixon's many Watergate coverups. At the time it was accepted by many, but there were skeptics, among them Harry Rosenfeld, a *Washington Post* editor, who said, "A man like John Mitchell doesn't give up all that power for his wife."

For the sensitive politician, an either-or struggle has always been present in many political decisions. Thomas Jefferson was forever conflicted between his private life and public duties. His wife was, by all accounts, forever pregnant and forever in danger of dying. As many of his children died in infancy and his wife often lay ill, Jefferson turned from public office—only to be derided by other politicians for abandonment of duty. Some historians feel that had his wife lived he might never have pursued the presidency. Jefferson wrote in the depths of melancholy despair to James Monroe, "I think public service and private misery inseparably linked together." Unfortunately there are many political families and politicians who would say the same today.

2

"I Feel Secure in the White House"

SOMETIMES the exploitation of the wife and family can be simply neglect. Even the present First Lady found politics a draining and demeaning life for several years and sought psychiatric help. Her "salvation"—the White House—will come to only a few political women. As First Lady there is loss of privacy and anonymity but there are also a direction, a well-defined role, and an exalted celebrity status of her own, unparalleled for any other woman in this country. It is a far cry from being the wife of a Grand Rapids Congressman. That she was stricken with breast cancer so soon after blossoming into a person in her own right seemed an ironic tragedy, but only weeks after her September 1974 operation, Mrs. Ford was talking about campaigning for her husband in 1976. She also had lost none of her candid humor that so captivated those used to dealing with her sphinxlike predecessor or a public used to canned and predictable First Lady comments. The most accessible First Lady in modern times, she is divesting the role of some mystery and much of its ridiculous façade. Following the mannequin mask of Mrs. Nixon, the glacial elegance of Jackie Kennedy, the resistance of Mamie Eisenhower and Bess Truman to public exposure, Mrs. Ford is astonishingly real. She freely admits to smoking, being divorced, seeing a psychiatrist, taking tranquilizers, drinking with her husband, and, heaven forbid, sleeping with him. One afternoon after her operation, she talked with me on the phone and giggled at how practically all the world saw the Fords' king-size bed being moved into the White House. Declining the White House tradition of separate bedrooms (Mamie and Ike also ignored the tradition), Mrs. Ford had said with amusement that she could do only so much for politics. "That," she said, "is just too far to go." That breezy comment, she told me, resulted in letters "from all across the country from people who feel it is very immoral for us to be using the same bedroom." I said, "You're joking," and she said, "I'm *serious.* I guess if you're President that part of your life is—I guess you're supposed to become a eunuch," she said with a laugh.

At one time before her operation, Mrs. Ford sighed, after countless interviews, "They've asked me everything but how often I sleep with my husband and if they'd asked me that, I would have told them." When reminded of that line several months after she was in the hospital, Mrs. Ford shot back, "As often as possible!"

Mrs. Ford said she had "long ago" gotten used to both invasion of privacy and criticism. While some people argued that it was tasteless to discuss details of her illness or her earlier psychiatric help, Mrs. Ford took the view that "if you have to have something like this, why not have some good come out of it. I think the publicity has helped other women. I never resented any of it." Instead of shunning her own one-time need for psychiatric help, Mrs. Ford as First Lady spoke at mental health meetings. "I think it vitally important for us to make sure our mental health is as important as our physical well-being," she told me. "Someone at one meeting told me that fifty percent of our hospital beds are occupied by people who are really mental health cases." She added in the easy, joking manner that is her trademark, "There are probably a lot more that should be."

Mrs. Ford decided she would not act out of character to avoid possible criticism. She regards it as an inevitable adjunct to her role and says she will not change. "I think it's silly to live a fictional life."

There is an important lesson in the irony that had Congressman Gerald Ford initially sought the highest office through *election*, Mrs. Ford would have been considered a minus. So used is America to the monolithic concept of the American Political Family as a perfect unit that a woman who could admit to having had problems is less than an asset. Mrs. Ford agrees that much would have been made of her past had there been a full-blown national campaign.

But the events that moved her into the White House were so unique, and the disclosures about Mrs. Ford were so after the fact, that for the first time the country had a chance to see how unimportant such personal matters were. Helping to neutralize the public's reaction, of course, was her candor. Of her first marriage, which lasted five years, Mrs. Ford said, "It is a marriage I could have easily skipped." (Mrs. Ford is only the second divorcée in the White House. The first was Florence Harding. Mrs. Andrew Jackson was divorced but died before Jackson took office.) Mrs. Ford has answered all questions about her mental and physical health, and she has made, above all, no attempt to gloss over the hardships of political life.

Betty Ford's entrance into the White House coincided with a time of change in the country's attitude toward political families. "I think what's happening," said one Washington psychiatrist, Dr. Zigmond Lebensohn, when we discussed the new perspective of the American voter, "is that Middle America is giving up its romantic love affair with the 'ideal family' in the White House—'momma loves poppa and poppa loves momma and poppa and momma love the kids', etc., etc. Interestingly, the one real uptight character we had, Richard Nixon, with his uptight wife and two uptight kids, has given us the biggest scandal. People are seeing that this hypocritical family image has no bearing on what happened."

Mrs. Ford had two years of psychiatric counseling—at a time when she had lost her sense of "self-worth"—to become a more confident person, but neither she nor her children forget those days when she was essentially the sole parent. The Fords decided early on that he would tend to politics and she would tend to the family, the traditional division of labors for political couples. All the children share an open sense of guilt for not understanding the toughness of their mother's role when they were younger. As they moved into the White House, daughter Susan said she hoped never to marry a politician. "I've seen my mother go through too much. Having to raise four children by herself is just murder, and I hope not to go through it, 'cause she's been left at home with, you know, everything on her shoulders and that's not the way I want it."

Jack, the Fords' twenty-two-year-old son studying forestry at Utah State, talked with me after his father became Vice President and said he could "imagine no greater tragedy than having Dad become President. It places added burdens on—well— on Mother." He has some regrets about his teenage years and "how hard I made it for her. Boys are unruly at that age. Nobody knows better than I. I was bigger than my mother even at that age. How she put up with it all I'll never know."

He sees his childhood as "different" from that of his friends. "The most difficult time, probably, was once my father became minority leader. He wasn't home. I was in the seventh and

eighth grade and I was without a father often. That was somewhat difficult. My father was in Congress before I was born—I
never knew anything else." Although he defends his father,
mentions that he tried to make all of his football games, he says,
"When I have kids, I'll be a different person," as far as spending
more time with them.

Tall, husky, blond, and attractive, Jack Ford wore blue jeans,
boots, and a silver bracelet. He dislikes Washington and is more
at home in Utah. "Washington doesn't run on reality. It runs on
ideas and power. I don't understand how Steve can live with it,
myself." (He was referring to his younger brother, who was in
Washington when his dad became President; Steve quickly
went west, giving up a plan to attend college in Washington.)
"It's quite different at school, you sit with your friends and talk,
do a little skiing after class. Everything is very much down to
earth. I can't wait to leave here."

Jack realizes he could not work in a Republican campaign
like any other college volunteer. "I'm known as Gerald Ford's
son. It makes it hard to establish person-to-person *real* relationships. The older I get the harder it is to make me Gerald Ford's
son," he adds with just faint rebellion. Jack has found some
girls take more of an interest in him now—"Mostly in Washington. I immediately pick out the ones who are interested in me
only because of Dad. And the funny mail you get. As if I could
say something and get him a million dollars for the project."

The presidency and the White House represented the unknown, with all its attendant fears, but everyone in the family,
including Betty Ford, seemed after the first six months to enjoy
it far more than they had imagined and were bemused at the
reluctance they had shown in previous months. "Now, after all
those years of dirty work, she's a celebrity in her own right,"
said son Mike. "When Dad came home we were so excited to see
him we'd just fall all over him. I was at fault for just assuming
that's the way it was and not appreciating all the love and care
Mom had for us kids." One wonders how aware Ford was of
helping to create such an atmosphere in which his sons would
"just assume that's the way it was."

Mrs. Ford is entirely outspoken about those years of "dirty
work," and although the family is a close one, she does not hide
the bitterness about the secondary role she took in her husband's life in the past. Gerald Ford put politics before every-

thing else—the Republican Party is his Elks' lodge, his Rotarian meetings, his weekends fishing, his nights of poker, his evenings at the theater with his wife—you name it, his everything.

With that in mind, consider the things she has said. Asked who had the most influence on her when she was growing up, Mrs. Ford answered quickly, "My mother—and my children should say the same thing. Their father's always away." Or, "Naturally I've done most of the child rearing. Particularly since he's been minority leader. His travel practically doubled then. I thought maybe when he became Vice President that the traveling would be cut back, but unfortunately it's doubled again." Asked if the children ever discussed politics with her, Mrs. Ford laughed. "They don't think I know anything about politics, and that's fine with me. I've carried enough of the load without having to handle that too."

The Ford children are a testimony to her ability to have raised them in a difficult political life. Susan moved into the White House with her blue jeans and favorite cat and said that if she continued her babysitting there it "might take some of the stuffiness out of the place." Steve waited three hours to make sure the movers handled his stereo set with kid gloves. He continued to wash his own car, even though it meant photographers and Secret Service agents looking on. One Secret Service agent, guarding Steve during his summer lawn-mowing job, joked, "This is some duty—watching a sixteen-year-old cut grass." When I interviewed Jack, his mother walked out of the room saying, "I think he'll be freer to say what he wants to if I'm not here." Months later she said she could not imagine why he viewed his father's then possible presidency as a disaster, but added that it was his right to say that. Then she quipped, "Maybe he wants the presidency himself!" She once said she "assumed" her children had tried marijuana, only to be called by four furious children who said they had not. "How was I to know? They never told me," she said. "They joked I probably got a lot of votes with young people."

Above all, the Fords are not the cream-puff, happy family that the Nixons tried to portray. Susan says no one talks politics at dinner because it "just comes to a huge fight." When Ford was Vice President, he openly chastised his wife for being late three times at public functions. At the time, I wrote that it seemed a humiliating thing for him to do, particularly since

Mrs. Ford had good reasons—being late from a doctor's appointment once, and having an emergency phone call to make to her daughter. But Mrs. Ford says she was chronically late until White House activities forced her onto a regimented schedule. "Jerry says if he ever has a heart attack it's going to be because of waiting for me to show up."

The Fords acknowledge differences and they acknowledge love. Not the canned togetherness of campaign photos. The boys easily put their arms around their mother. Susan says of her father, "He lets you learn by your own mistakes. I love him dearly. He's just great." After Ford was sworn in as President, Mrs. Ford whispered as he kissed her, "I love you." With TV cameras trained on him at their home that evening, Ford absentmindedly patted her on the fanny. "Our marriage has been very successful," said the President. "When I look around and see some others, I just thank God Betty and I were able to get together."

Politics was Betty Ford's life from the moment she married Ford in 1948, during his hectic first campaign for Congress. Ford showed up late for the ceremony, shoes dusty from campaigning. Their honeymoon came only after they attended a football game and then a speech by presidential candidate Thomas Dewey. After Ford became House minority leader, in 1965, he was gone more than two hundred nights a year on the campaign trail. Mrs. Ford, who had her first child after she was thirty, was facing adolescent rebellion and menopause at the same time. "The boys were playing football, breaking legs and collarbones, and our daughter was in early adolescence. After three boys I was unsure with her . . . I tried to be everything to them, and I completely lost my sense of self-worth."

After she developed a pinched nerve in her neck, doctors recommended that she see a psychiatrist, on the theory that her emotions were causing much of the problem. The psychiatrist made her realize she was "giving too much of myself to my family and the problems of the family and not enough consideration for my own personal feelings."

At the time she told me this, Mrs. Ford was still living in their suburban home and was into the first crunch of activities as a Vice President's wife. She was taking three Valiums a day. When I interviewed her one afternoon she wore a long blue robe and little gold slippers, the kind that fold up and go into a travel bag. The robe and slippers didn't go with the rest of her. Her makeup and jewelry were all on—wristwatch, bracelet, gold earrings, necklace. She was like an actress resting between the matinee and the evening performance.

Mrs. Ford's psychiatric visits even became the subject of her husband's Vice Presidential confirmation hearings—which points up the interaction of a politician's private and public life. The Thomas Eagleton Vice Presidential fiasco of 1972, when Eagleton brought forth his own history of emotional breakdowns after being pressed by the media, was still fresh enough for Ford's questioners to ask whether he had ever seen a psychiatrist. He said yes, but was quick to add that it was only in connection with problems that his wife was having. His wife denigrated herself and emphasized that "he didn't need a psychiatrist. It was just his dumb wife."

An aide at that hearing recalls a remarkable scenario between Ford and his wife. At one time he came over, bent down, and told her the session would be over soon and she had better "get ready" for the photographers. Betty Ford then went to the ladies' room, put on fresh lipstick, combed her hair, and returned to the hearing room. When it was over, Ford came to her, bent down, and whispered a one-word command as he started to kiss her on the cheek for the benefit of photographers—"Smile."

It was unquestionably an awkward pre-blooming period when Betty Ford was thrust into the difficult role of Second Lady during one of the most turbulent times in American history. There was a studied, frankly tranquilized look to her during those early days. This was, after all, a woman who had extracted a "blood oath," as her husband called it, that he would leave politics after one more term in the House. I asked if he would go back on that promise and her eyes glazed over with terror at the thought. "I certainly hope not," she replied.

But once in the White House, a fascinating metamorphosis took place. I recalled how Jackie hated politics until she got the White House to play with; how Pat Nixon was protected by a staff who let her see only the good mail—what a way to feel safe and loved even as beyond the barricades they are demanding your husband's head. Even the most sympathetic wondered, however, about the endurance of a woman with past problems who didn't want the job in the first place, but Betty Ford had strength and assurance to overshadow any such vulnerability.

And Betty Ford, as she prepares in 1975 to campaign heavily to keep her husband in the White House, says about that oath not to run: "That original promise was regarding his running for Congress again. I feel very secure here. I can see from my part in history how exciting it all is; what just my appearance at a luncheon can mean. I do like a challenge and with all the children away I really needed something. I had planned to do some sort of volunteer work—I consider this a twenty-four-hour-a-day volunteer job."

Mrs. Ford invested the First Lady position with a sense of purpose not seen since Eleanor Roosevelt and managed at times to stir controversy. She said that abortion was acceptable in certain cases, and she spoke out in favor of the Equal Rights Amendment. Despite the heavy negative mail she received for her ERA stance, she continued her support and wore a large ERA button at several public functions.

Betty Ford's odyssey may be of little help to lesser political wives whose role is similar to her old one of sole child rearer and lonely helpmate. Very few of them will ever have a chance to find their sense of self-worth in the White House. There is, however, a hopeful legacy of this first "appointed" First Family, something invaluable for future political families, and that is to let naturalness prevail.

3

"I've Been a Mistress Always"

MARION JAVITS had taken over her husband's Senate office for a few hours. When phone calls came in for her she sat in his chair, twirling it in a half-circle as she leaned back. Earlier, she had announced to me, "You *must* be here by a quarter of one. I have only one and a half hours free this afternoon." When I got to the office, I had ample time to examine the portrait gallery of United States Senators from New York that adorned the outer office—Aaron Burr, Martin Van Buren, John Foster Dulles, Kenneth Keating, Robert F. Kennedy, Rob-

ert Wagner. Mrs. Javits kept me waiting nearly a half hour
while she talked on the phone in the inner office.

Marion Javits in the spring of 1974, when I talked with her,
was a slim forty-nine-year-old with brown shoulder-length hair
and a penchant for wearing whatever is stylish. She had on cork
platforms, slacks, shirt, and sweater vest, and when we got
ready to leave, she slipped on a short, chubby fur coat and
pulled a crocheted cloche down on her head.

She was, at that time, planning a dinner to honor Senator Javits and help raise money for his upcoming campaign. (She was
annoyed that a picture page of the Javits family had been left
out of the program.) Mrs. Javits, who makes the gossip columns
frequently, made it again. Eugenia Sheppard mentioned the
dinner, then added, "What could be more ironic than Marion
Javits, wearing a grey jersey dress by Jean Muir and surrounded by beautiful people like Suni Agnelli and Oscar and Fran-
çoise de la Renta who *can't cast a vote?*"

People have been talking about the Javitses for a long time
now. He is twenty years older than she, and one wife of a former Senator remarked, "I have always thought of her as an old
man's darling." The view in Washington is that Marion Javits—
with her radical-chic friends, her open dislike of a national capital she finds pedestrian, her discotheque-hopping with other
escorts—could only be a Manhattan phenomenon. She would
be too much of a thorn for a Senator from any other place except, possibly, Los Angeles. Still, even those in New York political circles consider her "Jack's cross to bear," said one acquaintance. "Everybody in New York politics knows what she is. In
the very beginning, when he ran for Congress more than twenty years ago, she refused to let him have political parties at
home. She was 'of the arts'—and thought his political friends
were a bunch of bums."

While she may at times be the Senator's agony, she is also his
joy. "When I get to be a stuffed shirt, she gives me a kick in the
tail. If I'm youthful at all it's because of her," he says admiringly. Marion Javits, who says she has a "wicked" sense of humor,
once joked, "If I ask him a serious question, he buttons up his
jacket." She has also been known to be verbally vicious with him
on social occasions.

During our interview, Marion Javits was given to posing in
profile, talking to a far wall rather than looking directly at any-

one. As she sees it, her friends—aggressive and successful in New York's society of the new, the "in," and whatever is considered current talent—bring an important dimension to her husband's life. The Senator is in some agreement about their social life. Sometimes he objects to Marion's guest list, but, he says, "If you don't have the jet set, you have something else—like bores or relatives." She said, "He felt I was valuable to him in opening up his options. He could have his political friends, as well as the excitement of New York's intelligentsia." She pronounced "intelligentsia" with a hard *g*. She said the word three more times, each time using a hard *g*. So forceful and certain of herself does Mrs. Javits appear that I got to thinking she must be right and I had been wrong all these years. (The dictionary shows soft *g* is the preferred pronunciation.)

The extravagant use of such a word as "intelligentsia" to describe one's friends and the affected pronunciation are an attempt to mask the slum-hard childhood that Marion Ann Borris tried to run away from early. One male friend said, "Marion likes to compare poorsies," but when I talked to her she was nonrevealing about her background to the point of being both petty and hostile. She compared her husband's humble beginnings with hers. His was Lower-East-Side Jewish poverty, with a janitor father who lived in the Talmud and urged education, a relentlessly driving older brother who was determined little Jakela was going to make it big. "His kind and my kind of poor were something else. His family had pride of knowledge—his family traces back to sixteenth- and seventeenth-century educated in Europe. His education was stressed. Mine was not. I always said, 'I was too poor to be Jewish.'" When I asked for a few details she said, "My parents were divorced when I was ten. I had a kind of zigzag life." I asked her if she would describe her childhood. "Never mind. I'm not giving *my* book away. I'm going to write that myself." I said I would just like a few details to flesh out the profile. She snapped, "Look, I'm not going to give up my own book." I said that I would no doubt be able to get some of her background from other articles and sources but that I preferred her own details. "You can skulldug if you want. My point is I'm not answering you—okay?"

Hers is the checkered background of a relentlessly ambitious person who has looked endlessly for a pursuit in which she could excel. Her way to escape the slums was the theater. Shortly after the war started, she went to the West Coast, where she hoped to be discovered. She failed as an actress, took flying lessons and thought of becoming an army ferry pilot, but decided to go back to New York instead. Once married, she dabbled in the theater, took painting courses at night, and learned to play tennis. "I don't paint and I don't play tennis. I don't feel confident enough to do either. I adore the art world."

Although she refused to move to Washington, her beautiful-people butterfly image emerged later in her life. For several years she played the somewhat conventional role of a well-to-do New York mother of three youngsters. "I felt nourished in that role," she said, and now that all three are grown, she wishes she had a younger child around—"just to make up the gap until I have grandchildren." It is a surprising sentence from a woman who works so hard at being "with it," but Marion Javits is a complex person.

She views herself as a tough street fighter who feels uncomfortable with people less strong. Her husband has a reputation, not only of being one of the most intelligent men in the Senate, but the most arrogant and presumptuous as well. "He and [Senator John] Tower take the cake," said one Capitol Hill restaurateur. "The first time Javits came in, his staff called ahead and demanded that his dinner be ready—he would be there in five minutes. A martini straight up and a steak, rare. Well, he showed up an hour later. That happened one more time and then we learned. Now, they still call, but we don't put anything on until he walks in the door. He demands service and attention and after all these years, he barely says hello to me. I feel like saying 'Who do you think you are?' but that's life." His wife can be as arrogant, with the condescension of one who doesn't really know any better, or perhaps is insecure. "She makes life miserable for everybody who works for Jack," said a longtime acquaintance. "She assumes they are her minions and treats people like she *thinks* upper-crust people used to treat their butchers. She's really an uneducated girl, but she has a lot of native intelligence and is quick and bright." She tangled openly with Javits's former aide Dick Aurelio. It is said that she will storm into the office on her occasional trips to Washington and demand the decor be changed. She wins in arguments because in the final analysis she is Javits's *wife* and therefore an extension of him—he backs her up. But the other side of Mrs. Javits is that she can be "very warm and kind" said one Manhattan acquaintance. "When I had to go to the hospital for surgery she insisted on going with me, getting me a book, sitting with me. Then, a year later, she was capable of saying unkind things to people about my second marriage."

While some friends see an ambivalence in Marion Javits—enjoying all the prerogatives of being a Senator's wife and still wanting to be somebody on her own—she insists she's solved any conflicts. Javits has been in politics all their married life. He was elected to Congress in 1946 and remained eight years. He was elected attorney general of New York in 1954 and was elected to the Senate in 1956. They met through mutual friends when she was "trying to become an actress." After a few dates, she recalls, "he was sunk" by her vivacious, attractive youth. He was already a force in the liberal branch of the Republican Party, and she says, somewhat coolly about her attraction for him, "I was interested in his point of view. I remember he liked the fact I'd meet him wherever he was speaking. It never seemed too difficult for me to meet him. Isn't that what it's like during a courtship?" Today she likes to be there when he's making an important speech. "But I don't follow him all over. I suppose it's the same with a theater couple. In the beginning of a marriage, when the husband is sent out of town to travel with a show the wife will go every time. Later it cools and you find other ways of making the marriage more binding."

Mrs. Javits recalls in their early days of politics that an Ambassador's wife, advising her on the long absences of government men, said, "Just remember, his work will always be his mistress." Marion Javits reversed the order—she says, "I am his mistress—his work is his wife."

She continues, "I've been a mistress always. . . . That's been my role." When she is "about eighty-three years old," she says, she will write the full story of their "separate" life but she isn't going to now. Is it true, as some have said, that they seriously considered a divorce at one time? "I don't think I want to answer that question," she said, very definitely and firmly. Later she said, "I realize you want to make it a whole story—well, I'm not going to give you that."

Although Marion Javits no longer considers Washington a cultural backwash, she still feels she has a separate identity in New York that she could not have in Washington. "I'm background in Washington and not really me." Dinner parties are filled with performing "authorities"—"you have to have a couple of Senators, a couple of journalists, and then you have very few audience. I think the worst part of politics is the feeling that others have as much claim on my husband as I have, in the personal sense. And the deprivation it has meant to the family and family life that I covet very much. If the wife stays too much in the background, the husband pursues his politics with staff and sycophants—Washington is very much like Hollywood twenty years ago and the big star is the Senator. I think that that does bring about slight splits in terms of the great intimacy that normally would be." But, on the other hand, if the wife pushes in too hard, it can also be a negative. "When you're equal and up there fighting it real hard, your relationship changes," she contends.

"The wife who accompanies the man who shakes the hands knows what 'impersonal' means best of all. She is completely left out."

So Marion Javits opted for a separate mistress-wife existence in New York. To protect their time when they were together, she "put a stop" to staff telephone calls. She is not the only one to insist on the privacy of the home. Eleanor McGovern said she never let their home be an extension of the office. Carrie Lee Nelson said she puts an evening at home before social activities: "We never consider anything a command performance—not even the White House." Mary Lindsay took the phone off the hook at Gracie Mansion for one and a half hours every night of the week while her husband was mayor, unless it was during a crisis. While all callers—from politicos to cranks—got busy signals, there was enforced leisure in the Lindsay household.

Marion Javits's distinct pattern for marriage "grew out of a wife being alone." While women like Joan Mondale don't mind many nights alone in which to do the laundry and cut the grass, Marion said no. "I was left alone for years. When he was in Congress he was literally living on the shuttle. I had a choice of being alone in New York, where I knew people, or being alone in Washington, where I didn't know people. People became the other half of my existence. I built my life with friends and my children. He respects my way of life totally. He never objects when I appear in restaurants with a man separately and privately. He agrees that if I'm alone, why not! While some people might criticize this, it's a fact of life. I prefer that to being alone." There were sometimes tensions when she would make plans with her crowd and have Javits suddenly appear in New York because of canceled engagements. "That has been difficult. Because then I have to cut out on all the arrangements I have made and be available to him. It's been more difficult to do as the years have gone on. He made a choice to move more and more away and into politics. That's when I moved into my own 'condition.'" She smiled a sly smile and said, "that's put very delicately, I think."

Even as a wife-mistress, one problem is competition from hangers-on, the "teeny-boppers who surround, are in awe of and somewhat worshipful of the candidate." (Mrs. Javits amended herself and said most of the women in Washington were intelligent and competitive rather than teeny-boppers.) If a young girl threw herself at Senator Javits, Mrs. Javits said, "I don't think that would get in my way particularly. What is the difference between a politician having an affair and a truck driver who has an affair?" She paused, "There is one difference. The press."

Marion Javits has an upper hand in their relationship and that is her relative youth. She repeatedly mentioned that she is twenty years younger than her husband. She'll never face the problem of becoming an elderly woman who hovers in the background while her husband of the same advanced age—in keeping with accepted mores and who is desirable because of his power or position—swings out with any young thing that passes by. "As a mistress/wife I am more of a romantic object for him to come home to when he is here. I think, like pugilists who have to 'neutralize' themselves so the fight will be better, politicians are inclined to give their intensity to the strivings and involvement of their work. The relationship at home may take off the heat—but it is hardly the one they *really* care about."

The press is one reason why Marion Javits does not speak out in public on issues. "They are trying to get at my husband through me," she feels. She works behind the scenes, considers them to be partners. "I have *one* Senator to lobby." She pushed him to take a stand on Vietnam and to help introduce bills that would aid the arts.

Once on a television show with other political wives, Mrs. Javits contended that older women should take their cue from the young and wear less expensive but more interesting clothes.

Jane Muskie, her contemporary, but conservative in a turtle-neck sweater and suit, hair carefully sprayed, had just been talking about the necessity of having to buy more expensive clothes that hold up through constant wearing on the campaign trail. Mrs. Javits looked contemptuously at the other Senator's wife—a look that clearly said that, to her way of thinking, Jane Muskie was out of it—and continued with her premise. Later, I talked with Mrs. Muskie, whose eyes flashed on recalling Mrs. Javits's cavalier dismissal of her point of view. "I resent the fact that *she* was telling me what I ought to wear campaigning—when she's never done a day of it in her life."

On one hand that was a trivial difference of opinion on clothes, but on a deeper level it emphasizes how distinctly apart Marion Javits is from other Senators' wives. Jane Muskie can slog through the small towns of Maine shaking hands and meeting people; Marion's idea of campaigning is to help put together a New York fund-raiser for her husband—and then sit with her beautiful-people collection.

She never played the Senate wives' game—"I never rolled bandages. I think it's the most fruitless, ridiculous thing the women could do. If we wanted to help, I always thought we could go to the hospitals and read or help in some way. I like the person-to-person situation." For her, the plus in politics is that she and her husband have "shared trying to make decisions for the world condition. And I feel I work with a creative man who is really trying to make change possible."

A decade ago Javits was seriously being considered by the Republican Party for the presidency. Then, as now, Javits presented a contrasting personality; he is a different man in New York than he is in Washington. In a perceptive profile on the Senator and his wife, columnist Milton Viorst described their Marion-dominated high life in New York: "The Javits apartment on upper Park Avenue, a complete turn of the earth from the Lower East Side, is neither big nor ostentatious, but it too is thoroughly Marion. The living room is dominated by her full-length portrait, in profile, which does more than ample justice to her tush and is tactful with her little-girl bust. Marion has a small antique desk in a corner of the study, where she and her two-day-a-week secretary prepare her correspondence. Javits doesn't have a niche of his own in the apartment. When he wants to work, he sits at the dining-room table. To take a phone call, he goes to his wife's desk, where he gazes at a snapshot of Marion in a bikini. But Javits shows no sign of discomfort because it's *her* apartment. He also thinks of it as *her* city and because *she* is his, so is New York."

Javits uses fancy restaurants like other men use their clubs—in the sixties it was the 21 Club. One overheard telephone conversation in his office went this way. "I'm taking the eight o'clock plane up and going directly to Twenty-one. I've got to see some people there. I plan to spend the whole evening. Come in anytime after nine o'clock. I'll be delighted to see you. We'll have a chat. You might have to wait a few minutes, if I'm with someone else. Yes, Alan, Twenty-one. Anytime between nine and, say, one or two A.M."

Mr. New York he may be, but Mr. Washington, he isn't. As Viorst wrote, "with brains, money, dedication and loyal supporters, Javits really ought to get on better in Washington, where political and legislative excellence *are* respected. But he has the bad fortune of neutralizing many of his assets by being a stiff. On closer examination, Javits is not so much ill-humored as humorless, not so much pompous as proud, not so much distant as detached. From Javits emerges not the condescension of aristocracy but the priggishness of insecurity.

"Javits, a man with no time to waste, wouldn't think of passing an evening at a movie, just for diversion. Javits is, quite literally, unwilling to have an idle moment, for fear it might reflect on his importance. He can be charming when he tries, but he rarely bothers."

He does not have the ability of many politicians to turn political enemies into personal friends, and so one anecdote that made the rounds of Washington was highly relished by other politicians and observers out of proportion to the incident. It marks the night Carrie Lee Nelson had her last drink of bourbon. (She takes only white wine now.) She was at a party at the McGoverns' and, having had a few too many, was introduced to Javits. It was possibly more, but it was at least the eleventh time they had met. Mrs. Nelson even dutifully complimented Javits and established her identity by saying that her husband, Gaylord, respected his work on a certain committee. Javits was busy casing the room, with that politician's smile—the kind that never reaches the eyes—and did not even reply. Finally, Carrie Lee said, "You bore me." He looked at her, unhearing and asked, "Ah, what?"

She repeated, "I *said*, Senator, that you *bore* me. When I'm talking, goddammit, you listen." About that time, Eleanor McGovern came up and guided the two of them away from further conversation. Later, Carrie Lee said, "I just thought if I was going to sound off like that, I better not touch the stuff again." Her actions, nevertheless, endeared her to many who had wanted to say something similar to Javits; but, understandably, it was annoying to Marion. "I don't like anyone hitting my husband so hard . . . only I can do that. Yes, there may be a failing on his part not to listen, but he really has such a fund of stuff going on in his head all the time. People want to feed off of that all the time. I can see his point of view. He's got eighteen million constituents and one half of them he's 'met' and the other half are his 'best friends.' He tries very hard to remember. But he could come into the apartment and shake hands with *me*. Yes, he is distracted. No, he's not the most intimate with people."

For all their differences and their separate lives, it hardly seems an intolerable existence for either. To some political wives, in fact, Marion Javits is someone to envy. New York and Washington are close enough so that their enhancing separateness can be altered very quickly by an hour on the shuttle. He takes pride in her somewhat vague career as an "art consultant." She explains, "I try to get corporate support for artists, and I work at it professionally now. I feel that the new support and acknowledgment for the art world will come out of corporations." Her career just "evolved" from her early days of helping him do the original research on the arts bill. "In 1963 I produced a play, *Hang Down Your Head and Die*. It dealt with capital punishment but was a huge flop." Her interest in art led to art classes and to art consulting and some rather obscurely allied projects. "TWA hired me to do a small study on food and the stewardesses' role, and I did a very handsome report. For Pan Am I did a small film, and then I did a study on Olivetti." She is also pushing what she calls "living art." One idea is an attempt to soften day-to-day living in a technological society. She thinks it would be "lovely" if office workers when they empty out at 5 P.M. would be greeted by a performer in the lobby "playing his saxophone or clarinet very softly, very gently, or somebody reading poetry. Frequently people go up and down on the elevators and never look at each other. They've become mechanized in this technological society."

Reflecting on her life, Marion Javits said, "I think that because I almost grew up out of the ground, because it was such a struggle, all of it, until I was twenty-two, I really only started to grow and, actually, to become younger since then. In the last fifteen years I've grown happier, younger, more rewarded and more understanding. As a kid, I grew up frightened and uptight. When I had *my* children, *my* marriage, *my* shelter, then things began to change."

And her separate life makes it possible for her to know a certain kind of people and to play a certain role. Other Senators' wives may not aspire to it, but it's what she wants. An example was a telephone call she took in the Senator's office; it was mostly about an after-theater affair she had attended the night before: "Ursula! How *are* you? Did you come late? Oh, it was very boring. It was very dull. *Never* do an opening-night party. They're the *worst.* You only know the star and he's busy talking to everybody." There were some pauses, then, "Oh, *terrific!* Oh, *divine!* Then I'll see you then. Big kiss. Bye-bye."

4

Team Wives and True Believers

　　　　TO make a political marriage work, one contention is that the wife has to want it all as much as the husband does. The political "partner" wife can describe her supportive role with pride. To me, Joan Mondale, the wife of Senator Walter F. Mondale, epitomized the team-player wife when she said with an automatic smile, "I bask in reflected glory."

Many team wives see themselves in an honorable calling of service to their country and lobby their husbands for social legislation. And many partner wives have more status than they would ever have had on their own or in another marriage. For them, it is worth any sacrifice. Politics can also be an outlet for their own drives and ego. When they speak, it may be about their husbands, but the applause is for *them.* A very few experi-

ence resentment and insecurity—carefully concealed from constituents and the press—about being considered mere extensions of their husbands. Team wives are often shrewd, exact-
ing, intelligent—and frighteningly ambitious.

The degree of involvement in the political process varies
from family to family, often dependent on the ages of children.
The team wife sometimes gives speeches, sets her own schedule, runs his campaign or his office, or, at least, tells him whom
she would like to see fired. In contrast, other wives run through
campaigns in an undemanding, compliant, self-effacing manner—rushing through teas and coffees and handshakes like
perfect automatons. These are the ones who are careful to wear
the right clothes and speak as if the voice is canned and operated by a button pushed from deep inside. Most of these team
wives say, "Oh, I could never say anything on my own because it
might reflect on my husband." Some are as sweet as their images, others are sugar-coated black widow spiders. Most team
players are, above all, in command of themselves—a madden-
ing situation for anyone who cares to plumb their inner motivations.

To the romantic, the emphasis on the less personal, carried
to the extent some of these team couples do, seems too great a
sacrifice. Those couples who "run in harness" view campaigns
not as necessary evils, but part of a shared, driving, and compelling way of life. The wives close their ears to any talk of sexual straying on their husbands' part and live lives of deferred
pleasures, or so it seems to those who value leisure time—walks
in the woods, long talks in front of the fireplace, leisurely lovemaking, evenings with friends or books or children—or each
other.

Some people find solace in the view that the normal out-
growth of a long marriage is a far different kind of love than romantic love. No one in his right mind does what the Duke of
Windsor did; they would quickly say you have to be an abdicated king to place a white rose on your wife's pillow every night.
A ludicrous example, of course, but there are relative barome-
ters of distance in long-standing marriages. I once joked that
you could tell the couples who had nothing in common—they
were the ones that entertained all the time to fill the house with
something other than themselves With that framework in
mind, many team wives consider themselves lucky. Instead of a

life of shared boredom once the children are gone, they continue to plunge into the mutuality of shared political experiences.
Sometimes there is genuine companionship in that life, sometimes there is a whistling-in-the-dark acceptance of a lost relationship, and sometimes there is almost pure fraud. When the
doors close some of these couples are antiseptically impersonal
with each other—as, for example, we now know Eleanor and
Franklin Roosevelt were—but the image for all the world is an
exalted union. Some wives are tough behind a helpmate façade,
or are maternal figures of support who couldn't care less if
their husbands find fun and games with other women. Their
own role is too satisfying to bother with that aspect of marriage.

For those team wives who are *true* believers (unlike those who
merely act the role) life must be enviably simpler than for those
women who find their interests and desires moving in conflicting directions. The team wives may appear stifled and restricted to freer spirits, but if they totally endorse their lives, then
lack of choice itself brings a certain security. It is much like a
doctrinaire religious or political movement follower who ad-
heres unquestioningly to the church or movement dictates.
Self-doubt and the turmoil of confusion or examination of that
role are gone. These are the women who get most disturbed
and resentful and are the most protective when people point
out dissatisfaction on the part of other political wives or the
anti-wife stance of politics per se, or that many other people
view them as unliberated. I asked one such congressional wife
why she felt so threatened by such an examination if she was indeed so happy. She said, "Because the government so *desperately*
needs good people! If the women sense it is a hard life and not
fulfilling for them and their families, they are going to dissuade
their husbands from running."

In the last analysis, the political wife's sense of reward or
fulfillment depends on how much the husband and wife have
going for each other. If the husband truly values her opinion,
then she can make a legitimate contribution and share as an
advisor in his political decision-making.

It is often the case that the wife's value is unknown or undis-
covered until her husband is thrust into national prominence.
Mrs. George McGovern, out on her own more than any other
presidential candidate's wife in 1972, was not fearing those two
words that grip so many candidate's wives: "I think. . . ." Still,

she wrote in her book, *Uphill,* that until 1962 she "had never felt more than a spectator on the public scene." When her husband became ill during that campaign, she took over his public appearances—although "always leaving the heavy stuff to good Democratic friends." At the end of that successful campaign "my self-confidence was soaring; this really was 'our' campaign, not just George's. For me there was a special *secret* triumph involved."

"Fortunate to be on the fringes of power; even if it meant scouring pots and pans one minute, it sometimes meant chatting with the nation's most erudite public men and women the next," Eleanor McGovern wrote. "I was able to convince myself easily, even when overcome with weariness from coping with our absolutely chaotic household, or with loneliness for George or with apprehension about being the faultless mother my own mother had been, that I was in the right place at the right time doing the right thing." This lasted for some years when he was a Congressman. Then, in the next paragraph, Mrs. McGovern explains her championing his first Senate race in 1960. "Anything was better than campaigning for reelection every two years, living with one foot in South Dakota and the other in Washington with a preoccupied husband and five growing children who had no idea where they belonged." The intervening traumas or depressions that must have come with that change of thought are left unexplained. In describing their life Mrs. McGovern said, "Certainly 'togetherness' was not a prerequisite for what we shared with each other. It was true that sometimes political life stretched out the physical and emotional distance between us; yet our ties were more compelling than uninterrupted personal felicity. Politics and family were everything, and we were unabashedly idealistic about both."

That kind of dedication coupled with a seriousness of purpose is often at war with humor, frivolity, or just plain joyousness. Many such "messianic" couples have had to *work* at cultivating a wry look at themselves and their lives.

One would have to search far to find a more obvious example of political dedication overshadowing one's private life than an incident Eleanor McGovern relates so solemnly. She was in labor with her fourth child. "George had brought along the newspapers so that between contractions he could rub my back and we could read about Adlai Stevenson and the forthcoming 1952 presidential election. There was no doubt in our minds that a person with Stevenson's monumental integrity should lead the country. As we quietly browsed through the newspapers, George said suddenly 'Well if it should be a boy, why don't we name him Steven after Stevenson?' Now, in my mind, July 27, 1952, the birthday of our son, Steve, symbolically marks George's beginning in politics." The momentarily impending birth was, albeit, a fourth one. Still, I can't imagine too many women fitting themselves into that scene.

Although women like Eleanor McGovern emerged as individuals with strength and a freedom to express themselves, there are other team players who adhere to the doctrine that political wives should be seen and not heard.

Picture this scene when an interviewer was locked in a fandango with Mrs. Ronald Reagan. Her husband, the former governor of California, is mentioned among the 1976 presidential aspirants. Mrs. Reagan in the White House would bring a revival of Pat Nixonia, if this interview in a magazine called *Girl Talk* is any example. Mrs. Reagan seems totally innoculated against today's rebirth of feminism and emphasis on self-fulfillment and accomplishment for women.

"Why, my joy is being Mrs. Ronald Reagan." Does she ever see herself as a separate person? "No, I never do. Always as Nancy Reagan." She continues, "My life *began* with Ronnie."

Asked what she would be doing had she not married Reagan, Mrs. Reagan is startled into silence. "Oh heavens!" she finally says. "I don't know, I've never thought of it. I don't know what I'd do . . . Kill myself!"

She sees her role as doing volunteer work with the aged, the physically and mentally handicapped, and to "act as a buffer" for her husband. "I think a wife is part mother to her husband. To me, it's just a natural part of it." After a dinner speech she is the one who urges him quietly out the door. "I just keep pushing. Pushing and smiling!"

How would she help if her husband ran for the presidency? "Well, I don't give speeches. I'll do questions and answers, but I've never given a speech. I'd feel very presumptuous doing that." And last, would she like to be First Lady? She smiles. "I just want to be Ronald Reagan's wife. Whatever."

One prerequisite for "happy" political life is to be the daughter of a minister, or at least that is the message that comes through when talking to Joan Mondale. Her childhood as a clergyman's daughter prepared her for a life she views as one of worthwhile service and a marriage to an often absent husband.

"I was very lucky—my father was never home. He traveled six months out of a year, so I'm not accustomed to having a man around the house doing things. I don't expect anything. If I had a father who sat around with a mother bringing him pipe and slippers, if I had a father to make household decisions, to do the bills, I might feel differently."

Mondale—particularly in 1974 before he stopped trying for the presidency—is gone what seems a staggering amount of time for a marriage his wife terms as "extremely close" and "strengthened" by politics. In 1974 he barely saw his family and this was one reason he decided he didn't want the presidency enough for the grueling pursuit of it. During Senate races he is also gone every single weekend. The number of nights away during the week vary with speaking engagements and other appearances. When I mentioned I knew *divorced* couples who spend more time together than that, Mrs. Mondale seemed mystified. I joked that they might have hit on the solution to happy marriages, just not be around each other much. What does she do when he's gone all the time? "Cut the grass, put on the storm windows, do the laundry, drive the children wherever they have to go." She has help once a week. Joan Mondale said she also likes being alone. "I do exactly as I please during these empty hours. I do a lot of volunteer work; I wrote a book [on arts and politics]. I could do whatever I please with this time, and I am very satisfied and I feel that I earn part of my husband's income because when I go out and speak for him and when I campaign that's work. And I don't get a penny from it. I mean I don't get a paycheck." Their life in Washington beats their earlier years. "When he was Minnesota's attorney general he was home two nights a month." Unlike many pediatricians, who feel both parents are needed in the earliest infant years, which are important for developing a sense of identity, Mrs. Mondale remarks, "Fortunately the children were babies and didn't need him."

The recollections of a zealous, do-gooder ministerial life are in play when Mrs. Mondale says her husband is in politics "to make the government responsive and to do something about the problems in our life and times, not for personal gain or ego.

Then you figure it's all worthwhile—the good with the bad, the fatigue with the rest." She reiterated on TV, "I believe in social justice and I'm very proud and happy that I have a chance to help someone who is there voting on the floor of the Senate. I don't know many wives who feel they can contribute to their husbands' career the way political wives can. And if I can help keep him in the Senate that is my contribution to these issues." Mrs. Mondale said that on a television show with Martha Mitchell—a disillusioned woman if there ever was one, who practically named Nixon and governmental power as corespondents—looking skeptical beside her. I was on the panel and both Martha and I asked Mrs. Mondale how she feels she is effective, how does she really know she actually helps keep her husband in office? Because their role is so ill-defined, and the ability to gauge that effectiveness is so amorphous, many political wives have doubts that all their work ever gained their husbands a single vote. Mrs. Mondale agreed that she "couldn't take credit for my husband's remaining in the Senate. I hope that I can keep him there—by not embarrassing him, or saying something that wouldn't be, you know, acceptable."

Again her childhood training is a plus, although her explanations remain a mystery to more outspoken people. On one hand, Mrs. Mondale professes, in public, the view that she can speak "freely." She immediately turned around and told me in a private conversation that a politician's wife has to be "so careful." Dropping her voice to a whisper, she said, "You can't totally say what you think in politics. I don't think it's hypocritical to not say exactly what I think. There are a lot of things we all know that we don't talk about. I would feel the same way as a minister's daughter. My father is a minister." I asked her how she could feel "free" if she was also "afraid" of speaking out? She saw no conflict. "I can censor myself." I protested, "That's not 'freedom' if you feel—" Mrs. Mondale disagreed. "No, my husband censors himself. We all censor ourselves—what's polite, what will be, you know, well received." I asked, "What will keep him elected?" Mrs. Mondale: "Right."

The Mondale life means planning seven weeks in advance simply to have a family weekend. Martha Mitchell said, "I'd rather have a husband home during the weekend where I've got him for two full days than a few hours during the week." Mrs. Mondale protested, "No political wife can ask her husband to stay home on the weekends. That's when he goes home and campaigns. And if he doesn't go home and campaign, we'll move back to Minneapolis. He'll be defeated."

Martha Mitchell said a bit wistfully, and as if it might have been a good idea for her own marriage long ago, "Well, that might be true." Mrs. Mondale said, "Well, *I* love Washington. I want to stay here. I'm glad."

And that is a very telling point. A life of few vacations, little time together, campaigning, financial concerns, self-censorship is worth it to a woman like Joan Mondale because she "wants to stay here." For many, Washington beats back home. Politics is fortunate to have those who genuinely do like the life. However, Mrs. Mondale has one problem with those who cannot identify with her. People who know her well like her very much, but those who do not often think her never-waning enthusiasm simply cannot be all that real. "In Minnesota, they sometimes call her 'Phony Joanie,'" said one newspaperman who lived there for a time before returning to Washington. A woman newspaper reporter asked me, "What is it with her? Is that all an act? I find her unbelievable." A producer of one TV show featuring a panel of political wives said, "She wins the vanilla cream-puff award—she was such a disappointment—I think she was very unreal. No one would have so few real views." To me, the image she presented seemed too consistent to be anything but real. Bright, somewhat gushy, Joan Mondale is a discreet, disciplined, well-organized, programmed, and safe team player.

When I interviewed her at home, Mrs. Mondale said, "Let me get my biography, that'll save a lot of time." She returned from her basement files with her biography. "I'm on two new boards—I'm so *excited* about it I can't stand it." One board was raising money to give away free paperbacks to poor children.

She answers the phone. "Oh, I'm *really* disappointed I can't do it. But I'd like to suggest someone I think would be nice. She is a congressional wife, beautiful, blond, tall, beautiful, poised, and I think she would be a *marvelous* model." (After the conversation she said, "I'm just getting out of a fashion show.") Mrs. Mondale is tall, angular, with close-clipped hair, and speaks in italics and exclamation marks. She has clearly endorsed the political world and didn't back off in the slightest from her husband's pursuit of the presidency—"That would be fine with me." Other wives fear the First Lady role but Mrs. Mondale really wanted it. In the days when her husband was running hard, she said, "That's putting the cart before the horse. It's a daydream . . . look at all the women in this town who *envisioned* being First Lady! The odds are so great," she said, lowering her voice to a whisper, "why get your hopes up? The pitfalls are too great to imagine that—unless you get there."

The Mondale home is an old Cleveland Park stucco in northwest Washington, Danish modern furniture and uncluttered; not even a book out of place. One pillow says "Love is beautiful." Over the mantel is an amateurish painting of Fritz and Joan Mondale as Caesar and Cleopatra with the slogan "All Hail Mondale." She is holding a "vote" sign. This was given to the Mondales in Minnesota when they moved from a district where she was chairwoman of the Democratic Farm Labor Club.

Mrs. Mondale regrets that she "doesn't read as much as I should. I cannot sit and read a paper until the house is done, and that's very bad. My mother said when I was going to marry Fritz, 'Either her standards go down, or she's going to have a nervous breakdown.' My standards went down." Judging from the immaculate house, it was more an anecdote than reality.

The Mondales do not live over their means and plow any money they have left back into his political campaigns. "Fritz earns the money and I spend it. I do the bills. Campaigning is very expensive—we have to have fund-raiser after fund-raiser—it is very expensive. You have to raise your own money. People are constantly saying, 'When are you coming to Minneapolis?' My trips are paid for out of grocery money, except in a campaign year when there is financing."

Mrs. Mondale admits to one special strain in a political marriage and that is lack of job security. "The first thing is that every day your job is at stake. If you're a politician you just don't have the board of directors to please. You have the entire state, or district, or the country. It is not a homogeneous constituency. Everyone has an idea of what you should be. The first thing you realize is you can be swiftly removed. You're judged day by day. A lot of people like Fritz, they just don't like his politics. Whenever he gets rapped for inconsistency, he says, 'You have to vote on two thousand measures every year. How can you possibly be consistent?'"

Although campaigning is "fatiguing" she brightened even

more as she said, "On Sundays [back in Minnesota] we have receptions. It's *marvelous*. You stand in line and shake hands. I love politics, I get all the fun and none of the decisions. I bask in reflected glory." Much of it can become automatic, she admits. "I remember in 1960, Jane Freeman and Muriel Humphrey and I were all over the place—teas, five coffee parties a day, shaking hands, smiling and meeting strangers. You'd go into a home and shake hands and smile at a hostess you didn't know, look at the name tags, and give your little three-minute speech about how wonderful your husband is and then leave. Later, I went to a shower—on a personal basis—and I practically went around the room shaking hands. I was all programmed to do this. Can you imagine? I don't know what they would have thought of me!" Mrs. Mondale has not been asked explosive questions while campaigning. "I don't know, if asked, what I would say."

We discussed abortion. "It's very, very difficult. I can understand the Catholic thought, but the non-churched view against abortion is more difficult to understand." She feels abortion should be the choice of the woman and the doctor, but seems definitely relieved that she was never asked this while campaigning. I said I thought it must be tiring to always be worrying about what you must say. She said that "fortunately" she and her husband agreed on issues. Besides, "It's in a woman's own self-interest to promote her husband. What you say reflects on your husband all the time. You hope you present a good side."

I was wondering about their time together, what they laughed about, what they fought about. "We don't fight or argue," she said with a shake of her head. "Never. I usually get my way. That's the goofy thing. We agree. There is never this head-to-head difference. I don't know what people fight *about!* I would suppose raising children. But we agree. I have a friend whose daughter wants a horse. She thinks the daughter should have it simply because it's nice to have a horse. Her husband says no, she should not get a horse unless she gets A's and B's in school. When she gets D's and F's again, what do you do, sell the horse? It's a false sense of value and it's bribery. They're getting a divorce and I can see why."

Joan Mondale freely admits that politics takes the spontaneity out of their private life. I asked what they give up for politics. "The nonessentials." What are those? "Oh, you give up a lot of pleasure. You'd better find pleasure in your work—if you don't, heaven help you." The Mondales average two dinner parties a week but give up the impromptu things in life. "Movies—that's what you give up. We used to go to the symphony when we were first married. We used to go to a lot more plays— but you never have that feeling, what am I going to do tonight? You never have to worry about, shall we go play tennis or go to the play or take the children for a drive? You *never* get that chance. If you do something with the children you have to plan it, arrange, it, chart it. You have to be superorganized, and plan six months in advance. You clear the deck of ten million speeches, but that weekend is *inviolate*." Surprisingly, she calls her husband a "family man." I asked her how often he gets to be a family man? "Once a year." There is a week of skiing and then in the summer the family all goes to Minnesota for three weeks—about half of that time Mondale is out shaking hands. Mondale sees his children for an hour a few nights in the middle of the week. "One hour is better than nothing. He's funny and loving when he's home. He says the prayers with the children, lies down on the bed to talk to them. He's on the phone about a staff meeting or watching news on TV but he's also very conscious of the private time with the children. They know they're being cared about and he knows what they're doing. That is the secret of his success as a father. There are very strong family values." (We tried to get together for a family evening with her husband home but the first night we could arrange it three weeks in advance, had to be cancelled later. We never did get the family together.)

I asked if the three children—two in their teens and one younger—had any qualms about the life. "They don't *expect* him at home. If he's around they'll say, 'What are you doing home this weekend, Daddy?'" Mrs. Mondale often tells a story which she thinks is cute, about her daughter, Eleanor, when she was younger. "Fritz came back from a trip and said, 'Did you miss me?' and she said, 'Were you gone?'" (That reminds me of the story one political aide told. His boss had an unexpected night free so he went home. His wife saw him come in and was so surprised that she said, "Oh, children, you're father's here." They replied, "What channel?") I mentioned that some sons, particularly, have experienced feelings of inadequacy when measured against their politically prominent fathers. She protests, "That's the son of *any* successful man. It's not unique for a politician." But is it different for political children? "Oh, absolutely. The limelight. You do the best you can and not regret it. Teddy's sixteen years old and very complex. I don't think he's rebelling—he's just sports-oriented."

Another time, talking with me, Mrs. Mondale said she thought political children had a great deal of pride in their fathers. "Why, our daughter was picked to model for *Seventeen* magazine and she *knows* that would not have happened if her Daddy was not a *Senator!* That's a wonderful experience for her." I asked if she didn't have some worries that the child might someday feel upset and insecure in the knowledge that the "only" reason she was picked was because her father was a Senator? "Oh, no, you've got it all wrong! And she simply goes up on the ski lift and she just corrals those men on the chair lift and asks them, 'What do you think about Senator Mondale? Don't you think he's marvelous?' She's very proud of him." I thought that was excessive overt enthusiasm, Mrs. Mondale found nothing unnatural in it.

The time for Joan and Fritz to be alone is obviously rare and it was clearly an awkward subject. "We're alone together sometimes. It's never a period of time you can predict. It's always unpredictable." She is defensive about this area. "Just because you're physically alone doesn't mean you have your husband's attention. That sort of thing is very personal. You work out what you need from each other." She looks at campaigning as a "courtship." "You're not together all the time and when you are, it can be very, very sweet and nice." I brought up the fact that many political couples realized too late that they had grown apart sexually as their separate lives increased. She seemed embarrassed. "I think you can be romantic and be a political wife."

Do they ever walk together or take a drive into the country in the fall? "Never. That's a luxury; we *can't* do that—but you never get the feeling you're useless or not accomplishing anything. You free yourself from a sense of purposelessness."

This constantly sunny disposition—is it there in the hard times? "Bad times? Well, I've not thought about bad times." She puts her hands up to her face and thinks. "Well, I'm trying to think of bad times. Everything's gone so well for us. The children are okay—today—in this day and age you never know about tomorrow. We haven't had any personal bad times. We've had some career bad times."

Joan Mondale is so much the political wife that her remembrance of the worst time in their life was when her husband was unknown. "The worst time was when he was appointed attorney general and nobody *knew* him!" Her eyes widen at the horror of it. "I mean, *nobody knew him!* It was so bad. Fritz would say his name and tell people he was the new attorney general and people would say, glad to meet you and call him by the name of the man he had replaced. What do you *do* to get them to know you?" she asks rhetorically. "You go and go and go and you drop dead. Six months. Oh! It was so terrible. You had to make yourself known. Had to go and say, 'I want your help.' It was a major stumbling block."

The fact that both were clergymen's children played a large part in the Mondales' instant understanding. "Our life values were the same. We did not have to talk about money, career, how to raise children. As two ministers' children, we understood." She recalls her husband's wandering childhood. "Fritz moved every two years. Not only was he the new boy in town, he was the new preacher's kid in town. When they moved, he had to be beaten up by the boys. That's what you did," she says philosophically, "you beat up the minister's son." And Joan learned those rules of life so carefully applied today. Her mother lived by that old saw about never discussing politics or religion in public. But she saw nothing wrong with it inside the family. "We always discussed politics at dinner. Mother was the conservative," Joan Mondale jokes. "She was for Roosevelt. Father voted for Norman Thomas. I am no black sheep [by being a liberal], I'm just paddling along in the family tradition."

An uncle was director of the Cincinnati Art Museum and in her sophomore year in college, Joan says, she got interested enough in museums to consider this as a career. "My uncle told me, 'The problem is women get married and leave. I would not consider you for an important administrative position.' And he's *right!* I don't care what women's lib says." Later on in the conversation, Joan said she felt those attitudes were changing. She does not want a career today. "I worked for four years. I *had* my own career, thank you just the same. I'm not very fashionable, but I feel this way. Women's lib says I should feel deprived but I do not. I have car pools, PTA board meetings, and give guided tours of the National Gallery on a volunteer basis. I just adore it. I just *love* it. I *am* so lucky. I have my job and I can share Fritz's too!"

She feels it is almost impossible for women married to politicians to have full-time careers. She recalls when Mondale was appointed in 1960 to the attorney generalship to fill out a term, which meant he had to run for the office the following fall. She was thirty. "As I said, he was out every night except maybe two a month. Everyone always wants to know why can't you come to our meeting—and you have to go. It's hard, so hard. But the babies didn't need their father. He didn't change their diapers. But it is very *very* difficult when you're first married and have young children. The most important thing is those little babies—every little burp is wonderful. Then you realize that you as a wife are no longer the focal point in your husband's life. It's very difficult." She said this matter-of-factly. I wondered if she ever felt bitter. "Oh, I try to forget it. I don't think about it."

We talked about the growing number of divorces in politics. Mrs. Mondale said, "Divorce is a social indicator. Toffler's *Future Shock* is illuminating. The whole pace of life has picked up. The human body can only take so much." Her guard was dropping, slowly. For the first time there was a feeling that she was often measuring herself to the "competition" in Washington. She feels she is "not as well informed as Marvella [Bayh] and Bethine [Church]" and wishes she could go to Senate hearings daily, but her youngest child comes home for lunch. "Your children come first." In a "speeded-up life—everyone has to be beautiful, intelligent, young, perfect, and blessed with upward-achieving children. It is too much." There is some bitterness. "It's worse in this city. Look at the competition—brains, beauty, money. There is always someone more smart, more beautiful, with more money. It's true of everyone in this town."

Does she worry about the "star syndrome" and the adulation of female groupies? She answers quickly. "Adulation doesn't bother me. It doesn't bother Fritz." What about other women? The answer is crisper still. "Fritz isn't like that. Fritz isn't Mr. Big Time when he walks in the door. He doesn't thrive on adulation." Does she think it can be a dividing factor in political

families? "Oh, I think it's there. Some people are more suscepti-
ble than others."

I asked if she ever wanted to be a politician herself. "No!" she
answered sharply. Why? "Because I'm a woman." For an instant, I thought she meant women shouldn't aspire to the political life, but I was wrong. Through all the bliss of her helpmate
role there is a final acknowledgment of the differences that separate women who seek office from men who do. Her face goes
as hard as it possibly can and the smile is not there. "There are
too many disadvantages—such as your sex. Why, they talk
about you 'sleeping around.' " (She says that with a disgusted
look.) "Or, 'Why aren't you home taking care of your children?'
That's one of the reasons there aren't many more women in the
legislative body."

Later, on the phone, she elaborates on the male-dominated
systems of politics and society. "What are you going to *do*? Are
you going to run, and then what if your husband, because of his
job, has to move, for crying out loud?" What happens to your
district or your state? Women are absolutely trapped." Washington is not an easy town for a woman, she feels. "Washington
is a status town and the Mrs. has status only from her husband,
even if she is, say, a chief scientist." What if a wife does care
about her career? "You'd find yourself fighting all the time for
an ego of your own." What about the woman aide who gets satisfaction from her job? "She still gets her *status* through her
boss." While Joan Mondale acknowledged the problems of a
woman who wants a career, she said, "It doesn't bother me—
because I'm not trying to be anybody."

Her parting comment was, "I hope I haven't said *anything*
that would make it difficult for Fritz or sound wrong."

5

To an Elected Politician There Is
No Such Thing as Indecent Exposure

FOR the elected politician, there is no such thing as
indecent exposure. There is immense interaction between the
star syndrome, the role of the press, and the role his wife is ex-

pected to play. Out of that comes the long-standing myth of the All American Happy Political Family and the demands, both real and inferred, of constituents. All of this adds up to considerable strain on even the most idyllic of marriages, and forces a hypocrisy on those unions that are not so idyllic.

By the star syndrome I mean both the media hype a politician gets and the kind of fawning attention he receives—from aides, secretaries, lobbyists, and constituents who want something, and those who need a proximity to someone they feel possesses importance if not power. It is all relative. If you're President, it's nations; if you're a Kennedy, it's masses. If you're Congressman Zilch, it's a handful. You have only to stand in a Washington hotel lobby and watch a visiting Rotarian saying, "Hello, Mr. Congressman," and then see him introduce Congressman Zilch to his buddy to know that everyone is getting his jollies out of the meeting. The visiting Rotarian is impressing his pal, who will then brag at his local country club that "my Congressman is going to help me on that deal." And Congressman Zilch sorely needs that hand-holding because he walks around Washington with a terrible complex. He knows that in Washington power circles he's a cipher unless he has moved into a committee chairmanship or some other visible sign of importance. Still, as hard as it is for national reporters to realize, even the nerdiest Congressman from Keokuk has his domain. "Back in Cowtown, he's Walter Cronkite" is the way one Capitol Hill aide put it.

There are political groupies and girls available not only for superstar politicians but for most other politicians on the Hill. It is not unlike the rating system that used to prevail in college fraternities and sororities. Low-life pols just get lesser girls. Just as boys trade baseball cards, bodies are swapped according to rank. "There is such status tripping here," said one pretty brunette receptionist to a well-known Senator. "One girl bragged that she went out with a certain legislative assistant and I said, 'So what? Big deal. I went out with his *boss.*'"

In today's media-surfeited society politicians are the closest thing to show-biz people, filling in the Vicarious Living Gap that was created when Hollywood began to sink slowly in the west. The woman's magazines now write the kind of cover teasers about public figures that used to be associated with *Modern Screen* and *True Confessions*: "Mieke Tunney: How Washington

Ruins Marriages." "Joan Kennedy: The Tormented Kennedy." "Julie Eisenhower: The Nixon that Never Stops Fighting." "How Much Does Jackie Spend on Clothes?" "What the New First Lady Is Really Like." "How Happy Is Happy?" In *Parade* magazine's "Personality Parade" page, questions about politics and political families consistently make up half or more of the questions. (Two weeks running it was eight out of ten.)

Some women experience great difficulty coping with the constant public scrutiny of Life in the Limelight. Both Joan Kennedy and Margaret Trudeau felt enough emotional stress to be hospitalized in 1974.

With the advent of television, it was only inevitable that politicians and attendant media members would become celebrities and everyone would exploit one another, even more so than in the days when newspaper columnists such as Westbrook Pegler and Drew Pearson wielded so much power.

We are in an era which Robert Brustein, dean of the Yale drama school, calls "news theater." In news theater, news *makes* the politician as often as the politician makes news. The pressure and presence of the media contorts politicians into artificial whirling dervishes in a spotlight. Sam Irvin became the homiletic rustic philosopher during Watergate. Martha Mitchell converted what genuine pain and embarrassment she felt over her publicly disintegrating marriage into a coast-to-coast performance. For a while she became everybody's favorite daytime talk show host substitute; and, like every other Washington celebrity, no matter how unenduring, was writing her memoirs.

Nothing succeeds in political news theater like high crimes and felony. Jeb Stuart Magruder sold out autographed copies of his book long before the lines ran out just a few days before he waved at the cameras as he went inside the prison gates, looking, in his alligator-emblemed shirt, like a tennis pro for the minimum-security prison. Egil Krogh and his happy family did a happy family media jog when he came out of the same prison. Agnew sold a novel for an outrageous sum. To top it off, he was considered for the part of Warren Gamaliel Harding in a proposed Broadway show. Agnew's lawyers seriously announced they would consider the offer. In 1975, John Dean got $3,000 per speech.

In typical news theater reverse, many ex-politicians just continued to expose themselves—former Cleveland Mayor Carl Stokes went to work for NBC and New York's mayor John Lindsay became a commentator for NBC-TV.

One can only imagine how the Aaron Burr-Alexander Hamilton duel would have been covered today, using all the current media hype techniques. Bleacher seats would go for five dollars and Howard Cossell would bring you the play by play on Wide World of Sports: "Here we are, folks, on the Jersey Palisades overlooking the Hudson River on the Weehawken dueling grounds. That's the Vice President on the left, as we see him, chatting with his second, just moments before we are about to witness the greatest duel of the century before a packed, sellout crowd that's waiting, just waiting for the action. . . ."

Cossell, it should be noted, at one point felt that his mouth was enough of an asset for him to briefly consider running for New York Senator James Buckley's seat in 1976. But Cossell apparently recalled the James Breslin-Norman Mailer dynamic-duo political flop, as well as the words of David Brinkley, successfully unseduced by political office. He commented that most TV-created media celebrities found out when they ran for office that they most often lost. The public viewed them with the good judgment it often renders. The voters had sense enough to know what these media messiahs didn't: that they were simply, and nothing more, "famous for being famous."

Senator Proxmire, who had a face-lift as well, talked about the political need for such cosmetics as his hair transplants. "When a man is thin and bald, I think he shows up as ready to be buried somewhere. And in politics you don't want to quite look that bad. People photograph on television in a peculiar way if they're bald. Your head sometimes can look three feet high. You look as if you just stepped off another planet or something. The main impression that people have of someone these days is what they see on television. They don't see you personally very much, even if you get around a whole lot, so for that reason I thought it might help."

One country that eclipses the United States in celebrity politics is Japan. In 1974 the citizens of Japan elected a professional joke teller, a movie queen, and a TV newscaster to the upper house of their national parliament. Partaking of the free-flowing sake and joy in his victory campaign headquarters, the professional jokester, who was elected under his stage name Columbia Top, said, "The fact that a comic like me is elected shows how far removed today's politics is from the Japanese people."

In America, those who argue for public financing of campaigns reason that this media worship heightens the candidate's need to look good to those people who spend money on his campaign; you're only as well known as your last press release or TV appearance. Therefore, obscurity is a dirty word and almost all exposure is decidedly decent. A few bemoan the fact that they have no anonymity—can't go out to dinner unmolested, can't tell a heckler to go to hell, can't get so publicly drunk as to get caught at it—but most are willing to sign away their private lives to become public property. Then sooner or later, mostly sooner, they become media junkies, and the adulation of the masses is far more nourishing than anything they can get at home.

Consider the scene played out daily in the summer of 1974 between House Judiciary Committee members and the reporters who stared down a long corridor in the Rayburn Building at the closed doors behind which the committee pondered the impeachment of Nixon. When the doors opened for a recess, Congressmen raced for their favorite reporters and vice versa.

Other House members watched with awe, amusement, disgust, and not a bit of envy. One day Representative Bella Abzug surveyed the picking and plucking and chuckled, "Vultures."

Curiously, there is a paradox in that many politicians who seek the limelight are actually shy loners. "I call it a 'loud shy,'" said one political aide. "Most of them just don't come alive until they get in front of a crowd."

There are those who see a danger in the ego-swelling political-star syndrome. While an actor creates a world of make-believe, the politician star affects people's real lives through legislation and other political action.

Expedience and temerity in the politician's decision making can and do follow when the trappings of office become so desirable that the thought of doing anything that might lose the job is unimaginable. "The whole ego corruption begins when you first walk up on that Hill and those elevator operators—who are *instructed* to memorize your face and match it with your name—

call you by name," says former Maryland Congressman Carlton Sickles. It is the little pluses that give you one up on the rest of society, like the congressional license plates, that can sometimes do it.

Those special plates give you special places to park on the Hill—drive by on a busy day and you can see policemen guarding empty "reserved" parking spots. Congressmen also get special parking at National Airport, while everyone else drives around in manic fear of not finding a place before the plane departs.

Andy Jacobs, Congressman from Indiana, said, "Hell, there are some of these men that are incredible. I actually was in a car with one Congressman who announced himself to the gasoline attendant," Jacobs said, modulating his voice to pear-shaped tones. "'Hello, I'm Congressman so and so. Give me five dollars' worth of gas.' That sounds like going up to a bubble-gum machine and introducing yourself before you drop in the penny."

If you're feeling nasty and particularly childish, there is a mean game you can play while walking through the Capitol or the House or Senate office buildings. You see this man coming toward you and you know he is a Senator or a Congressman because he walks important. Faster. More purposeful. He is ever ready with his greeting. Quickly, quickly, you see him trying to recall—has he talked with you at some point? Well, if he doesn't know you, you certainly must know *him*. So the smile is in place. And then you look past him as if he might be just any other stranger. The smiling mouth drops to a thin line across the face. One less moment of recognition.

A friend of mine talked about coming back from Texas on a plane one day with Senator John Tower, who positioned himself in the front seat of the mobile lounge that takes people from the plane to the Dulles airport terminal. "Tower should have been the first one off but instead he rose and stood watching as all the people filed past, basking in the recognition of those who did recognize him. I just gave him a cold stare because I had never seen such a brazen act of egomania." (Tower, one of the least liked by staff on the Hill, takes a different young thing to lunch almost daily at the Monocle. One story is that Capitol Hill secretaries voted him the Senator they'd least like to get stuck with on an elevator.)

One receptionist, now with a Senator, said, "I worked for Congressman Silvio Conte for one day. I was new on the phones, and he called into the office from the floor and asked for his A.A. [administrative assistant]. I asked, 'Who is calling, please,' and he exploded on the phone. 'What do you mean who is calling? This is the Congressman!' When he came back he came looking for me and shouted that if I didn't recognize his voice on the phone, I had no right to be there. I was in tears. And then I quit."

All those silly little daily acts of special treatment present a decompression problem when the politician comes home and his wife asks him to take out the trash. Few political wives are as witty as Rita Hayworth, who supposedly said of her ex-husband, Orson Welles, "He expected me to applaud him when he stepped out of the shower," but they do say such things as "If I were the only person in the room he'd ask me for my vote." The wife of former Senator Albert Gore got tired of his sitting around when the phone rang. He expected someone else in the house to answer it. She finally said, "I'm not your secretary, dear."

But, more important, such special treatment serves to set these people apart from the rest of society. The most obvious case, of course, is the presidency. George Reedy, Lyndon Johnson's White House press secretary, once wrote that the President "is a form of king and no one argues with a king." In a mass society, people are reduced to statistics, and in a mass communications era, the politician—while he can be viewed by all these statistics via television—cannot himself reach them, or get any feedback. It also results in a hero worship of the worst sort; people bowing before cosmetically appealing apparitions that loom larger than life in one's living room or bedroom. In an age that has lost its magic, there is this hopeful dream that maybe the images—just as if they were mythical gods and goddesses on Mt. Olympus—can solve our problems.

This collective hope is, paradoxically, coupled with negativism and apathy, so that a scrambling politician faces insult and blame as well as praise.

There is also the "negative" factor to voting. People in their jealousy and envy will find some way to extract a payment from politicians whom they perceive to be living glamorous lives. They may use any rationale, however weak or illogical, for not

voting someone into office or for keeping him there. A controversial wife or an ugly divorce may not mean much alone,
but it can be used as an excuse.

And then, as one aide said, "There are an awful lot of ass-
holes who just got reelected by apathy. I think they stick it out
because they have dreams of becoming Senators."

Often the vote that propels a man into public office is a pure
protest vote. One Michigan aide said that was Senator Robert
Griffin's situation. "There was this daffy woman named
Thompson in Congress, and she kept promising this Air Force
base all around her district. Wherever she made a speech she
had that base located—it was going to be in Cadillac, Traverse
City, Manistique, Frankfort. The people got pissed at her, and
the Air Force got pissed and never did build the base. The people voted for Griffin, whom they didn't know from Adam, as a
protest against her."

While there are other professions with high ceremonial content where the wife is expected to do her bit and any deviance
from a cautious norm could be damaging to her husband, there
is not the same amount of attendant publicity that comes with
politics. The spotlight is on the minister's wife, and the corporate world still grades wives. June Bingham, a biographer and
the wife of New York Representative Jonathan Bingham, interviewed young foreign service wives about their growing rebellion against what they consider servile roles. Mrs. Bingham
feels that "being the wife of an Ambassador is harder than
being the wife of a Congressman. You use many of the same
muscles but the hours are longer and need for discretion is
greater." In the military the admiral's wife is practically Queen
Victoria and all wives of lesser officers are supposed to do her
bidding.

Still, no matter how degrading and stifling such roles must
be, the "constituency" is far smaller, there is more room for private idiosyncrasies, and there is no press to record faux pas or
ask embarrassing questions. And no potential voter to tsk-tsk
over the question of whether a politician who "can't control his
wife can control his country," as the saying goes.

When a politician becomes an international figure, the mass
adulation, curiosity, and often hatred reach paparazzi proportions and life is never, ever again the same. Often the wife and

family are the only leveling influences left, influences he may need, but reject. To know what he really is and has left over inside while being constantly on display is an immeasurable and constant struggle. And for the wife who is also escalated by virtue of her husband's position, it can be a strain beyond belief. Two prominent casualties of political fame and power in 1974 were Joan Kennedy and Margaret Trudeau.

Joan Kennedy has been in training as a political wife all her married life, but, no matter how pleasantly she smiled, the vicissitudes of life as a Kennedy became too much for her and in 1974 she sought rest in private sanitariums at least three times, following a number of psychiatric sessions. Simultaneously, the wife of Canada's Prime Minister, Pierre Trudeau, vivacious twenty-six-year-old "flower child" Margaret Trudeau, was hospitalized for "severe emotional stress."

But the two women handled their problems entirely differently. Margaret Trudeau, like Betty Ford, gave a long and candid interview that made her sound intelligent as well as naïve, and endeared her to many who did not before understand the strains of her life. The Kennedys, however, who have been used to publicity all their lives, have also been used to manipulating it. It had been Ted Kennedy's decision consistently to quiet his wife, and she complied. Her friends feel he has done her a disservice by not letting her speak out. Her image is that of a wispy, inaccessible creature, ignored, to the thinking of many, by an insensitive chauvinist husband who cannot sympathize enough with someone who does not thoroughly enjoy the rough and tumble of Kennedy living. One of Joan's major problems was the haunting fear that he would run for the presidency. Friends and advisers said her emotional condition and fears were Kennedy's prime consideration for announcing in September of 1974 that he would not be a 1976 presidential candidate. The second consideration was the desire to spend as much time as possible with his son, Teddy Jr., whose right leg was amputated because of cancer of the cartilage. A third reason was the always lurking worry of assassination. And finally, the specter of Chappaquiddick, the tragedy in which a young woman drowned in a car Kennedy was driving in 1969, was always with him. He knew it would be rehashed and those who felt an explanation was still necessary for his actions would not fail to pursue it. Kennedy did not want his wife or children to be pulled through that again. When he announced his decision—which was made after conferring with his wife, mother, his sister, Jean, her husband Steve Smith—Joan Kennedy, barely out of a California hospital, sat beside Kennedy. Her hands were folded in her lap and she showed the smiling control Americans have come to respect in their political wives. When Kennedy said, "My primary responsibilities are at home. It has become quite apparent to me that I would be unable to make a full commitment to a campaign for the presidency. I simply cannot do that to my wife and children and the other members of my family," Joan blinked back tears. Later that evening, as she greeted him at home, she had one word for the way she felt—"relieved."

(But a few weeks later Joan was in the newspapers again. She failed to stop her car in time as she was driving to her McLean, Virginia, home one afternoon, and crashed into a car in front of her. Although the driver of the car was unhurt and commented on how "apologetic" Mrs. Kennedy was, police drove her to a police station where a test revealed enough alcohol in her system to qualify her for driving under the influence of alcohol. She was fined $200.)

There was a time, several years ago, when asked how she would define herself, Joan Kennedy had come up with the same sort of one-word clarity: "vulnerable."

When she first came to Washington, Joan Kennedy was everybody's golden girl, though it seems she didn't know it. She always had seemed the most likable, the most sincere and kind of the lot. I remember, when I first met her, the hair was not so bleached blond, she was truly a natural beauty, and the press was focusing in on her as the newest Kennedy arrival. I asked a rather stupid small-talk question and did not realize the significance of her answer at the time; something about would she be seeing a lot of Ethel and Robert Kennedy. Her smile stopped. "We have our *own* friends."

Years later when talking of her extensive psychiatric visits, she revealed that she had struggled for a niche and fought her feelings of inadequacy—that she could never be the superstar Jackie was, the supermommy that Ethel has been cast as, nor the tough, politically savvy woman Eunice is. Her search for a niche in the Kennedy world, to reassure herself that she could manage, began long before her husband was the sole remaining son and successor to the throne. She was not always helped by the rough and tumble, competitiveness, and boisterous teasing that marked life among the Kennedy clan. One frequent visitor to Hyannis and a Senator's wife when Robert Kennedy was alive recalls, "They all really got on Joan to the point where I felt sorry for her. I remember one day we were all going sailing, and everyone had on old blue jeans and Joan came down in a leopard-skin bathing suit. Ethel said, 'Really, Joan, did you expect the photographer?' Everyone snickered. Joan was helpless, unable to quip back with some smart crack. That's what you had to do. I got along because I didn't give a damn, was not in awe of and wouldn't play a lady-in-waiting to Ethel."

Joan Kennedy's adult life has included adulation and success, but the tragedies have been many. There have been difficult pregnancies and three miscarriages. The latest grief, something that would shatter any parent, was the cancer that forced the amputation of then twelve-year-old Teddy Jr.'s right leg above the knee.This was the explanation given for her three-week rest at Silver Hill Foundation, a private sanitarium. It was followed only days later by a second visit. Her husband's office explained that the repeat trip was part of the treatment.

Silver Hill treats patients with mild psychiatric disorders, victims of stress, and alcoholics in need of drying out. Close friends insist she was not "freaked out" but "worn out" and under enormous strain.

Silver Hill is expensive ($700 a week and up) and looks like a resort with its forty acres of trees and lawns, swimming pool and tennis court. In the late 1950s Silver Hill began a program to aid business executives under great stress in taking "emotional inventory." One political observer commented that the pressures on a Joan Kennedy were at least equal to the pressures on an executive. The difference is that the pressures are played out in public for the politician or his wife. A businessman who goes to Silver Hill may be stigmatized to a certain extent by his colleagues but this is becoming less an issue as people become more enlightened. Yet, the political wife admitting her emotional problems is still a direct detriment to her husband's career. While Kennedy bowed out of the race in considerable part to save her from the ordeal, there was no question that her illness was looked at politically as a two-way street. Political aides, even former aides to JFK, were saying in Washington that Kennedy's chances for the presidency were quietly diminished by Joan's Silver Hill visit.

Meanwhile, Joan was struggling with the reactions to international publicity her Silver Hill stay created. When she joined family members at a graveside ceremony marking Robert Kennedy's death, people were constrained. "I didn't go up to her because I didn't know what to say," said a friend of Ethel Kennedy.

Joan was hardly out of Silver Hill for the second time when she went to Capistrano-by-the Sea, another luxury hospital where she underwent treatment for emotional problems. Both hospitals specialize in treating people with drinking problems, but Capistrano-by-the-Sea uses massive doses of vitamins—a treatment that an American Psychiatric Association task force said does not work. Reportedly, Mrs. Kennedy decided to go to the California hospital against the advice of doctors who had been helping the family.

Despite her car accident, friends insisted that Joan Kennedy was doing marvelously, particularly after Ted bowed out of the presidential race. A rare sight was to see them having a leisurely lunch in the middle of the week at the San Souci shortly after the announcement. That appearance underscored the kind of treatment she constantly receives. She looked terrific, better than people remembered in some time, in white slacks, a black sweater, and red jacket. As they left, she was stared at in a restaurant noted for its celebrity clients, who are usually discreetly ignored. She walked up the stairs, head high, looking straight ahead, until an old friend called to her from a table. She went over to embrace him and talked gratefully and enthusiastically. There was something about her stance and her manner that made an observer realize that *she* knew she was being scrutinized by everyone in that room. Since a private illness and a private recuperation are impossible, close friends argue that she ought to be allowed to speak out to clear the air. "I wish they'd let her talk. She is really controlled by Kennedy's press office," said one close friend, not apparently making the connection that it is Kennedy who controls the press office. "They overprotect her. If they let her go she'd make a fine impression. All that stuff about her having a nervous breakdown and drinking too much is all wrong. All she needs is one drink and she's a wee bit tipsy. At a reception that looks bad." Another friend also said she has a low tolerance for alcohol.

Even Joan's own successes, reciting "Peter and the Wolf" and playing the piano as a TV guest star, have filled her with concern. One time she murmured to a friend, "Would they have asked me if I hadn't been Ted Kennedy's wife?" After one performance, when a close friend of Rose Kennedy, Marie Greene, came backstage to compliment her, Joan eagerly asked, "Would you write a letter to my mother-in-law and say I was good?"

Ironically, if one wants to judge a person by those political-trooper qualities so admired by the Kennedys, Joan is considered one of the best even by her mother-in-law. In October 1970 in Massachusetts, I watched her and talked with her for a few days as she campaigned for her husband. The cannonization of the Kennedys was still evident, even post Chappaquiddick, in this world of the Irish. She plowed through an exhausting schedule that included a pat little speech and a "home movie" that looked as if it had been produced by MGM.

"Since Ted couldn't be here and neither could the children, I brought a home movie film taken on Cape Cod. I thought it would help you to get to know us." A sailboat shot: "There's Ted." Audience claps. "There's my sister-in-law, Ethel." Louder claps. The boat was awash with children. "Most of the passengers belong to her." Laughter. Film cuts to a county fair with Ted and Ted Jr., then nine, on a roller coaster. The Senator is then seen fondling a huge rabbit. "Isn't he the fluffiest rabbit?" Artful shots of the handsome family on the beach, accompanied by the roar of the waves, totally enthralled the unquestioning pro-Kennedy people of Massachusetts. It took an outsider to dub it the "Chappaquiddick antidote film."

People in receiving lines carried their Instamatic cameras. Kennedy aides, so used to the ritual by then, would take the camera and stand the person next to Joan—a Kennedy, remember—and take the picture, hand the camera back, and the receiving line would move on. Joan took her shoes off and bowled with a group of women who had their hair up in pink curlers and giggled a lot and said, "Isn't she cute?" In the car she said she felt the people of Massachusetts had forgotten Chappaquiddick and everything would be all right if the press just got off the subject. She was, in a word, game.

A Boston political operative once raved about Joan Kennedy

for being "cooperative, a joy to work with. Never complained. Never was selfish. One time we had her at a Christmas party with some Mexican kids and they had this piñata, and they were hitting it to break it with this bat. And she kept smiling away while the photographers were taking pictures. Then afterwards she asked if she could sit down a minute and I saw she had a big bruise on her forehead. One of those kids had accidentally hit her, and she never even mentioned it."

Sometime after that 1970 campaign she began to consult a psychiatrist regularly. At one point she was seeing two different psychiatrists a week—wanting to check out each other's analysis. At that time she told Lester David, a writer, "I had really lost my self-confidence. The only thing I knew, that I was sure of, was that I was a very attractive young woman and that I had a pretty good figure."

She was unconfident during her performances and instead of maximizing her differences, worried and fretted that she was not good at the Kennedy competitive world of athletics. She was allergic to horses, but she tried to ride anyway. She once confided, "They're so good at everything and I'm a flop." She once said her husband should have married her younger sister, Candy—"she was always the female athlete." Her miscarriages caused more than the usual emotional trauma; Ethel and Eunice were having their children and her own husband had once said he wanted at least ten children. It was just another sign of failure to Joan. She went through a period of dressing with inappropriate exhibitionism by Washington standards—silver minis to the White House when everyone else was in long gown. This at least caused a first. The unbending Mrs. Nixon was photographed with her face almost slack-jawed and her eyes on Joan Kennedy's hem. Then it was a leather skirt and boots and a see-through blouse. Another time gaucho pants. She was signaling that she needed help, not attention, but it had taken her some time to convince her husband, of traditional Boston Irish Catholic stock, that a psychiatrist was needed. That was something politicians did not do, certainly not Kennedys.

It was not just life with the Kennedys that bothered Joan. Although on the surface she accepted the role of political "prop" wife, she admitted it had never been her idea of how to live her life. One male friend told me, "Joan should have married a successful, nice businessman and lived in Westchester."

From the beginning of her life with Kennedy, there seemed

to be a conflict. Joan wanted their 1958 wedding ceremony performed by her favorite priest, the Reverend John Cavanaugh. The Kennedy family picked Cardinal Spellman, and Joan later wistfully recalled "that was that." Her indulgent and overprotective parents seemed bent on making sure Joan Bennett made a "good catch" of a husband and were not above pushing her into what they felt were important careers, such as modeling. One woman who grew up with Joan in Bronxville, New York, told me, "She was the nicest, most sincere friend, but I always felt her mother had great ambitions for her. She used to sew all of Joan's clothes—and then stick in Henri Bendel labels." Ginny and Harry Bennett sent her to Manhattanville, the college for bright, well-bred Catholic girls. It was a sheltering time. Her father, unlike Joseph Kennedy, told her he did not expect her to be first in the class if it was at the expense of a little fun. On a Bermuda spring recess she became a beauty queen and not long after her businessman father was urging that she meet Candy Jones, head of one of the most important modeling agencies. Joan modeled for eighteen months and made several thousand dollars before she graduated and soon married Ted Kennedy.

In what must have seemed a gauche performance to some, Joan's father, according to Lester David in his book *Joan Kennedy*, arranged to have St. Joseph's Roman Catholic church lit up with floodlights at the sides and in front of the altar and the November 29, 1958 wedding was recorded on film.

There were some unhappy times in the Bennett family, which shook Joan's sense of security; her parents later divorced and Joan's mother at one time visited Silver Hill herself.

Although she enthusiastically threw herself into the early campaigns—for John, for Ted, for Bob—the assassination tragedies lessened her already waning interest in politics. There were countless nights of staying home while Ted was gone. Unconditioned to take the blows of life, as the Kennedys were (it was Jack who said "life is unfair"), Joan staggered under the crushing blow of her son's illness. He is a brave boy who uncomplainingly accepts the treatment, which brings bouts of severe nausea, but, as any mother can understand, having to stand by helplessly is a devastating anguish. With her husband's decision to forgo a presidential campaign, perhaps Joan will have the semblance of the normal life she naïvely thought would be hers when she married a young law student.

And yet it seems as if that life will always be haunted by public rumors. As scandal magazines continued to make pronouncements that Joan and Ted were through, even to the point of naming the "other women," politicians and the press refused to believe Kennedy's bowing out of the presidential race was final. The political pressure was off of Joan for a few months, but by summer of 1975 the word in Washington was, flatly, "Kennedy is running."

For Margaret Trudeau, her life will begin when her husband leaves office. "I long for the day I can just be Pierre's wife," she said after her hospitalization for severe emotional stress. What led to her seeking psychiatric help? "I felt myself trapped in a role I didn't feel very fulfilled in." She was "completely unprepared" for her life as the wife of a Prime Minister. "It was a total catastrophe in terms of my identity," she said, speaking in a lilting but childlike voice that sounded younger than her twenty-six years. She didn't quite know what to do with the servants—"I certainly wasn't going to order them around. I'm too much of a flower child for that." She wasn't prepared for the interest of the press, nor was she prepared for the Royal Mounties who are her constant escorts. "I sometimes escape but I am sometimes chastised. They say it is a great risk, but you just *long* to walk along and not hear footsteps behind you. I don't have that freedom. I'm never alone. And I sometimes like to be alone. Lots of times. I feel like I'm in a prison, but what do you do? You must accept it as one of the realities." A more subtle concern was the unvoiced "expectations of other wives and political organizers. Things are vague. Nobody's going to tell me what they want. I'm pretty much a straight-out-front sort of chick and I get pretty confused. They should just tell me what they want." She does not like the "formality" and "posturing" of political life. "It's not a glamorous life; it's a lonely life. It's not a free life."

The press was a burden. A very private woman who had given birth to two children in quick succession, Margaret Trudeau astonished and then captivated Canada with her speechmaking campaign that was credited in no small part with his 1974 victory. "I didn't feel the image makers, the press, or the people really understood what a kind man he was." Her job was to "round out the hard edges" and help people understand this "shy and private man." Trudeau had to convince her that organized politics was a way to contribute something worthwhile. She decided that as long as he felt that way, she would rather have "someone like him in office." But after her political campaigning, she felt the press should leave her alone.

"I am such a private person and I opened up so much in the campaign, I felt I deserved a rest. I found this [the press] an intrusion at the time [of her illness and after the campaign]. Yet again I had to deal with the expectations of people trying to figure me out—when I was trying to figure out myself." Living up to her image of a beautiful, perfect mother and perfect wife of a Prime Minister became too much. "I was beginning to believe I *had* to be [perfect] and the strain was just too much. I get as angry as anyone; I have as many problems as anyone. I can't be perfect and I can't please everybody."

She became depressed and began to cry a lot. "I didn't feel sick, I just felt very, very weary and emotionally tight." Seeing a psychiatrist was a "very positive thing." She had been repressing her anger and her emotions "until I didn't have any more campaign elections to fight." People treat her with more respect now that she has asserted her feelings, she said. She received letters from people who told her they had been through the same thing. "You tend to feel cut off from other people and think you are the only person who is suffering."

Margaret Trudeau said she wanted to try a career at writing and photography at the time of this interview with Carol Taylor of CTV news (the commercial Canadian television network). But a few weeks later she said her photographic career was being halted "for the time being." It seems it was too much on top of her role as mother and political wife.

6

The Happy-Political-Couple Myth and the Role of the Press

THE public has long subscribed to a curious paradox concerning politicians. The individual one votes into office—i.e. "my" Senator or Congressman or President—is supposed to act like a paragon. Yet, at the same time, the public, responding to polls, lumps all politicians together at the bottom of the integrity barrel along with used-car salesmen. That these "bums" are expected to behave like "saints"—and their wives and children along with them—is the traditional, unrealistic, and hypocritical belief that bolsters the Happy Family political pattern.

For years, the politician and his family, on the surface, eagerly went along with the Happy Family image, sensing political ruination if they did not. And the serious press, for fear of sounding like *Modern Screen*, often went along with the act, too. No matter how much a politician might be attacked, his marriage supposedly was sacrosanct. Those members of the press who did not go by the rules were often vilified by a public who wanted nothing more than to believe in an impossible dream, a dream that they themselves, in many cases, could not attain in their own lives.

The public reaction to the revelation that Franklin and Eleanor Roosevelt enjoyed a less-than-perfect union exemplifies the desire to believe in the myth. Westbrook Pegler was attacked for being more scurrilous than his enemies usually regarded him when he mentioned that a woman other than Eleanor—Lucy Mercer—was spirited out of Franklin's death room by the Secret Service. And generations later, when Roosevelt's son Elliott offered insight as well as revealing a less-than-flattering picture of his parents as a couple, he was criticized as an ingrate, ne'er-do-well son unworthy of his parentage.

The Happy Political Family, in the beginning, not only corroborated an ideal, it was actually in step with and fit the pattern of the rest of society, the nuclear and extended family that held early America's social system together.

But as industrialization and urbanization created shifts and breaks in family patterns, the political family was still not allowed to move out of the Victorian mold. Even today, as people struggle to create new ways of life out of old ruins (one out of every three marriages fail, but the "rate" of divorce is increasing; Masters and Johnson predict 40 percent of all marriages performed in 1973 will end in divorce), the politically glued-together family is still some mythical model, a parody of roles. As Senator Robert Dole, whose divorce hurt him in his 1974 senatorial campaign, told me, "We're not expected to be normal."

When you live in relative sophistication or at least in urban anonymity, it is hard to find anyone who would vote for a man on the basis of whether or not he has a good marriage. In a time of uncertainty about the future coupled with disillusionment about the past, many young people—and many older people, once their children leave home—search for alternatives to a way of life that seems to have become too hypocritical to retain. Many people who divorce remarry. There were four and a half million people married in 1973, an unknown number of those remarriages. There were also 913,000 divorces, a jump of 74,000 over 1972. In many cases, simply living together is a growing pattern, with "his," "hers," and "our" children coexisting. Younger people in their marriage contracts don't opt for "till death do us part." Our pop magazines, ever in search of the trendy and in, tell us that "bisexual chic" is the latest on college campuses.

So isn't there now room and time for candor on the part of political families? Don't all the free livers of the world, even if, by Iowa standards, this means only the divorced, constitute a constituency of sorts? Why still the conforming to an archaic mold? Don't people see through the hypocrisy of fawning wife and husband and respect the politician less for such an act?

The pollsters that I have interviewed indicate otherwise. There are still a lot of Mrs. Grundies out there. And it's not just the Mrs. Grundies, but others who view urban life as impersonal, tend to romanticize the "back-to-the-land" philosophy, and are wary that their representative might change and get "uppity" when he moves to Washington. Wander through Disney World and it's difficult to imagine the divorce statistics as you see the double-knit generation, 4.2 family, clean and wholesome and incredibly Aryan-looking (I saw very few minorities of any sort), flowing through the gates. And then there is apparently a large number who don't care what their politicians do of a private nature, as long as they don't get caught at it.

As for women politicians, the double standard is at work in the most covert and insidious way. While the Kennedy moviestar handsomeness is an asset for males, a beautiful woman has problems. "She can't be a buxom blonde and run for office," said one pollster. "She can be moderately attractive and make it, but she better not be stunning."

And although there is much of the star syndrome attached to

political life, there is one vast difference. "It's okay for movie stars to be 'kicky' or 'decadent.' In fact, they are expected to behave on that level," one pollster told me. "When you go to a movie, you go to see a movie and you don't give a damn if Robert Redford is off screwing fifty people other than his wife. And the kids can be slightly cuckoo." (Jane Fonda's antiwar stance never hurt her father, Henry Fonda, who merely "played" politicians in movies.)

"The Protestant ethic is alive and well," said one political researcher. Most pollsters, admitting to an inexact science, have not gotten around to questions that probe a politician's moral fiber beyond financial and political corruption and, more lately, divorce. "How do you tap those feelings? Do you ask, 'What do you think about a Congressman who plays around or drinks too much?'" questioned one pollster. They might learn that most people don't care, but like the blind leading the blind, politicians and their families are still wary of rocking the boat, and many give the public appearance of having been wrapped in aluminum foil and flash-frozen in the 1950s. That was when, if you've forgotten, a movie called *The Moon Is Blue* was almost banned because the word "virgin" was used.

It is this 1950s image that so strongly reinforces the teamplayer political marriage as we know it today. Despite the woman's movement, despite the fact that Alcoholics Anonymous annually tries to get the secret alcoholic housewife to come out from behind her empties stashed in the pantry, despite the working-mother statistics, (nearly 14 million women with children under 18 worked in 1974), despite divorce and open marriages and no marriages, despite more women deciding to run for power rather than marry it, the "correct" political couple is still by and large a monolithic stereotype.

Today's political couples are, in fact, not unlike the uppercrust Edwardians, whose broad pretenses covered a multitude of actualities. Many politicians and their families said they would talk to me only anonymously—they have a deep fear of repercussions. One close friend, a wife of a Congressman, who smokes marijuana on occasion and takes a few Alice B. Toklas brownies to get through "some of those God-awful functions," said, "Oh, hell, put that in. It's about time people knew we were real and alive." Two days later she called back and said, "You know, no one would give a damn in Washington, but you better not use my name. It would get my husband in deep trouble back home if those local papers get ahold of it."

People don't vote for a politician in a vacuum—they vote between a *choice* of individuals. And although people are fond of saying, for example, that divorce is okay today, that it does not cost someone the presidency, as it may have Nelson Rockefeller in 1964, to many it is still a fingers-crossed affair. And political opponents play a subtle form of dirty pool in the divorce stakes.

If one politician can present a spouse and children and the other can't, it helps. "The wife is a tremendous asset," says Peter Hart, a top political analyst. He said that even if the marriage is a total farce, "I think the use of the wife [note the word "use"] is a tremendous humanizing effect. I'm sure a lot of the people we poll are divorced, but there is still the double standard; it's okay for me, but not for my politician." One national reporter said, "The role of the political wife for years was to show that the candidate wasn't a fag. Do you remember all those things they said about Adlai Stevenson? A bachelor was suspect."

Whether revelations about his private life hurt enough to cost a man his office depends on a number of variables: how he handles it, the strength or lack of strength in his opponent, the degree of sophistication and tolerance of his constituents, how the press treats it.

Senator William Proxmire—divorced once and separated for three years from his second wife (they reunited in the spring of 1975)—seems to have no problems with his constituents because the only urge that seems to get the best of him is work. There is never a hint of scandal about him and another woman. He told me that in the case of one Wisconsin politician given to healthy sexual urges, a whisper campaign and fear of public repercussions kept the man from getting his party's endorsement for a state office. This in 1974. And Gaylord Nelson, the other Senator from Wisconsin, said, "Don't kid yourself—if I got arrested for drunken driving, it would really hurt me back home."

One political analyst and adviser thinks the politician brings a lot of this on himself, overselling himself as a hero, using today's mass media techniques; just as the public buys charisma over character and then is disillusioned. "Politicians have set themselves up as gods. Look at all the Charlie Guggenheim films [slick, attractive footage used by political candidates to advertise themselves]. They portray themselves larger than life. God, you feel like you're looking at the greatest human being. I tell all my candidates, 'Don't overpromise!' This is the time of the underpromise. You have to be real."

But one Senator says, "The public doesn't want reality; well, maybe in other areas, but not when it comes to the family." Instead, the public likes a careful *imitation* of reality.

No one knows when the first political wife did her first political tea. Wives were often silent and not so silent maneuverers in politics from earliest times—Abigail Adams, Dolly Madison, Mary Todd Lincoln, down to Eleanor Roosevelt and Lady Bird Johnson. Active campaigning often depended on regional and ideological patterns. (Some Southern women still remain very much in the background.) Some wives of Middlewestern populist politicians were giving speeches several decades ago.

But for the most part, until recently, what most people wanted out of the political wife was simply her presence. (Jacqueline Kennedy Onassis, criticized for her lack of political interest, managed through her glamour to focus great attention on the political wife.) It was as if these wives went into intensive training—given by the wives of retired politicians—to learn how to smile forever. A political wife's most controversial statement has long been her meatloaf recipe. She is homogenized to a blandness rivaled only by an old State Department hand's wife, whose chief preoccupation was to be profoundly innocuous.

Although urban papers have switched from women's pages to sections of overall interest, named View or Style or Portfolio, many smaller papers still segregate the "women's" pages and ask the wives of politicians their favorite recipes and how they furnish their homes. Even when the conversation creeps into private corners, there are "candid" admissions that "yes, it isn't always easy having the man-of-the-house away a lot." But these are quickly followed by "it's all for a good cause" stiff-upper-lip phrases.

So brainwashed are these wives to their back-of-the-bus status that what seems aberrational to others seems normal to them; the wife and family needs rank without question far below political considerations. And so, even as Abigail McCarthy (the now-separated wife of former Senator Eugene McCarthy) was rushed into X-ray when complications developed after the birth of one of their children some years ago, her husband, she recalls, left the hospital to get to the Hill for a vote. The doctor was shocked; she wasn't. And in 1958, the wife of the Wisconsin Senator, Ellen Proxmire, gave birth to a son, only to see him die the next day. She recalls that the Senator took off for a convention the following day. He recalls that the convention was two weeks later.

Senator Birch Bayh's wife was in Europe when she heard that her alcoholic father had shot and killed her stepmother and then himself. When the plane bringing her home landed in Boston, the papers were brought on board. The headline said "Senator Bayh's father-in-law in murder-suicide." She stumbled off the plane, to be met by aides. She waited with aides and friends for several hours at home. Her husband could not be there, he was guiding the most important debate of his political life, which led to the defeat of G. Harrold Carswell's nomination for the Supreme Court.

Even wives with a reputation for outspoken individualism argue that when it comes to issues, they feel uncomfortable speaking their minds. Abigail McCarthy said the fear that you might say something to endanger your husband is practically enfeebling. Few have the nerve and style of Mary Lindsay to reply, as she reportedly did, about disagreeing on an issue with her husband, John, New York's former mayor: "Just because I sleep with him, I don't have to think like him." For the wife there is the added pressure of wooing the press, yet not saying anything to damage her husband.

Political wives sometimes complain that the media examination is excessive today. Although the press has upheld the happy-political-couple myth in general, *famous* political wives have been written about disparagingly throughout history. Mary Todd Lincoln was criticized all her life by what she called the "vampyre press" for her political meddling, as well as her shopping sprees during the Civil War when people were starving, and for her sorrowful meanderings as the widow of a martyred president. There was little attempt to understand that she was a sick woman. Martha Mitchell had the midnight telephone; Mrs. Lincoln, her midnight letter. She would write that certain officers and cabinet members should be fired. Some of the press caricatured Mrs. Franklin Roosevelt unmercifully, the homely do-gooder who went down into the coal mines more times than anyone could bear. (Her unhappiness in her marriage forced her, like many political wives, into seeking fulfillment in a more active public role.) Stories circulated for years about Mamie Eisenhower and her supposed drinking problem. Jackie Kennedy was criticized for the money she spent on clothes (inspiring her wry comment that she couldn't spend that much if she wore sable panties). Lady Bird was caricatured for her accent and her "beautification" projects. No one ever understood that these wives may have been reaching out in their own ways to compensate for an incomplete private life with men who needed the roar of the crowd more than private acceptance.

A perfect example of someone who was damaged unnecessarily is Mrs. Edmund Muskie. She was riding on a campaign bus one icy night with four women reporters after an exhausting day of campaigning in New Hampshire. She explained to me later that everyone was nervous and tired and a little scared of the slippery ride and she tried to cheer them up. And so, she said, among other things, "Let's just sit here and tell dirty jokes," and referred to her husband as "Big Daddy." "That was the only time I ever called him that and it was totally in jest." Jane Muskie may be breezy and informal, but she is as correct a political wife as you could find. Kandy Stroud of *Women's Wear Daily* wrote it up. No one else did at the time. Other national reporters on the trip said they had understood that "the whole thing was off the record." One said, "I fault Kandy for making it impossible for us to get any background 'feeling' on these people any more; they don't dare be relaxed or unguarded at any time with us." Mrs. Stroud said she had no impression of its being off the record. At any rate, the situation escalated when *Newsweek* plucked those specific phrases from the *WWD* article and gave a false impression of Mrs. Muskie.

William Loeb's right-wing *Manchester Union Leader*—Loeb hates all things in general and Democrats specifically—wrote an editorial about "Big Daddy's Jane," reprinting the *Newsweek* information, saying she sneak-smoked, drank, and used off-color language on the press bus. The rest is history. Muskie, who was having his problems with the then mysterious gremlins at work sabotaging his campaign, stood on the back of a flatbed truck in a near blizzard, attacked Loeb as a "gutless coward" for writing about his wife and cried.

I, for one, don't have the same macho view of what political campaigning should be. It is repression of self in the extreme. If George McGovern wants to say "kiss my ass" to a heckler—as he did—I found it one of the better, nonvacillating things he said.

To cry in public, while it seemed horrifyingly bad politics to old pros, showed some humanity and compassion to me rather than weakness. But who really knows how the voter will react? On election day I was doing a story about the New Hampshire primary and I asked one woman as she came out of the polling booth if she had voted for Muskie and the answer was no, "I don't want them tears in the White House." A woman right next to her said she saw nothing wrong with it and wished her husband would defend her that way.

Male reporters wrote that this was unseemly; that Muskie's notorious trigger-happy anger and his crying made one wonder about his ability to "handle" things in the White House. The judgment, once again, of the man who someday might have to push that "little red button" called into question.

Occasionally Jane still reflects on the campaign trials and the depression her husband went through afterward. "It took him about six months to get back to normal. And I sometimes wonder if I had really inadvertently started all that." Then, referring to such espionage tactics as the fake "Canuck" letter, she says, "Now we know there were so many other things that went into it."

Even before, and certainly after, the Jane Muskie incident, political wives had nightmares of saying or doing the wrong thing. Many can't help but think that the bland image, no matter how insipid, is preferable. Today, this creates a gaming tendency on the part of the press, who look for cracks that will enable them to look into the real households. But some years ago it was considered in bad taste to print any occasional slip, no matter how much more telling it might be than all those correct statements.

I will never forget a 1960 interview with Mrs. Lyndon Baines Johnson for a profile I was doing on her husband, soon to be inaugurated as the Vice President. I was new to Washington and politics and was asking any number of naïve questions. I asked Mrs. Johnson, "How does he relax?" That is the kind of question guaranteed to set off the Political Wife Filibuster.

Her smile widened. "Howah does he relayax? Weyull, he weahs his boots. He weahs his boots like othah men weah theyuh moccasins. And there isn't a thing he wouldn't do for his two darlin' daughters. Why, ah just . . . " Suddenly there was this clomp, clomp, clomp of Lyndon's boots coming down the stairs, accompanied by what can only be described as a bellow. "BIRD! If ah tol' you once, ah' tol' you a hundred times we got those people comin' for that inaugural, and you don't have those cots or innything." Mrs. Johnson leapt up as if she had just discovered herself sitting on a tarantula, and shot for the hallway. "Ohhhh, Lyndon," she said in a fluttery tone, followed by a stage whisper. "Theyuh's ah reporter heyah to see you." Silence. Johnson appeared around the corner. Came close. Held the hand in greeting. Looked through beady eyes, down his bulbous nose as if down the barrel of a rifle. "Haih. Glad to meet yew. So sorry ah cain't stay and chat a spell, but ah gotta go up on the Hill and do mah work." As Mrs. Johnson walked him to the door and the waiting limousine, there was a sotto voce parting shot from him—"Like ah said, about those cots. . . ."

Mrs. Johnson came back, sat down, crossed her legs at the ankles, and began to carry on. "Now let me see, where was I? Oh yes, his boots. . . ."

The press corps used to look in vain for some sort of emotion to pass between Pat and Dick Nixon; observers looked for anything that spoke of warmth. When she ventured out on her own as First Lady, a frothier, breezier Pat emerged. She could tease her staff or the press corps, using her college-days slang such as "kiddo" and "big deal." But whenever she was around her husband, she would revert to "plastic Pat." She was on her way home from South America in March of 1974 with a case of the flu, when she learned that her husband had scheduled a birthday celebration for her at the Grand Old Opry in Nashville. It was imperative that Nixon stay on the good side of the South in his impeachment battle. His wife's birthday celebration was pretty much sidetracked most of the night as Nixon concentrated on what was to be his finale of the evening—playing a yo-yo onstage. "It hurt me to see it," said one of Pat's aides. "He ignored her all evening while he messed with that silly yo-yo."

Three reporters who covered her constantly related two identical incidents that struck them as peculiar. "One time we were getting off a plane in San Antonio and he gets off Air Force One and we all meet on the Tarmac. Senator John Tower is with Nixon and he comes up and gives Pat a kiss. Then Nixon comes up. And shakes her hand." The second time this happened, she was on her way back from her first solo trip. The limousine pulled up to the front of the White House. Nixon was there to greet her. She got out. Again, he shook her hand. Mrs. Nixon, then, holding his arm, pulled his face down for a kiss on the cheek, which the photographers duly captured. "I have never seen two people with less rapport," said one observer.

Mrs. Nixon was kidded unmercifully and cruelly (one joke went, "on trips, she takes her hairdresser and her embalmer"). But she was also praised for being America's Political Pinup Wife, as unreal as Miss America. The pinnacle of political wifedom, she was devotedly admired by even those who hated her husband. Admired for, quite simply, being a monumental façade. That she could have used her First Lady clout to do something of value for the poor or retarded or diseased seemed not to matter to those who universally praised her. You heard the phrases all the time: "She's amazing. She's got strength. She doesn't crack under the strain." Is there anything wrong in cracking under the strain just a little bit? To many people, a lot, apparently. So she shook the hands of all those countless "ladies" who visited her on afternoons, some wearing gloves and hats, and she was a "brick" and she wore a smile of pinched emotions.

She and Richard Nixon epitomized the American Dream that so many had dreamed: the self-made man and the self-made woman who would rise together from their Whittier garage apartment to the White House. It was a dream that Pat Nixon clung to longer than anyone, as she pleaded to the last for her husband not to resign—knowing that in her husband's destruction there would be a legacy of shame and disgrace—for her and her children and their children's children.

That she seemed to believe in her husband to the end made

people pity her, but it was inevitable that a woman like Pat Nixon *had* to believe for her own salvation. She had invested too much of herself over too many years of grief and pain as well as glory to admit that he was not what he seemed to be to her or her daughters.

And there were others that did not see her as some hapless victim, those who knew of her steel-like toughness. At one point, Mrs. Nixon urged her husband to burn the Watergate tapes because "they are like love letters."

As Nixon gave his maudlin and tear-stained farewell to what was left of his White House staff, Pat Nixon stood next to him as she had in so many crises. The tears glistened in her eyes and the hollows in her cheeks seemed deeper and she would look off to the side to distract herself. Some inner command kept those tears from falling. One wife of a member of Nixon's administration said, "It's as if she has an extra duct to suck them back in."

It was an emotional end to a life that had been so carefully lived that no one in Washington could ever say they knew the real Pat Nixon. I remember a Senate Ladies luncheon in the early summer of 1974. It was something of a pre-impeachment lunch. Wives of Democrats were clearly there for one final look at the White House under Nixon; reporters had come to see if the famous mask would slip. Pat faced her visitors in a pink and white dress and white patent shoes with little bows. Shaking hands as she had for so long. Smiling as she had for so long. Pat Nixon, for all her appearance of locked-in emotions, is also a toucher. She hugs children and she hugs adults she feels some rapport with. It is an impulsive and quick gesture. She can also stiffen when there are those around she doesn't like, but the gesture is so subtle that the only clue is in the eyes. They turn as cold as cobra's. On that day she reserved that gaze for the wives of the Senators she regarded as her husband's enemies—Jane Muskie, wife of Edmund Muskie, and Lorraine Percy, wife of Republican liberal Charles Percy.

Mrs. Nixon once described politics as a "life I would not have chosen," but she gamely went along. Occasionally a trace of bitterness would flash, so quickly that people were not sure they had heard her correctly. When a reporter once suggested she had a "good life" Mrs. Nixon paused and said, "I just don't tell all." When asked if she wanted her daughter Tricia to marry a politician, she answered, "I'd feel sorry for her if she ever married anyone in politics."

7

The Plight of the Political Helpmate

FOR the first time in political history, the public saw a real-life nationally televised soap opera—"The Political Runaway Wife"—in the early months of 1974. For weeks following Angelina Alioto's seventeen-day disappearance, she and her husband, Joseph, the mayor of San Francisco who was running in—and would in a few months lose—the Democratic primary for the governorship of California, were trailed by TV cameras and photographers and reporters who wanted more and more of Mrs. Alioto's true confessions.

She responded as if she were Betty Hutton, the aging movie star who was "rediscovered" serving soup in a Catholic parish in 1974 and was brought into the warming glow of the spotlight for a New York charity event of Hollywood-style hugs, tears, and attention.

Mrs. Alioto, fifty-eight and the grandmother of eleven, poured out her grievances coast to coast. She had run away to "punish" him. She was "neglected," left alone twenty-five nights a month in the mansion. "Joe doesn't always tell me the truth." She needed some "thoughtfulness."

It all began January 18, when her husband forgot to introduce her at a political function in Palm Springs where he was the guest of honor. It was one thing to be a prop. But to be a nonintroduced prop was more than she could bear.

She was so "furious," as she recalled, that she sped off into the night, not telling anyone where she was going. When she returned, seventeen days later for the moment of triumph, to be courted by TV cameras and autograph nuts, it was obvious that her husband hadn't the foggiest idea what had happened to this little bonbon of a woman who appears the antithesis of the women's movement, with her carefully bleached hair, expensive jewelry, designer gowns. Her "gilded cage" is a Valentine box of a mansion, all gilt and marble floors with showy

French and Italian antiques, red and gold flocked wallpaper, heavy velvet drapes; not unlike those opulent movie theater lobbies of the twenties and thirties that linger in memories though most have been torn down for parking lots.

In the aftermath of his wife's public revelations, Alioto's male companions worried about the mayor. "He was publicly humiliated, and it was obviously a shameful thing for him. He seems a troubled, burdened man," one of his friends told me. "He hasn't been the bombastic dynamic whirlwind of a man that he was before this. He keeps to himself and doesn't say much.

"I think this may have a long-standing effect on his marriage, and certainly his political future," his friend continued. "He is a macho Italian type, and you must remember that for San Francisco Italians, the family is close-knit, and the father really runs the show. It isn't like Mrs. Lindsay, for example, standing up and saying she's mad at John. Besides, the mayor isn't the kind of man who likes to share the limelight. In those first ten days after her return, it was Angelina everyone wanted for speeches, TV, autographs. He just had to stand there. It was tough duty."

All of a sudden Mayor Alioto was wearing the stiff grin that political *wives* are supposed to wear. It was *he* who had to be the ever-smiling, all-forgiving, constantly supportive appendage. He did not handle the role well. "She was bound to be the heavy—the pop-off wife," said one pollster, "except Alioto flubbed it." The mayor could think only of his own humiliation and could not turn this startling deviation from the norm into anything positive. In the first few hours of her return, Alioto did not anticipate that women all over the country would write his wife, to tell her, as one wrote, "Someone has finally voiced our anguish and frustration at being overlooked, ignored, and forgotten by our husbands."

Later Alioto tried to regroup by talking about "the problems of women" in his speeches and would say "there are a lot of Angelinas out there"; and his aides, with wistful desperation, referred to her explosion as the "human touch," but Alioto's first reaction was the one most widely caught by the press and public, and therefore remembered.

When Mrs. Alioto complained about her husband's neglect, the lack of being consulted on political matters, her husband gripped her hand and gave a feeble semblance of a smile. "No one likes to be used. That was part of my anguish. I want to be wanted for myself." A woman reporter asked Alioto, "Do you understand what your wife's trying to tell you?" Alioto's damaging answer was no.

While no one would ascribe his defeat solely to the Angelina caper, most California politicos admitted it was a factor. They differ on its importance; but his reaction to her did solidify an image of a man behind the times, an out-of-date politician.

At their joint press conference the mayor said almost apologetically that he was guest of honor at a Palm Springs function. "He," she said, "was on cloud 101," as she darted a poisonous glance at the mayor. "My son and his wife and I were stepchildren at the dinner. I thought we would be assets and he seemed to be trying to hide us." The mayor flew back to San Francisco, apparently unnoticing of and unconcerned about her "anguish." "He left me with anguish, and I took off."

It was Alioto's decision to hold the press conference, and then to go on a subsequent nationwide television show, during which his wife continued to give him hell. To some observers, the whole thing was in intriguingly bad taste; others thought her balmy. Others thought he should have handled it better. Any number of people were amused and, since she was so obviously a rich little lady who had played the game so correctly for so long, it gave credence to the belief that politics—at least that kind where the wife is not a team partner—is a stifler for wives, and that some of them were not willing to put up with it any longer. Still others, such as Abigail McCarthy, unwittingly told more about the political system than she realized when she said, "Of course, the life came as a shock to her—she'd only been in it for six years." In other words, unless you go through a lifetime of training as a public wife, it is possible to get the bends if public life comes late to a marriage.

When Alioto took office as mayor in early 1968, there were no apparent hostilities in Mrs. Alioto, who had lived more than twenty-five years as the wife of a nonpolitician. (They were married thirty-three years in 1974.) There were the ritual interview teas, with such prescribed headlines as "Mrs. Alioto Takes New Role in Stride."

In May 1968, a few months into her new role, she showed off her home, built in 1914 of Italian Renaissance design, in which she and her millionaire husband and their six now-grown children had already lived for twenty years. It was suffocatingly opulent. Crystal chandeliers, more antiques than a small museum might possess, gilt and flocked paper, and such little touches as bonbons in a candy dish held by two china cherubs, the tea cart with its gleaming silver service. Mrs. Alioto was in her apricot crepe Yves St. Laurent at-home pajamas, and she was attended by three maids who looked as if they stepped off a 1930s movie lot in their black dresses, white aprons, and white caps.

For the first one hundred days of his term in office, Mrs. Alioto shunned publicity, was upset when visitors, thinking the house was like Gracie Mansion, where you could tour the rooms, streamed up the marble front stairs (which are guarded by two bronze lions).

But by May, she was saying, "I wanted to keep my home private and I still do, but I have changed in attitude. I saw the need for leadership of my husband's caliber, and I decided to go along." At that time, she was the personification of the kind of political wife who is going to be helpful and staunchly inoffensive.

She became a board member of the opera association, the De Young Museum Society, and the Patrons of Art and Music at the California Palace of the Legion of Honor. At least two days a week she worked in the office of the Rice Growers Association (Alioto is president of this organization, in 1968 one of the largest cooperatives in the world). She acquired a real estate license (without telling her husband she was taking the courses) to handle family business transactions. She opened an antique shop and traversed those San Francisco hills in her Mercedes.

Both of the Aliotos are of Sicilian descent, but she bristled at frequent references to her husband as "the son of a Sicilian fisherman," though his campaign literature called him "the son of an immigrant fisherman." She grew up in Dallas, where her wealthy father was in real estate and wholesale produce.

A syrupy article stated that "Mrs. Alioto has definite ideas on definite things and behind her attractive mien there's a keen mind." In a section on "topics she speaks up on," the quotes made her sound about as profound as Kahlil Gibran. "On living: A person shouldn't live in the past or too much in the future . . . otherwise you miss out on so much of the present."

As for politics and her husband, she said he was "not a politician . . . he's a civic-minded gentleman who's trying to run a city."

Six years later she was ready to say she was jealous of politics. "This politics is a real bug. It's worse than golf . . . ever since he's been in politics, I haven't felt like a real person; and I'm jealous of it because it's taking him away from me. He always says 'the city I love,' 'the state I love,' and I know he loves me but . . ." Her voice trailed off.

Mrs. Alioto exemplifies the theory that politics puts special stresses and strains on a family and heightens problems, brings out a lust for adulation that was more in balance before. While many people argue that it is not politics but the success drive that makes men neglect their families, Mrs. Alioto does not sound like a person, however old-fashioned, who would have stayed unprotestingly in a marriage for thirty-three years had she felt as neglected as she did in the last six. She might have *stayed* but not without protest.

When Mrs. Alioto "took off," as she said, it was not a new experience for Alioto. He was not even too concerned at first, according to a close friend of his who said, "She had done this before. At least once a year" (while he was in office). Alioto apparently never thought those earlier bids for attention meant enough to examine or change the pattern of their life. The only difference was that this time she stopped telephoning her daughter to check in after the first few days. Associates say that in the first week political repercussions were foremost in the mayor's mind as well as theirs. They ruled out her being hurt. "We felt we'd hear about that" was the rather dispassionate comment. The mayor's concern for her grew, and he cancelled some appearances, using the excuse that his wife had laryngitis. Meanwhile, Alioto and his aides were checking fat farms and facelift parlors. That she would hide herself away to have a face-lift seemed plausible to them. Impending older age, yes, that would be it, that womanly thing about "age" *must* be the reason.

Political embarrassment was building along with the tension as days went by. But publicity was the last thing the mayor and his staff wanted, and so police were "very quietly" dispatched to look for the white Hertz Rent-A-Car she was driving. Then on the sixteenth day, it began to dawn on everyone that she might be hurt, or kidnapped. This time, an all-points bulletin was issued. Mrs. Alioto heard it in Santa Cruz and called home, then drove up to the mansion in the early hours before dawn.

Aides offered to go through a mock press conference with her, as the President of the United States often does, to drill her for the possible questions that might come. Alioto did not think that necessary. According to one political consultant, Alioto only decided about ten minutes before the scheduled 2 P.M. press conference to "tell" his wife what he thought she ought to say. "They had quite an argument. Three times they started down the stairs and then went back to the bedroom to talk some more," he told me. "They were thirty-five minutes late. It was quite obvious Joe didn't know what the hell she would say."

It was a full house, and Mrs. Alioto was quick to tell them that she was frustrated over being cast into the background of the mayor's blooming gubernatorial campaign. The press listened in skeptical disbelief at what they thought had to be a press aide's inspiration. Traveling as Angelina DiPuma (her grandmother's name), she had made a pilgrimage to the California missions. But they grilled her and it was true. "I have no regrets whatever about taking off," she said. "I now feel better educated about California."

She said she was sick of being "pampered" and that her husband had not consulted her about running first for mayor and then for governor. She loved her husband and thought their marriage had been a success until politics entered. "I feel now as if the six children and I are cornerstones—places to hang hats, foundations. I don't want to be used," she said, "that's part of the anguish. I was frustrated over being used. I wanted to be wanted for myself. I have to be here alone in this place with my housekeeper twenty-five to twenty-seven nights a month. I feel neglected."

Someone asked her if she had ever planned to leave her husband, and Mrs. Alioto giggled before replying, "What woman hasn't planned such a thing? I even planned what I would wear." Then she paused, and added a joke, of sorts: "Actually it wasn't dissolution I was thinking of. It was murder."

There were the obvious comparisons with Martha Mitchell, and Mrs. Alioto complimented her East Coast sister with, "She was the only truthful person in the whole [Watergate] affair.

She wasn't believed because she was a woman. I am no women's libber, but I greatly admire her." The mayor, who had gripped her hand tightly throughout, weakly tried a joke, saying that his wife was a "cross between an Italian mama and a liberated mama." Mrs. Alioto was not amused. "What the hell is that supposed to mean?"

The saddest aspect to the Alioto road show is that their private communications had so broken down that she felt forced into a public confrontation because, from her story, she never got the chance to confront him alone over the kitchen table.

As calls, telegrams, letters, and comments gushed forth, Mrs. Alioto did another burn. Her eyes flashed as she told one reporter, "The other day down in L. A. a television reporter stuck a microphone in Joe's face and said, 'If you can't control your wife, how can you control what happens in Sacramento?' Well, I got so mad at him. I said, 'The mayor's not accountable for my actions. I'm not a robot he can wind up like a little car and send across the floor.' Why, the idea! It makes me so mad."

Whatever truly brought about the rebellion of the "little political helpmate" remains locked inside Mrs. Alioto. She gives all sorts of explanations and motives, and people who know her well say, "Something snapped; she simply had had enough." The build-up was at least six years in the making, and her private story revealed so much more than that blatant press conference.

In an interview with Lacey Fosburgh of the New York *Times*, she still had all the trappings of a kept wife—the diamond earrings, blue lamé Nina Ricci gown, the beringed hands—but the words sounded more like Nora's farewell in Ibsen's *A Doll's House*.

"He does all the little things, takes me to dinner, gets me anything I want; but I have never felt included in the big things, and I'm getting tired of it." She says, "When I ran away I thought I was so secondary to his life, he was so busy campaigning, I wouldn't be missed." Even as she said her sojourn had made him more tender and understanding, the mayor was still pulling the strings. He personally cancelled two of his wife's appointments with the *Times* that had been set up through his office. Mrs. Alioto said she had never even been informed about the meetings, cancelled or otherwise.

"You know," she said, sadness showing in her face, "I have been my mother's daughter, my father's daughter, the wife of my husband, the mother of my six children, and grandmother to my eleven grandchildren; but I have never been me. But I am now because I went away. I am a changed woman in eighteen days."

The fidgeting and the anxious swing of her little feet, hanging over the edge of the library chair stopped. "I have learned"—and she paused—"to say no for the first time in my life. And that's important for me. I've learned to say no to my husband and no to my children, and saying no is a big step for me because I never dared to before. I've been a very tolerant person. I've been taken advantage of. While I have been very discreet the fools have tried to make a fool of me. . . ."

Mrs. Alioto's husband was beaten badly in the June primary. All seemed quiet on the home front until the spring of 1975, when Mrs. Alioto suddenly filed for divorce. A few months later, they were back together. A close acquaintance doubts that they will split. "I think Angelina used this public stuff as a way to keep Joe in line. I think she wanted more spending money and this public act was a way to get it. Once he gets out of office she won't be able to pull such stunts because no one will give a damn."

Most political wives, imbued with a sense of personal discretion, but equally ever mindful of constituents, would not do what Mrs. Alioto did. When your husband's job depends on votes, when several thousand strangers make the difference of whether you stay in the house you've just gotten used to, whether the children will stay in the school they've just gotten used to, something *has* to happen to a woman. In such a precarious and public life, the woman's *choice* of how she will live and act is largely taken from her.

Art Buchwald's wife, Ann, a witty and outspoken person who is a literary agent, said to me, "I don't have to like Kay Graham or Ben Bradlee or anyone at the Washington *Post* or the Los Angeles *Times* [which syndicate his column] or pretend that I do. I can say and do what I please. They're buying Art's *column*. But if Art's job depended on several thousand *votes*, think how differently I'd have to feel. That's why I'd hate being a politician's wife. I *like* to have choices."

Traditional political wives for the most part have given up their freedom of expression and are so trained to be correct at all times that they either become nonentities or give that impression publicly. In Washington, where everyone else has an opinion on controversial issues, people tend to treat these wives with disdain for playing what they consider a hypocritical role.

Despite the traditionalists, there are the beginnings of change in the attitudes of politicians and their families. While the slug-it-out-via-your-favorite-media political wives—such as Martha Mitchell, Angelina Alioto, and Barbara Mandel—are still a rarity, a virulent strain of candor is beginning to spread through the political world. Quieter and more thoughtful revelations are increasingly expressed by political families. Prominent, recently divorced Senators and Congressmen will tell you they would have divorced their wives years ago except for one reason—they felt it would hurt their political careers. "Let's face it," said William Ford, Michigan's divorced Congressman, "politics forces you to take a lot of crap from your wife that another guy would walk out on."

Caution still runs deep, however, and oftentimes the candor is "qualified candor"—expressed only after there is assurance that their views will be shrouded in anonymity.

There are many factors causing a slow chipping away at that monumental façade, the stereotype political helpmate—the women's movement, a vanguard of outspoken wives, changing attitudes of the public, the caliber of better-educated young politicians and their families, a press more aware of political family hypocrisy than in the past, more freedom in society in general. But change was and, to some degree, still is a long time coming.

The attitude of our Founding Fathers, who, after all, never included women in their framework of who was created equal, died hard. Thomas Jefferson castigated the females of French aristocracy who took an interest in the politics which led to their country's revolution. Writing from France at that time, Jefferson penned, ". . . Our good ladies, I trust, have been too wise to wrinkle their foreheads with politics. They are contented to soothe and calm the minds of their husbands returning ruffled from political debate. They have the good sense to value domestic happiness above all other." Jefferson himself apparently never gave up his own interest in romance to the exclusion of politics. "All is politics in this capital," he complained of Paris. "Even love has lost its part in conversation." (That comment of Paris could be made about Washington today.)

Before turning to the newer breed of political wife it is important to hear from the traditionalist wives. Many of them want things to stay the same for a variety of reasons. As I have indicated, many feel challenged and fulfilled in their secondary positions. Others have curbed their personalities for fear of eclipsing a jealous husband. Another kind finds personal glory through a helpmate role that can disguise martyrdom—"Darling, I'm doing all this for you"—which breeds more resentment on her husband's part than she often realizes. And a great many accepted their role as a necessary and unquestionable one.

Talking about a lifetime of losing campaigns, Mrs. Endicott Peabody, the wife of the former governor of Massachusetts, told me how wives traditionally went along with politics whether they wanted to or not: "I had the thrill of driving Eleanor Roosevelt to Groton school, was it twenty-seven years ago? Good God, it must have been. I had just gotten married to Chub, and he was in law school and I told her, 'You know, he's going to run, is there anything you can tell me that I should know?' She looked sad and said, 'I think it will be a lot easier for you. You're pretty, you move around easily. I was very scared, very frightened.'" Then Mrs. Roosevelt told her how little choice she had in her life. "You know, these men, they're born with it," she told Mrs. Peabody. "I know so many men who want to run for office, and they say their wives would never let them. I don't think Franklin even thought of that. He just *expected* you to be there. I can't possibly describe it to you. I just went along with it. . . ."

And Muriel Humphrey, who was uninformed of her husband's final decision to run for President in 1968, wired a humorous jab, "Let me know if I can be of help."

Many who invested their lives in a role that is now being questioned are particularly defensive or protective. Conversely, the political wives who never played the same game are often contemptuous of the role playing of their less free sisters.

One Senator's wife said, "A lot of those gals feel very self-important because their husbands are Senators, and they play the role to the hilt. They have no credentials in their own right, so maybe that's why they throw their weight around. I'd say more like the attention and the campaigning than not. Somehow they see it as a feather in their cap. I don't think they're aware that they reveal, ever so casually, their feeling of self-importance. At business meetings of the Senate ladies, weeks would go by where they'd wrangle over the silliest things, like reserving the front seats in the visitors gallery for Senate wives. I remember Betty Fulbright saying, 'I've told *my* Senator [meaning her husband] never to take a constituent there. Those seats are for the Senate ladies.' Who gives a goddam who sits in front or back?"

Another Senator's wife said, "I was at the beauty parlor, and there was Carl Albert's wife saying, 'As the *Speaker* said to me the other night.' Can you imagine anything more asinine?"

This is why so many of them are categorically dismissed as unimportant but pompous parasites in Washington. Frank Mankiewicz, top press aide to Bobby Kennedy, George McGovern's campaign manager, a columnist, author of books, and one-time candidate himself, said, "Most of those women are so dreary that they deserve everything they get. At parties, I avoid them. I'd much rather talk to a journalist's wife or a doctor's wife or a lawyer's wife. They are intelligent, have their own interests, and say what they think."

Dr. Phyllis Magrab, chief pediatric psychologist at Georgetown University Hospital and a mother of three, said she noticed political wives seemed less individualistic in general than many wives of men in other professions. Among her own acquaintances, she sees far more families with joint careers in the fields of medicine, law, and journalism than she does in politics. Columnist Ymelda Dixon, a Senate daughter who grew up in Washington, emphatically thinks most political wives are "parasitically" dependent on the emoluments. "In some ways, they are just like their husbands. They come here such sweet people, often very provincial. They quickly learn and adapt—although some never do—and all too soon they are self-important and full of themselves. Cars, staff, security guards, fawning attention—they soon think it is their right. Naturally there are exceptions—and all of them are my best friends," she adds laughing.

Abigail McCarthy sighs and says, "It's open season on the political wife. There is very little sisterhood extended to her by women who have careers. There is almost an irrational animosity toward the political wife by women who work on the Hill and in the press."

There is a queen-bee syndrome among older women who have made it professionally in tough fields that holds no sympathy for a complaining wife. "Oh, they make me sick with their trials," said one woman political columnist. "It's all so much bull. They're there because they love it."

The famous anthropologist Margaret Mead sputtered through the phone at me when I asked her about a quote attributed to her that a politician needs a full-time wife. "Well, there are certain roles as life is set up at present, those offices with high ceremonial content, where wives are needed full-time. I don't think it's beneath one to be a wife of an important man." If she feels that it is beneath her, the political wife should have married an executive and had two swimming pools and lived her own life, Dr. Mead thinks. Herself a figure from myth, to many, Margaret Mead stands on a mountain, looking contemptuously at times at the ants below who had not the curiosity, drive, energy, intellect, passion, or talent to perceive what they could do or even what they *wanted* to do in the early decision-making days of their lives. When I protested that many political wives feel there are stifling aspects to their lives, she said, "Oh, I think they're just having an attack of women's lib, frankly. Every woman in the world thinks she could have been a great sculptress if someone had discovered her at the age of twelve. I *know* what they were doing twenty years ago. They weren't willing to do a stitch of work, except to get husbands. It seems to me if she is really committed to the job she's doing, it would not be belittling.

"Any man who has something important to do, an educator or a political figure, for instance, needs a full-time wife to make it possible." This traditional role, so at variance with her own life experience, is to be left to those who "enjoy" it, she intones. "We ought to cultivate people who enjoy devoting their lives to other people—to husbands or children—and who really enjoy it."

In *The Future of Marriage,* Jessie Barnard writes that women of talent and motivation are often "selected out" of marriage by men. "The talents it takes to achieve the best-paying jobs—

including competitiveness, aggressiveness, drive and will to succeed—are precisely those not wanted by most men in wives, at
least in the years when mates are being selected." For a man
with the drive and competitiveness needed to make it in politics, this is certainly a factor, and the wife in either conscious or
unconscious fashion, must have woven those considerations
into *her* selection of *him.*

Like ambitious men who envision life at the top in business or
a law firm, many politicians, I believe, pick noncompetitive,
nonthreatening women who will maintain a good, careful image. Many wives of Congressmen told me they were noncompetitive and not desirous of pushing for individual goals or careers. As the young wife of William Cohen, Congressman from
Maine, told me, "Billy could not have married anyone who is
competitive. There is room for only one prima donna in the family," she added with a laugh. Like most politicians, her husband readily admits he is inordinately competitive—had to be
first in all sports when he was in school. He is a perfectionist,
like his father, a baker, who, Cohen says, is "still looking for the
perfect roll." But Cohen's saving grace, at least at this point in
his career, is that he is sensitive to the family destruction political life can cause, his wife said. Of political wives, Diane Cohen
said, "I resent us all being pigeonholed." And still, she admitted, she had made friends more often with newspapermen and
women than the congressional wives in the 93rd Congress, the
majority of whom, she feels, are too stifled to be interesting.

A full-time career is a rarity among political wives. Most feel
it would be too time-consuming to mesh with the demands
placed on them as mothers and as the wives of politicians. Some
try real estate and writing, but few give more than part-time
consideration to their own interests. Just as with the wife of an
Ambassador or wife of a company president, the wife's participation is almost but not quite formally institutionalized. These
wives are expected to give acknowledged public performances.

Mary Jane Dellenback, the wife of a former Congressman
from Oregon, says there are a "lot of identity crises for congressional wives" because the life is so "stressful." Those who make
it as far as national office often feel they have worked out the
stresses and consequently have strong marriages. Mrs. Dellenback does not gloss over the problems nor deny them, but she

likes the life and feels that many other wives do, too. She notes
that every other year a Congressman has "three full-time jobs—
legislative, attending to constituents' demands, and running for
reelection." This stress plus the financial load (maintaining two
homes, clothing, travel expenses—the wife's trips home come
out of pocket—the cost of entertaining constituents) and the
difficulties of planning one's time create extreme pressures.
Her husband was as conscious of the problems as she was and
tried orientation sessions for both husbands and wives who
were new to Congress.

As a study for her degree in psychology at George Washington University, Mrs. Dellenback polled 477 congressional wives
to determine how they felt about political life. She received 190,
or 40 percent, replies. Half of these women were pursuing the
education that was interrupted by the full-time job of running a
home and caring for a family in the early stages of their husbands' political careers. Mrs. Dellenback said, "I don't think
those who replied were all candid; the older they are the more
they have deluded themselves that everything is keen; but the
most striking thing is that more people said, on reflection, that
they were a lot happier than they thought they were." Many of
them, particularly the younger, expressed resentment at lack of
privacy and the feeling of being a public possession. The predominant frustration was the impossibility ever to plan—"never
knowing what time their husbands were coming home for dinner, how long Congress would be in session, never being able to
plan a vacation because the Congress might preempt it—and
the shortage of family time together." Most of these women are
wives of lawyers and they state emphatically that their husbands
had more time for family life when they were practicing law. As
for the pluses, the women felt that, unlike with their husbands'
law practices, they were now able to participate in their political
careers—"they had a feeling they had aided in an important
and significant career."

Remembering her early days, Mrs. Dellenback said that as
soon as they arrived in Washington she was "dumped in Potomac [Maryland] and my husband had to leave on a ten-day
speaking tour. You can't believe it. You don't even know how to
find the grocery store." Those first months were "just horrible
for everybody," but later Mrs. Dellenback came to look on her
husband and herself as "ambassadors from Oregon to Washington."

Those who are politically oriented, as she is, like the power. While her husband was on the Hill, she said, "I think I like being even close to where the important decisions are being made. I lobby when I have views, but I pick my issues carefully. I cared about the Equal Rights Amendment, the slaughter on highways from drunk drivers." She would not exchange it for life as a small-town lawyer's wife, when she had no part in his work. "Suddenly I was reading his speeches, talking issues, that's a tremendous plus." A minus is that they had more *time* together when he was in law. "A very universal complaint is a need for more free time." Some of her colleagues, however, paint a less happy picture. "One of them wrote that she had to find her own niche, ice skating, skiing. It was either she fulfill her interests completely on her own or it would ruin her home," Mrs. Dellenback said. "She has a rigid, strongly opinionated husband who probably wouldn't brook any disagreement with his views."

And I can't help but wonder about those 60 percent, the other 287 who could not bring themselves to answer this anonymous questionnaire sent by one of the sisters. (Mrs. Dellenback says, "Sisterhood is growing among political wives.")

After eight years on the Hill (her husband was defeated in 1974), Mrs. Dellenback said, "It was a very difficult period. We were in limbo. For a long time we were not in *anything*. It is hard to live with uncertainty." Later that spring her husband was named director of the Peace Corps. Staying in Washington and in politics seemed important to the Dellenbacks. Going home to practice law was "one of many options we were considering," but she admits "it was not terribly high on the list."

Abigail McCarthy is a staunch defender of her former political sisters and says that "like their husbands, they are able and interesting and a cut above the people they may be said to represent—in education, in appearance, and in the general skills of life."

She feels most are well educated and that many left interesting jobs. "Few people have any idea what we really are." They of course, cover a spectrum of American life—from Chicago Poles to blue-blooded New Englanders. There are small-town girls and moneyed sophisticates. There are young mothers in Washington suburbs with the duties of chauffeur, gardener, house cleaner, manager, and all too often the sole parent in

their young children's lives, in addition to the political obligations they have.

"In a close election, the wife who campaigns effectively makes
the difference of fifty to one hundred votes in every precinct,"
Abigail McCarthy contends. "I don't think I ever felt stifled;
many women find an outlet for their own talents in politics. I
found it absorbing and interesting. It was challenging to my intellect. If you believe in your husband, as I did, and in what he
is trying to do, I don't think there is anything more important
that you could be doing."

She also says, on the other hand, that the personal sacrifice
can be too great. "Recently there has been an emphasis on human values and their importance, and efforts to privatize one's
life again, but for those of us who were brought up to 'save the
world,'" she says with a self-conscious laugh, "nothing was too
much to sacrifice. It was only when you found you were just
flesh and blood and couldn't do everything that you began to
see no one person should give up that much. It's a very hard
line to draw."

One cross many bright political wives often bear in silence is
the fact that they get little praise for what they do. The political
husband often leads that silence. The fact is, many politicians
seem to resent all the bush-beating their wives do for them.
They have a hard time when the wife is excessively praised.
George McGovern respects his wife's views and her efforts, but
some who know him well felt he did not take kindly to people
saying, "Eleanor should be the one running." A female friend
of Birch Bayh's says, "He always praises 'marvelous Marvella' in
public, but I think he sometimes wonders if he could have
made it without her, and that causes resentment." It is not unlike the old saying that if you want to make an enemy of a
friend, do a favor for him. Gratitude, particularly when the
wife can say in a fit of anger, "Look at all I've done for you," can
be a burdensome thing.

Some political wives, such as Bess Truman, were unknown to
the public as the strong political advisers they were behind the
scenes. "Although it went unsuspected by nearly everybody in
government, Bess Truman entered into nearly every decision
the President ever made," J. B. West and Mary Lynn Kotz
wrote in *Upstairs at the White House*. Sala Burton, wife of California Congressman Phil Burton, is known as a tough politician

who was active in San Francisco politics and acts as a "lieutenant" for her husband. Bethine Church is a total politician.

Wives often protest that there is true camaraderie in participating in their husbands' lives, and yet I had a revealing set of separate conversations with a husband and wife who have been regarded as the epitome of team partners. After she extolled the virtues, happiness, and rewards of being an active political wife she finished with "What you newspaper women don't realize is that some of us *like* the supportive role."

Then I mentioned to her that her *own* husband told me he felt the team-player wife had a tendency to overrate her performance. She quickly rejoined, "But they begged me to campaign! Well, their own egos won't allow them to admit that they need us!"

If success comes in politics, it is coupled with massive adulation and massive hatreds. There is hardly a public man who has not had both. This brings another strain unmentioned by most wives. The wife who "knew him when" has her own anguish as well as her own glory when she sees what that outpouring of love and hatred can do to her husband.

"I love my husband, but I find this whole seeking of votes so *demeaning*," said one wife. "I was always embarrassed when I would see him out there shaking hands. I know he has to do it, but I would say to him, 'You have so much going for you. Try to be a little more aloof, standoffish.' He was so *eager* for the praise . . . and yet he's so magnificent when he loses—and he's lost an awful lot. It seems he enjoys the losing more than the winning. It's the *battle* that appeals to him."

The wife sometimes has to stand by watching the "real" person being eroded by his public life. To criticize, no matter how constructively, when everyone else is puffing him up—or encouraging him when he has been roundly defeated—is a difficult task. Even the most traditionalist political wives will chirp along well enough for three hours or so. But then, lowering their voices, they will speak confidentially. . . .

She leaned forward, almost whispering, in the den of her home, even though her husband had left for the Hill and we were alone. "You know, he never gets enough of it." Of what? I asked. "The attention. I thought after he was on the Watergate committee and got national attention that would be enough.

But he feeds on it, basks in it. We go to airports and people from all over the country come up and say, 'Aren't you Senator ——?' And, my god! The swelling and puffing! He gets jealous of me when I get attention, or when people find me amusing." A profound sense of loss came over an otherwise cheery face. "I tell you, it's a real trial."

Another wife, who believed strongly in her husband's goals and moved through the exhausting months of a national campaign, said, "It used to hurt me to see him looking for someone to shake hands with. I felt he was too good for that; he didn't need to do that. He was such an integrated person before. It seems to me it just escalates. The bigger he got, the more he needed that attention."

One result of the straining political life is that couples continue to be separated by the wedge driven by lack of intimacy. Just as political wives turn to one another more and more for companionship and for understanding, politicians often become lonely and seek the companionship of fellow politicians. This becomes a vicious circle with the male "clubbiness" further threatening whatever time there is left for the family. Hubert Humphrey told me, "I've said the Senate is a 'sinful monastery.' We *live* in here. We see more of our colleagues in one week than we see of our families in three months. We eat together, walk together, exercise together, swim together." He paused: "The only time we don't see each other is when we go home."

8

No More "Mrs. Nice Guy"

THE phrase has been around for a long time now, and is attributed most often to Chief Justice Oliver Wendell Holmes and/or his wife. It is the all-time put-down of Washington wives and it comes in various versions: "Washington is filled with men who are famous—and the wives they married when they were young" is one. "Washington is filled with men who are successful and the wives they married when they were not" is another. Anyway, the message is clear: most political wives are weary and dull and small-town and the appendages of clever public men who, for reasons of political safety, must endure these unions.

Some muse in wry wonder how so many incredible "mismatches" could ever have occurred, even back in precinct-level political days.

The maverick political wife—regardless of the protestations of some political wives or any women's liberation urging for being one's distinct self—is still the exception. Considering the number of political wives, I doubt that the catalogue of the mavericks could fill a book as large, even, as a compendium of World War II Italian naval heroes, but luckily for those who come in contact with political wives, they do exist. To my joy, I discovered a number of "closet individualists," those wives who maintain low profiles in public but possess private personalities of humor and candor.

There is also a small band of political families who defy rigid patterns. When Fred Harris, former Oklahoma Senator, was first running for office, one of his largest contributors said he thought there was just "too much LaDonna" in the campaign. Harris told this important money man that he better get used to his wife because her views and her presence were both going to be prominent. LaDonna, half Comanche, led an Indian crusade that received publicity, particularly when her group warned then Vice President Agnew that there would be trouble if he did not meet with a national council for Indian opportunity. Neither she nor her husband minded that she was singled out, as a Senator's wife, by those who questioned the tactic. Their disappointment was in the fact that the government didn't respond enough. LaDonna continued to attack the government's "paternalistic" handling of American Indians, with her husband's backing when he was in office.

Back in 1970, I witnessed a "typical" morning breakfast in the home of Senator and Mrs. Philip Hart of Michigan. After juice, cereal, toast, and an interview, the Senator went off to the Hill—his major responsibility that day was to vote no against the nomination of Judge G. Harrold Carswell to the Supreme Court. After he left, his wife crammed for a couple of hours for a noon exam—she was working toward her master's degree in anthropology at George Washington University. Mr. Hart had also glanced at a morning newspaper filled with accounts of how she and seven other leaders of an antiwar mass at the Pentagon had been found guilty of violating federal regulations governing the use of the building. Two years later, Mrs. Hart refused to pay the first-quarter installment of her estimated income tax of $6,200. Any "lingering doubts" she had about being a conscientious objector were "dispelled" when the United States invaded Cambodia. She wrote the IRS: "I cannot contribute one more dollar toward the purchase of more bombs and bullets." She had some private agonies for her husband's job, but everyone in the Hart family—and that includes eight children—is a strong libertarian. There is much talk of "following your own conscience." One Senator's wife sniffed that Jane Hart didn't have to be the "perfect" wife because she gave Hart something most wives couldn't—her very considerable family money. But that woman, who herself spent a political life agonizing over saying the right thing, missed one major point. The money brought financial security, but Hart is secure enough in his own right not only to admit that, but to say with ease as well as sincerity regarding his wife's actions: "There is an order of priorities in your life. The first one is following your conscience. Other things are of lesser importance—votes, inconvenience, what have you."

Jane Hart defies a world of congressional luncheons and teas. She is a flying ace and the first woman to get a helicopter license in Michigan; the mother who goes off to classes on her Honda; fought for women to go to the moon; marched in antiwar protests; pilots a boat; breeds horses. She is a Catholic who is for birth control and finds homes and havens for dissenting priests. "I get letters excommunicating me quite often," she said. She is also an active campaigner for her husband, who seldom speaks on anything except issues. Senator Hart doesn't have to run again until 1976, so in 1974, she took off for three months on one of her many trips. She and a friend plan to sail around the world, doing it in stages. She will report on some of the trip for the *National Geographic*. Although her children are grown (only one is still in high school), Mrs. Hart makes no attempt to gloss over two important factors that have enabled her to pursue her free-wheeling life-style: (1) money and (2) a long-standing housekeeper whom she calls an assistant mother.

Betty Talmadge, wife of the Senator from Georgia, makes $3 million a year selling hams and is shrewd as well as friendly. "I always say the best politickin' is no politickin'—and the best ham sellin' is no ham sellin',," she said with a wink. "When I meet a prospective customer I never ask for a sale." She paused for emphasis. "My salesmen come in later and do *that*." She also turned out to be a delightful closet feminist who, despite the Southerner surface role of acquiescence, sounded off about some aspects of political life—*after* her husband had left for the Hill.

Carrie Lee Nelson, the wife of Wisconsin's Senator, is warm, earthy, funny, and irreverent. She has such a following among the press that there are reporters who joke that they wish her husband would become President just so Carrie Lee, a welcome antidote to the perfect wife, could get in the White House. While team players talk about how much they've helped their husbands, Carrie Lee Nelson says, "Oh, that's so much shit. I wonder if those women dare stop to think how much they *really* helped? I may have *lost* Gaylord votes, but I can't remember ever doing anything that got him one damn vote—even when I campaigned." Mrs. Robert (Nadine) Eckhardt, the wife of a Texas Congressman, is another one who can be counted on to say the outrageous before the bland.

Some maverick wives are also at times a political plus for their husbands. Nearly everyone thought Martha Mitchell's midnight phone calls to the *Arkansas Gazette* were the ramblings of an inebriated woman, but she told me in 1974 that her antics were a put-up job by the Nixon Administration to call attention to their enemy Senator William Fulbright. "I also changed John's 'image' when I told the press he was 'cute and cuddly.' No one ever thought of him that way before. I meant it at the time," the estranged wife of John Mitchell added. Fred Harris said LaDonna enhanced their shared liberal views by speaking out at times when he couldn't as a Senator.

Wisconsin's governor, Patrick J. Lucey, is considered one of the most politically astute men. When his volatile wife started sounding off on issues—she verbally attacked a group of welfare mothers and another time antagonized the trucking lobby—many wondered whether Lucey was, in fact, controlling the situation. Her action with the welfare mothers looked like political dynamite, but many in Wisconsin politics felt that it in fact helped counter her husband's very liberal image with some of the more conservative and work-oriented ethnics of his state.

I asked Lucey about that and he joked that "sending up Jean is like sending up an unguided missile. Believe me, she speaks her *own* mind and only her own mind." But he did add that her view in this instance was probably a plus in some circles. The welfare mothers had chained up the gate to the governor's mansion. Lucey avoided a confrontation—he went by boat across Lake Mendota to his office. His wife, however, drove her car down to the gate, got out, and spoke to the women. "I told them to get off their you-know-whats. I said, 'If you're clever enough to agitate, you're clever enough to work.'"

Jean Lucey is one politician's wife who never followed traditional concepts of her role. "I don't think I lost my civil and human rights just because he got elected governor. I'm a pretty independent person and I make some people a little nervous, but I don't think a wife costs her husband votes." She thinks that "this country is dying for a little candor and frankness—they're sick of political double-talk. Whether from husbands *or* wives." Still, Mrs. Lucey admits that an outspoken wife is a jolt to the political world. "Men have always suggested that if a political wife gets too involved, too outspoken, she's a little 'kooky.' The press, which is mostly *male,* is so lacking in ingenuity and creativity they make me a little sick. If you speak out, they immediately say, 'She's another Martha Mitchell.' How can they compare me to Martha Mitchell? I hate the telephone. Besides, I deal in issues."

Unlike most politicians' wives, she loves to become embroiled in controversy, and in 1974 she lobbied openly against the truckers who want heavier and longer trucks (65 feet or longer) permitted on Wisconsin's roads. When she sent out some literature on the subject, the truckers' lobby attacked her for using taxpayers' money. "They are trying to scare me and shut me up. I'm lobbying for the little people—who don't have a lobby. It's all right for them to spend thousands *against* the public interest, but as soon as I spend fifty dollars I'm doing something wrong."

A prosperous realtor before her husband became governor, Mrs. Lucey says, "I can't be a hypocrite and arrange flowers and pour tea. Some wives are just great at that and, well, they can do it. I did not take on any of the roles previous wives did. I decided I was not going to be trapped by precedent. I was not going to sit around in this mansion and show the real estate." She announced there would be no tours of the mansion. "The kids were home—they were at that age when they were just getting over their alienation of everything, and I felt that I couldn't ask them to live here and every so often say, 'Disappear because a few busloads of women are coming to tour the place.'"

The public has backed her up. "They're all having trouble with their kids," Mrs. Lucey explains. "I said my first duty was to my family and I wasn't going to abandon them to pick up a few votes for my husband. Some governors' mansions are set up so that you can show some rooms. Our is not. There's one dining room, one kitchen. If you're showing it, you can't prepare meals. The kids couldn't have their friends over."

There is more often than not a built-in staff-wife animosity over who gets what part of a politician's time, and some wives and some aides square off openly. Mrs. Lucey said to the staff, "You don't own my husband after five o'clock. Maybe you think you do, but you don't. Some wives are so awed by it all they don't say anything, but after all, the whole American family is disintegrating and I just feel that politicians can't get away with not seeing their children." For awhile the staff ran off two sets of schedules—a fake one for Mrs. Lucey with the weekends free, and one for the governor with the scheduled appearances. She said, "They tried that—*once*. It didn't last long."

Jean Lucey was sympathetic about Mrs. Alioto's 1974 outburst, although she questions the propriety of ironing out her problems in public. Mrs. Lucey says, "I understand why she did it. There's a real change, and it's coming from these gals who are so deeply frustrated. She felt abandoned, and that's true of every political wife. We *are* abandoned." Mrs. Lucey's own publicized "incident"—the time her husband locked her out of a room and the police had to be called—undoubtedly eliminated Lucey from McGovern's list of vice presidential possibilities. As one McGovern strategist said to me recently, "That was really enough—just that one story. Particularly because it was so close to the convention. It didn't sound exactly presidential." But that thought hardly bothers Mrs. Lucey. She now laughs and says, "I'm glad they made the decision *that* way—otherwise, we'd have been blamed for his losing. I thought the whole campaign was sort of goofy. God knows, the last thing I wanted was my husband on that team." (At the press conference at which her husband endorsed McGovern, Mrs. Lucey went around telling everyone that she preferred Muskie.)

Close friends feel that the locked-door fight was the kind of quarrel most couples can—and do—have, and that the Luceys are a happier couple than the always-loving political duo. But, once again, the publicity and political ramifications pointed up how much a public person's private life is subject to scrutiny. When we talked two years later, Jean Lucey referred to the night of the locked door as a "dumb little misunderstanding." She would not discuss what happened, and elaborated only to the point of remarking, "We are living in a job with tremendous pressures."

The Milwaukee *Journal* account of that mid-March night in 1972 stated that, according to police, the governor's wife called the Madison suburban police department of Maple Bluff at 11:09 P.M. Officer Hugh Morrison was quoted as saying, "Jean Lucey was upstairs kicking at a bedroom door and shouting and swearing at her husband, who was inside. It appears that both Lucey and his wife had been drinking and had an argument. She wanted the door open so she could get some of her things and go to their nearby residence." (The Luceys kept their old home when they moved into the mansion.) Morrison said he "maintained the peace until Mrs. Lucey left." One friend said, "I am convinced they have a good marriage. They understand each other. She made it possible for him to have a political career. When he was traveling in the early years, she stayed back in Madison and ran the whole real estate business. Once I asked him to sum up her contribution to his life and Pat said, 'If it weren't for Jean there would have been no 1970 campaign.' I asked her what she thought of that and she came back with, 'Well, if it means I stayed home alone and took care of three children six days a week while he was gone—then he's right.' "

Mrs. H. John Heinz III is the mid-thirties wife of the young Pittsburgh Congressman and pickle, soup, and ketchup heir. She's surprised that her husband, coming from his wealthy Republican background, turned out so well. "When I think of what he *could* be, from his background," she says in wonderment. "But he has it here [she touches her head] and he has it here [she touches her heart]." When he ran as a political novice in 1971 his wife agreed to campaign, but on her terms. "They told me to be sweet, smile, pick up kids, and I felt that was a bloody waste of time, so I refused. I had something more to do with my time than that." A stunning brunette with freckles who wears little makeup, Teresa lived an international, affluent existence for most of her life in her native Mozambique, East Africa, and in Europe. Along the way, she learned to think for herself in several languages. When campaigning she talked about issues, her husband's capabilities, and bawled out audiences for not working to change politics. In one speech she told women to "get off their tails." She recalled, "I just socked it to them. I said, 'You cannot *dare* to leave it to your husbands to do the mending of politics. You're mothers and don't apologize for what you are. Love yourselves, but for God's sake, do something.'" She also attacked the men and sounded off on the apathetic who don't vote. "I never voted in my life—I lived in a dictatorship." She also attacked machine politics—"The Democratic machine in this country is putrid." In one sector, because some "damn dictator" dispensed so little money, she said, "Half the homes didn't have running water." Not that she's a Republican—and "I'm not going to be. I'm an independent." While other wives say very little, ever about other politicians, Mrs. Heinz said before the 1972 election that the Democrats were "playing it too careful. I want to see somebody with balls." Nixon she "didn't trust" but she added, "Ted Kennedy I don't trust either." Mrs. Heinz, who once had a bleeding ulcer, finds that swearing is a good way to relieve tension. Her personality is in marked contrast to her husband, who wears 1950s conservative-style clothes.

While Mrs. Heinz will say the country's priorities are "all screwed up" and decries tax loop holes for corporations as "intolerable," her husband comments cautiously, "If I had my druthers, there would be meaningful tax reform." No matter the striking contrast, Heinz makes no attempt to curb his wife, and he openly admires her. She can be herself, she says, because she draws a clear distinction: "I speak only for myself. I keep him free of me."

Teresa Heinz was educated at the University of Johannesburg and the University of Geneva, learning five languages and studying history, government, international relations, economics. It was a life filled with international friends and Heinz was "just an American" she met on a tennis court when he was working at a Geneva bank. There followed several years of phone calls, letters, and meetings for ski weekends. Then Tere-

sa came to the United States to see if she could live here. "I went
to Washington first and hated it. Most of the young men I met
were so busy trying to become something that they were the
most dry, boring people I ever met." Washington was like
Geneva, she felt, full of political "opportunists." She then went
to New York and the UN as a twenty-four-year-old consultant
to the Trusteeship Council. She was twenty-seven when they
married. Although she likes Washington better now ("I'm
learning from the people I get to meet"), their first years in
Congress were rough. When certain groups urged him to run
for governor of Pennsylvania she discouraged the idea. Although her main interest is education, she sharply curbed her
outside activities after her husband's election because her
young children had experienced some traumas owing to his absences and her own heavy campaign schedule. "I really have
some anger in me right now—I think the women's movement
has got to reverse itself on the motherhood thing—it's important and necessary that a mother stay home and be a mother for
the first few years of a baby's life." She seems more sober and
reflective than when I met her in 1971. She has "systematically
disciplined" their life to reserve time for important "spur-of-
the-moment things like a movie" and to be with their children.
"Our number-one topic is time with the family. I tell John, 'You
haven't done enough with the kids this month or this week.'
He's cut down on a number of things and that helps. We never
go to big hotel dinners—you could go four times a week if you
wanted to. We curtail the social schedule." A nonclubby woman, Teresa has litttle interest in the diversions of the idle rich.
Asked to join the Junior League, she rejected it as passé. Most
of her friends are in the academic world.

While she recognizes and supports her husband's desire to
remain in politics, she flatly refuses to sacrifice either her family
or her individuality for it. "I can only make a statement based
on my impression, but I think a lot of politicians' wives are as
ambitious or more so than their husbands are. I feel I am a rarity. I know some couples who stay together only for politics. If
Ted Kennedy holds on to that marriage just for the Catholic
vote, as some people say he does, then I think he's a perfect bastard."

Teresa gets along with the staff but she makes no bones about
"discussing" her needs. "Since they schedule him, I want them

to know my limitations—how much I can live without him, how much the children can live without him. But I am not jealous of them. They are people who have given up a lot to work for him."

Mrs. Heinz makes no apologies for her financially free life, one that most congressional wives do not have. "My husband is very demanding—the house has to look good, the food has to look good, the conversation has to be good, so that is why I don't feel guilty about having help. I use what we have to help make us happy, but I don't need a fancy house to be happy. To know your identity and what you can do—that is important, not being Mrs. Heinz. I'm me in *spite* of being Mrs. Heinz. As Mrs. Heinz, it's much harder to be me. I was me until I was twenty-seven and I like myself."

She laughs and says she'll never run for office herself. "I couldn't put up with the bullshit. Or those stories written about politicians, not based on fact, but innuendos. That would destroy me, the kind of person I am. I get so angry, and I am emotional. I savor too many things, even the time to do nothing, to successfully play that role or to be ensnared by it. There are too many things essential to my being me. I was myself a long time before I was Mrs. John J. Heinz, and I like being myself. Fortunately, John understands and admires me for what I am. But to be a politician? I'd go loony. There are so many bullshitters and, well—I know what price I had to pay just to be the minor public figure that I am."

One Washington wife not married to an elected official, but whose life was touched very directly by the elective process is Cathy Douglas, the pretty young lawyer who in 1968 married a man old enough to be her grandfather, the brilliant and controversial Supreme Court Justice William O. Douglas. Because of their marriage, one Senator suggested that her husband be impeached. Many recall the time when Representative Gerald Ford wanted to impeach Douglas for, among other things, his writings that some construed as advocating dissent and that appeared in such erotic magazines as *Playboy* and *Evergreen Review*. Hardly anyone remembers that other impeachment suggestion when he married Cathy, then a twenty-three-year-old student. It was not so much his marriage but his long-standing defiance of social mores and his consistent choice of young

wives that upset his critics. Cathy laughs as she recalls, "We
were on our honeymoon and we were in Cliff's Meat Market in
Yakima, Washington, when I heard it on the radio. I just
laughed. It seemed so funny. Bill didn't laugh quite so hard."
She reserves particular glee for the amusing irony of the situation. The Senator who suggested that Douglas was a lecherous
old goat unfit for the Supreme Court was South Carolina's
Strom Thurmond. Not very long after, Thurmond, a few years
younger than Douglas, married a woman young enough to be
his granddaughter.

Cathy said her husband tried to prepare her for Washington,
but after several years here she recalls, "I got surprisingly decent treatment. There were sufficiently few hostile reactions,
everything considered. I've never been terribly panned in the
press." She also feels her treatment points up "the difference of
people's reactions when your husband is in a position of power.
I am not so sure I would have been treated as nicely if he
wasn't." She is modestly not considering her own beguiling,
pleasant, and easy manner that disarmed everyone—except
Joan Crawford. The aging movie star, who everyone assumed
had had a little more to drink than the Pepsi-Cola she pushes,
verbally attacked Cathy Douglas at a White House dinner. Everyone came to Mrs. Douglas's defense after the incident was
reported in the press. Cathy laughs as she recalls Joan Crawford making loud remarks about the "little girl" at her table and
officiously showing Cathy how to remove the doily from her
plate. "I still can't imagine what I did to offend her," muses Cathy.

If Cathy had planned a life of only official functions, she says
neither her marriage nor her life in Washington could have
lasted. "There were some hard times with some political
wives—I was only one year out of school, after all, and I must
have been a shock to some. But if I was insulted by a woman, I
just didn't see her again. If we had lived only in the Washington
circle, I might have run into her, but my life was so filled with
law school and my own friends and Bill and his fascinating
mind and work. If I'd tried to retreat to a life of lunches and a
variety of social situations I couldn't have made it even for two
years."

Mrs. Douglas says of official Washington, "The wives get so
little part of the show." She could not be content with being just

a wife. "When I was young I was just so afraid I would get married and end up in the suburbs of Portland, Oregon, and that would be it."

We talked about the effect of Washington on women. "Often it is very debilitating by and large. Politics takes on an exaggerated sense of importance, and that makes insignificant the talents of people not involved in politics. The importance placed on the traditional male political role makes it hard to feel successful in other roles. Everything else is thought to be very very secondary. The political wife on top of this has the worst of all traditional roles. There's not that much money and too much work, and she can't say anything because it will reflect on her husband. Her only sense of self-worth is her social position. It's all part of that cloak they have to take on. They must not be flamboyant or extraordinary. I know some perfectly extraordinary women who do their darndest to cover it up. In fact, I never found, as a group, women more educated. I should think in the future we will have husbands and wives running as a team for a single office." She laughed and said, "The Court is the best of all worlds—you're appointed for life."

It is tempting to say there is a new breed of activist political wife, but that is not entirely accurate. As one political wife said, "Most of the young women who are really independent-thinking are now planning on political careers of their *own*, not their husbands'." (A 1974 feminist poster says "Women Belong in the House"—underneath it is a picture of the White House.) Mrs. McGovern said that in the 1972 campaign she was asked by some feminists why she could "support a male candidate"— even when it happened to be her husband. (She could not buy the feminist point of view, nor could most spouses of politicians.)

Also, among the younger politicians and their wives there is a growing number who have worked out various forms of "open marriages," which help them to deal realistically with the problems of long absences and "separate lives." One beautiful young Congressman's wife told me, "We have an understanding. I love him deeply, but I know we could not survive in a traditional marriage. We could have if he were back home practicing law, but he is simply gone too much for that kind of life. I am forced to live my own life, but I also go along with the political life and I enjoy it—there's a certain titillation about going into a room and knowing people find you attractive. At first, it was because of who he is, but then we started to be invited back five and six times. I've met Ambassadors and Senators, and it is so much more expanding than my life at home.

"I know men find me attractive and my husband knows they do, and that's good for both of us. He may have a fling with someone because he is so good-looking and women are more attracted to him now that he is something of a celebrity. I feel stifled back home because there I am as well known as he is, but in Washington I can also have my private life. I need that. And if it includes men, he knows that's the price. I am not going to stay home all the time he's gone."

These women are also much more free in their conversations about sex than their more "correct" team-player colleagues. One such wife sits with her legs curled up under her in her Georgetown den, with its zebra rug and bentwood rocker, and sips wine and lets fly with all her views on politics and life. She is very good-looking, around forty, with almost a flapper-girl face and an easy, gurgling laugh and high irreverence.

"Well, I don't know how the other women handle this, but I get mean as hell." She was talking about her Congressman husband having affairs. "I found out he was running with an old friend of mine in New York and I just wrote her a letter and said, 'You can just forget about your dinner party with him, and you can forget me as a friend.' I just told her I didn't care what the hell she did, but just keep her fucking out of my life. Of course, he denied it, but he got the message." The woman is also one of the few wives who admits that she will have an affair if she is neglected. "You have to work at a marriage—and that goes both ways. Now I didn't realize he was getting a little mad about all these young men who hang around over here—they're really just friends. But still, they kept him on his toes. When he finally said something, I said I'd be glad to get rid of all my 'Valentines'—that's really all they were—if I could see him more often. I told him, 'You're the only man who means anything to me,' but that I was just sick and tired of being left alone. He got that message, too."

She is also a "political animal" who works hard in their district. She presents a different face for constituents; keeps her swear words to a minimum. She suspects she still gets talked about but doesn't give a damn.

It is her second marriage. She said, "A woman's ego has to be in good shape before she can put up with a Congressman husband. Most of them fear getting older—and they like being around the chickie babes." She has an advantage—she is several years younger than her husband. "He wants to hang on to me and we both know it. Besides, except for a little stuff here and there, politics *is* the other woman."

The woman laughed as she recalled some of the "stag" functions lobbyists serve up for Congressmen. "Some ex-governor of Kentucky sent an invitation for my husband to come to dinner on a private railway car. I thought to myself, 'Now, honey, wait a minute.' So I called this little character and identified myself. I said I wanted to know what the plans were for the wives. He replied, 'Well, Ma'am, at this point, no *ladies* are invited.' I said, 'What you mean is that no *wives* are invited.' He got all flustered and said he'd call back. We never heard from him," she said with a laugh. "Of course they'd planned this stag thing for Congressmen and those girls—you know, the ones with the piled-up hair and the white go-go vinyl boots, who always manage to show up. My husband roared when I told him. He wouldn't have gone to that thing anyway, but I just think it's time the wives tried to put a stop to that stuff. I told that man I talked to that I knew all about the railroad lobby and if they wanted to talk legislation that was no way to do it. You know, I think the wives might fit in more than people realize, if they gave them a chance. But first you got to cut this stag shit out. Some of those Congressmen look so damn silly, if they ever stopped to look at themselves. They all think they're important in their districts and they're absolutely nothing up here in Washington. I suppose some of those dumb stag things given by some whore-producing lobbyist are all they can get invited to."

And another wife, Nadine Eckhardt says, "I feel the political wife cannot operate in any of that old framework anymore. Times are changing. They're all busier, the girls are more available. If the wife doesn't *demand* some of him she's going to get leftovers. I put it down to genes. Politicians just have different glands—once that massive adulation starts, there's no turning them back. You've just got to fight for your rights."

When Mieke Tunney spoke out, not with venom, but with a desire to reveal and therefore hopefully change some of the hypocrisy surrounding political life, many of the Senate ladies who roll bandages wanted to throw them at her. However, other wives spoke up and defended her view that politics stifles their identity.

"The few incidents that become public property are only the tip of an iceberg," wrote Kathleen Kilgore in *Boston* magazine in April 1974. "The unvarnished truth is that in an age of women's liberation, the candidate's wife is little more than a stage prop, who should look attractive, shake hands sincerely, and speak banalities."

Writing out of her own experience as a neophyte political wife (her liberal husband, Don Houton, ran unsuccessfully against Louise Day Hicks for Congress), Ms. Kilgore explained how she received "guidance" for her husband's 1970 campaign from a Republican National Committee booklet with advice for candidates' wives sent to her by a Washington congressional wife. She memorized its major prohibitions: don't be photographed with a glass or cigarette in your hand; remove your name tag when being photographed, *never* give your views if they differ even slightly from your husband's, never mention your own work or interests. She adds, "The Republicans' views of white gloves and hats [wear them at all times] I thought could be safely ignored in 1970." Her husband's campaign manager added some more no-nos: she was not to mention that she was a Protestant, or, since he was trying to get elected in a predominantly blue-collar district, that she had gone to college or grad school.

Then she went to a garrulous Irish advertising man who started in on the cosmetic overhaul of a fledgling political wife. Circling a few pictures of her that had been taken for the campaign, he began to explain a political process whereby the wife *and* the public are both used, interspersing his lectures with Kennedy anecdotes to prove a point. "When Jackie Kennedy was going to be married," he told Mrs. Kilgore, "her mother told Jack, no pictures, no press, just a discreet notice in the Newport papers. And he told her, 'Look, your daughter is marrying a public figure, a Senator, a man who may one day be President. There are going to be photographers whether we like it or not. So the idea is to show her to best advantage.' "

The man told Ms. Kilgore her hair would have to be cut—too long, "the hippie image." "People look up to men who have attractive wives. It shows they're successful men. You want him to project an image of success." Promising that "you won't know yourself when we're through," he asked, "Where do you get your dresses? The one you had on the other night in Cambridge was awful, if you don't mind my saying so. It was too big, for one thing. You're not pregnant, are you?" Her answer was no, they had just gotten married. "Too bad. It's a Catholic district. Tell you what, when somebody asks you that, just give them a little wink and say, 'Well, I wouldn't be surprised if I was.' And then give them a nice smile. They're great people. Now that purple dress. Don't wear it again." After promising that his wife would fix her up, show her how to wear makeup, and then new pictures would be taken, the ad man give her a final piece of advice: "Just remember. You're the *wife*, you can't help that much, but you can hurt. You smile, you go to all the events, you be careful what you say, you look good—there's nothing to worry about! Remember, he's the one who's running. You defer always, always to him."

Another Boston political wife, Maggie Bellotti, whose husband Francis X. ran unsuccessfully for the Democratic nomination for governor in 1970 but made it for attorney general in 1974, told Ms. Kilgore, "Once they've been in politics, they can never leave it alone. It's an experience that marks them."

Ms. Kilgore said it had changed her, too. Four years after her husband ran and lost, she finds herself sticking to old political habits—the "extra firm handshake, the conservative clothes, the big smile in front of a camera even when it's just Daddy filming Thanksgiving dinner. . . . At anything public, from the Boston Bicentennial to a Mothers' Rally, when anything goes wrong, my first thought is always, 'Who advanced this one?' And I still wake up occasionally at 3 A.M. and think about my first campaign. What if I'd been the ideal pol's wife? If I'd been beautiful and charming? If I'd been rich enough to buy a big, slick media campaign. If I'd always given him the right advice and then always deferred to his opinion? If I'd worn the right clothes? Would it have really mattered?"

When I wrote in a *Newsweek* column that the political wife is often looked on with contempt as the ultimate nonliberated lackey, I added that if these political wives are to have many defenders, it is up to them to show that they are fed up with the confinement and hypocrisy of their second-class roles. The replies varied from those who thought I was cuckoo to political wives who praised me. Some said I held only the Washington view; that these women were immensely popular and valued in their home states. Mrs. Hugh Scott, wife of the Senator from Pennsylvania, a gentle and retiring sort of person, was so mad that she called *Newsweek* to complain. (I then tried to reach her to get her viewpoint for this book, but she did not return my call. When a television show asked her to be a guest, a secretary said, "Oh, Mrs. Scott never speaks out in public." I regret that; I would have liked to hear her views.) Some protested that I "completely failed to mention the benefits of being in politics." "My husband has been a state representative for almost two years. In that time we have enriched our lives because of the many people we have met and the experiences we have had together as a family," wrote Linda L. Christman of Englewood, Ohio. "This is one family that enjoys the political life."

Joann Bloomquist (Mrs. Gary) of Seattle, Washington, wrote of me, "With her elitist views of women, it's a good thing for women that she holds no greater power than the ability to peck out silly articles on her typewriter." But there were others. From Laila Uhlman, the wife of the mayor of that same city (and formerly a state legislative wife for eleven years), came a different tone. "Thanks for recognizing the plight of the forgotten woman—your column on political wives is excellent. After much careful thought and sixteen years of 'political wifery,' I've decided that the best alternative to second-class status is to find my own career, especially now that our children are no longer babies. We have always tried to concentrate on the positive aspects of public life and to ignore the less pleasant influences as much as possible in order to maintain both marriage and sanity. So far it has worked!"

Elizabeth Steele of Vernon, Connecticut, wrote, "You smacked at an issue with which, I am sure, many a political wife will concur, myself included. Although it is difficult to surpass that second-place role . . . or third . . . or fourth (beneath the campaign manager, the contributors, the delegates, ad nauseam), it is not hopeless. And, as you said, it is up to us. The most positive thing to do in rising above that 'prop image' is to create our own identity, absorbing ourselves in something completely separated from our husbands' political arena, something that will give us some self-satisfaction, confidence in our own abilities, and a sense of accomplishment and something for which we can be known for ourselves and not just as our husbands' wives. There is no need to disclaim the sense of pride we have in our husbands and their accomplishments, but why not also be proud of what we can do? For a personal instance, my salvage has been a seat on the local board of education." She ended with, "The next step forward for us lackeys would be to attach a wives' amendment to all the campaign reform bills being proposed statewide and nationally: Campaigning can be done only once a week, so that husbands can share a little more of the homefront activities . . . and maybe be an appendage to us when we are called upon to perform publicly."

One young wife, Gail Lewis, whose husband, Delano, was an aide to both Senator Edward Brooke and D.C. Congressman Walter Fauntroy before he ran unsuccessfully for the D.C. City Council in 1974, said, "People come up to me and say they hear that '*we*' are going to run. I say '*Del* is—I'm not.' " Intelligent and pretty and the mother of four active young boys, Gail is torn between her sense of "equality" in a marriage that allows her husband to do what he wants to, and a protectiveness of the family. She regards politics as the "rape of the family. If he gets this, I know it's just the beginning." Del says, "One friend said the only thing that would stop me is Gail walking out on me. He's right. If she really says she can't take it, I will get out."

And Burnella Jackson, the wife of Atlanta's first black mayor and the first black mayor of a major Southern city, Maynard Holbrook Jackson, has been active in her husband's political career from his first defeat in 1968 to his next two successful races. "But," she says, "I am very sympathetic to San Francisco's rebellious Mrs. Alioto. The politician's wife has such a peculiar role to play. You have to watch what you say. Your life is planned for you by your husband's staff; and sometimes when he gets home he is so talked out I have to read the paper to find out what is happening."

"I didn't choose politics, and I don't know what I may be like after many years in it." She spoke for many younger political wives who do not intend to acquiesce through life. "Just because I married a man who has made a public niche for himself doesn't mean I don't want self-fulfillment."

In recent months some political wives, facing a money crunch and identity problems, moved out on their own. Antoinette Hatfield, wife of Oregon's Republican Senator, and Texas Republican Senator John Tower's wife, Lou, sell real estate. Maryon Allen, wife of Alabama's Democratic Senator, lectures on period furniture and writes books. Ann Stevens, wife of the Alaska Senator, opened a plant store. Some of the wives are clearly in rebellion about their expected roles. The all-smiling helpmate has become No More Mrs. Nice Guy. Mrs. Tower said, "I just came to the conclusion that I had more sense than I was using going to teas and lunches every day. I'm fifty-four years old and I've decided I want to do something on my own." Mrs. Allen, a former women's editor for four *Sun* newspapers in Birmingham, was automatically placed in the "dumb-bunny category" nevertheless when she became a Senate wife. "People expect you to say nothing and know nothing." Those command performances—teas, luncheons, bandage rolling, and the like are in the past. "Honey," she drawled. "I've done my bit. I've done all the charity balls in Alabama. And if I have to go to another fashion show, I'll slit my wrists. Now I'm going to do the things that please me."

Not all of those who seek a change in politics are young. The wife of an older Southern senator is one of those "closet feminists" I mentioned, lurking behind a careful smile. After several hours of conversation and coffee she said, "You know, I was asked to be on the board of a black college. Some of my friends said, 'Oh, you can't do that! It could hurt X.' I said, 'Well, it might hurt and might not, but I'm sick of having to make my decisions on whether it hurts his politics or not.' I've done that all my life," she said, with a pause. "It's time for me to do something I *want* to do, and I want to be on the board of that college." "Are you going to ask him?" I asked. "No. I'll just do it—and then I'll tell him."

Jane Butler, wife of a Virginia Congressman, retorts to any pressure to be anything but herself, "If my husband doesn't like my image, he can get a new model. If his constituents don't like my image, they can get a new Congressman. I feel my part is to have a solid family."

Some of the younger wives have rebelled even more from the pattern, and I think that is a healthy sign of change.

One wife who shook up her sisters was Roscoe Dellums, the

stunning and outspoken wife of California's Ron Dellums. "They thought I was going to be Angela Davis and stand around calling everybody 'honky.' They were just so *relieved* to find out I was a human being." But after a few years, she spoke out on television in the fall of 1974 about the "plantation mentality" toward blacks on the Hill, the "do nothingness" of political wives and the stifling roles they are expected to play. When she went to one Democratic wives' club board meeting after that show, she was asked to get up and apologize for her remarks, like a chastised sorority sister. Roscoe Dellums said she could speak only the truth and she stood by her comments. At the end of the meeting, some of the women were agreeing that what she said needed to be expressed.

"I stopped going to one congressional wives' group. I found it meaningless." The diverse political natures of their husbands and their districts, in addition to innate caution, made them unwilling to take up any meaningful causes, Mrs. Dellums said. Older wives were used to what she termed "beaten-down roles." "Some of those people who came here in the 1950s with those 1950s ideas are still here." She went down with the Quakers protesting the war at the White House. "I brought food to the people who were keeping the vigil. That blew everyone's mind. They'd say, '*You're* not supposed to be doing that.'

"Right now I want a job, but no one takes me seriously. They say, '*You* don't need a job.' How can anyone express *need* for me? My husband is not independently wealthy. Politics makes more demands every day on politicians to donate money to causes. No one heard of 'black affluence' where I came from. We lived a simple life in Berkeley. The women I used to be with at home were thinkers and activists. I think the feminist movement helped me see things a little clearer. It was easy to fall into the whole trap before, but now Ron has had to deal with my new consciousness. I didn't do a traditional campaign this time. I went with a group of feminists. This is where my head is. I get really offended at the idea of traveling three thousand miles, dragging the kids out there and pulling out all the props to be the 'happy couple.' Marriage is *bad* enough without all that. Those politicians are behind the times. They kept trying to push me alongside Ron to be close for pictures. I wouldn't move. Staff people would whisper, 'Ron's tie is crooked, would you straighten it?' That old image thing. They could not *under-*

stand why I was not standing alongside. I was very aggressive in his first campaign. I became a registrar to get new people to vote. I gave up my job [she was teaching adult education courses]. Ron's was a very symbolic run and I believed in the need to change government. Had it been someone else with his head screwed on like Ron I would have been for him. Those people had no idea who I was. I felt very different; I could give a good spiel for Ron, the candidate, but not as Mrs. Dellums. I separated that concept of political helpmate wife from me, a political activist trying to get a good politician elected."

Another new type of wife is Ruth Harkin of Iowa. When her husband was elected to Congress in 1974, they decided that she would not move to Washington. She, in fact, seemed slightly astounded that anyone would consider her doing that. This would mean giving up her *own* elected position—as prosecuting attorney of Story County, Iowa.

She holds the opposite view of team-player wives who cling to a sense of importance in their role. "I think the role of the wife is overrated—and a lot of times is overrated by wives. I don't consider as wives that we are assets to an election. We are used as pawns to acquire press and that is okay. It doesn't bother me, but who cares what we really think? We're not a *voting factor*. I feel I help Tom on a psychological basis. He likes me to be on the campaign trail so I go with him. He says people like to see me and all that but as far as I see it, it's just one more time the name gets in the paper. Because of my job, we have pretty good name recognition in this one county, more so than if I were known only as Tom Harkin's wife."

Ms. Harkin can't imagine the women who feel fulfilled totally through the supportive role. "God, my life would just be superboring if all I had going for me was thinking I was helping to get my husband elected. It just *isn't* that exciting." At thirty, Ruth also has some cynicism about Congressmen. "My God, you know what most of them are like in Washington. I joke with Tom, 'You may want to run for Congress—but I've got my peer groups to consider.'" She said that very few team-player political marriages seem truly believable to her. "I just can't see it. A good case in point is those wives who haven't done a damn thing and yet they're so defensive—they're trying to convince their husbands they're campaign assets." When I mentioned that many political wives accepted as a matter of course a "caretaker" role for the family because their husbands were gone every weekend of the year, Ms. Harkin said, "That's incredible." Despite the separation necessary now that her husband is in Congress, she sees theirs as a marriage between equals with similar interests. They have no children and she said they were going to have to make a decision on whether or not to "pretty soon." She can also see some conflict of interest as a lawyer if her husband develops a prominent congressional career. "Unfortunately, that's when we'll have to decide who's going to do what in their career. At this point, I'm doing what I want to."

To some of the freshmen congressional wives, the clubs for political wives are hopelessly passé. Ruth Harkin said she couldn't believe it when she received her "Homecoming 1975" invitation from the Democratic Congressional Wives Forum. The only concession to today was "Welcome Fresh *Persons*." The rest of it was a play on words of the minutes of sorority meetings twenty-five years ago. "Our first social event will be our *rushing* luncheon for the cream of the new crop coming to *U of D.C.* The *rushees* are definitely the type the DCWF [Democratic Congressional Wives Forum] wants as its *pledges*." The announcement relayed that they would "sip a bit of sherry and hold a remarkably short business meeting" (Ms. Harkin noted, "Short to match our intellectual capacity, no doubt"). The main discussion was about the role of political wives, "the most vital question facing our members today," but even that was couched in cutsey gobbledegook: "How to be a Wife in Action on the Hill Without Alienating Her Reason for Being on the Hill—or, What Gives With the Political Wife?"

The invitation was decorated with raccoon coats and pennants. Perhaps the new freshman wives, taking their cue from the freshman members of Congress who helped stage the January 1975 revolt against the seniority system, could bring a bit of relevance to the political wives' clubs.

Ruth Harkin uses her campaign appearances as a forum to inform. She feels that not enough women are rejecting the stereotype role of political wife. "Most wives of candidates out here are still pretty much in that traditional role of helpmate, regardless of their age. They *never* talk about issues, and that's all I ever do. At a typical coffee, you call the shots. You can talk about issues or chit-chat." One of her pet areas is public financing of campaigns. She thinks the quality of political family life would be "drastically" changed and improved if there wasn't the constant hustle to raise money. "In 1972—those people who *lost*, but got 45 to 49 percent of the vote, spent $109,000 on the average for a House of Representatives campaign! And those were the ones who lost.

"I am very much interested in separation of a private life from a political life. To keep a healthy balance is a real challenge and certainly requires a huge amount of self-discipline. Politics would require much less time if we had public financing and if the public were better informed. As it stands now, a candidate or a public officeholder is under constant pressure to keep his or her name in front of the public so that contributors will view your candidacy as a viable one."

Ms. Harkin is ambivalent about the progress she sees for women's causes. On the one hand she said the fact that political wives "allow their lives to revolve around their husbands is indicative of women in our society. A political wife is no better or no worse—she just gets more publicity. The feelings are still in our society that the man provides and the woman is grateful for his position in society and the money that he brings into the home. Time after time there are cases of educated women allowing their lives to be controlled by men. Our local bar association has about fifty-five members. I am the only woman in the organization. So you see, it isn't just political wives. In the case of my colleagues, the women live strictly through their husbands' careers and have no outside interests of their own. All political wives I know have never worked outside of the home since the time of their marriage."

But Ruth Harkin is still optimistic about the future. "Five years ago, I would have been a freak in Iowa as a political wife, but I think you can be elected without having children, being married or if you are divorced." She isn't so sure politicians have caught that message. "They still perpetuate that image. I saw [Iowa Senator] John Culver's TV ad and I was appalled! I like the way he votes and everything but he had this damn ad—it's only thirty seconds long. There he is, and his wife and their four kids. He introduces each one of them—and that's the damn ad!"

Active in the National Women's Political Caucus, Ruth Harkin has spoken to conservative women's groups about the discrimination in many of the state laws. "Often the response is positive. Hopefully, we are educating women to think of themselves as potential candidates—rather than potential candidates' *wives*."

9

Political Sons and Daughters

NO matter how much they respect or admire their political parents, few children I talked to felt they were close or truly intimate with them. Sometimes political parents will ruefully admit this as well, but often they are unaware of their children's feelings. For other parents there is a subliminal awareness and deeply buried guilt about the political drive that meant reaching for the public hand rather than the private understanding of a child.

In some ways, the political family simply exaggerates the devastating "norm" played out by success-oriented people: fathers absent for career reasons, wives frustrated by secondary positions, children alienated.

But the irony is that the political family must, publicly, appear to have it all together. That children seldom become close to their political parent is carefully hidden in that ceremonial rite, election night with the family. The children are placed in a back-up position on the platform where they are to smile worshipfully at their elected parent and are usually referred to in passing, along with praise for the political spouse.

It makes an admirable picture and most political families dance the ritualistic gavotte. The children and the wife and the dog pose for the All American Family photos to be used on campaign literature and the Christmas cards that will adorn the mantels of constituents.

Eugene McCarthy remembers in the 1968 presidential campaign when Bobby Kennedy entered the race, the Kennedys use of the family—capped by a visit by Mother Rose to Father Flanagan's Boys Town. "That had nothing to do with issues," McCarthy murmurs today. But it had a lot to do with getting elected.

That toddlers hit the TV sets in anger when their political fathers are on, as Sharon Percy Rockefeller mentioned, because they see their fathers more on television than they do at home; that teenagers refuse to campaign or attend public dinners for their fathers because they have had to share them so much with the public are behaviors that get a hush-hush treatment, along with the fact that a teenager may be experimenting with marijuana.

If your state's Bicentennial dinner falls on your child's birthday, so be it. Political survival means wooing the electorate.

Constituents come to town and expect to be taken to lunch or dinner, not knowing there is no government budget for those meals, or caring if the night out is one less for the family. Every elected official or his spouse has a story about how some constituents walk into the house and expect attention from their representative. Congresswoman Julia Butler Hansen, Democrat of Washington, announced her retirement in 1974. She said she was going to "do as I please, hang up the telephone or take the damn telephone off the hook, and when people I don't know appear at my door and walk in without knocking, I'll have the great opportunity of telling them it is my private home." She recalls, "I was bathing my son when he was a baby and an irate constituent showed up and told me in no uncertain terms to drop him because she needed me and demanded my time."

The single-minded opinions of small-town voters often include the idea that politicians ought to be idyllically "good family men." There were countless interviews with disbelieving rural Republicans who felt Nixon could do no wrong; he was "such a good family man."

The set of standards for one's private life in Peoria are often incompatible with the more sophisticated mores of Washington, and politicians and their families, particularly from rural areas, are caught in a schizophrenic juggling act; operating in a world with one set of accepted life-styles and values while being held accountable to those who live in another. This is an added burden that makes their situation unique.

Time and again political children have told me that they were afraid to get in trouble because it might hurt their father's careers. The public does not give a damn if a journalist, lawyer, doctor, or businessman plays around, drinks too much, fights with or leaves his wife, or has kids on dope—or conversely, chooses to spend a lot of time with his family to what appears to be the detriment of his career. In the long run, they may not care that much about it in a political family, either, but *psychologically* the burden is there.

Families of an executive do not have an investment in his personality and image; they have an investment in Daddy's status or money-making prowess. A doctor's children have an investment in his ability, say, as a brain surgeon, a writer's children in the fact that he can make a living with his talent. In politics, however, there is enormous investment of personhood, and everyone combines in the family to bolster this identity that gets bread on the table. "If it weren't for me and this identity, we'd be starving somewhere," the politician implies.

"There is a consummate worry to present a consistent self across every screen," said Dr. Isaiah Zimmerman, a specialist in clinical psychology who has treated about a hundred elected and appointed high-level political families in the past several years. He theorizes that "this is very bad, usually, for family life. Family life should be the training ground for intimacy skills, and how are you going to learn intimacy skills when father and mother collude in saying, 'Dear, there is no difference between our public and private life'? There is a complete blurring of differences between intimate and public life. A young child, particularly in early adolescence, begins to feel a very powerful discrepancy in the family myth of 'nothing to hide' coupled with the loving façade, when in reality he knows his political parents can have an absolutely sexless, hostile, nonspeaking relationship. The kids are hurt because they don't get a balanced picture of family life with its mix of frailty and solidarity, craziness and sanity, the give and take, good and bad that goes on in intimate lives." And why? "Because the family is being processed for public consumption."

"My public life is the same as my private life" is a recurring theme in the utterances of politicians and their wives. Former President Nixon, in arguing that gifts given by politicians should be tax-deductible, spoke a telling sentence: "Public men seldom do anything of a *personal* nature." Mrs. Gerald Ford said when her husband was picked as Vice President "It's no effort for me to discuss personal things. After 25 years our entire life has basically been public anyway." And Dick Drayne, Senator Edward M. Kennedy's press secretary, when I told him I wanted to talk to the Senator about the effect of politics on his private life, retorted, "In the first place, he has none." Then he added, "And what little private life he *does* have, he wants to keep that way."

The politician often thrives on his publicness, but the political wife and children are helpless at being constantly on display, frustrated cogs in the myth-making machine. In certain areas of the country, these families truly become the hostages of an ever-prying constituency. Evelyn Moakley saw her husband Joe work his way up the ladder in one of the most politicized neighborhoods in Boston (state representative, then state senator, and then defeating Louise Day Hicks for Congress in 1972). He is a weekend shuttle fixture between Boston and Washington. Now, because of their bigger constituency, Mrs. Moakley says, they have to be more careful of their "image."

"I wanted to put the Christmas tree in the window so the people in the nursing home next door could enjoy it—they're the ones I really decorate for. But we thought, well, people might talk because of the energy crisis and all. So I just put up a few little lights and put the tree where you can't see it from the outside. It sounds silly, but I've found people do notice even little things. Our neighbors downstairs told us people asked them why we weren't ever home in the evenings because they'd driven by our house at night and no lights were on. It's a strange feeling to know you're being watched so closely."

Dr. Phyllis Magrab, feels one definite problem for a politician's child is to perform as "Little Miss or Mr. Perfect." She has treated one Senator's family where the daughter had been raised as a china doll. The expectations and the pressures, not unlike those imposed on the children of clergy, were placed on her to always remember her father's position. In her adolescence, a rebellion, coupled with the assurance that she couldn't possibly be that perfect, led her into a promiscuous, sleeping-around, dropout state. The child's real self had been stifled all her life.

When Julie Nixon once slammed a locker in anger in high school, Tricia cautioned, "Remember Daddy's position."

Ann Hart, the daugher of Michigan Senator Phil Hart, is now in her mid-twenties. She recalls that while growing up, "I was very conscious about being a Senator's daughter. It is very intense in the home state—you can't budge." Although she has picked acting and music—performing arts—she sees a difference: "Your *whole life* isn't made into a public spectacle."

I remember election night in New Hampshire, 1972, trailing the Muskie entourage through a small hotel kitchen to the stage. As the revelers stomped on crushed beer cups and cheers went up I felt trapped just being on the periphery. I wondered about the children. They were dealing with this very tough thing that happens to children when their parent is completely taken away from them by the outside world and they too are being displayed and examined. Ned, then eleven, threw up his dinner. The next day the two teenage Muskie girls were sick and nervous on the plane going from New Hampshire to New York. At the airport there was a poignant scene that points up the excruciating demands of time and the press in politics. Whatever goodbyes there were on parting were said in the family cabin. As we got down on the runway, slicked by rain, the family moved as if on command. Muskie, like all politicians, as if drawn by a magnet, headed without hesitation to a forest of microphones and cameras and press. His wife and her assistant moved to a waiting limousine and their own set of interviews. The press piled onto a bus. The children? They stood there, the three of them, together and alone. An aide came up and sorted out the children's luggage and moved in to take them back to Washington. Their mother and father would not see them for several days. Although some of the five Muskie children are still somewhat alienated from politics, Mrs. Muskie says the whole experience brought them closer together as a family.

Although Dr. Magrab hesitates to say political life causes more problems than other children have, she does not hesitate to say there are "different" problems for a child of a political figure. In addition to the on-display factor, there is a more subtle problem—sharing that parent with so many people. "A child's sense of identity in that parent's world can get a little shaken," says Dr. Magrab. "And then, not only is that parent a public figure, but a public figure who *leaves* a lot." There can often be pride in what that parent is doing, but also a real sense of loss. One Senator and his wife appear to have a perfect image—even to the closest members of their staff. Of all political families, I felt they had managed to be good public servants, yet remain privately together. I was shocked when their daughter told me, "I hate to say this—they're both wonderful people—but we have been screwed as a family. He is a magnificent Senator but he works very hard at it. This business of politics is really destructive to intimacy. There is a great deal of showmanship. Solving the world's problems leaves no time or interest for solving the problems you have as children. Without the help they hired to replace them as parents, this place would fall apart. The assemblage occurs for the photos and that's it."

The daughter admits that some of her friends are bitter toward their own parents who are not in politics. They have felt the neglect of wealthy or social parents. She knows there are compensating factors in having parents who, she said, "stand for something I can be proud of." She insists, however, that "the public life took away from the intimacy we needed as children. In one way, it forced us to be tough, but at a great expense. Those of us who survive—and I'm not so sure all of us will make it—will no doubt be strong and independent thinkers."

A daughter of a governor from a far-western state said, "I knew my father as mainly someone who came to dinner occasionally." Now a successful journalist, she has an ambivalent feeling toward her father. On the surface, there is a very good relationship. A close friend said, "Her dad's a great guy and that's why she feels guilty that she has so much tension and resentment toward him. She has a great need for being close, a great need for attention and assurance because it wasn't there before. She has a supersuccess drive and a great need to develop an ego and identity of her own.

"Another thing that fucked her up was always having to be on her best behavior, and not experiencing a normal childhood." One time when she was double-dating, the conversation got around to childhood things. The other woman made some comment about her babysitting experiences. The governor's daughter said, "I never did anything like that." One of the people in the group said, "Well, it *would* be rather strange, driving up to the governor's mansion to pick up the babysitter."

Her friend said she never got the chance to really know people. When she was young she saw them as masses who either booed or cheered her father at rallies, but she was protected—and insulated—from them by the state troopers at the door.

Sometimes the special trappings can make a child feel more important than his peers, and the perceptive parent may do something to change that.

When Bess Abell, former social secretary to Lady Bird Johnson, was a child, she was known mostly as the daughter of Kentucky's governor Earl Clements. One day her father countered any sense of arrogance she might have gained. He called her into his study and showed her the globe. He twirled it and showed the entire world. Then he pinpointed their state. "It's a pretty small place, isn't it? And it's a pretty small thing to be governor of that state—or to be the family of that governor."

Often whatever arrogance might accrue to the child of a famous politician is offset by the insecurity of not being able to establish a private identity. "Politics has nullified my personality," claimed Joy Dirksen Baker. "The problem started with my father, who was famous [the late Senate orator Everett Dirksen]." Then her husband, Tennessee Senator Howard Baker, was "catapulted into prominence" during the Watergate hearings. His wife said, "I *always* felt I was sort of an appendage."

But others take the view that politics pulls the family together. Sharon Percy Rockefeller, wife of John D. Rockefeller IV, former secretary of state of West Virginia and unsuccessful candidate for governor, is also the daughter of Senator Charles Percy of Illinois. Recalling her childhood on the "Not for Women Only" television program, Mrs. Rockefeller told host Barbara Walters about passing out pamphlets with her four brothers and sisters at county fairs where no one knew her father, who had been a highly successful businessman. "We would go back to the motel and the five of us would sit there and sob at the stupidity of these people who didn't seem to crave my father. Then it turned around and, in a year, all of a sudden you're very well known. You can't go anywhere. You can't go into a restaurant, a movie theater, anything. You end up going to movies a lot because it's dark, to get away from public adulation and people coming into your life so much. And yet I think in the long haul it has kept us together as a family better because we've been through the glories and the defeats. You are isolated as a family. But you tend to withdraw from others, therefore go in together."

Mrs. Rockefeller noted in 1974 that of her three toddlers, the oldest, four, "already is rather self-conscious. He went up during the seventy-two campaign to the television set when an advertisement was on for my husband and began hitting the screen. And he was only three. He was angry. He absolutely sensed there was something wrong in the fact that he saw his father more on television—that our house was being used as a laundromat and a cafeteria on Sundays and that was it." In political life, she said, "Everything around you is trying to almost destroy your family and tear it apart." Mrs. Rockefeller said, "My entire married life has been based around election years. But that's all right; you become conditioned to that kind of thinking." Her children were born in off-election years, and she said, "I can't say it's coincidental."

Speaking of self-conscious children, an example was the eight-year-old son of Jeanne Dorsey Mandel, mugging and generally acting spoiled as he stood on the platform while his mother's new husband, Marvin Mandel, accepted victory as the reelected governor of Maryland in 1974.

During a spell of teenage rebellion, when many children prefer to remain temporarily alienated or at least independent of the family, the political child often feels pressured to make those public appearances. Often a son—searching for his own identity at that age—has a more difficult time of tagging along in his father's campaign than a daughter. Many politicians purposely do not push for their involvement. "Our oldest and our youngest, both girls, always took an active interest in politics," said Fred Harris, who seemed surprised at the lack of closeness in political families. "The oldest, in law school, is like our closest friend." While in office, he cut down on weekends in Oklahoma to be with the family. During his campaign for the presidency in 1974, his son Byron, eighteen, decided on his own to join them in New Hampshire. "I'm real happy he decided to," Harris said.

The Ford sons fled from political life—studying the ministry, living on a ranch. They all feared the loss of anonymity, the ever-present Secret Service. John, raised to be open and honest, told me he could think of "no greater personal disaster" than his father's becoming President. When Ford did become President, John continued to be hounded by reporters to speak out on issues and he did—amnesty, the President's pardon—until his father felt compelled to say publicly that his son's views were not his.

Conversely, the only Ford daughter, Susan, seventeen, seems to have lost her initial fear of the White House. For one thing, her father is now "home" more than at any time she can remember in her life, since he lives and works in the same place. Somehow, Susan and her father weathered the extreme absences, as some other political parents and children have managed to do. "We care about each other and we understand each other," she said. "He lets me express myself, and doesn't always expect me to agree with him." She remembers his infinite patience during those few times he could spend teaching her sports, shopping with him for clothes for her mother, and being the apple of his eye. When she was six he used to call her with a jingle: "Susan, Matusan, you're the girl of my choosin'." She says he is a "perfect" father and, "He is always siding with me. He used to stand up for me against my brothers."

In school, the political child is always expected to know more about politics and current issues. There are, of course, bonuses to political life of untold value if the child wants to get involved in current events. They often do have unique experiences at an early age. Chase Church, son of Senator Frank Church, often goes to dinner parties with his parents, and as a teenager had already accompanied his family to Russia and India. The chance to meet newsmakers in your parents' living room is remembered as an important asset by some political children. Sometimes the children of altruistic politicians surprise their parents. Ted Proxmire, son of William Proxmire, who fights big corporations, went into big business because he wanted to make money. And Chase Church shocked his parents when he said he might eventually go into politics, but first he would go into business "and make money. My father is a politician—someone has to support the family."

It helps, of course, if your political parent wears a white hat. One who was for ecology, against big spending, and against the war commanded a certain respect from the peers of college- and high-school-age political children in the late sixties and early seventies. But no one could feel anything but pity for the sons and daughters of Nixon's followers who found themselves eventually visiting their fathers in jail. Some principals of schools had to call in children and tell them not to tease the children of Watergate defendants. My son, then nine, came home from school during the Watergate trial and said of one of his friends, Tracy Magruder, "She is so brave. She tries to act like nothing's wrong." He almost pleaded with me. "It wasn't her father's fault, was it? Nixon really did it all, didn't he?" They were difficult questions to answer.

Eleanor McGovern recalls the problems her children had; it was a "real jolt to these young people to hear someone speak disparagingly of their father." In her book *Uphill,* Eleanor writes, "Our own children, we know now, were more personally touched by early campaigns than we thought: little Susan, hurt and astonished, passionately muttering, 'I can't *stand* it!' as she switched off a TV program critical of her dad; Teresa, gregarious, competitive, who bought candy bars for a nickel and sold them for nine cents to swell our congressional campaign chest; young Steve, a sweaty little hand in mine, holding back as we entered a Republican-owned store for Cub Scout equipment, saying, 'Aren't you *afraid* to go in?'; and the same young boy, during a winter in Washington, asking, 'Mommy, when are we going to move back to the house in Mitchell where Daddy used to play with me?'" Steve had the hardest adjustment. The four girls were involved in their father's 1972 campaign, but Steve "just could not do it. He was totally opposed to his father running for President. I think that he has felt throughout the years that maybe his father did not pay enough attention to him. He was going through these very difficult years in his life, and as an only son, it was especially hard for him. He tells us now, 'Well you know, if I had thought Dad was going to *lose* I would have campaigned for him.'" Teresa, on the other hand, decided to campaign "because I wanted to show that I believed in him; I wanted him to know that I believed in him." While Mrs. McGovern believes it was very hard for her children, she also saw their political involvement as a rewarding experience: "They forced theselves to do things they'd never done before. . . ."

Her husband said he would have given up politics if his wife had ever told him it was too difficult for his family. In 1972, McGovern said, "It's all been so uphill all along. Eleanor's opposition would have been just too much opposition. Those long days away, particularly when the youngsters were little and really needed me—that is a source of sadness. I've had times when I wonder if it wasn't too big a price to pay." Mrs. McGovern's sense of resentment at "being both father and mother" came when her children reached adolescence. She was a concerned, worried mother, like many these days, and her children told her she overreacted to their teenage problems. When Teresa was arrested in 1968 for possession of marijuana, the McGoverns learned the stiff fact that political children who do things countless others do, and who get caught, pay the penalty of publicity. The case was dropped because of a legal flaw, but it became a national issue because McGovern announced only days later that he was going to run for the presidency. Rather than look at the problem as a personal or family situation, as some other fathers might, McGovern took to saving the world. He told his wife, "If the country is so mixed up that even our daughter is playing with drugs," he should perhaps go into national politics. Mrs. McGovern said, "My own experience of watching a child use marijuana and LSD to cope with the unpleasant side effects of life has made me skeptical about the drug culture." She experienced the pain of many parents, even though her daughter made it to self-reliant adulthood through therapy—"I still wonder what I could have done as a parent to be more helpful."

Mrs. McGovern is insistent that political life is not that negative. "In the long run they are very proud and I think my children, in spite of the fact they've had many problems—and I don't think more than the problems of friends of mine who have not been involved in politics—they have a keener awareness of social problems and social needs. They never, never again will be apathetic or unconcerned or uncaring. That is one of the great benefits that my children have achieved over the years."

Both Mrs. McGovern and Marion Javits say their two youngest daughters, Mary and Carla, are determined to run for the presidency, but Mrs. Javits says that Carla has had problems coping with her father's identity as Senator. "She really wanted to feel that her father was precisely that to her." In 1974 she refused to go to a big fund-raiser where he would be the Senator, not the father. "She did feel somewhat alone and neglected as the youngest. I think he almost cried," said Mrs. Javits. "He wanted the family there and she was saying, 'But I love Daddy as Daddy.'" Mrs. Javits also feels the child is hampered by publicity. When Carla, daughter of a Republican Senator, was wearing a McGovern button out on the street, Mrs. Javits was told about it. She felt that Carla could wear the button privately "but if it is picked up by the press it becomes something else." Later she said, "I never knew if I was suppressing her point of view."

Mrs. Javits supports the theory that sons have the more difficult identity crunch. "I think Joshua has felt the sorry feeling of not having been as close to his father, on a personal level, as he might. My son was a leader in high school, but I think when he went to Yale, he conked out. He felt that anything he did—well, we were very surprised to find that he wasn't active or a part of the life of the university at all. I feel there is something that's thwarted, something that's missing, as a result of being a son of the father—even though he is politically oriented and speaks well and campaigns for his father."

The Harts of Michigan, with their eight children, emphasis on human values, and his lack of presidential ambition, seemed likely candidates for a close-knit family; yet Ann Hart said, "The public requirements came at times to take precedence over real-life communication. We've all come to this realization; in many ways we know what happened now. My father is certainly spending much more time with us than he did before. We've come to realize that the getting through, day-to-day business of life, year by year, is the means by which you become intimate and somehow or other, because of the demands of public life, that was short-circuited. Dad loves us and I love him; it's just the *continuing* force of daily support or interest isn't there. It's a subtle thing, but it can be very destructive."

Cathy Gilligan, daughter of Ohio's former governor John Gilligan, worked in Washington as an advocate for penal reform before her marriage this year. In her mid-twenties, Cathy is bright, articulate, and has a sense of humor about herself and the political childhood she remembers. One anecdote involves her as a girl of twelve handing out literature. "There was just violent fighting between various factions in the Democratic Party. That day of voting, tempers were running high and my dad's opponent greeted me and another girl passing out pamphlets—by spitting at us." She laughed. "That's mature politics for you.

"I don't really think until I was much older that I ever compared it with anything else. I only realized there were some real strange elements as I look back." Gilligan, a highly respected liberal, had a public personality of aloof erudition that helped bring about his defeat in 1974 and, with it, his presidential aspirations. He was regarded in his own well-bred "nice family" circle as a bit crazy for wanting to go into politics. "Most of my friends' parents hated my father. I went to a private girls' school and there were fairly wealthy families. He was kind of a rebel to them. I knew from the point I was very young we'd be getting this flak." She was buffered by two brothers. "There was this great sort of coming home and reporting what so-and-so said and getting a lot of support. Another thing helped. At an early age I learned to be very sarcastic and very verbally defensive. Nobody really messed around with me very much. But in a sense they had a threat against me—'My father won't vote for your father,' or 'My father hates your father'—and I knew it was true. The constant newspaper criticism was much harder on my mother, but I was very aware from an early age that someone else has the ultimate say. Whether father was good or not did not matter—other people could fire him every few years. There was always the uncertainty that his job depended on a lot of people I didn't like."

She remembers also being treated as "too special" during campaigns. The volunteers were her age but she was set apart as the "boss's daughter." During her teenage years when her father was a Congressman in Washington, "It was a tough time for Mother, dealing with the boys, to have Dad exit from the scene." While her father was in the governor's mansion, Cathy said she never felt as if she were going "home" when she would commute from her Washington job. The family goes to Michigan for Christmas.

She fought to get a job on her own. "I didn't want someone hiring me because I was Dad's daughter so I didn't go into politics." Her brothers may not go into politics. "I think they might be threatened by who their father is." She said, "I don't know if I'd want to live that kind of life. Especially as a wife. Maybe I'm totally wrong, but there is something about politics. The woman's official role is as the man's wife. *Period.*

"I guess what I disliked most was this defending aspect. No one else I ever knew was called upon to do that for their parents. I really wanted people always to love Dad the way I loved him." Her father would always be "Don Quixote," she said. It was "groovy" when she was in college and he spoke on her campus as a dove, but it raised hostile reactions in Cincinnati. "I don't basically like the public official that is my father. I like to spend my time with my father, not the governor of Ohio. But luckily he can turn it on and off."

The insecurity of a father getting reelected is felt at very young ages. My eight-year-old daughter's close friend has a Congressman for a father. In November of 1974 my daughter said, "Her dad has to win *something* tonight, or he won't have a job. Would she still live here for me to play with?" (He won.) And a few years ago when Evan Rees, son of California Congressman Tom Rees, was eight, he could only dimly remember California as a place to live. He had grown to like Washington and his friends. One day, he came home from school with a shaken look, went to his room, and shut the door. When his mother tried to find out what was wrong, he would only say, "Something terrible happened on the playground." She got him to say it was about his father and then he blurted out, "There was a kid on the playground and he kept teasing me." In a sing-song, taunting chant, the boy kept saying, "Your father's going to lose, your father's going to lose."

When the children are too young to understand that a very good father may have gone down to defeat over a principle, defeat can bring confusion, guilt, and shame.

The wife of one former eastern governor, who lost far more than he ever won in his lifetime of pursuing politics, said, "The children used to hate election night. It would tear them to pieces. When he ran for the Senate and lost, our daughter was a little older and her great worry was that her father had not been able to fulfill himself. When she was at school she would plead for me not to come in the gate if our chauffeur was driving. But her brother loved it. He's the only one of the three who did. The other son is like the daughter. He despises politics and can't bear to see his father ridiculed anymore. I think if he had been more successful it would have been easier on them growing up. Our daughter wouldn't touch the newspapers when he was governor because they always criticized him. Our oldest son, the best adjusted, would just say, 'They're not too good this morning, Mother. Why not have your cup of coffee first.' One time after an election when his father was beaten, again, he said he couldn't go to school. He was just a little thing and he didn't want to face the other kids. He was crying and said, 'I don't see why Dad can't be like other fathers.' And I shouted back, 'Like what—the drunk on the corner?' Then I calmed down and picked him up in my arms and he sobbed and sobbed and I cried. I said, 'Daddy is never going to change. He *has* to do this. You've got to fight for him. The only people he's got are us. You're just going to have to go and push that guy's face in.' "

Their daughter spent years seeing a psychiatrist who told the mother, "She has built a wall around her and I'm not about to break it down. She needs it desperately. She hates her father." The daughter told her mother that she never got any guidance from her father and felt he therefore never deeply cared for her. "She had her problems with me, all right, and there is some hostility there, but she said to the doctor, 'We always knew where we were with Mother. Either she was for or against us on something. With Father we never knew.' "

It is probable that Julie Nixon Eisenhower would not have made it on her writing talents alone, and it is certain she would never have been asked to host the "Not for Women Only" national television show had she not been the daughter of Richard Nixon. One acquaintance said, "She is so bright but so sheltered. She has been brainwashed and conditioned all her life." She has also been criticized more than any other woman her age in America. Her life has turned her into a poised, frighteningly unshakable person who people are willing to bet will enter politics despite her protestations to the contrary. "When you are in politics you have to open up on a lot of private things that other people are not expected to come forth on. I'm not going to feel this obligation anymore to have my life an open book," she said when her father left the White House in shame. Her idea of "freedom" out of the White House is to be without her bodyguards. She sees freedom in what many average people regard as the tacky inevitables of always having to cope for yourself. "I can walk alone in an airport at twelve midnight and feel adventure and feel like, gee, I'm really a big girl, and I'm going to stay at this motel myself tonight, and I'm going to make my own travel connections, and it's just as silly as that. Getting into your own car and going somewhere."

One woman who lived a normal, happy, and loved childhood

is Margaret Truman Daniel, the daughter of President Harry Truman. She admits her father was a political rarity. "The family always came first with Dad. He was there most of the time, except when he was campaigning and we went with him. He always put the family first—if you'd read my book you'd know." Mrs. Daniel is vivacious, with a flawless complexion, an abrasive wit, and frankness that seems formidable at times. She hates Washington, where she now lives with her husband, Clifton Daniel, Washington bureau chief of the New York *Times,* and their four sons. "It's much phonier than New York." She was saying things like that back in her White House days. She knew she couldn't take an ordinary job—"The publicity hullabaloo would be resented and would disrupt the efficiency of the office. But the only alternative was the life of a social butterfly and I was fed up, bored to death with the so-called Washington social whirl," she said in 1950.

Instead, Margaret Truman passed up a frivolous time for a difficult career as a concert singer and became the first President's daughter ever to set out as a single woman on a professional career of her own. She considered using as her professional name Margaret Wallace, after her mother's family, but realized she would hardly escape her real identity and learned to capitalize on it. Unimpressed with her White House address, music critics roasted her considerably: "It is not possible to sing so incorrectly after working at it for years unless the entire method of vocalizing is wrong to begin with." Paul Hume of the Washington *Post* wrote that she was "flat a good deal of the time." He continued, "There are very few moments during her recital when one can relax and feel confident that she will make her goal, which is the end of the song." Margaret took the criticism in stride, but "Give-'em-hell Harry" did not. Hume got a letter in which her father, the President, wrote, "I never met you, but if I do you'll need a new nose and plenty of beefsteak and perhaps a supporter below."

Margaret was skeptical of the men who might be interested in her when her address was 1600 Pennsylvania Avenue. She formed no close attachments until she was out of the White House and she married Clifton Daniel when her father was no longer President, in 1956. Her advice, she once said jokingly to a friend who asked about whether she wanted her sons to go into politics, was, "I'm not so sure about politics *or* the newspaper business!" Although she went in a White House limousine to and from classes at George Washington University (she graduated with a B.A. in 1946), she said she never felt a sense of isolation in the White House. "Of course not!" she said, to that question. "I had my same friends. No *new* ones," she emphasized, "but the same ones I had before. And they're *still* my friends."

Lynda Bird Johnson, however, felt a cocoonlike existence. "Sometimes it is hard to break away from the White House," she once told me. "Living here is somewhat like living in a small city. It's hard as the President's daughter to go to another place. You're afraid people will like you because you are the President's daughter, not because you're a nice girl."

As the caricature of the All-American Family is played out by political families—many could be stand-ins for the Brady Bunch or the Partridge Family—any number of conflicts arise but are not often dealt with effectively because of other demands. Geneticist Leon Kass says, "The family is rapidly becoming the only institution in an increasingly impersonal world where each person is loved not for what he does or makes, but simply because he is." But in the political family such intimate acceptance is often eroded because of those three big elements—impermanence, the emphasis on myth making and the exaltation of surface appearances, and the lack of private time together.

When politicians do go to counselors to help their family or marriage, it is almost always triggered by a crisis. Few, according to most psychiatrists and psychologists that I talked with, go because they ever simply sense a problem, and few stay on to effect any real change in their family life. Sometimes the decision to devote more time to children comes in a very graphic way. One Congressman, whose child attempted suicide, was jarred to the point of decreasing his campaigning, turning his whole schedule around to receive counseling for him and his child, taking speaking trips to be near the child's boarding school. Another, whose kindergarten-age child became withdrawn due to his campaign absences, resisted offers to run for higher office, cut down on his time away from home, and as his wife said, "learned to get to know his children."

One Congressman's child developed disturbing fears that exceeded the normal fears of a four-year-old. Through therapy, the mother learned that he had felt abandoned when both his parents were out campaigning. "It was my first campaign, and I wanted to do so well. I would sit at table with him at least one meal a day, and then I'd have to change and go out again. When I was with him, I was so nervous and tired. At the school they noticed my little boy seemed withdrawn. He started wearing hats, especially helmets. The reason he was wearing the helmets was not because he wanted to be a football player or soldier, but because he felt hidden and secure wearing them. His IQ was much higher than his attention span." The irony was that this woman, a warm and feeling person who has worked with disturbed children in the past, said, "I never thought it would happen to my child. I felt guilty beyond comprehension; worse than guilty. I thought I was a damn fool of a mother if I couldn't see what was happening to my own children. I felt he was much too young to catch the concept of why I was gone."

When her husband made it into Congress, she decided to get some counseling for her now five-year-old son. They found out one of the reasons his fears were so easily heightened was that he had extreme depth perception—"If he drew a Ferrari it would be in 3-D, with the carburetor and everything." Consequently, every monster in a fairy tale illustration or TV characterization was extremely real to him. She feels that had she been home more she could have helped him. "The doctor was very good and would see my husband in the morning at 7 A.M. before he went to the Hill. The adjustment to Washington was hard for the children. Congress is one example of this mobility in America, which is one of the most destructive elements on family life. It is a totally foreign life, no intimacy, no neighborhood, no friends." (This woman, by the way, is beautiful, gregarious, well liked by all who know her, and is considered among the most popular in Washington.) Her husband "really carried a heavy burden, he was very supportive to me and the children; and here he was trying to put the office together, learn about the legislation. Even so he made giant efforts to spend time with the children." She has cut back on her activities to stay home.

If politicians have any psychological problems themselves, they are "given more to depression than any other syndrome," said one psychiatrist. They have a quick rationale for it—the stress resulting from enormous responsibility, or they see it as the burden of the office. They don't see a lack of intimacy, or the lack of being *valued* as an intimate as a spouse or father as being a factor. There is the "office" team that is publicly plausible, and there is the "home" team that is publicly plausible, and there should be no difference.

Interestingly, the office team often comes down the hardest on politicians for their non-family-oriented life. One female aide said, sarcastically, "I hear all about the neglect of the family in ghettos—but the place to start is with our government officials."

Harry McPherson, former aide to Lyndon Johnson, wrote in his book *A Political Education* that an "intense concern with politics" may reflect an unwillingness to come to terms with one's personal problems. The distinct and verbal, if complex, political issues are safer; dealing with "one's parents, wife, children, boss, colleagues and friends was far more threatening, as it involved dark tides of emotion into which one might be swept at any moment." His analysis seemed to be borne out in the careers of many political men, McPherson wrote, whose failure as husbands and fathers matched their success in public affairs. "Brilliant in the arena, eager to engage in contests of ideas and rhetoric, they must have avoided the necessary intimacy by which a family lives—so starved and hostile did their women and children seem."

Wes Barthelmes, an aide to the late Robert Kennedy, felt Kennedy was "good with his own kids—it's just that he saw so little of them." I asked Barthelmes about the happy political marriages. "I think most of their private lives are disasters. Occasionally you'll find a private person in a public profession like politics, and they try to maintain a home life. Church goes to his cabin in Emmetsberg [Virginia] as much as possible. I think they have a reasonably good family life. But for most, the whole business just seizes them. Everything is directed to votes, and it's very destructive of personal relationships. I know it's a cliché, but most of the ones I know are insecure; politics provides the external things to make them secure—or feel it. A big demand to go on a TV show or a warm reception from an audience replaces a walk in the woods that you or I might want. I'm not saying there aren't some compatible team political marriages. There are a few who can work well together, but what they *feel* toward each other is something else.

"It's very hard *not* to go wrong. Most get caught up with the services, the free haircuts, just the whole matter of someone getting your tickets, or picking the wife up at Woodies [Woodward and Lothrop department store], the invitations to a Kennedy Center opening. Some of the wives like it, but it's very tough on families. If you're married to someone just out of law school and he gets into local politics and suddenly gets a thirst for state legislature or Congress, if you have no taste for it you can go absolutely nuts. I think the children suffer worst of all. Most of their lives are very messy."

I asked Joe Califano, former White House aide, if he knew any politician who had really put it all together with his family. He said, "No." Another former aide agrees. "It's a fuck-up for the kids. I'm sure every male kid wants to be like or better than his father, and he gets a sense of inadequacy. He reads the papers and his dad's in them all the time. Now Eleanor and George McGovern, I think, are really in love. He has immense respect for her and her advice is treasured by him, but they gave up completely with Steve in that seventy-two campaign."

Hubert Humphrey, a political animal from teething days, said, "Our hardest years were when the children were young and we were young. As we became older and more adjusted to public life, it got easier." He sat behind an ornate desk in his Senate office, this man who became Vice President and then tried so often to break through to the presidency. "I have always felt pity and understanding for people who are new to Washington; they come to Washington after being quite known in their own district; respected citizens, lots of friends, the kids have adjusted to local schools. All at once they come to Washington, and it's a foreign land and a foreign language. I felt some of that, and I'm sure my family felt some of it." He shook his head as if remembering the shock, disappointments, alienations, unmatched expectations. "You come from a rural district and you have two or three children you had to take out of schools and Mother doesn't know anyone. This is a fast-moving city, a power city. It hurts, sometimes." He paused. "I often felt very, very discouraged, very lonely."

The Humphrey children were raised in a predominantly matriarchal household. "I knew I wasn't going to have time with the family and Muriel made up her mind she would," Humphrey said. "We were not very social when we first came to Washington. It was hard for us to just pick up and 'go.' Muriel made up her mind to be with the children. She, ah, was the one who took care of the children."

And yet, as one psychiatrist says, "Many achievement-oriented people spend enormous time away from the family, and often for escape reasons; but you and I both know political figures who hardly see their families at all. If he has a reservoir of sentiment in him toward his wife and children, chances are he *cannot* spend all that time away. If he did, he would be the world's most unhappy man." (Many children told me when their fathers were home, they would have to share their fathers with the telephone, or aide, or briefcase. Others said they resented and hated dinner out with their fathers because they were always shaking hands or talking with people who stopped by, and there was never a private moment.) "If he does have such feelings and he still is gone, then he has to have a defense mechanism; to insulate himself against the need for that exchange of sentiment—whether that exchange be a loving look or a spat that has to clear the air or whatever. Very few political figures are tightwads with their families, most are quite generous except when it comes to that reservoir of sentiment."

Of course, some politicians and their families are sensitive enough to question their roles and the dehumanizing factors in our society. Some make a concentrated effort to spend more time with their children.

Some would like to see the rules governing their work changed, with three weeks of each month spent on the Hill and a fourth week in their district. That would free them to be with their families on weekends. "It's run by old-men's rules. They don't have families," said a father of four. Some are giving at least lip service to examining ways to change their life-style. Missouri Congressman Jerry Litton proposed in the fall of 1974 a "congressional school" as a controversial and tentative step toward change. Because congressional recesses seldom coincide with children's vacations, Litton said, "it forces a member of Congress to choose between the family he loves and the people he represents." He has two children, ten and eleven, and he was upset in his first term of office when he realized that divergent time off from work and school put congressional families "back in his home state three summer months when he is here, and puts him back in the state three winter months when the family is in Washington. These six months of the year could be spent together if school vacations coincided with congressional recesses." Litton emphasized that the average age of congressional members gets younger each session. For those cynics who say it would make no difference—that the Congressman would be out politicking and ignoring the family anyway— Litton replied that they would at least be home at night in the same state.

The children, it seems, should be interviewed to see if they would embrace the specialized nature of their school chums and school life. Litton proposed the cost not exceed per-pupil cost of public schools in the District and that all employees of the House and Senate, including staff members, elevator operators, custodial employees, and anyone else whose working time is determined by the time when Congress is in session, be included.

Even if such a school were born, no great change would be effected until politicians raised their own consciousness about the treatment of the family. In general, Congress legislatively treats the family with supreme indifference. As Colman McCarthy wrote in 1974 in the *Washington Post,* "Arguments that make the case for families—for easing the pressures that cause so many of them to break apart, be strained or stand undefended—are usually the last ones to be considered, if at all, when government policy is debated. It is as if the laws were to be passed and felt by anonymous classes, groups or mixes— known as the 'public'—and not by mothers, fathers, and children with blood and emotions running through them." A case in point was the then-current debate on strip-mine legislation and what would happen to family life among the ranchers of the western coal states if their land was allowed to be taken over by coal companies. The question was much on the minds of the citizens of those western states but, McCarthy wrote, "Appeals to Congress have been mostly brushed aside as sentimentalism."

He concluded, "To say that the government has no family policy is not entirely accurate. To ignore the pressures on families, to look away from the immense costs—both in terms of public money and personal suffering—to mistakenly believe that families can make it on their own; that becomes the national policy."

It is also, all too often, the *private* policy of elected officials—
the mistaken belief that their own families can also "make it on
their own."

10

Surrogate Wives

THERE is one person who can be more threatening
to a political marriage than a mistress, more of a rival to a political wife than the most doggedly devoted secretary. This person's role is symbiotic and complex—surrogate wife, alter ego,
fueler of the narcissism endemic to a politician's life and, zealous devotee to the one thing the politician reveres most: himself. I am referring to the male aide.

In elective politics, where personality is so exalted (principles,
issues, ideas, values are all personalized and exemplified
through the most popular vote getter), it is not only the President who is considered royalty. Every Congressman, Senator,
Governor, or Mayor is cosseted by a staff of "handmaidens and
foot rubbers," as one former Senator's aide put it, whose excellence at this art reaches paramedical proportions. Like satellites
around a sun, they revolve, twirling, hopefully, into their own
special orbits. For one who is—or wants to be—a most valued
political aide, it is in his own special interest to make his boss
look good; his tenure is measured by his ability to perform one
or more of a variety of functions in the pursuit of that aim—
from getting good press, writing the most effective speech or
the best piece of legislation, offering the best political advice,
running the best campaign, being an alert tactician and master
organizer, on down to reinforcing the candidate on how well
he's doing, brushing the dandruff off his shoulders before he
makes a speech, covering and sometimes pimping for him and
his sex partners.

Aides do not serve a company or a newspaper or a law firm;
they serve *one* person and, therefore, the Hill is a more modest
version of what happens in the White House. Politicians tend to
be surrounded by sycophants and hangers-on; the insecurity
fosters, as one political consultant said, "a lot of ass kissing." An

aide, no matter how capable, often finds himself vying in a natural rivalry for his boss's time and attention. Jealousy and hostility among the staff and, often, between the aide and the wife,
are the result.

"Let's face it," said one wife whose husband ran for national
office, "during a campaign they actually hate the wife and the
children or any person who might take him away from their
twenty-four-hour goal of getting him reelected. They want to
get him elected, so they can have a job." In turn, aides grumble
that wives have no understanding of what goes into timetables
or issues.

The battle can erupt in full force during a campaign—particularly a tough statewide struggle for the Senate or a national
campaign for the presidency, when the wife and aide are both
protective of their own prerogatives. Wives have thrown aides
out of hotel rooms when they felt their husbands were tired.
Abigail McCarthy said that after going from dawn until dark
during her husband's 1968 presidential campaign, "The campaign staff would hold a conference in the living room and expect us to give them coffee and talk to them. They had no idea
we had any right to rest. I was far from hospitable and just simply retired."

Eleanor McGovern, who was praised by her husband's 1972
presidential campaign staff ("I never saw her angry at George,
and she was wonderful with all of us," said one man), felt frustrations nonetheless. "I think for the most part my husband's
staff has been very cooperative with me—until 1972," she told
Barbara Walters on her "Not for Women Only" program. They
were eager for her to campaign "because they heard from
sources all over the United States that I was helpful. On the
other hand, they were very reluctant to give me any information that was helpful to me. I had to beg and plead and get
down on my hands and knees to find out what George's positions were on things. I had difficulty even finding out what he
had said the day before in order to meet the press the following
day. And I think the reason is, they don't quite know what to do
with the campaigning wife." She said the greatest problem was
in scheduling her—"because they don't know what you do best,
what you want to do, how much time you can devote to it." Nor
do they consider the fact that there are children at home, she
says. "If I was to campaign again, as in 1972, I would have my

own scheduling staff, I would synchronize everything with my husband's campaign."

The staff and wife are often natural antagonists, working at cross-purposes, desiring entirely different things.

Robert Hartman, adviser to President Ford, has found that the First Lady's pleasant demeanor masks a steely will. "Bob and I don't always jibe; I'm willing to admit that just as well as he is. I think perhaps my resentment of Bob comes from his trying to run my husband's life—and yet I think he is very valuable to my husband. Perhaps I feel he oversteps his boundaries."

Harry McPherson, long an aide to LBJ, said of Lady Bird Johnson, "I've known Mrs. Johnson a very long time, and I never felt that she liked me. Since he's been dead, I feel we'll at last become friends. It is as if you are competing for this man. I have always felt a lot of hostility on the part of wives toward a staff. It's probably one way they can vent their spleen at those other than their husbands. And I think we bring a lot of heavy-weight anxieties to their doorstep. For example, I spent a lot of Sundays briefing Ed Muskie in the days when he was deciding to run for the presidency. We'd go over to the house to see Ed, and I just got the feeling that Jane was thinking, 'Oh, shit, here they come again.' Any chance for a home relationship was gone for all those months, even before the campaign. You know, these past months, when I see her, she seems genuinely happy."

Marion Javits and Marvella Bayh have reputations for being "demanding bitches" who, according to former aides, were motivations for them to quit. Mrs. Javits says that reputation stems primarily from Richard Aurelio, a former administrative assistant who worked later for Mayor Lindsay and who, she says, "I think had very personal ambitions." While Mrs. Javits admits she can be a "difficult and complicated lady," it was Aurelio who said publicly, "Oh, she'd drive the staff up the wall." She says, "I felt that if I was doing that, it was for valid reasons, because I really was relating to what Jack had to do, and what I felt also had to be done, and they didn't feel at the time that my role was the significant one to watch."

Mrs. Javits said the staff constantly called her husband at home. "As soon as he came home from work, there would be like three telephone calls, until I put a stop to it. They wanted to talk about his schedule or somebody that he had to talk to. And I had to say, 'No more. When you're home, and when you come home, at least a few hours of privacy.' And you have to fight hard for it."

Marvella Bayh is one Senator's wife who refers to "my" secretary (one of her husband's secretaries types her letters and arranges her campaign schedule) and feels the staff is there to help her on matters concerning her husband's political interests. There are rumors that she got certain people fired. One ex-aide said thinly, "All I know is I tangled with Marvella and shortly after that my fortunes went downhill." Jane Muskie, who gets a gold medal from awed staffers who have experienced Ed Muskie's towering temper, has tangled with the staff, especially when she has felt he was being "overworked and overscheduled. We had a big flap in 1968. The majority of the staff was determined he should campaign around the country and forget Maine, that we had it sewn up. I fought that bitterly. I felt it was my duty to remind him that I felt he should be there." However, most of the time, she says, she feels more like a buffer trying to ease tensions.

Even though a former aide to Frank and Bethine Church feels they have "one of the few happy marriages on the Hill," he recalls, "We occasionally had to remind her that there were only two Senators from Idaho—and she wasn't one of them."

One veteran political consultant growled that "the two people I'd like to see thrown off a major campaign—the ones you always have trouble with—are the wife and the finance chairman. The wife invariably wants to go beyond her role, becomes a prima donna, and the goddamn finance chairman is someone who usually doesn't understand politics and argues about how you spend the dough." A friend who was listening and who has been on several campaigns, volunteered, "It's best to get the wife off on her own. She tightens him up every time. I've never seen a candidate who wasn't freer when his wife wasn't around. She knows him too well for him to feel comfortable with all that bullshit he dishes out and all the adulation, and he knows it."

The first consultant said, "Yeah, a perfect politician's wife is the kind of woman who would have helped run a Mom and Pop store—staying in the back room when that role was called for, taking over to help serve the customers when that was needed."

Implicit in that comment is the idea that the wife should avoid anything that looks like an assertion of authority.

Some wives feel aides are jealous in part because, no matter how important a behind-the-scenes role an aide plays, it is the wife who gets the recognition. She can write letters to constituents telling them how much she and her husband liked their point of view, or be his substitute speaker, or be on television or give an interview, extending the reach of the one-man band. Primarily because of her last name, she has an out-front niche that no aide can occupy; and when she is good at it, some wives feel, this creates envy.

Of course, the degree of infighting varies with the individuals—the aides, the politician, his family, the strength and security of everyone's position and, most important, how much the politician expresses, implicitly or otherwise, his devotion and respect, or lack of same, for his wife. The staff takes its cue from the rapport of husband and wife. If she is regarded as a valuable political asset, confidante, and adviser by her husband, the staff sometimes sighs, but accepts it. And some wives and staffs respect each other and coexist as friends. But if a husband's indifference to his wife emerges, this encourages aides to erect invisible walls to keep the wife out of the way.

What some wives probably do not care to admit is that the staff can provide an alluring diversion from the wearisome text of familial concerns such as mortgage payments, Billy's flu, plumbing that's shot. The aide is focused on what the politician wants to talk about, what he must get into his speech, or how he can get the most publicity out of something, or what he must know about a bill before he votes. "The whole *place* is set up as a mistress," says one man who was an aide to three top Democratic Senators. "There's a wife, who is treating him like an average human being, but the whole staff, particularly the males who are working on issues, are serving the function of telling him about all those things that bolster his image of being an important presence on the Hill. Most jobs don't compete with a man's personal life, except for his time. Here is a permanent organism, the staff, that is competing constantly for his time, energy, his interest, his body, everything else."

Another friction is that wives see in their husbands and aides a sort of beer hall "out-on-the-town" camaraderie that excludes

wives. Aides admit to me that they have been partners in seeing, speaking, and hearing no evil when it comes to the sexual
peccadilloes of their bosses—hardly a role to cement friendship
with an intuitive wife. If the politician has a particularly swinging image, aides use their male "helpfulness" in that department; it can smooth their way to becoming intimate confidants
to the politician.

"Let's face it," said a former aide to a Senator who is not noted for saying his rosary at night on the road, "the get-close syndrome, the jockeying for position counts. To fall into the category of 'friend' is the ultimate. When you're traveling, he feels
he can trust you. The ultimate in this job is intimacy—and the
ultimate of intimacy is pimping. You have something on him,
and you both know it."

If the marriage is solid and the wife is realistic, the staff counterforce can be just an annoyance; but if the husband wants to
use his work to escape home, the staff is often used as a buffer,
an excuse maker, a . . . well . . . liar. One former wife of a
Congressman who is a ranking member of an important committee said, "They all knew about his girl friend [now his second wife] in that office, and because he thought she was the
Queen Bee, they did, too. His aides just built a wall—the secretary'd call and say he was having a business dinner with his A.
A. [administrative assistant], a guy I'd known all these years,
and well, how was I to know?" While wives speak of barriers,
aides counter with gritted-teeth remarks that most wives, if they
had their way, would turn the aides into chauffeurs—for them.

All of this is not unlike the Machiavellian maneuverings of
ancient courts, and the aide's world is a tangle of egos, jealou-
sies, and competition. On a national campaign, advisers know
the press is watching them to see which one sits closest to the
throne—the last person seen hopping out of a car with the candidate, or having breakfast with him, or sitting next to him on
the plane would seem to have his ear. They dream of the position they'll have if he gets the Big Apple. On the McGovern
campaign there was enough snarling and sparring by males to
make Clare Boothe Luce's *The Women* look like *Rebecca of
Sunnybrook Farm*. For those outside the intrigues, there were
some hilarious sequences.

Hangers-on escalated in direct proportion to McGovern's rising popularity. As each primary became more significant, the people who wanted to appear on the platform during the victory speech increased, until that platform was like the campaign itself—an overloaded, sinking barge. It was fascinating to watch which staffer's head would appear behind the candidate's left or right ear in the photos or on camera, sometimes with a look of benign innocence.

Anyone who chooses to be a political aide does not do it because of a lust for security or with the idea of collecting a pension. It is a career founded on the quicksand of personal interplay; the aide serves at the bidding of his one and only boss—there is no union, no civil service appeal if he gets canned. If his boss is defeated in November, he is off the payroll on January 1. (That some are near pension status, having hung to the coattails of doddering and ineffective octogenarian Congressmen, is testimony to just one more failing of the seniority system.)

The aide's role is highly supportive, subordinate and acquiescing, and could be classified as the stereotypical "feminine" or "wifely" role. The relationship has its peculiarities. More than one former aide described the union as "man-child" or "master-servant," which reminds me of a conversation in a cab I shared with two men going to the Hill. They were young and obviously trying to impress one another as much as me and the cabdriver. They discussed a couple of pending bills, as knowledgeable insiders, you understand, and then one asked the other, "What does your man do? What committees is he on?" You would have thought you were listening to two English valets.

The job is characterized by a love-hate ambivalence. The security of the aide's job depends on keeping his boss there, which necessitates the constant pursuit of making him look and sound good, and all the while that is going on, the aide nurtures some special feelings of neglect, ego loss, and lack of identity that a job distinguished by anonymity fosters. Many aides say they enter politics with the altruism of supporting a person whose goals for the country seem sound and just, for the experience or excitement of it all, for the money, for the chance to wield some behind-the-scenes influence on issues. They can become disillusioned and feel demeaned when they find their identity is inherited, that their only status is gleaned from the status of the person they serve. Some in this group are frustrated politicians who end up running for office themselves. Others find solace in word-of-mouth appreciation or within a special circle where they have their own influence or in the knowledge that the press seeks their counsel. Many realize, as one says, that they "haven't got what it takes" to be a candidate. Others realize that, but still smart when they hear their words being delivered by someone else.

The animosity between wives and aides may in part be caused by the subtle acknowledgment that both groups function precisely the same way in one area. Serving and feeding the ego of a man who is selling only himself means being careful not to intrude on the limelight. In reacting to their roles, there is little difference, for example, in the words of Mieke Tunney, the former wife of Senator John Tunney, and those of Del Lewis, the first black professional hired by Senator Edward Brooke and then top aide to Walter Fauntroy, Washington's first Representative since Reconstruction. "You have to subdue your own personality. You cannot shine," says Lewis. "As a good political wife, you have to stifle your own identity and play second fiddle," says Mieke Tunney.

I found most political aides to be interesting, likable, cynical, hard on themselves and politicians, more introspective and shyer than the people they serve, bright, articulate, able to stand back and observe as well as participate.

Seth Tillman, highly respected and well known on the Hill as former Senator William Fulbright's principal foreign policy ghost, instrumental in shaping a policy credited with helping to turn Congress and the country around on the Vietnam War, said that after thirteen years with the Senator he recognized that "you get a little bit hooked on that power and the proximity to it, but at the same time I have a fairly clinical view of it." We talked about defeat and Tillman said, "Just about anybody who gets bounced out of here makes good at something. It's the *power* that's tenuous. It's not so much the fear of loss of money, it is the loss of power or proximity to it that is being taken away. It's an intoxicant far more addictive than you realize until it is taken away." The best aides realize they would have no power on their own. "It's the Senator with the authority and influence of power. You may write the stuff, but if it were marketed as yours, it would be lost in the mill," says Tillman.

Some find this not so easy to take. Del Lewis said, "Most of

them really want to be in positions of power. They may not
want to be a candidate but it comes through in other ways.
Brooke's A. A. had his Ph.D., a real nice, quiet guy and then
one day he said, 'Del, I'm ready to leave.' He knew all the stuff
about arms control. Brooke didn't know what ABM meant, but
Alton did. He finally just said, 'I'm tired of writing those
speeches with someone else's name on them.'"

Most speech writers have learned that it pays to be studiously
anonymous, and could have probably prospered in the CIA,
but still it can be tough. Bob Shrum set a record in 1972, working consecutively for Lindsay, Muskie, and McGovern. All of
them lost. A 1974 Fellow at the Kennedy Institute of Politics,
Shrum recalls "one moment of pure unalloyed joy. I wrote
most of McGovern's acceptance speech. And then comes the
crashing realization, 'Nobody would listen to *me* if I had said
it.'" Speech writers who do not share the consensus on anonymity have ways of surfacing. As Jack Germond, a top political
reporter before becoming an Assistant Managing editor with
the Washington *Star-News,* says, "Somehow we always learned
about it when Dick Goodwin or Bill Safire was the ghost."

Some aides reach heights of pomposity and self-importance.
"What really gets me about that kind is the way they always say
'the Senator,'" comments Mark Shields, a highly respected political gun-for-hire who helps candidates on a consulting basis
and used to work for Senators Proxmire and Robert Kennedy
and for Governor John Gilligan of Ohio. "What is that shit? I
always ask, '*Which* Senator? There are one hundred of 'em, you
know.'"

Most aides are realistic about their secondary position, but
some politicians with big egos make the role especially demeaning. Stories abound of bosses ordering aides to do menial
chores, of expecting them to take the blame when things go
wrong, of never complimenting them when they do well. For
the lucky ones, a relationship based on mutual respect develops. Others establish more symbiotic ties. Like remora fish,
which attach themselves to larger fish, they hitchhike through
life. My son's easy-reader book, *Fish Do the Strangest Things,*
provided a delightful analogy to some of the more parasitical
political aides: "The remora holds on with the top of his head.
The top of his head is flat. There is a suction cap on it. With this

cap he can quickly fasten onto another fish. He cannot fall off unless he wants to. The remora rides on sharks so much he is often called a 'shark sucker.' Sometimes many remoras will ride on the same shark at the same time. But remoras will ride on almost any big fish. The remora gets a free ride. And he also gets free meals. When the big fish catches his dinner, the remora lets go. He swims around and eats up the leftovers."

Abigail McCarthy says, "A lot of insecure people attach themselves to candidates. I never realized the terrible competition around a Senator. If it weren't so hectic it would be amusing," she said. "Those who want to touch, be near, be important. Even though they would like to be known as advisers, most all are yes-men. They're afraid of losing their influence and afraid the wife will tell him something they don't want him to hear. I feel the Senator is badly served, since it seems to happen on every staff. All the jockeying and so on deflects from the aim." (There are those Senators, like Birch Bayh, who say they look to their wives for the most honest answers and guidance.)

An authority on Hill bosses who has worked for Congresswoman Edith Green, Representative Richard Bolling, Senators Frank Church, Robert Kennedy, and Joe Biden feels staff people get "vicarious gratification." "A lot of staff people may be as capable or talented; but they don't have the drive, the competitiveness. They feel if they're working for good people, they're accomplishing something. The appeals are very high. Their own egos can be enormous, but for some reason they don't want to go it alone. They want to ride up on somebody's back. It's a sort of psychic weakness." On the other hand, those fortunate among the so-called professional staff—the good press aides and legislative and administrative assistants whose opinions are valued—draft bills, write speeches, hear their own words on radio and TV. "Some chafe to get the credit but others are content to powder, diaper, blow their noses, and send the member off to the floor," said Wes Barthelmes. In lieu of real power, some indulge in their own power plays, such as keeping certain reporters from seeing the Congressman.

Mark Shields says, "Your whole identity is through the man. The ultimate is intimacy. It is man-child: 'He noticed me!' 'He chewed me out!'" This relationship stems from the absolute power a politician holds over the staff. "A politician is under no one's aegis. Even in a corporation or the navy, there is someone above you, unless you're Henry Ford or some admiral, to put yourself in perspective. In Congress, you're not under anyone." Still, Shields gives the elected official credit for more courage than any aide. "Those guys are willing to lay their ego on the line, and we're not. We can sit and grumble, but we're not taking the chance. It isn't as if I lost my job or you lost yours, and we'd have our friends and family who would know. If we were politicians, everyone reading the papers would know you lost for Governor, and I lost for the Senate." As for being a self-effacing aide, it is hard to imagine Shields ever repressing his personality for anyone. He is a round Irish leprechaun with a manic wit who missed his calling as a stand-up comedian. Mark says he's been lucky in that the people he works for appreciate his humor. (He and another friend, Mike Barnicle, used to pipe Sargent Shriver aboard the campaign plane to the tune of "Hail to the Chief"—on kazoos—during the 1972 vice presidential trek.)

While power can be a high, it can also make one feel inferior. "Deep down in your heart you kinda wonder about it all. That's what one Senator told me when we got drunk as skunks one night on the campaign," said one aide, who repeatedly had to bolster his politician's morale.

This is no doubt one reason why some chew out staffs or test their power on them or resent any attention they get. Senator Fritz Mondale surprised some friends one day and caused them to doubt his own inner security when he said, not bitterly, but simply as a matter of fact, "If I get an aide who wants to see his name in the paper, I tell him frankly to get out and run for himself."

One aide said, "So I'm a ghost-writer. If you write a good speech the response is fascinating. After you give it, the politician will look right through you as if you're not there. Or he'll sorta mumble, 'Great speech—I hope you won't spread it around that you wrote it.'"

Tony Smith, a long-time friend and writer for Senator Barry Goldwater, said, "I once worked for a guy who said, 'I'd like to invite you down for the speech, but if I look across the room and see you sitting there, I just wouldn't like the feeling. It would tighten me up.' So you console yourself that you're *paid* to be a ghost. But if the speech falls on its face, or if *he* delivers it wrong and it bombs, then you're a bum."

Like many an aide, Smith is a former newspaperman who went into politics for the money. Another such aide is Dick McGowan, a caustic, chronically disgruntled former New York City reporter who looks and acts as if he had read *Front Page* once too often. Although you never know, you get the impression that McGowan's practiced cynicism is a study in not letting his soft side show.

At the time I talked with him he was in Senator Lowell Weicker's office, and he was unhappy. Weicker has an equal proportion of good-looking secretaries and pictures of himself with a mess of astronauts. Huge pictures are autographed by the crew of Skylab, and there are slogans such as: "Lowell Weicker was present at the landing of Apollo 11, July 16, 1969." There are also the ritualistic pictures of the All American Family. I had a 4:30 P.M. appointment, and I was still waiting at 5:15. This is far from uncommon on the Hill, and I am always amused by the minor functionaries who answer phones or run in and out of doors while you wait. Some are cordial, apologetic, or offer you Cokes. Many, however, act as if it is your just reward to wait forty-five minutes to see the king. This isn't a penance reserved just for the press. In Humphrey's office, Admiral Zumwalt was backed up and waiting just as long as I was. And Governor Mandel kept a group of interested citizens with an appointment before me waiting one hour. Most people anticipate the delay and bring something to read. To be kept waiting is one thing, to keep a Congressman or Senator waiting is quite another. A couple of times, trying to find a place to park—most of the Capitol Hill parking space is restricted for you-know-who and the staffs of you-know-who—I was late by about ten to fifteen minutes. The staff outrage at my audacity was comic.

In the spring of 1974 I was sitting with McGowan, who was on the phone fending off speech requests because Watergate had made Weicker a pop hero. Two girls sitting on the floor of the crowded office counted impeachment telegrams—1,010 against 8 to impeach Nixon, they droned. McGowan glared at the telephone as he hung up, and said, "I can ask him, but by God, I just know he can't."

I asked him how he liked his job. "Frankly, I find it degrading. There is a certain amount of independence and freedom as a newspaper man. Your ego gets satisfied. Here you're dealing with egomaniacs. At one time, people came here for the salary, but newspapers pay enough now. 'Ding dong' happens to be a cheap S.O.B." I gulped and said, "Oh—ah, don't you like Weicker?" (Many aides or former aides conform to the same unwritten code that former wives and wives do—no zapping your politician or a former politician. Complete candor can only hurt the aides when they try to catch on with someone else. McGowan just didn't seem to give a damn.) We returned to old "ding dong." "Nahhhh, it isn't just him. There was no doubt in my mind after being here less than two weeks how and why the executive branch seized all the power. They're the most egotistical group of jerks I ever met in my life. I'm talking about the whole lot of them. They're moribund. Chasing their own tails. At least the House has to explain itself. Every two years they have to explain themselves to constituents. They're reelected on Tuesday and back campaigning on Wednesday."

Tillman, an aide who enjoyed a close relationship with Fulbright, said of politicians, "Many of them really are very egotistic and narcissistic. That's why they're so tiresome. Everything is about themselves. There is a fantastic preoccupation with publicity. The effect of that is that a contagion of power spreads to the press, and it becomes more and more like the people it is dealing with—self-righteous, aggressive, moralistic."

McGowan, embittered by his experience, said, "Most feel they don't have to rely on the staff. They use people up. It's totally a 'What have you done for me today?' attitude. There is really very little sense of accomplishment." His eyes were expressionless as he answered another call. "I know he'd like to do the show, but I'm positive he'll be out of town. Pick another date, and I'll nail him down."

Weicker came out of his office, and there were a few moments of awkward chitchat and then, like a flagship surrounded by its flotilla, the Senator barreled down the hall with his staff for a command performance at a publication party being given for a book of Watergate cartoons. It was held in that same hearing room where some of the Senators had donned sunglasses in the TV glare, but now the main attraction was a bar and a table of cocktail meatballs and stuffed tomatoes. It was a bomb of a party, a strange group of non-Washington people, including a woman in a blue lace "tent" and silver spike-heeled slippers. They all came up to Weicker, hard to miss as his six feet four inches towered above the crowd, to shake his hand and have their pictures taken with him. I said goodbye to McGowan, who had done his duty for about five minutes and then walked with me to the door of the Senate Office Building. "I have no ego here," he said. "It hurts."

The Hill at night is soft and pristine. The marble buildings, finely etched, gleam like the false fronts on a Hollywood set for the archetypical Washington movie—it could be *Mr. Smith Goes to Washington* or *Advise and Consent* or any of a dozen others. I was remembering the phrase that had been used so often by people who work on the Hill—that it is a fantasy tinsel town: "It is all so unreal. What happens within the office is there are so many personal ties to the member. Cronies, campaigners and others, hacks and all. Everyone using everyone, including the aide who is 'using' the member to learn the office scene." Or: "The member is the absolute center of attention, and it's like no other office in government or private enterprise. That's his *personal* staff; the result is it is run in a personal way with all the problems such a thing can bring. Corporations can be vicious— I've worked for one—but not as vicious as the Hill. I live a fantasy all day long." And still another Senate aide comments: "The whole office is dedicated to making that man look good. There are ninety-nine 'enemies' out there."

It is difficult to understand how some politicians can so totally lose perspective on themselves unless you observe the setup of Capitol Hill. There are only 435 members of the House and 100 Senators, but 14,000 people keep this world of theirs functioning. There are plumbers, electricians, barbers, doormen, masseurs, public relations men, carpenters, elevator operators, janitors, tax lawyers, charwomen, waiters, machinists, messengers, tour guides, manicurists, secretaries, aides, upholsterers, repairmen, handymen, librarians, offset press operators, typewriter repairmen. There are gyms and steam rooms and restaurants and an arboretum that furnishes greens for the offices and an aquarium and a power plant. The names for some of the jobs are, to say the least, inspired. A fellow on the House payroll is described as a "venetian blind technician." He makes $9,200 a year for cleaning them. A lot of staffers are friends, relatives, and political workers of the Senators and Representatives.

Then we come to the staff and committee aides, the "pros" who can earn up to $36,000. There are 900 such professional-level jobs on the Hill. White males still predominate. A generalization made by Hill observers is that there is more professionalism and brightness not only in Congress today, but also among those who work for Congress. The reason is that demands on Congress are greater.

"I don't in fact understand why some of them stay here," said Representative Richard Bolling, chairman of the Select Committee on Committees, that has tried—with mixed results—to reform the House committee structure and operations. "They could be more comfortable, freer, and better paid elsewhere. We treat first-rate people absolutely awfully." Some of them stay because they see accomplishment. Charles Ferris is chief counsel of the Senate Committee on Democratic Policy. As Mike Mansfield's nosecounter and chief adviser on domestic legislation, Ferris finds satisfaction. Among other things, he helped shape civil rights legislation.

No one today has the clout that Robert G. Baker had a decade and a half ago. A poor Southern boy of Snopesian lineage, Baker sniffed out power better than anyone, became indispensable to Lyndon Johnson as secretary of the Senate, and was respected for his ability to count. He always had at least "ten senators in my pocket" and seemed to have many more girls ready anytime for a party. Baker, who was fired in 1963 by Johnson's successor, Mansfield, later served a prison term for larceny, fraud, and tax evasion. Likable and glib, Baker still has many friends in Washington.

To overreach in the pursuit of power and ambition when others are doing the same all around you can be a large temptation. Perhaps no other group so collectively believed in their right to misuse their power than Nixon's White House aides.

After he was sentenced, Jeb Stuart Magruder told me how he felt after he first heard the transcripts. Like a discarded lover, he suddenly said of Nixon, "I realized then that he didn't love us! he *never* loved us! And of course we all loved him. We could not have done what we did if we hadn't."

The shame and trials Nixon aides brought their families is not a common fate of aides' families. However, in the quest of giving their all for some politician, their own families are off in left field, neglected, and with none of the sense of participation afforded the politician's family.

The wives and children of aides live an uprooted, insecure existence. Wives often see their husbands turning into jack-in-the-boxes, leaping up the second their bosses whistle. There is very little warmth in "reflected" glory four times removed. Many aides have shattered marriages; a large number of those I interviewed are divorced and are trying a second time.

Joe Califano says his wife, Trudy, still complains about his hours as an ambitious lawyer, but that it is nothing like the White House days. "You can't imagine what it was like, especially working for a guy like Lyndon Johnson. He expected you to show up on Sunday on that *Sequoia* if he asked you. You'd say that Trudy and the kids had other plans, and he'd say, 'Bring 'em along.' He never understood that the boys wanted to play basketball, that their idea of an outing was not a bunch of adults talking political business on the President's yacht. Trudy came once and said never again."

A more "devastating" problem is "you lose every element of the day with your children," Califano said. He would leave for the White House before his sons, then five and six, were awake and came home rarely before 10 P.M. He worked all day Saturday. On Sunday he would go to church with his boys and then go back to work. "The few times you are home the phone is a monumental intrusion to your wife." Finally, even going to church was invaded. One Sunday, after Lyndon tried unsuccessfully to get Califano, the President told him, "From now on, you take a White House car with the phone in it to church. And sit in the back so the driver can go in and get you." Califano said, "The grind is more persistent than in any other work. It never lets up. But at least wives of aides know it's for a finite period, that it will be over someday. With Senators and Congressmen it's forever."

One aide, now divorced, said, "When I got off the campaign plane one night in 1972, another of the guys said to me, 'My wife's probably thinking, "Here comes that dumb shit with a suitcase full of dirty socks and a hard on." I expect to get bounced out of the house any day now.'"

One problem that contributed to the collapse of the aide's marriage was "the availability of single, young, horny women. It's the usual office games that go on, except there are so many more. The makeup of the Hill just means more social activity, the kind I was unused to as a newspaperman. There's always some function going on in Congress. The endless rounds of receptions. You drop down, have a couple of drinks, and before you know it, you make a date to go out." His card with his name—and the U.S. government seal—"is perhaps one of the most traveled ones in the world. I don't know a stewardess from here to California I didn't pop it on." I asked him if it worked. "I used to get a lot of phone calls. You just can't imagine the respect being with a top Senator commands." And what about all those polls saying everyone is disillusioned with and distrusts politicians? Apparently they never interviewed any political groupies.

Another divorced aide said, "In politics, the temptations are always there. On a campaign the roar of the jet plane taking off drowns out the noise of wedding rings being dropped into change purses." For all that, the music stops eventually. He held a top job with the Democratic National Committee, but he says, "You get tossed out like an old Kleenex with never so much as a thank you. It's undignified and degrading."

A former aide to Senator Bayh said, "I remember he was making a speech, and then he had to go to a dinner and he had to change into his tuxedo in the car. I noticed his black shoes were caked with mud. I started wiping them with a handkerchief—'Gotta make this guy look good'—and I said to myself, 'You're becoming a valet, you little S.O.B.'"

Aides joke that they stay with Senators because it impresses their families. "My father was at a hearing, and the Senator motioned me to come over during it. My being there impressed the hell out of him." A second aide said that when he decided to leave Senator Proxmire, his father said, "But, son, you're not going to quit working for a *Senator!*"

The need to look good back home, the glamor you are often credited with in other circles, as an extension of your job, keeps people in positions that necessitate putting up with a lot. The Kennedy glamor has commanded a disproportionate share of willing lackeys, and the Kennedys trade on that. Eunice Shriver had a revolving door of aides who couldn't get along with her when she was campaigning for her husband. Another Washington woman said, "I got sick of being one of Ethel's ladies-in-waiting. She expected you to be there whenever she wanted you to."

An aide to Phil Hart said, "One day I am sitting at the far corner of the table at an antitrust hearing, and I hear this sound. Someone is *snapping* his fingers. I look over; and there is Ted Kennedy snapping his fingers at me to come over and get something for him. I hesitated, but up here, a Senator *is* a Senator, so I went over." This aide spoke of being "spoiled." She works for a man conceded to be one of the nicest on the Hill, Phil Hart. "He is a delight to work for, one of a few. You'll see him carrying his luggage, and he'll mumble that he's going to the airport. You jump up and offer him a drive, and he'll say 'Oh no . . . I'll just take a cab.' He seems embarrassed to put anyone out."

While Lyndon Johnson could cull more political mileage out of his down-home origins, he was one son of a bitch to work for when he felt like being one, which was not infrequent. "An indefatigable worker himself, he saw his staff, and Senators themselves, as fungible parts of an army whose purpose was to serve, equip and sustain its general in his infinite tasks," McPherson wrote in his book. One time McPherson prepared a long list of questions for a hearing and he watched anxiously as Johnson thumbed through his memorandum. "He looked up; I caught his eye; he motioned me up to the dais with him. Excited, I rushed around behind Senators and staff and bent to hear him whisper: 'Go up to my office and get me a few of those orange sourballs.' I was furious; but I did what he said, bringing them back sealed in an immense manila envelope which, I hoped, he would have trouble opening discreetly."

Aides put up with it in part because they are "participating in history" and partly because it gives them a certain cachet elsewhere. McPherson had radically changed his mind about Senators as a group—thought them more ethical and intelligent than he expected. Besides, "If a senator was an activist, if he served on the right committees or simply had the right interests, his legislative assistant moved in a high-pressure world of cabinet officers, academicians and Washington lobbyists."

McPherson talked about the emoluments of a high staff position and what they do to a person. No matter how the boss may treat you, the payoff is in the way others treat you. "When you're a top aide, you're treated differently when you are away from home. You're treated with unbelievable deference. There was that White House car every morning. It would wait thirty minutes outside while you had your second cup of coffee. Then you'd go down to a world where telephone operators can handle anything and are willing to do so," he said. "There's an enormous difference between that world and the one you left. *You've* got the chauffeured limo—whereas *your* car always had mechanical trouble. I laid that and a lot of things on my wife. I was always able to say, 'I can't do it, I've got to meet with the *President* or the *King* of Siam.' It creates anger and hostility on the part of the wife and a good deal of defensiveness on the husband's part. Even the kids think you're getting special attention and resent it. Jim Symington had some tickets to a Redskin game, and he asked me to join him. My son, eight, was pouting that there wasn't a ticket for him, too, and he said, 'You get to go because you're powerful and you just told him to give you those tickets.' "

One late afternoon I sat with two lawyers who had long experience in national politics. The two partners were interesting because they represented both poles of the major argument I had heard since I started this book. Bernard (Bud) Fensterwald worked many years for Senator Estes Kefauver and was staff director of the Senate Antitrust and Monopoly Subcommittee headed by Kefauver. In 1973 Fensterwald represented James McCord, the Watergate conspirator. His partner, Gordon Harrison, Jr., possesses memories of Washington as a "sleepy little Southern town," pre-World War II. He was on the staff of the late Senator Theodore Green of Rhode Island.

Fensterwald feels that pampering aides are in a direct way responsible for alienation in political families. "I think Senate wives are among the most to-be-pitied people in the world. Their husbands are invariably wedded to their jobs. Then all of us 'handmaidens' compound this. I call 'em the handmaidens and foot rubbers; we spoil them rotten. They get to be like children after a while. Can't even get themselves a cup of coffee. It gets to the point where you wonder, 'What's the trouble, are you crippled?' " "Were you a foot rubber?" I asked. "I was a foot rubber," he said, with an engaging grin. "Why would you do that sort of thing?" I inquired. "Hell, we wanted interesting jobs! That was a part of it. No job was perfect and that part of it was a mess. You always knew that you could be a chief petty officer—which you were—but you weren't ever going to be a commanding officer. It's an incredibly clear-cut organization."

He took a slug of beer and said, "I remember once in Pocatello, Idaho—now, goddammit, I'm telling you the truth, Pocatello—and it's 3 A.M. and Estes dispatches me to find this screwy cigarette holder he used. Hell, I went and woke the druggist up! Never did get those goddamn filters. Kefauver probably was the least imperial of all I worked for—but he had some peculiar quirks." I said I heard that he sure liked women. Fensterwald's grin spread archly and widely over his face. "I've heard those stories, too." He wasn't about to embellish them. "I think Nancy [Kefauver's wife] made up her mind years earlier that he was married to his job. She's one of the few Senate wives who had her own career [she was an artist] and she was certainly successful at it."

Fensterwald feels that the "two institutions, the U.S. Senate and marriage, are incompatible. They should all be bachelors. Hell, Kennedy had a grand time. He and Smathers. Kennedy got the nickname 'Mattress Jack' in those bachelor days. I don't have a particularly high view of that august body. I think most of 'em would starve to death in the outside world. They're lousy family men. The average son of a Senator is neglected. His father simply isn't there."

Harrison protested that if you took one hundred men in the business or legal world, you'd come out with the same type of kids. Fensterwald shook his head. "In the first place, the average Senator's wife is so busy going to lunches and parties and bandage rolling and all that crap they feel they ought to do, that she can't be there. And I think Senators are just physically away more."

Harrison protested again that Fensterwald was exaggerating everything, that almost every successful person has both difficult working hours and someone to massage his ego. "A doctor, or a reporter who has to go out of town, or a CPA at income tax time—all of that strains a marriage." Fensterwald argued with a wink: "You'd be amazed at how many women throw themselves at the feet of a U.S. Senator as opposed to how many throw themselves at the feet of a CPA."

Some aides retain an independence as well as a sense of achievement in their roles. Wes Barthelmes said, "I've been lucky. I've always worked for good people." He left Edith Green's office "when she decided to turn on everything she stood for." He ghosted two books for Bolling—"I think that was an important academic contribution"—and worked with Frank Church on the Church-Cooper amendment to end the Vietnam War.

While he feels that "Robert Kennedy was one of the great people of our time," Barthelmes did not have the temperament for the all-consuming job of being his press secretary. "It wasn't worth that much to me to turn my life over to someone else. After a year or more, it became apparent that the job was going to consume you, seven days a week. It's all in the service of God and country, but you don't have any private life."

Some aides are not content with their secondary positions and go on to be politicians themselves. And then there are the also-rans, wasted by high living and alcohol, who take jobs on the Hill after they've wrecked their political chances, and, often, their marriages. One such man lives in his dreams of past power. He is a heavyset, Faulknerian character with brooding dark eyes who works for a Southern Senator. His childhood was Deep South prep school and some family money. Nervous and arrogant, he banged his crème de menthe glass on the tabletop. When no one looked up from the bar, he banged again and shouted, "Boy, fill it up." Taking a swipe with his large hand at the hair falling on his forehead, he muttered, "The guy that knows me here must be off duty."

His static, run-on manner was disconcerting as he started talking about how he'd always had political ambitions and how he had early visions of being an Abe Lincoln. He met and married the "ideal political wife." "The first real big trouble we had, I graduated law school and we stayed in Washington one more year. Then I announced we were going back to——" (He mentioned the state.) "She was graduated from a fancy girls' school and she was addicted to the arts and the cultural pursuits of Washington. She was into all the art galleries and acting groups around at that time. She opened in T. S. Eliot's—oh, Jesus Christ, what was the name of that damn play he wrote? Well, anyway, she threw a conniption fit. But I always remembered the advice that to get ahead in Washington, you had to go home first."

He got his wife to go home; and he decided to run for the state legislature, all the time with the idea of getting back to Washington as a Senator. It was a financial strain and an emotional strain, but his wife knocked on doors and asked people to vote for her husband. "I was so damn tired by the end of that damn campaign, campaigning you can get so damn tired sometimes, I'd just drive down to New Orleans to get away from everybody. I'd drink and go out with shady ladies. You just gotta get rid of that tension, and you couldn't do it at home with three screaming kids." He was elected, but a depression set in for five or six weeks. "I'll tell you what that damn depression is about. Paying the goddamn bills. Your damn law practice goes dead while you're campaigning." To counter the depression, he said, "I slept a lot. I don't have to tell you that doesn't help your relationship with your wife."

Did he feel any power and glory in his job as a state senator? "Oh, shit, yes. I loved it. As I say, my depression cleared up as soon as I took the oath. Yes, I liked the power and glory. What the hell else do you get out of it? You get to be called 'Senator.' You walk into a state agency and they quake. I was on a top finance committee and among nineteen of the most powerful people in the state." He was on his third crème de menthe. "And then you get your picture in the paper for introducing some bill or something, and somehow, mysteriously, you meet these ladies. At first you're very surreptitious"—the word was slurred. "You know, sneaky. And then you . . . well, we have a saying that Cutty [as in Cutty Sark] makes you invisible. It's the same way with an office. You get to feeling that way, and you don't give a damn."

In 1960 he was among a Southern faction that was the first to support John Kennedy. He was riding high, and he went to that convention with the Senator who is now his boss and he was going day and night.

"I spent that damn election in the veterans' hospital, in the mental ward." He tapped his head. "It all just got to me." Afterward, he worked in the governor's office. "I swear I like to killed myself there. I tend to overwork; I'm hyperactive." By then his marriage was disintegrating. His wife refused to move to the capital, so he lived in a hotel. "We had five children—I always joke that she was a 'passionate Presbyterian.' Well, she started to form her own life, got involved in the theater."

He was convinced that he would snap under the pressure if he ran for office again. He is perhaps an extreme case, but it tells something about the syndrome of the psychological makeup of the aide. "I had no trouble working for others; only when I ran myself. I think it goes back to some childhood pressure. Suddenly it's *you* who has got to make all the decisions." As he continued to talk, he reminded me of Peter Gent's novel of the doped-up life of pro football players, *North Dallas Forty.* "Hell, most candidates' wives are on something. They're all on tranquilizers. The governor's wife, hell, I'd lose my temper and she'd give me a Librium to calm me down. Then you'd go out and drink to get a high."

Despite his concerns about flipping out, the aide said the pull of elective office was too much. The governor was concluding his term in 1968 and couldn't succeed himself. "I was trying to figure out what the hell I was going to do. I decided to run for lieutenant governor. I resigned from the governor's office, opened my own office, and campaigned six weeks. Then the governor—who couldn't succeed himself—the *son* of the man who brought me into politics as a kid, decided *he* was going to run for lieutenant governor. I didn't have a chance. In the interim, my wife said if I ran for lieutenant governor, she was going to divorce me. Although I withdrew, *she* kept her word. She'd had enough of this goddamn life. She married some professor of drama—she's back home with her thespian." The aide, in his mid-forties, is "going with a girl back home, but she hates politics." He says he dates around a lot.

A political addict who weaves his way through convoluted dates and political personages like some boys know baseball statistics, he was clearly on his way to a massive hangover. Not totally resigned to working on the fringes of power he, nonetheless, knew it was his only choice.

11

Old Mistresses Never Die, They Just Fade Away to the Mimeograph Room

A vigorous social life with a locker-room quality to it—drinking, brawling, and womanizing—has been one of the least lofty but enduring cornerstones of American politics. Men in power have often equated a little jocko-macho sexual prowess with voter appeal—and so have the voters, to say nothing of the women who find that sleeping with power is the next best thing to having it on their own.

The rules for political sex modify with whatever is the current social trend but some of the most consistent are as follows: (1) On the Hill you are not very bright if you run with a girl in your own office. (This is often violated.) (2) You are also not very bright if you are especially blatant about your womanizing—unless you have the panache of an Estes Kefauver, Lyndon Johnson, John Kennedy, "Gorgeous" George Smathers, Adam Clayton Powell, or Earl Long (whose longtime companion was stripper Blaze Starr). (3) The campaign trail is an accepted place for liaisons that, no matter how ardent, are never expected to last past the first week in November. Men and women of relatively faithful bent find themselves engaged in frenetic woomanship in that crazy, encapsulated world called a presidential campaign.

There are also some recent, totally unscientific findings on the whole business of sex and politics.

1. The major one is that most politicians really aren't all that good in bed. At least that's what many wives and girlfriends say. Their lust is for power—sex is secondary. Psychiatrists add a few high-sounding remarks about the same drive that got them into politics being the same drive that gets them into bed, but generally admit that the sex itself is no more intimate than many of their other *private* but *nonintimate* relationships, such as marriage and family. Some wives have to cope with compulsive infidelity but the act is seldom anything as serious as "making love." As one psychiatrist said, "Many of these politicians play a phallic game. It's all part of his seeking of adoration and approval; he wants a relatively immature form of sex, one-night stands and new admirers but no commitment."

One Texas writer, a former aide to a young, dynamic politician who was riding the wave into national politics before he wiped out in a financial scandal, recounts the story of one of his former boss's conquests.

"I had fixed him up with her, after he had practically devastated all the females in the auditorium with one of his turned-on speeches. She told me later that he came in, took off his clothes, got in bed, screwed her and left. The whole thing took fifteen minutes—and he never said a word to her."

Most women know that kind of performance can only be classified, on a scale of 1 to 10, as *zero*. William Masters, of Masters and Johnson sexual rehabilitation fame, once told me that the secret to good sex is the sharing and giving of a mutually responsive couple. That means forgetting yourself long enough to include the other person in your thoughts, something that politicians have had little practice doing. As Masters said, "Good sex takes two—and in their case, only *one* is important."

For years, attractive Georgetown women had a certain cachet in being able to drop the knowing hint that John F. Kennedy was a major disappointment—his bad back, you know—but those Camelot days are finally fading in sexual importance.

2. Another finding is that the Hill does not jump as it once did. Several Senators' wives have told me what it's like to see their husbands not only fair—but *open*—game in an era of so-called "new morality." Jane Muskie said, "You go to a party alone and when your husband arrives you see all those women advancing like vultures. Well, that does something to a man that's not normal." Another wife said, "It could be devastating if you really *cared* about your husband."

Roscoe Dellums, the stunning wife of one of the Hill's major sex symbols, California Congressman Ron Dellums, said of those women who flock around her husband, "If I could tell them how awful it would be if we changed places—they'd be startled if I said, 'Forgive me, he is *yours!*' But I refuse to be frightened to death by all of that. And yet that is happening to wives of politicians. One wife, seven months pregnant, begged her husband [newly elected], 'Don't take me to Washington and ditch me.' The now divorced wife of another Congressman told me she said the same thing when they came here. These men are finding they can get reelected no matter. They are getting very, very arrogant. We live in a progressive district and the people couldn't give a damn about his leaving home."

Still, longtime male observers and sometime participants say that sex is not the good old game it used to be for two reasons. Before the women's movement, a certain "class" young woman, with a good education and intelligence, populated the Hill because the jobs were exciting compared to what she might get elsewhere. If she also enjoyed a "good time," it was with a certain congenial rapport. Now women of that caliber refuse to settle for such jobs as "personal secretary" to a Congressman.

They vie for the still relatively scarce top positions open to women on the Hill. "They want to be advisers on foreign affairs or they just don't come here," said one male. The vast majority of secretary-receptionist jobs are now being filled by, as one man said, "little teeny-bopper groupies. All rock 'n' roll girls. They're really dull or jail-bait, practically. These very young ones have no real interest in politics, look at their work as 'just a job.' Their social life is more downtown in singles bars or in their high-rise apartments. There isn't that same glamor attached to the figure of a Congressman any more."

Sid Yudain, editor of *Roll Call,* a weekly magazine for the Hill, reminisced. "They used to have those congressional staff parties and there would be millions of guys and millions of girls, and Congressmen would come in making the rounds. Now the parties are half full."

Another major reason is an escalated work load which doesn't leave as much time for parties. A constituency educated by watchdog consumer organizations and TV to "write your Congressman" places far more demands. "Oh, yeah, Congressmen are still sleeping with secretaries but it's not the way it used to be—you don't have the open, partying fun you had. Now it's all sorta sordid. The goddamn place is becoming as dull as IBM," sighed another lover of the good old days.

That, and the dreary sexlessness of Watergate, is why so many people quickly latched on to Wilbur Mills's escapade as one of the brightest bits of news in 1974. His drunken evening with his "friend," a stripper named Fanne Foxe, the Argentine Firecracker, whose closing number was to jump fully clothed into the Tidal Basin, ultimately destroyed Mills's political career, however.

Accustomed to his lordly role as powerful chairman of the Ways and Means Committee, Mills was still trying to be in command the night of the 1974 incident. When police refused to let Mills drive the sopping stripper home, he shouted, "I'm a Congressman and I'll have you demoted."

The scandal was destined to take its place in the randy-old-goat division of Capitol Hill folklore. It shocked many on the Hill who had considered Mills a man of impeccable reputation whose idea of fun was to sit home at night analyzing the income tax structure. Still, there were those who had noticed changes in Mills's behavior. As his once distinguished career foundered, this man, known as rigidly moral, escalated his erratic behavior and heavy drinking.

He seemed gripped by a dual personality. With Fanne Foxe at his side, Mills often frequented the Silver Slipper—a sleazy strip joint where dancers shake down to their G strings to the thundering thump of amplified music and B-girls cadge $2.75 drinks. A confusing and kinky note was added when it was revealed that Mrs. Mills also made the scene at times. A sedate, retiring, former vice president of the wives' congressional club, Polly Mills at a strip joint seemed unbelievable, but so many reporters heard the story from so many independent sources, including Fanne Foxe, that they gave it credence.

When Mills tried to explain the evening away, he stated that Polly, who had a broken foot, "blamed herself for not having accompanied us that night." Once again, a most extreme case of the wife used by a politician in an attempt to look respectable. With Polly at his side, Mills campaigned vigorously in Arkansas to get reelected, but shortly after that he followed Fanne Foxe up onto the stage of a Boston strip joint to kiss her. That was the final blow. Mills repaired to a hospital for treatment for alcoholism and colleagues speculated on his emotional and mental condition. Mills became a pathetic figure as he resigned his chairmanship in late 1974.

The Mills incident points out what many political wives fear about the numerous chances for extracurricular fun accessible to their husbands. One ex-wife of a Congressman moaned to me about her husband—also an influential member of an important committee—and how he was wrecked by fawning lobbyists who created trips for him and the women in his life. I thought it might be a singular story or an exaggeration, but a few former public relations men for major corporations told me, "If they want some action, they sort of farm it out. It's sort of included in with those speaking engagements to trade association deals. I think since Watergate a lot of guys are being more discreet and aren't going to play around either in Washington or in their home states. If they do it, they'll do it in conjunction with some kind of business trip. The girls come with the speech, if that's what they want."

Another former journalist and assistant secretary of defense is skeptical. "It would have to be a pretty stupid Congressman

to put himself into that compromising a situation and accept
those kinds of favors from the American Panty Hose Convention or some such thing. As for taxpayer-subsidized sex on
official travels, I think it's mostly a myth—and Wayne Hays and
his type are the exceptions that everyone recalls. I'm not saying
some individual doesn't make out on junkets, but it is certainly
no consistent thing."

Although the candidate may be the drawing force for interested women, some reporters and staff aides have more fun on
campaigns than he does. One former aide to a presidential candidate said, "The girls were all interested in him, but he never
had the time." A reporter who covered the same candidate said,
" the fallout is just incredible."

An older aide defined campaign sex as similar to World War
II sex. "There is this insane excitement and sense of adventure—it's like screwing in London with the air raid sirens and
the bombs going off. It's the most fantastic thing ever because it
may be your last. There is the same sensuousness in a campaign
when it's truly an exciting one." (In real fact, those who have
the greatest reputation for enjoying each other, unencumbered
by the distraction of political decisions, are the stewardesses
and the Secret Service.)

A speech writer for Democratic candidates said, "It's inevitable; if a guy is in a position of glamor and away from the family,
he's going to screw around." A former Senator's aide agreed.
"The good ones all hump—you have to put humping time into
their schedule." Well, not all. One aide on the Shriver campaign said, "Shriver was twenty minutes late one morning, and
I asked one of the other guys why and he said they had spent
the time looking for Shriver's rosary. Honest."

Still another campaign manager said, "If you examine it, the
whole concept of a campaign is sexual. The guy balls the crowd,
turns 'em on, revs them up; that's what it's all about." A former
reporter who worked at the Democratic National Committee
said, "I was on the platform with Bobby Kennedy once and so
help me, this girl in the front row really turned on. I watched
her throughout the whole speech, and she was ready to faint.
That's pretty good—from thirty feet away."

A former top official in the Johnson Administration said, "A
friend of mine refers to it as 'prestige pussy.' Everyone gloms
onto people in prestige positions."

The only one who really knows for sure is a participant and most of them just don't talk about it. One former aide to a midwestern Senator who maintains an image of Boy Scout goodness said, "We were at this one rally and after it was over, there was a party. I noticed this one girl was just staring at the Senator; and it wasn't lost on him, either. Later in the car we started talking about the party and I mentioned this girl. I said, 'I think she has the hots for you.' He said, 'Why don't you arrange a meeting?' So I did. That's as much as I know, that they met for a drink. What happened later I don't know. But when he comes out with that public shit about his great wife I always think of that night." One columnist laughs about his naïveté during the 1960 campaign with Jack Kennedy. "We were at this party and Kennedy and I were talking. A really great-looking woman came up and flirted with Kennedy. Then she actually dropped her hotel key down the low front of her floor-length evening gown. I saw it on the floor, so I picked it up. And gave it back to her. Later, Jack said, 'You idiot—don't you know that was for me?'"

"I used to escort Senator ——'s chippies," one former aide recalled. "Once in Florida he asked me to stay over a few extra days, and I said, 'I will if I can fuck her, too.' He said, 'What?' He was outraged and I said, 'I'm not kidding. Listen, I really don't like this business,' and I left." Shortly after, the aide quit. "It gets to the point where you lose your self-respect." The aide says this man's wife used to flirt with him. "I always felt she knew about everything, and she was getting back at him by making up to me. Boy, did I feel uncomfortable!"

While most politicians protest that they are too busy, exhausted, and what-have-you to play around on campaigns, "swordsmen" stories persist and are regarded as commonplace features of all campaigns, not only for the politicians but aides and press. "I always say morality is not so much a matter of willpower as it is opportunity," said one political consultant. "A truck driver may be making it with a waitress, but a politician sure has more opportunity."

On a campaign the candidate is always the subject of gossip. Ed Muskie had a reputation for being the straightest. Rumors about George McGovern and one top female assistant were so rampant in the press corps that campaign strategists took her off some of the trips to quiet the stories. A former Senator recalls Hubert Humphrey saying to him during his 1968 campaign, "Goddamm it, everyone on this goddamn plane is having more fun than I." The man said, "Let's face it, being a candidate means you are isolated. One night we were all out drinking and there was this fantastically good-looking woman with us and we called Humphrey and he said for us all to come up and have a drink. He thought she was pretty fantastic too, but he was Vice President at that time and believe me, everybody, *including* her, went home when the partying was over. I think, psychologically, two things happen to you by the time you get into national office. First, it's just more dangerous, and second, you get some sophistication. You get used to the idea that a lot of grown-ups go to bed who aren't married."

An important element, he said, is that there is probably less action than there is public flirtation on the part of politicians. "The ultimate applause is to know you can screw every good-looking girl in the room. There's not always the follow through, though."

The serious women on the Hill, dedicated either to their own careers or their own marriages, resent the blanket connotation that all women there are easily accessible. The attitude toward woman is incredibly chauvinistic—she is either sex object or patient drone.

A married woman on a major committee said, "I'm no secretary, but those Congressmen are such chauvinists that when they see a woman as they stride into the hearing room they'll call out, 'I want coffee, black,' and automatically expect us to wait on them. The thing that struck me up here is the total infidelity. There are the drinkers and fanny-patters. One Congressman who was going through a divorce corralled a girlfriend of mine on the elevator after a party one night and practically ripped her belt off. I had a problem with one Congressman—right in the middle of a hearing. I was sitting where I normally sit and he came up, sat next to me, said, 'Hi, there!' and put his hand on my knee. I was surprised and said I'd appreciate it if he took his hand off my knee. I learned later that this was his standard proposition to a new staff member. Some girls are really on the make. I don't know if anyone is ever hired as a specific groupie, but I know of one woman—and she is one of the few female attorneys up here—who was after a divorced Congressman and then she went after another who was married. When I said, 'But he's married,' she just said—'Well, not forever.'"

Infrequently, stories surface about call-girl rings on the Hill but, as one twenty-five-year resident of Congress said to me, "I've never seen anything 'official.' The girls just come and they go." Another said, "Occasionally you get a group who seem to be passed around and are augmented by two or three hookers. But even though Bobby Baker had such a reputation for supplying girls, I remember him calling me a couple of times and asking me if I knew any. Floyd Spence [Congressman from South Carolina] had some girls who were real party girls, but I don't think the office gives rise to it as much as the girls themselves. In fact, some of the old farts with the most lecherous reputations have real straitlaced, older office help." "Who needs call girls now that sex is so easy and free?"asked one aide.

The Hill was a more casual place years ago when the atmosphere and leisurely working schedules made a vast difference. In the 1920s and 1930s Congressmen would spend only three months in Washington. The wife and children would stay home; legislators would come to Washington on the train and stay for three months and then go home.

"This place must have been a lot like the state legislature then," said one Senator. Mention state legislatures and nearly everyone acquainted with them has a booze-and-sex story. One Senator, who started in politics on the state level in his twenties, said, "I wasn't there a week before I realized that, by god, everyone in that capitol was fucking. By the time I ran for the U.S. Senate, the opportunities were immense but the stakes were higher. And hell, by then I felt it wasn't such a big deal and it doesn't seem worth the intrigue."

Some straight politicians wonder, "How in the hell can those guys screw around without getting caught?" I asked an aide who said he used to pimp for his Senator. Although his former boss has quite a reputation, only once did a story surface in the papers. "There are all kinds of ways to avoid being caught. Sometimes you do incredible things. You check into a hotel— give one set of keys to the girl and give him another set. They are never seen together. They just meet in the room later. It's the easiest way in the world. The only problem the Senator has is hiding in the closet when the room service guy comes in. He's lucky he's just serving breakfast—and not a banquet."

The caliber of men on the state legislature level, often local businessmen who don't earn their living from the legislative post and don't take it that seriously, leaves much to be desired. The camaraderie with chickie babes at end-of-the-session parties is legendary. One Washington reporter remembers his greenhorn days covering the Maryland legislature and being bowled over by a groupie who had planted herself firmly on a bar stool in one of the hotels where a general free-for-all was taking place. She told him she had made a solemn vow to herself some years before and that was, "Never to cry on election night—and never to fuck a Republican." (That's loyalty for you.)

There is a fear that a post-Watergate morality binge may produce a scrutiny of politicans' private lives unknown in modern American politics, alhough it was common practice in earlier days when "muckraking" was an amorphous umbrella for all kinds of writing, sometimes needed exposés, sometimes just plain scandal. One inherent danger in this is the election of a "squeaky clean" candidate, a self-righteous type of limited scope.

In writing about private lives, one must be aware that much of the supposition about a politician's character can be only accusatory at best and libelous at worst. One of the most difficult judgments to make is whether inebriation or womanizing—for example—impairs the man's ability to carry out his office. For years there were some drunken Senators and Representatives who could barely navigate the aisles of Congress by late afternoon, much less navigate their way through a speech to make a point.

In 1974, Speaker Carl Albert, the Oklahoma Democrat, held his breath until Ford was confirmed as Vice President, because Albert did not like the scrutiny he was getting in his "heartbeat-away" successor role. The question of Albert's drinking and his fitness for the office had been raised. In 1972, Albert was driving a car on one of the major avenues in the District just before midnight. It struck two vehicles. Several witnesses, including a law student and a psychologist, were quoted in the newspaper as saying that Albert was "obviously drunk." According to witnesses, Albert yelled as police approached, "Leave me alone. I'm Carl Albert, Speaker of the House! You can't touch me . . . I just got you raises!"

Albert denied at a press conference that he had been intoxicated. He guardedly acknowledged that earlier in the evening he "took something" during a cocktail party. His meeting with reporters was so brief (about one minute) that it quickly was tagged the "hit-and-run" press conference. Other stories about pint-sized Albert began to circulate. One was that he liked an Oriental woman on his staff who was a frequent companion, and another was that he frequented the Zebra Room, a college-age hangout on Wisconsin Avenue, near the scene of his accident. Mark Russell, political humorist, quipped that if Albert got the vice presidency they would "hold the Inaugural under the table at the Zebra Room."

(Another pint-sized colleague, Senator John Tower, who thought of himself as a fluke one-time winner in 1960, told a friend, "I'm going to be here for one term so I'm going to live it up." His friend recalled, "And he did. He was the partyingest guy in town. He loved to play games. In fact, one time, fooling around in the office, a big gal turned a desk over on him."

"I'll never forget old Russell Long in his drinking days," said one former Senator. "We were out in the cloakroom and you could hear this loud voice and so we all went in, and there was Long up there, flailing around, and there was Stennis, pulling at his coattails trying to get him to sit down. The debate was about giving governors the power to appoint their antipoverty program heads. Long was just so drunk and yelling. He opposed it, saying his 'goddamned governor would appoint this goddamned guy who was nothing but a "hot check artist"' and he called him by name. I thought, 'My lord, Long's had it for good.' The press gallery was certainly not empty. I thought if I'd done that, I'd really be in the soup back home. Well, the next day there was nothing in the papers or on TV. His staff worked all night, apparently, to change it all." (The laundered statement in the *Congressional Record* bore no resemblance to anything he had said.) The former Senator said, "The next time I was talking to one of the big TV correspondents, who had been there, I asked him why Long's performance didn't get written up or commented on on television and he just said that that was the way things were."

Not all reporters are impressed, of course, with senatorial privilege. One night, Morrie Siegel, a sports columnist and TV commentator, was giving a group of men a ride back from a function where Siegel had been a major speaker. All of a sudden he felt this hand clapping him on the back of the head and this drunken voice urging, "Faster, boy, faster." It was Long. They went one more block, and when Long did it again, Siegel stopped the car and ordered an astounded Long out of the car, which won Siegel a few medals from members of the press.

It is interesting that Russell Long is now regarded as a new man, and the person credited with that conversion is his new wife.

Most reporters, at least those who can put their glasses down long enough to say a few words, admit they shy away from stories about politicians' escapades with sympathetic understanding.

Journalists often feel a collective collusion and guilt. Washington reporters know how often they have neglected their own families. To do what? Cover politics. For a sensitive man, this is a guilt that weighs heavily. He then gets defensive about the peccadilloes of the men he is covering and about himself. "It's just plain self-defense," protests one Washington journalist. "If you start writing about who is a drunk or screwing around or anything like that, he can turn around and say 'How about the time you were so drunk with that girl out in Pocatello?' Hell, you've got your own family, remember? Besides, what does that have to do with how he votes on welfare? Wouldn't you rather have a screw around than someone like Nixon, for Christ's sakes?"

It's a good question and it gets debated often by the press, now that there is a realization that there is a somewhat obsessive interest in the moral price exacted by fame in this country. The complexities and ambivalences of probing the area of the politician's private life are factors the press will have to deal with.

During the Watergate hearings, John D. Ehrlichman struck a profoundly moralistic tone in defense of White House snooping into the personal habits of political opponents. "Someone with a serious drinking habit is of doubtful fitness for the kind of heavy duty . . . that any Senator bears." The political opponent of a congressional drunk had "an affirmative obligation," Ehrlichman maintained, to bring such facts to the attention of voters during a campaign. "You can go over here in the gallery and watch a member totter onto the floor in a condition of at least partial inebriation," Ehrlichman said. He also said the press covered up such private areas as the sexual and drinking habits of politicians.

Even if politicians were absolute teetotalers and faithful husbands, stories about them would continue to circulate because of the nature of their public servant role. Scandals involving sex and/or drinking seemed not to hurt in 1974—almost all politicians with divorce, drinking, or sex scandals were reelected—and, as has been pointed out, sometimes a slightly racy image is a plus. During Nixon's days the joke was he could improve his image tremendously if he were found in the company of some woman instead of Bebe Rebozo. On Walter Cronkite's show Rebozo revealed their sophomoric level of humor when he told how he and Nixon played their joke on another friend, Robert Abplanalp. "We had a couple of these ladies' legs—it looks like real legs, they're skin-colored and all; they're blown up. And Abplanalp was going to come over and visit us so we decided to play a trick on him, and we borrowed a wig and a wig stand from a neighbor, put it in bed with the wig hanging over the thing, and the legs sticking out from under the sheet. Bob came in, and when he saw that, he didn't know whether to act like he didn't see it, or leave it or what, but it was quite a riot."

Scandalous behavior may not turn off the voters but it can make deep inroads in a marriage, particularly if publicity occurs. The national political scene creates an atmosphere that can be unsettling for all but the most secure, dumb, or disinterested wife, although there is some indication political wives are rebelling into affairs of their own. (The wife of a Texas mayor has been keeping close company with her young state trooper driver. The ex-wife of one Senator took up with a campaign aide. Other wives have told me that if their husbands are going to be gone all the time they are not going to stay docilely at home.) One Senator's pretty brunette receptionist said flatly, "I think it's hard for wives to compete. Now I hear Hatfield's real faithful—and he's good-looking and all!" I asked about her own boss, who was also good-looking. "Would you go after him if the circumstances were right?" She shrugged her shoulders and said, "Why not?"

A woman who cannot escape the stories about her philandering husband, which have escalated since his death, is Lady Bird Johnson.

Johnson's bluntness often did not spare his wife, but former aide Harry McPherson said Johnson also showed more genuine affection for his wife than anyone else he had met in politics. "You could have Johnson, McNamara, Rusk sitting around, and it made no difference if the world's future was hanging in the balance; when Mrs. Johnson came in to say hello, Johnson would stop everything. He'd say, 'Where'd you get that dress? The hem's too long in back, but I love that pin. Where's that from?' And he'd pull her down and have her sit on the ottoman, holding her hand, touching her back. That happened a lot—much more than I have ever seen happen with any other public officials." Harry paused and said, "She knew his faults better than anybody. She was tougher than he in many ways. He was more 'man' than anyone I ever saw in my life, but he was still a little boy. They could manage an open display of affection, in a way entirely okay to everyone else around. That's a rarity in any politician. They can't seem to risk those intimate feelings of hugging and warmth."

Still, the stories of Johnson's blatant appreciation for other women are legendary. Mrs. Johnson, who friends say spent much of her time playing the dutiful ranch wife around Lyndon, acknowledged those stories on a TV show in 1974 but glossed over any significance by saying that Lyndon was fascinated by people, male or female.

One night, late, after dinner in the White House, Johnson was looking at photographs the White House photographer had made. He got to a picture of a New York society woman and turned to Lady Bird and commanded: "I want her down next week, Bird." As he stopped, reminiscing about how she had befriended him when he felt ignored at a Kennedy party, Johnson turned to Lady Bird and drawled, "I don't like this picture of her, Bird. Her titties look too flat. See if there is something Yoichi [the White House photographer] can do about that."

Carl Rowan, former Ambassador to Finland and former head of the Voice of America, recalls talking with Mrs. Johnson on a balcony one time while waiting for Johnson. The President greeted Rowan with, "Goddamn, here I am waiting to discuss important matters with you, and you're out on that balcony diddling my wife."

At a party one night, Rowan told a story with great gusto that had his audience collapsing. Rowan said this girl came up to him at a party when he was Ambassador to Finland and said, "Oh, Mr. Ambassador, I need to get transferred *out* of the White House." Rowan said, "I asked her, why on earth? And she told about being at the ranch and, although she was surprised that there were no locks on the bedroom doors, she wasn't worried because of all the Secret Service agents around. Then, in the middle of the night, she felt the presence of someone in the room. She was about to scream, when this little pencil flashlight flicked on and she heard this familiar voice say, 'Move over—this is *yore* President.'" I asked Rowan later if it were true and he said, "You're damn right. I talked to Moyers, and we got her transferred to the State Department."

Friends marveled at the closeness Lyndon and Lady Bird seemed to have for each other throughout so many years of a consummately public, pressured and openly "flaunting" marriage.

Jack and Jacqueline Kennedy, however, or so the stories went, were another matter; she kept threatening to leave because of his playing around. Kennedy as a young bachelor piled up enough stories that would surface in years to come. One was that in 1952, when he was running against Henry Cabot Lodge for the Senate, Republicans got hold of a picture of Kennedy lying "bare-assed" on the beach with an equally disrobed female. The Republicans supposedly brought this to the attention of Kennedy aides, who went through the ceiling; Kennedy merely recalled the girl with pleasure.

Lyndon used to do a slow burn when he would see Jack and George Smathers leave the floor after voting, giving quick nods to exit to tanned lovelies who had waited patiently for them in the visitors' gallery.

Ted Sorensen after the 1960 election made a promise that "this administration is going to do for sex what the last one did for golf." Recollections continue to be embellished: Secret Service smuggling in high-priced prostitutes . . . skinny-dipping parties in the White House pool (Jackie supposedly returned to the White House en route to the airport and a New York weekend and found Jack and a Cabinet member frolicking with secretaries in the pool). During the 1960 campaign, a woman showed up in Washington newsrooms with pictures of Kennedy supposedly leaving a girlfriend's apartment; the woman in question, in true courtier fashion, later became a member of Jackie's White House staff.

The White House was such a sexual no-man's-land during Nixon's administration that Henry Kissinger—fat, short, egomaniacal (as well as witty and charming when he wants to be)—became an alleged swordsman practically by default. This was in remarkable contrast to the stories that floated out of that pristine white edifice when Kennedy and Johnson occupied it. One newsman who made trips with Johnson to the ranch recalled to another reporter, "He'd take people through the house and when they came to the bedroom he would pause, motion to the bed, and declare affectionately, 'Ah've had hundreds of women in my life, but let me tell you, nobody is better in that bed than Lady Bird.'" For years, Johnson had a special place for certain secretaries. He later was there to "marry them off," and forever thereafter played good old affectionate uncle to them.

It is difficult to gauge if blatant "friendships" can become political defects. One reporter who covers Senator Ed Brooke said, "I heard all over the place that he was playing around; his opponents used to whisper it at us. No one gave a damn." A former aide said, "I was always amazed that no one called him on it; he was really quite outrageous about it. When he'd fly somewhere, he often used to show up with some gorgeous girl. Everyone assumes his marriage is just in name."

Probably the most well liked in recent history for his sexual exploits was Adam Clayton Powell; his very openness was a plus for his constituents, who liked the fact that Powell was, in all ways, thumbing his nose at "the Man."

It took the more hypocritical to cast him out of the Hill, a place where the old lechers are dying off, but still abound. Congressman F. Edward Hébert (pronounced "A-bare") of Louisiana, was deposed in the 1975 House revolution as chairman of the House Armed Services Committee. Behind his opulent office is another, smaller room. Peering through his thick lenses the then seventy-two-year-old Congressman showed off to me his "seee-duction room," which contains a TV and a couch. He sometimes refers to it as a room that can be occupied only by two—"one adult and one adulterous."

While rumors of sexual adventures are a backdrop to practically every political campaign, there have been a few times when it hurt. Nelson Rockefeller's leaving home for Happy, who left her husband and children for him in 1963, was one example. Back in history, Richard M. Johnson was elected as Martin Van Buren's Vice President in 1836. He openly maintained three black mistresses, and Andrew Jackson urged for that reason that Van Buren dump him from the 1840 ticket, which he did. (Andrew Jackson himself was denounced as an adulterer but he clucked to Van Buren "how can he [Johnson] expect friends to countenance and sustain him when he shamelessly lives in adultery with a buxom young Negro wench?")

According to Drew Pearson's diary, Michigan Senator Arthur Vandenberg never entertained serious thoughts of the presidency for fear his active love life would be exposed. Pearson wrote, "I really think that it was his affair with [the glamorous wife of a foreign diplomat] that helped to prevent his getting the Presidency—though another affair with a beautiful British widow in Washington also contributed. The *Chicago Tribune* crowd claimed the British had planted these two women on Vandenberg in order to make him pro-British and cure him of isolationism."

Jefferson was hounded with political doggerel inspired by his slave mistress Sally Hemings and accused of adultery by another man. Fawn Brodie writes in her recent biography of Jefferson, "A myth persists that the British, to discredit George Washington during the revolution, had forged a letter having him describe the charms of his Mount Vernon slave women." Fortunately for the father of our country, Washington's love for Sally Fairfax, his neighbor's wife, did not surface until long after his death. Grover Cleveland acknowledged his illegitimate child prior to an election, and the Republican chants of "Ma, Ma, Where's My Pa?" did little harm. His opponent's public corruption (James G. Blaine of Maine) was less preferable to the voters, so Democratic rallies repeated the Republican line and added their own, too, "Gone to the White House, Ha! Ha! Ha!" Republicans unsuccessfully attempted to use unsubstantiated rumors of adultery against Woodrow Wilson in 1912. When he married Edith Galt, a ribald riddle asked, "What did Mrs. Galt do when the President proposed to her? Fell out of bed!"

There are at least three other cases in this century in which we will never know what damage might have been caused by revelations of sexual indiscretions. That Warren Harding had a White House mistress was never common knowledge until after his death. His love letters to her revealed his ardor: "I love you garbed, but naked, more!" The stories about Franklin Roosevelt and Lucy Mercer saddened those who thought the Roosevelts had a perfect marriage, but the affair was kept hidden until after his death. So, more or less, was the friendship of Eisenhower with his WAC chauffeur. And no one tried to make sex an issue during Kennedy's 1960 campaign.

Sometimes the accusations are completely false, as the 1972 planted insinuation by opponents that Hubert Humphrey and Scoop Jackson were no strangers to homosexuality. (There is an ancient saying of Indiana backwoods politics that a "candidate need fear only two things—being found in bed with a live man—or a dead woman.")

The puritanical code, which went hand in hand with hypocrisy, has been a curse to American politicians unknown in many countries used to generations of open sexual intrigue and debauchery at court.

In other words, the rule in America has been, if you've got it, don't flaunt it.

Historian Fawn Brodie writes that Jefferson had an object lesson in the "disparity between the French and American sexual and social codes." This reinforced his knowledge that seeing and escorting the married Maria Cosway (with whom he almost certainly became deeply involved) in Paris was one thing and "to travel about with her in America . . . quite another."

Mrs. Brodie writes that "the new French Minister to the United States, the Comte de Moustier, had embarked for the New World with the Beautiful Madame de Brehan, who was his sister-in-law and also his mistress." Jefferson wrote warm letters of introduction on her behalf to both Madison and John Jay describing her as "goodness itself" and "modest and amiable"— adding the covering phrase that her officer husband was "obliged the times to remain with the army." Americans treated the couple frostily, Mrs. Brodie writes. Madison stiffly wrote that Moustier "suffered also from his illicit connection with Madame de Brehan which is universally known and offensive to American manners."

This in 1787. Nearly two hundred years later, in 1974, I was having a talk with an old acquaintance, Pierre Salinger, whose second of three marriages broke up when he was himself a celebrity as President John Kennedy's press secretary. Now married to a French woman, Salinger lives most of his time in France, covering French and U.S. politics for *L'Express.* I said that it occurred to me that American politicians had no inclination for anything but the quick dalliance with an adoring camp follower; that they wouldn't take the time for a real give-and-take relationship. Salinger said, "No inclination or no time, perhaps, but it is also far too precarious a position." He described a French political scenario, on the other hand, not unlike the incident described by Mrs. Brodie. "In France, well, I don't know of an important French politician who doesn't have a mistress. It is well known, but no one cares. In France a politician can have an affair for twenty years, and you never hear about it. The Americans are not prepared for that. So politicans have to hide what they are doing."

One political analyst heaved a sigh and said, "I'd like to think that twenty-five years from now no one would care here, either. It would be healthier." Another commented, "If every one of us had worn scarlet letter As on our foreheads like Hester Prynne, it would be all over and done with by now." (As religious leaders, post-Watergate, speak of a beleaguered nation needing ethical and moral leadership it may not be the time for the wearing of scarlet letters.)

In deciding whether or not to print stories about sexual liaisons, newspapers in general emphasize that sex alone is not news; there has to be some "additional factor" to make it news. But if there is, heaven help the politician. A Congressman gets a paternity suit and it is news. While the incident may not get him out of office, the publicity is damaging and embarrassing to innocent family members.

And sometimes the "extra factor" is debatable. Brit Hume objected to an item he worked on for Jack Anderson's column about Randy Agnew—who moved in with a male hairdresser at the time of his divorce. Others on Anderson's staff argued that it was newsworthy because Vice President Agnew was going around the country posing as an expert on parenthood and decrying the way many parents raised their children. Randy has since remarried and could easily be seen as the victim of ugly sexual innuendo. Les Whitten of Jack Anderson's staff said, "Randy may have been an innocent victim, but really of his father's mouth." Anderson felt strongly there was political consequence in the inherent hypocrisy of his father's talk and Randy's choice in roommates. Many papers refused, however, to carry the Anderson column.

Chappaquiddick is an example of so many other things that whether or not Ted Kennedy was driving Mary Jo Kopechne to the beach for fun and games is totally beside the point. Not seeking immediate help at that nearby house, the ten-hour delay in reporting the accident, the conflicting testimony, all add up to an error of judgment and flawed character to many people, as well as strengthening the contention that preferential treatment and inept prosecution kept Kennedy from manslaughter charges.

The tabloids will always sell with their sex-only stories because people will always be titillated by the private dalliance of public men, but as for one's sex life counting in politics, today it seems this would be important to voters only if it was a proven factor in destroying or dominating his effectiveness in office.

Pure sex alone has never been a very powerful political weapon. But amazingly, every year some effort to discredit a person for sexual reasons seems to crop up. One of the most obscure and weird efforts of 1974 was that of Dennis Gregg, a young man running for U.S. Congress from Virginia. He stated that his opponents, among them Joseph Fisher, distributed campaign literature that had the word "sex" subliminally imbedded all over their pictures. Since Fisher, with glasses, short-cropped hair, nondescript suit and tie, looks like your average elementary school principal, any suggestion of "s-e-x" would have had to have been very subliminal indeed. Gregg even produced a copy of a letter from Dr. Wilson Key, assistant professsor of journalism at the University of Western Ontario, verifying "subliminal communications techniques" that affect people. Explaining "how they were imbedded in the materials," Key said, "subliminal imbeds in the form of the word 'sex' can be very lightly etched into the photographic portraits." The subliminal inductions, apparently, were to induce voters into thinking these candidates were sexy, therefore desirable, and therefore worth voting for. It all sounded like a delightful put-on, until a serious Gregg sent a letter to the Fair Campaign Practices Committee asking them to undertake an immediate and full investigation of the "unethical subliminal communications techniques being used by four of my opponents." Well, who are we to say Gregg didn't have something? The decidedly nonsexy Joe Fisher surprised Virginia, if not the world, by beating long-entrenched Joel Broyhill.

In politics you would do well to know who your bedfellows are, or at least which *politicians* know who your bedfellows are. They can really make trouble if they decide to testify. William E. Fornoff, a former top aide to Baltimore County Executive Dale Anderson, accused Anderson of accepting cash kickbacks from county contractors. In an attempt to explain Fornoff's accusation and to make himself look the figure of saintly rectitude, Anderson testified in his own defense in 1974 that there was bad blood between him and Fornoff because Anderson tried to break up an "illicit love affair" between his former top aide and a secretary.

Former aides *and* secretaries helped do in Baltimore County States Attorney Samuel A. Green when they testified at what became known as the X-rated trial of 1974. Green was tried and convicted of all sixteen counts of obstruction of justice, misconduct in office, and attempted subordination of perjury and conspiracy. But this was overshadowed by the titillating accounts of his alleged sexual activities. His former deputy, Stuart Hirsch, alleged that Green had sexual activities with at least nine of his secretaries in the state's attorney's office in 1968. At the time of this trial, it was announced that Green was also later to be tried separately on charges of "carnal bribery." For those unfamiliar with that term, it means that Green "demanded and received sexual favors from a twenty-five-year-old woman who wanted her shoplifting case favorably disposed of."

Hirsch contended that Green's office motto was a rhyme emphasizing that a position in his office was predicated on one's sexual interests and that "if you didn't participate in a sexual act, you've got to go." Hirsch was asked if he had spread stories that Green was a pervert. At first Hirsch said he didn't want to say anything to offend Mrs. Green, but then added, "If you were talking about how I threw out a can of whipped cream Mr. Green used in my apartment and a jar of apple jelly or ice cream that Green had brought over . . . " He was interrupted by snickers and laughter in the court before he could elaborate.

Two former secretaries also detailed life in Green's office. One said she was rubbing his back as he joked about sexual acts to others in the room and while he perused the morning mail. Green, with his wife faithfully by his side, denied it all and said they were all out to get him, then resigned from office.

New York Congressman Mario Biaggi had his own woes that year with a woman who slapped him with a paternity suit. Vehemently denying it, Biaggi moaned, "This sort of thing happens to public figures all the time." He was reelected. Tests later proved he could not have fathered the child.

Most politicians steer clear of casting the first stone for the reason, possibly, that they live in glass houses, but for another one as well. No one has ever figured out the public's reaction, and more often than not the sneaky attempt to get an opponent in the sack, a tactic proposed by White House plumbers, will backfire.

Only occasionally does some action of a political nature occur. Back in 1881, the New York *World* informed that a Senator Thomas Platt was observed in the arms of an "unspeakable female." The observers were backers of his opponent who went up the ladder to peek through a transom and then back down to report on their findings. Platt was forced to withdraw his reelection bid, but later made a resounding political comeback.

While the public does not always get to read sex stories, they are relayed as gossip constantly in Washington. The most outrageous stories are delivered with a "so-help-me-God-it's-true" earnestness. One is about an administrative assistant who had a good-looking wife. One day he came home and found his boss, the Senator, in bed with his wife. The Senator looked up and commented, "You should call before you come home." The administrative assistant walked out of the room, later divorced his wife—and went back to work for the Senator.

Warren Weaver, Jr., in his book on Congress *Both Your Houses*, took time out from a serious analysis of that dysfunctioning group to chuckle over some of those sex stories. There are old lechers who pinch bottoms and, occasionally, a little more. One aide to a now-departed Senator remembers a girl hired to type and look pretty most of the time. Then, about once every six months, the old renegade would come in with a gleam in his eye. The girl would promptly get a headache, just thinking about the prospect of a tussle with him.

Weaver wrote that one wealthy Eastern Senator, later defeated for reelection, provided X-rated entertainment for his neighbors one summer while he was between wives. "Because he never closed his curtains, a prime view of his living room could be had from the balconies of an adjacent apartment building. As the news spread, young people lined their railings each afternoon to watch the Senator and his current friend perform on the couch. On dull days, only she would be observable, making nude runs for beer from the bedroom to the kitchen. Occasionally the Senator would stroll up to the front window, unaware, and scratch himself. He was not an exhibitionist, just a nearsighted, wealthy man raised in houses so far from neighbors that it never occurred to him to draw blinds."

When Representative Frank Boykin of Alabama was in his seventies he continued to act out his motto, "Everything Is Made for Love." On many a restless morning, Boykin would leave his committee hearings and repair to the nearby Congressional Hotel where he would disappear up the elevator. Some thirty-five minutes later he would reappear in the committee room (his intrigued colleagues timed him) with a relaxed and serene smile on his face.

Sid Yudain remembered once hiding in a closet. "I am known as a good soup maker so I once agreed to make soup for one of the girls up here. She said I had to be out of there at six P.M. Well, at five-thirty there was a knock on the door. She told me to hide and I dashed into the clothes closet. In walked one of the supposedly most straight-arrow, sanctimonious, family-man Congressmen we had. I had to stay in that closet for hours while they screwed and ate my soup."

The politician's preoccupation with his office can lead to a pretty dull sex life, even for the girlfriend who tags along on campaigns and finds her time usurped by aides. For the wife, preelection time can be disastrous. There is one story of an ambitious Senator whose wife helped run his campaign. One night, during a brief halt for lovemaking, her husband looked down at her and suddenly asked, "How do you think we're do-

194   TILL POWER DO US PART

ing in Brown County?" The wife later divorced him and remarried his campaign manager, who presumably didn't care quite that much about Brown County.

Fielding sexual innuendos is part of the political job when you are a woman, especially a single woman. One of Robert Kennedy's "Boiler Room Girls" who was at Chappaquiddick is Esther Newberg. She served as Muskie's campaign manager in New York State, and in 1974 was executive secretary of New York's Democratic Committee. Very bright and politically knowledgeable, she despises the "Boiler Room" connotation. However she is accustomed to being regarded as a sex object and understands that acceptance on a sexual level comes before acceptance for intellect or ability. Her legs get compared to other women's legs—"They told me mine were better." When you're single, she said, men "assume that the reason you're in politics is for sex." She told Susan and Martin Tolchin for their book on women in politics, "I just had a guy on the phone ask me if I was going to Washington tonight, where was I going to stay, and that sort of thing." She shrugged off the advances. "I don't mind though. If there has to be fifteen seconds of that kind of bullshit, okay. It makes them bigger men. They are products of their background."

Men who continue to relate to political women only as sex objects heighten the struggle of serious women trying to coexist on an equal basis, but there still are not-so-serious women who not only expect but enjoy sex-object treatment.

One pretty brunette receptionist to a Senator alternated between answering the phone and twisting a lock of her long hair around her finger. She bubbled with a certain joyous exuberance, seemed happy and content to be a receptionist, was not interested in a political career, and wants to be an elementary education teacher "when I get married." She said with a giggle that "Congressmen talk about us girls more than we talk about them. One Senator calls me anonymously a lot." How did she know who he was? "Oh, I recognized his voice. He'd talk to me and hang up. And then there is a freshman Congressman who is so shy, so uncertain. He's from our state and he'd call me five times a day about where he should go. I could hardly believe he was a Congressman. Another would stop by the office and make up excuses to talk; ask me to sew his button on his coat, things like that." Is there a lot of dating going on? "Oh, sure. I'm dating a *single* Congressman now." Being a married, older Congressman means nothing, she found out when one befriended her. "He said he wanted me to date his son, and he was so nice to me. He helped me with my job when I was new and helped me move. Then one night he stopped by my apartment and I found out it wasn't his son he wanted me to date. When I found out that was all just an act, I cried. Their egos are so fragile, if you refuse to date them, they keep calling and persist—or else they act extremely embarrassed that you turned them down." For all the talk of glamour going out of the political role, there are still some women who view politicians with adulation and awe. When I asked this girl if she would consider marrying a Congressman or Senator, she replied, "I don't know. A lot of girls wouldn't even consider that possible. They just seem so far above you that it couldn't happen." She is in her early twenties and on a pleasure trip that leaves little room for considering the future. Or feminism. Women are still being paid far less for the same jobs on the Hill as men, but that is no concern to her. "My job is the most fun! Oh, I never have to stay late. I have no aspiration. I'm not climbing."

Another woman, named Leigh, has Raquel Welch sort of good looks, including false eyelashes at noon and a necklace with "LOVE" on it. An executive secretary to a businessman, she has "dated" some Congressmen and had an oblique pass made at her when she applied for a Hill job. "I'm not a women's libber. I mean, I'd be looked on as antiquated by them. I believe in chivalry. You know, a man standing up when you come in the room. I went up to the Hill for this interview. He was a very striking-looking man and he said, 'If you notice, none of the women in my office are pretty and there is a reason for that. I'd rather have those women around who are not a distraction.' The Congressman sparred around for some time and then said, 'If I were to approach you, what would your answer be?'

"I was sort of awed by him and I said, 'If you are speaking as a man to a woman, I'd be flattered—but as a boss to an employee, I'd be disappointed.'" She didn't get a job but she did go out with him. "I wouldn't want to mention any of the names of politicians I know. It's more important for men in politics to maintain a 'good' life. Just like Senator Kennedy. He got caught and that's all there is to it." When she dated a Congressman, how did she fit into his hectic schedule? "That's what I'd like to know," she said drily, "He would call me at the most with two days' notice, but often it would be that afternoon, and he'd say, 'Let's go out and have dinner.' We'd go to the good old Rotunda" [a restaurant close to the Hill that has dancing and dark corners around the bar]. She recalled one evening when she had a date with a man she referred to as a "wheeler-dealer lobbyist." They had dinner with a Senator and the Senator's 'wife' —as the other woman was introduced. "She was no more his wife than I was. She wore junk jewelry."

The popular opinion is that those women on the Hill who drift along are discarded as they get older for other younger women. Or, as one aide said, "Old mistresses never die—they just fade away to the mimeograph room." They seldom rat on their former boyfriend/employer. He has the power, they don't.

A caste system prevails and the intelligent, politically serious female aides look down contemptuously at the party girl or groupie. One former White House female aide who now works on the Hill said, "A lot of politicians seem superficially attracted to some chickie babe who's picking up what she can. This one girl bragged about a Senator she slept with. She was more taken with the sense of prestige and the sense of excitement and turmoil that goes with a love affair than with him. She figured, 'If you're going to have the turmoil, why not have it over a famous person?' Another girl said she had a thing with Ted Kennedy, gee, this was about four years ago. She was mooning around like she was really going someplace, and I wanted to dunk her head in a pail of water and say, 'Hey, stupid, who do you think you are? You're just one of a long line.'"

The woman, bright, witty, articulate—perhaps a bit too much so for the men who had populated her life—was approaching forty and unmarried. She admitted that "there is a great deal of jealousy and resentment about these girls who are falling in and out of bed—even though I can't stand it and wouldn't be like that myself. But she was the type he'd pick. Let's face it, Kennedy wouldn't pick me in a million years. She was sexy, easily overruled without being dumb, just enough star-struck. She was the type."

The woman, who has a reputation of being so bright and

efficient that she carried her male boss when she worked in the White House during Kennedy's administration, is an example of another kind of woman who is attracted to politics and can threaten the wife. The relationship can be antiseptically non-physical, but in that position of dedicated helpmate, the female aide or personal secretary assumes a function the wife fulfills in other marriages.

One Senator said, "I had a woman like that who worked for me for years, She'd do any goddamn thing in the world for me. I think my wife was jealous of our relationship because we were so damn close professionally." Senator Robert Packwood's wife complained that his female aides even picked out his clothes for him in the 1974 campaign. Angie Novello was Robert Kennedy's faithful secretary who lost a part of her own life when he was killed. Some former Kennedy aides said, "She was tough and very nervous and so protective of Bobby we almost had to kick her out of the campaign plane and activities. She didn't understand that we wanted the press to have access to him then." A warm, outgoing woman, Miss Novello now works for Washington lawyer, Redskins owner, and treasurer of the Democratic National Committee, Edward Bennett Williams. The unquestioning loyalty that political figures inspire in their personal secretaries was no better exemplified than in Rose Mary Woods, who took political humiliation as an ignominious end to years of faithful servitude to Richard Nixon.

While the political wife may resent these women, who, more often than not, remain single, the women themselves often later question what they gave up personally for a life of political devotion. One unmarried former White House aide recalled, "I had a boyfriend I used to break dates with all the time, and finally he said, 'I can't compete with the White House.' I thought for a minute and said, 'You're right—you can't.'"

Another female former White House aide said, "There's glamor, constant pace in your work, and honest to Christ, everything else seems dull. It's a lot of fun and great escape. I was unhappy all the damn time—falling in and out of love with the wrong people, they were always married, always important in politics—but I didn't know how unhappy I was." The woman later moved into Robert Kennedy's office, then continued to have important jobs in Democratic politics after his death. As people became more conscious of the back-of-the-bus roles women have traditionally been given in politics, there were moves to make her a top aide with titles equivalent to those the men had. Even though she in many cases had been doing the same work, she found herself turning down the titles. "I think I really put myself into situations I thought I couldn't handle. It would tear up my personal life and emotional structure, having to compete so in politics. Even to this day the White House sort of haunts me. If I bring out all I've done, people look at me differently. The younger girls seem so much more aggressive and sure of themselves. One in our office now has bopped around and gotten her master's degree and she's going someplace. She's twenty-eight—ten years younger than I am," the woman said wistfully.

"I don't know how to play the game—but I have survivability," she said. "Ninety-eight percent of your life is right there in that job. Your best friends are there. Politics can screw up your sense of values. You don't know who you are. When a campaign is over, or when someone like a Bob Kennedy goes, part of your life goes. I have a strong desire to leave, but I'm afraid to leave. I don't know what the hell else I would want to do."

As a woman in politics, "you pick up all the problems the men have had. My answer is to say 'fuck it.' I don't want to compete, I don't want to have ulcers. If I weren't so bright I would have settled for something less. It all gets inflated out of proportion. It's not enough to be bright and talented without being a hustler. I'm not a hustler. Would I like to be in love? Oh, yeah. Yes. I would very much. I would choose living with someone tomorrow."

Sometimes a political woman can be tagged with an undeserved reputation. The women who were in that party the night of Chappaquiddick, in the summer of 1969, have an undeserved "party girl" reputation that haunts them. Circumstantial evidence and the unanswered and sometimes conflicting testimony served to taint them as much as it did Mary Jo Kopechne, although those who know them regard them as bright, hard-working political professionals. One of them now in a prominent political job said she cringes when she sees strangers making the connection between her name and Chappaquiddick. One Senator actually worried about the effect of her reputation on his position when he considered hiring her. A Congressman took just the opposite view—"I bet she's a hot ticket, I should have hired her," he told a mutual political acquaintance.

This is an insult to a bright, well-bred woman who went on the Chappaquiddick outing in the spirit in which it was billed—a get-together of the women who had worked for Bob Kennedy.

She is around thirty and says, "I keep looking ahead, thinking about the future. I've changed a lot in the last six years. The Chappaquiddick incident forced me to examine the way people were evaluating me. I don't worry about not getting married; I only worry about not doing what will make me the happiest. When someone gets very close, I feel threatened. I had to come to terms with myself. People who didn't know me before have a preconceived notion. The reaction of people at home to my parents was, 'I'm so sorry,' as if I'd done something wrong."

She said, "One of the problems of politics is that people get involved in the king-making syndrome. It takes over their entire life. It's interesting how few men really count on women for their talent; there are very few women whose thoughts and substantive work stand up by themselves." (She is a key adviser to a Senator.)

"The Hill is such a funny place; where power is the only important thing. Where *Carl Albert* is a big deal! My reaction is to stand back and just look at it. It makes me a bit sick. People aren't looking at you individually. It's where you are, where you've been, where you're going. A woman has a tough time, it's a very thin line; being tough and yet being able to maintain your sensitivity. I find myself changing. I find I come on much more aggressive with people I don't know."

An interesting participant in the John Kennedy days is now incredibly metamorphosed into a radical feminist. One long afternoon we sat in her Manhattan apartment and drank white wine and talked about those days when she had been a mistress to one of Kennedy's closest friends and Cabinet member, and then switched to another high government official. "Kennedy set the example. Anyone in his following had to have his doxie." As for herself at that time, she said, "I liked power. You'd go to a party with one of the most important men in the country and you could see the hostesses were in a quandary. They didn't know exactly what to do about you. They thought of you as a mistress, and yet they had to be nice to you because they never knew if the man was going to leave home and marry you and *then* you'd be an important part of his title. Besides, it was a helluva lot of fun." She never dated elected officials, she said. "I stopped at the Cabinet level."

The woman, now around forty, heard two conflicting messages growing up in the fifties. Her mother was a powerful career woman and she learned to value women of accomplishment, and yet her idea of getting power was through a man. "I always wanted to be married to a President." She had met politically powerful men through her mother and was used to them in her home. Adventurous and given to dramatizing her role, the woman saw herself as a Becky Sharp; young, pretty, the stepdaughter of an enormously rich man and running with the Camelot crowd. There were the one-night stands during the Kennedy regime but some of the women were like this one— bright, Vassar-educated, condescending to the women who chose to be a married backdrop to a politician. The era was not without its Edwardian private brittleness toward public convention. "It was an expected game. The whole idea was to walk into the most glittering party and pick out the most powerful man and captivate him. My friend's wife hated Washington. These men are bright, outgoing, and driven. They find exhilaration in their public life and then when there are quiet times they are restlessly lonely. I didn't feel anything but contempt for the political wife. As the 'other woman' you generally feel brighter and certainly more into his political life than the wife. Now, I feel that political wives are the ones who are really manipulated and exploited. Like most women they were sold a bill of goods about security in return for sexual services and keeping the house clean, but they bought it to the nth degree."

The contrast in her present views and her past are staggering. "I used to spend a fortune on clothes; went to the dressmaker three times a week, had a facial once a week." One night there was a turning point. "I was in dull-white satin, a Dior ball gown, with shoes to match and a coat with a pouf collar, diamond earrings and necklace, and I looked at myself and thought, 'You're worth about fifteen thousand dollars on the hoof.' It all just seemed so absurd." She was ripe for the women's movement and, like all converts, adopted it with an intensity she had reserved for her former life. Her looks are now the least important thing, her hair is clipped short and there is no makeup—"I don't know anyone who wears makeup anymore." She is almost of the protesting-too-much school, but she insists she views men as the enemies of women.

When Jack Kennedy was about to run for the presidency, a longtime acquaintance and journalist asked his father, "the Ambassador," if the rumors about JFK's girls would be bad publicity. Kennedy's father replied that the American people did not give a damn who a candidate slept with.

Some observers agree, although their own perceptions can be colored. "When I see a guy who is screwing everything in sight on the campaign trail and then gets together with his wife for the All American Couple image at the victory party, and says something about how he couldn't have done it without the little woman, I feel he's a man who is just not in control of his private life," said one reporter. Another divorced reporter said, "When a man can be that hypocritical in one area, it makes it easier to be hypocritical in *all* areas of his work and I am skeptical." (The journalists who stay married and practice a little hypocrisy of their own are, understandably, more vague and less hard-line on the subject.)

And the woman, who was to enjoy the same view as the Ambassador while in his son's court, pointed out, today, an entirely new argument for the public's right to know, concerning the sex life of politicians. It could terrorize the male politicians if enough of her sisters shared it. "I want to know if a candidate is screwing his secretary. It matters very much to me." Why? "I belong to an oppressed class. It's called female. I want to know, just like a black wants to know, how the white massa treats his field hand as opposed to the house nigger. And also that tells me what he thinks of his oppressed wife. Now does that say it?" Ruling out the possibility of women being compliant and willing "victims," she elaborated, "How he treats women—if they are just a subjugated sex object—is not a *private* concern. It is a very public concern."

Part II

Candidates for Divorce

12

"They Can't Stand the Remembering"

"A married couple always presents an absurdly un-truthful picture to the world," wrote John O'Hara, "but it is a picture that the world finds convenient and a comfort. A couple are a man and a woman and what goes on between them the world never knows, could not possibly know . . ."

The fiction writer can, however, tell the world with the vivid freedom of fiction what goes on between a man and a woman. No matter how closely his characters reflect real people, fiction protects the author from cries of scandalmonger. Fiction also protects the reader from facing the disturbing realities present in the portrait.

To ask real people to tell you about the "disturbing realities" is to deal with inconsistency, half-truths, vague and undefined feelings. There are no absolutes when dealing with human feelings and emotions. Even the most sincere must be allowed to embellish, distort, and color. But even their most distorted concepts are of value, for they tell us how these people perceive their lives.

The examination of political divorces that follows is in no way the whole story. Most people realize that there is a covert dimension to their lives, that they are moved by forces difficult to understand and identify. This hidden dimension among political people is often deeply buried.

The reasons for marrying in the first place are complex. The collapse of a union is never simply a case of "we outgrew one another." In *Sex and the Significant Americans: A Study of Sexual Behavior Among the Affluent*, sociologists John F. Cuber and Peggy B. Harroff found many reasons why 437 success-oriented Americans, among them politicians, married the people they did. There were also many reasons for the divorces. Those who remained married or were remarried, presented an outward appearance of success in marriage. But their interviews were often studded with words denoting emptiness, pretense: a "settling for" of depressing frequency; staying together "for the sake of the kids," or "because of my career," or "because it's not as bad as being alone."

When pretense no longer serves, and a divorce or separation is the result, most couples do not have to face what many political couples often do—a public announcement. A lesser Congressman may get two paragraphs on his divorce in his back-home newspaper, but prominent political couples—Abigail and Eugene McCarthy, John and Mieke Tunney, Ernest (Fritz) Hollings and his first wife, William and Ellen Proxmire, Governor Marvin and Bootsie Mandel, John and Martha Mitchell—face considerable public appraisal of the decision.

Politicians are no different from other people in their often fumbling attempts to describe what went wrong. After some interviews I remembered a psychiatrist's words: "First I listened to her story, and then I listened to his, and I thought, 'Could these two two people possibly be talking about the same marriage?'"

Most former political wives saw in their ex-husbands a tendency to be overwhelmed by ambition and work, rejecting a more modest professional life and accepting the ultimate sacrifice of an intimate marriage for those goals. Many politicians agree. Representative Pete McCloskey, in an emotional outburst after his wife left him, said, "I've been crying myself to sleep every night. I feel lousy. She was right to leave me. Politics is a grueling business. You get so involved in causes, you lose your sensitivity to other people."

"I'm constantly amazed there aren't more political divorces," says one congressional wife. One reason, of course, is that divorce until recently was supposed to be the death blow for politicians.

While some political observers, such as Abigail McCarthy, now separated from the former Minnesota Senator Eugene McCarthy, contend that there were just as many political divorces twenty years ago, most consider there is a political divorce increase that mirrors the national increase. A 1972 Bureau of Census report states that the proportion of divorced persons in the United States—compared to all persons in intact marriages—has increased by about one half over the preceding twelve years. During this time period, the annual number of divorces rose by 80 percent.

And the divorce rate is still going up. The rate has increased as much in the past *four* years as it did in the entire previous decade.

House Chaplain Edward Latch said, "While I think there is definitely a more liberal attitude on political divorces, it's hard to say if there are more actual divorces. They get elected for two years, some lose, others come back, you lose track of them. But divorce on the Hill is not anywhere near as high as in the country."

Latch said he felt many were happily married. I asked him if by "happily married," did he include those who *stayed* married but had wives who deeply resented their husbands' work? "Oh boy, you're hitting on something now. I find the Congressmen are having to give a lot of their time and when they go home, they take work. It's bound to affect the home life and the wives have every reason to say the husband spends too much time. I think some wives understand that it's the price they have to pay to be married to a Congressman. Some get involved in projects; the prayer groups and the sewing groups help to fill some of the time, but it never takes the place of the relationship with the husband."

Latch has remarried about nine Congressmen, but 1973 and 1974 were unprecedented—four second marriages were performed in the Capitol Hill Prayer Room—Al Ullman, William Ford, Bob Wilson, Charles Gubser.

This prompted one ex-wife from a rural district to purse her lips and say, "What is this world coming to? They're turning that prayer room into Las Vegas! As for Dr. Latch's counseling, when I told him *my* husband wanted a divorce he just told me I might as well see a lawyer."

A partial list of divorced, separated, or remarried includes Senators Dole, Hollings, Russell Long, Proxmire (reunited in 1975), Tunney, Harrison Williams, former Senator Charles Goodell, Governor Mandel, former Senator Joe Tydings, McCarthy, Congressmen Ed Mezvinsky, John Ashbrook, Richard Bolling, Lawrence J. Hogan, Charles Diggs, Jr., John Dingell, Don Edwards, Edith Green, Millicent Fenwick, Pete McCloskey, Mo Udall, Al Ullman, William Hudnut (defeated in 1974), former Congressman Peter Kyros, Don Riegle, Larry McDonald, Gene Snyder, William Wampler, Garry Brown, Charles Gubser, Bob Wilson, Richard Ichord, Elford Cederberg, Andy Jacobs, Pete Stark, John Burton. At one time, no fewer than seven of the nineteen-member Michigan delegation were divorced. A considerable number of Congressmen were divorced in earlier years and remarried. Excluding those amorphous "separations" there are probably no more than seventy-five to one hundred divorced or openly separated Congressmen and Senators on Capitol Hill at one time, still well below the national average. (Even in Abraham Lincoln's time, divorce or at least separation in politics was not totally unheard of. Lincoln's close friend and antislavery advocate Senator Charles Sumner wed Alice Mason Hooper. The match combined fascination and hope on the part of Sumner, fifty-seven, and fascination and ambition on the part of Miss Hooper, twenty-seven. But soon after their marriage his pride and will collided with hers and they parted, he to contemplate suicide and never after refer to her as anything but *that* person.)

Nelson Rockefeller's bid for the presidency in 1964 was in part shattered by front-page headlines and ensuing public reaction to events that seemed insurmountably shocking at the time. Not only had he left his wife, but his second wife, Happy, left both husband and children to marry Rockefeller. A decade later, when he was named as President Ford's choice for Vice President, this was long forgotten. The late Adlai Stevenson had a bitter ex-wife casting assertions on his manliness, hardly a campaign plus, and according to Drew Pearson, Eisenhower refused to return from Paris to campaign in 1952, because, among other things, "he doesn't want to face the Kay Summersby charges." A friend of Eisenhower's, John Bennett, felt, "Mrs. Eisenhower never knew the truth about Summersby—namely, that Ike wanted a divorce." (Mrs. Summersby was a WAC officer and chauffeur to Eisenhower during World War II.) Former Arkansas Governor Winthrop Rockefeller's wife's three divorces sparked most of the criticism in his first campaign, but he later said, "Divorce is getting to be less of an issue, unless there is an open scandal."

Even divorce scandal-style did not dislodge popular incumbents in 1974. And yet many politicians contemplating divorce in 1974 were deeply fearful of the consequences. The second person they reach for, after the lawyer, is a pollster. The third person is very often the second wife. The stigma of the divorce is often removed if they quickly remarry. "People don't mind divorce, they just don't like the absence of the wife," said one ex-wife. The politicians are equally prayerful that the first wife remarries quickly, to take away the image of the "dumped" little woman.

People love to talk about political divorces, but whether or not divorce affects their vote is another matter. Two men killing a little time in a Giant supermarket gossiped like outraged backyard neighbors about Maryland Governor Mandel's divorce, but when I asked them whom they were going to vote for, they said Mandel.

There was a brief encounter between a silver-haired male customer and an equally silver-haired female clerk one afternoon in a Washington People's drugstore. The woman leaned on the cosmetic counter, surrounded by lip glosses and perfumes, and started in on Mandel: "He could hardly wait. Could you beat it? Thirty minutes after his divorce is final, he marries her. That's what we got running the country. And you take what we've got in the White House now. His wife is a divorcée *and* a dancer, and then, if you get the Rockefellers in, *both* of them are divorced."

I asked the woman if a divorced politician, or a divorced political wife, would affect her vote. "No, I don't think it has a thing to do with anything. I was just pointing out that they get away with everything today and poor Adlai didn't have a chance. To think they wouldn't let Stevenson in, and he was the best of the lot. And besides, he didn't have anything to do with it. His wife was the one who wanted the divorce." Did she think many people cared about political divorce? She said, "Well, maybe the elderly—the *real* elderly—but I can't see how much difference it would make."

In many cases the wife's social life was totally the result of her husband's position. One ex-wife said, "My husband's second wife tried to join the congressional wives group but the women were very cold to her and they kept inviting me back. She didn't come again and so I came back. These woman are *my* friends." For years the Senate Ladies' only crisis was how much gauze to order for their bandage rolling. Then in 1973 they had to face divorce.

Many lawyers claim that the "get even" syndrome of a marriage breakup practically blackmails the politician husband into a better settlement because of the threat of adverse publicity. One lawyer said, "My experience has been that politicians will sign away anything to avoid publicity." But many wives say that because of their children they are reluctant to smear their husbands. Few wives can escape the charge of being bitchy if they sound off in print, and husbands bank on both these factors. Many wives, in fact, argue that because of their husbands' prominence they have trouble getting lawyers to take the case back in their home states.

For several years now, women liberationists have said there is a natural affinity for the male-dominated legal fraternity to side with the husband in a divorce case. Two former Senate wives swear this was true in their cases. One said, "I went to the top lawyer in our state. He kept stalling and kept stalling and I finally realized that he was going nowhere with it. I found out that he feared political reprisals. He very much wants to be a judge. Then I found one who had no such political ambitions of his own and everything was fine."

The other former wife recalled that her husband asked a federal judge to try to pull her lawyer off the case. According to her story, the judge called her lawyer and asked to see him, regarding the couple's separation settlement. The lawyer asked if the judge was involved in the husband's case. The judge replied no, but that he was an "old friend of the family." When the lawyer asked the senior partner what he should do, the senior partner replied that the lawyer should go, but that the senior partner would go along as well. At lunch, just before the designated appointment, there was an interesting collision. At one table were the two law partners. At another table were the Senator and the judge. Pleasantries were exchanged. "From that point the meeting rather disintegrated and of course the judge couldn't ask for anything with both the partners there," recalled the wife.

One Washington divorce lawyer who has handled divorces of both politicians and political wives said, "When I represent wives of Congressmen here, of course the husband's position cuts no ice at all. But I suppose it's conceivable a lawyer back home might shy away from it if he wants a judgeship." I told him that most political wives felt that their husbands were leaning on their reputations and had a rather cavalier attitude about the settlement. "I think these wives are coloring the situation. Every wife I represent normally feels she ought to get more from her husband and he feels she ought to get less."

No fewer than three political ex-wives considered running for office against their husbands in 1974—Mrs. Mandel, Mrs. Gene Snyder of Kentucky, and Mrs. William Wampler of Virginia, but all backed off; all used the excuse that they did not want to hurt their children. All of their husbands were relected in 1974.

One Congressman joked that in rural America, just plain divorce and sex wouldn't ruin a politician anymore—"you have to throw a little Communism in with it." The fact is that ex-husbands and ex-wives now comprise a sizable voting block of their own. A newly divorced Senator was mulling over his chances for reelection when a close friend reassured him, "Look, don't worry. If you get all the votes of those who are divorced, or would *like* to be divorced, you'll be home free."

There are several other factors involved in how a recently divorced politician fares—how sophisticated his constituents are, how quiet the divorce, how secure he was in office before the divorce.

There are always some bizarre incidents.

One story is a marvelous lesson in chutzpah. It seems that Mrs. Mo Udall left, with custody of the Udalls' five children. Shortly after, she married a younger man who was in the army. While Udall was no longer her husband, he was still her Congressman. As a concerned constituent she wrote him a letter asking for special consideration that her second husband be exempted from further service. The grounds? That he had to support five children.

The uncontested winners for the most recent "Tacky Divorce Award" easily were Gene Snyder, a Republican Congressman from Kentucky, and his former wife. Their 1973 divorce and subsequent 1974 child-custody battle was one of the most vicious public fights in political divorces. Kentuckians agreed that the divorce didn't help, but no one thought it was enough to shoot down Snyder—a law-and-order, anticommunist, anti-gun-control favorite of his conservative constituents who elected him by a landslide the last time. He won again in 1974.

After Snyder divorced his wife, Louise, and married his red-haired district office manager, the ex-Mrs. Snyder called the papers and announced she was running against her ex-husband for Congress, throwing in for good measure that he was a liar and a cheat.

Snyder, an inconsequential Congressman in his mid-forties, is a sturdy six-foot-one and given to wearing ties with American flags waving on a background of deep blue. He is so anti-gun-control that at one time he packed his own pistol, or rather, pistols. He kept one or two of his large gun collection in his locked desk drawer at the Capitol, would stick the guns in his briefcase and take them home with him. When reporters asked how many guns he stashed in his office, he replied, "It's none of your damned business."

When his wife decided to oppose him in 1974, it was clear the motive was not to "serve constituents." She wanted to put pressure on Snyder to stop the child-custody battle for their then fourteen-year-old son, Mark. "I don't care about politics," she said. "When he filed that custody suit on me, I needed a platform. I'm doing this to protect my son." The son is described by those who know the details as the truly emotionally scarred tragedy in the case—bounced back and forth like a shuttlecock by his power-driven father and equally intense mother. Whatever were their sincere concerns for their child, the Snyders managed to hide them as they flung charges and countercharges at one another in print.

When she started name calling, Snyder countered that his ex-wife had "serious problems." He seemed to be including her second husband, a radio evangelist who saves people via the air waves. "I've done a little research on that new husband of hers," Snyder drawled. "If she runs against me I'll get the court to release the divorce file and they'll both have to leave town. It takes a pretty good case to get a kid away from his mother."

But Mrs. Snyder said that her husband had political power on his side and charged that the custody case was "rigged," and that her ex-husband had "bragged to that effect" on two occasions. The judge ruled that she was overly emotional. "When I heard Gene lying through his teeth, I did cry. All the time Gene was running around, I was home taking care of Mark."

Referring to his "serious problem" charge, she countered, "I did have a problem for five years, and her name was Pat Robertson. Now he has a problem for five years, and her name is Pat *Snyder*. He married her. Those politicians. Everyone from old women to young babies tell them how great they are. Then you get a red-headed secretary who knows all the ropes and well—you know. Those guys work twenty-four hours a day to build their image and the people really never know who or what a man is. Once he feels safe in office, he can do anything he wants to." After the custody battle she decided not to run for office.

Snyder said politics prompted his wife's use of publicity. "If I wasn't a public figure, she wouldn't use this kind of tactics." He apparently wasn't above using tactics of his own. "I've got a photo I took myself of her and this guy going into an apartment house back when we were married . . . No, I don't think this thing's gonna hurt me.

"Now I want to tell you something," he said, his voice getting lower and harder. "I'm fed up to you know where sittin' around keepin' my mouth shut. If you write a line, lady, you'd better let those lawyers clear it. I'm not going to take this any longer—my present wife has been maligned by her and I kept my mouth shut. She talks about photographs she's got but she ain't got none."

One Kentuckian said, "You could say that Snyder and his ex-wife are both, er, unusual."

From this Snopesian world, we go to the Wamplers of Virginia. Sometimes the wife's sense of the politically "sensible" is more finely honed. Mary Elizabeth Baker Wampler, of Bristol, Virginia, just shakes her head in disgust at the "stupidity" with which her husband, William C. Wampler, handled his separation from her.

First, he made a one-sentence announcement that he had separated. It seems that this is part of a new political practice of "separation fever." While sometimes it is an unavoidable and calculated step to diminish negative voters' reaction to the breakup of a mythical "happy marriage," it can be overdone. Some of them crank out the statement before anyone really knows or cares.

Mrs. Wampler, who would never have gone to the press with their separation, found herself being asked questions by reporters who had been given the statement by Wampler. Unfortunately for Wampler, his wife belongs to that group of frank political wives who answer questions honestly, a position that has to strike terror in the hearts of many a politician who espouses honesty and integrity from every platform.

When I asked her in 1974 if politics had broken up her marriage, Mrs. Wampler said, almost breezily and with humor as well as frankness, "No—just another woman!"

Then she started talking about her husband's political mistakes. "There's been a lot of gossip due to the way he handled it. He really had the world by the string and then to blow it over some stupid affair. If he wanted a divorce it would have been far more politically healthy for him to do it and get it over with. It's been a year now. Had he made a clean break, like death, it would have been final. But it's a prolonged separation and it's still hanging in the air. As for his political future, the people would have forgotten about it by now had he gotten the divorce." He also told her he was going to take a poll to see what effect the separation had.

Mary Wampler feels that his "separation" position was for political reasons. "He wants her, he still wants to run around, but he still wants to say that he has a wife and two kids. He's saying we're back together now—that's the farthest thing from the truth—but I guess he thinks it helps politically."

Wampler was not dealing with any political novice in his wife. Her brother is Howard Baker, the Senator from Tennessee. Mary, just like Howard, cut her teeth on Tennessee politics. When her father, a U.S. Congressman, died, her mother took his place to finish his term. She is not one of the children of politicians who is bitter about political life. "I think it's good. It brings the family together. I think you understand and I think you learn a lot about life very young. If you win, everybody loves you. If you lose, the next day you are absolutely on the bottom."

She said she herself has only begun to rethink the role of the politician's wife and family since their separation. "I do think the family has to give in to the father or husband—to the politician's whims, more than in other families. It's all right if it's something you really wanted to do. I love people and I love politics. I was very happy actually and I thought he was too. I'd be in Washington in the winter and at home in the summer." Politics is in her blood. "I love a campaign too." For a while she thought long and hard about running herself.

For her, as for many women who bought the entire package of family and marriage as their blissful lot in life, the sudden jolt of having it all overturned was devastating. "Maybe I'm lucky to be getting out. But after twenty years it really hurt. We have two really great kids, that's the worst part—one is seventeen and one fourteen. The younger wants to be President of the United States after his uncle Howard runs," she said with a mild laugh.

She feels there is no question of the negative effect of politics on marriage—the long separations, the availability of other women, the headiness of a campaign. "Oh, very definitely. It just makes your blood pressure go up."

There is a general feeling that political divorces are only signaling the end of an incomplete liaison—one in which the politician outgrew the spouse. This is not necessarily the case. All kinds of political marriages break up. There *are* the wives who stayed home and showed no interest in politics. Many of the so-called ideal team marriages also end, among them the McCarthys and Mandels. The young and the glamorous split up, as do political couples who are grandparents. Conservatives and liberals, Republicans and Democrats divorce. Those with swinging images, like John and Mieke Tunney, wound up in the divorce court the same year as former Congressman and preacher William Hudnut of Indiana. His wife filed for divorce just days after he presided over a White House prayer breakfast.

Some wives find lovers who make them feel more important and needed than their husbands do. One ex-wife said, "I was faithful for a long time, and then, he was gone all the time and I heard the stories about him and other women." She started to dress provocatively and attracted the attention of other men at parties, but this did little to change her husband's attitude. "And then I fell in love, and the minute that happened my love affair with my husband was over. I was too honest to play games. Of course he never thought I would leave *him*, but by then it was really all over. I had had it with waiting around for him." She lives with her lover and her children now, a bitter pill for her husband, but he swallowed it in order to avoid publicity.

She was determined to live life her style, even if it meant an open fight for the children. "He can have any cutie he wants in his apartment and of course no one says anything. Why shouldn't I have *one* man in my life? I simply do not want to marry again and I am no longer imprisoned by being a public figure. And besides, it is not bad for the children. What they cannot take is the lying and dishonesty that they see in most homes. My husband brought this up with his lawyer—he said I would be setting a bad example for the children. I decided to be frank with my teenage son. I said, 'Do you *really* think that I am setting a bad example?' He looked at me—do you know what his reply was? He said, 'No, after all, you're human, Mother.' They know a lot more than we give them credit for and I think they knew it was an unhappy life for me when I never saw their father."

One ambitious wife, a Washington reporter formerly married to a Maryland state senator, said the fact her husband was in politics "kept the marriage going an extra five years. The fact we didn't see each other as much as we might certainly helped. I loved politics. I pushed him into politics. I could always fantasize my waving to crowds riding down Pennsylvania Avenue, and yet I couldn't conceive of *myself* running, at the time we got married. So I enjoyed being the wife of a state senator. I felt there were more pluses than minuses. There was the convenience—you had a husband and yet you didn't—it gave me so much more mobility." She helped push his career through her contacts on newspapers. "I said to Mandel that my husband wanted to get on the finance committee. He got on the finance committee. As long as I was helpful he was delighted to have me around. Politicians want a wife who is like a dog, preferably a mongrel who doesn't require much care and attention, who will happily lick your face when you come home and won't make any demands."

Some of the reasons given by team-player wives who see their husbands move off for younger women are simply self-protective shields. And yet they are not always just bitter when they examine why their husbands sometimes cancel their life together as if it had never happened. Some political wives told me they could understand that their husbands felt the need to move on. But what they could not take was why they so quickly expunge the first wife, and even the children, as they do. Sometimes the *Congressional Directory* entry is revised to read that the man is married, but there is no indication that it is to a second wife. Occasionally the children by the first wife are not even listed.

Many women said the same thing, but Barbara Mandel summed up their feelings. "The reason they want to cut us off as if we never were is because they want to forget that we helped too *much*. That the wife helped make them what they are is too much for their egos." She paused. "They can't stand the remembering."

13

Instant Divorce

SENATOR ROBERT DOLE, tall and handsome in that dark-eyed, dark-haired way so fashionable in Hollywood in the late thirties and forties, has a reputation for irrepressible bluntness. He was one of President Nixon's most loyal yes-men on the Hill and was ever ready to shoot it out with any administration foe before he was unceremoniously sacked by Nixon's henchmen, Haldeman, Ehrlichman, and Mitchell, as Republican National Chairman. Dole attempted to turn his firing into a plus and, like many a Republican, sought to put much distance between himself and the sinking ship of the Nixon Administration in 1974. Nevertheless, his previously hyperactive loyalty to Nixon, his dedication to a national job, his divorce from his wife of twenty-three years, and an impressive opponent combined to put him in deep trouble in Kansas in 1974. His constituents tended to think he had become mighty uppity, and had neglected them as well as his wife while he pursued national attention as GOP chairman. They were also suspicious about his former alliance to Nixon and, indirectly, Watergate.

Unlike most Republicans, Dole had the plus—or minus—depending on your view, of wit as a weapon. When someone wondered whether Watergate investigators would be able to "get anything" on Dole regarding Watergate and Creep activities, he cracked that they would never have anything recorded on his telephone conversations with members of the White House palace guard. "I always answered everything by shaking my head yes or no." And when someone urged his successor, George Bush, to "hang in there, George, and we'll all hang with you," Dole spoke up, unprompted, with "It's just a question . . . of where we're hanging." Still, he had a reputation, however clever, of being ruthless and vicious and ever ready to attack and defend.

All in all, I expected not to like Dole, but even Bella Abzug, worlds apart ideologically, told me one day, "Dole can be very candid and pleasant when he wants to be."

And so he was on that day when he talked about his divorce and power and politics. There was more than a mild attempt at candor. He said incautious things, it seemed, for a man who had lived much of his life with the burning ambition of getting ahead in politics, who was self-absorbed and all-consumed by his job. He readily admitted the height of his obsession with politics—that he would have divorced years ago except that he was fearful of the consequences politically. He continued, "I was always feeling so selfish about my future and I wouldn't leave. Politics actually kept it [the marriage] together longer." Not in the sense of common interest, he explained. "If I hadn't been concerned about my future, I think our divorce probably would have happened much earlier."

Two and one half years after the divorce, his former wife would reply angrily and tersely to me on the phone that his professions of long-standing readiness to leave the marriage still came as a shock to her. "That's very interesting," she said, dryly. "I have never heard that one."

Dole's divorce was a shocker, in fact, to many people. He was so conservative; he had a reactionary constituency; there had never been a hint of marital discord. Why so quickly? Two views circulated: either he had a girlfriend and wanted to re-marry immediately, or he had higher ambitions and wanted to more or less sneak the divorce through in a hurry in hopes that it would quickly be forgotten. When Dole asked his wife for a divorce, Nixon was considered a cinch to try for his second term. Watergate had not begun to surface and Dole was emerging as an important Republican force on the Hill as a loyal advocate for the administration's Vietnam policy. A freshman Senator, Dole was forty-four when he was elected in 1968, but despite his lack of seniority, he had come so far so fast in the Senate there was even in 1970 talk among conservative Republicans of making him Republican leader—an unprecedented move.

The long and lean plainsman cast himself in the role of Palidin and used blunt force, sarcasm, and wit in his floor maneuvers.

Dole was the recipient of warm telephone calls and notes from Nixon and was a frequent guest at White House state dinners. In January of 1971 Dole was picked by Nixon as national chairman of the Republican Party. He was characterized then as the most ambitious, aggressive, and hungry of freshman Senators. Others refused the job, but the coattails of Richard M. Nixon seemed ample for Dole at the time. How he was to regret his alliance in 1974! When he asked for a divorce in 1971, 1972 was too close for him to emerge as a national figure, but there was always 1976. And if his future didn't lie as Nixon's running mate by the time he had to run for the Senate again, in 1974, a divorce might be forgotten. His former wife blames his national political role for their breakup and described her husband as a man who "began to believe his press clippings."

If Dole had indeed wanted out earlier, there were those who saw him callously using his wife. One Kansas newspaperman said, "Phyllis never did like politics much but she campaigned up one side of this state and down the other in 1960 for him. If he had any desires of divorcing her then he was a real dog for putting her through all that."

So aware of the political ramifications was Dole that he apparently discussed the divorce with his colleagues more than he did with his wife, if her expressions of shock and dismay were real. A concerned Dole went to John Mitchell and Richard Nixon. "I thought maybe I should resign as Republican Party Chairman," Dole recalled. Considering what came later, Dole delivered one of the funniest lines of the year. "They assured me that as long as there was no scandal involved, I would not have to resign." (When I mentioned that he talked to Mitchell, his former wife said, "He sure picked a great guy to discuss it with.")

The former Mrs. Dole's Washington lawyer said that, while she was dazed at the quickness of the divorce, she was not as much in the dark as her statements indicate. She said they had never been separated, but her lawyer insisted, "It was a long goddamn wrangle for property settlement—from six months to a year. And they were separated before that." I asked the lawyer, who preferred to be anonymous, why she would have insisted they were not separated, and he said, cynically, "You've got to realize women's lib. You women have to save a little face. When she got remarried she blew the best goddamn property settlement you could get." (The former Mrs. Dole married a wealthy small-town Lincoln, Kansas, banker, Lon Buzick.)

The actual divorce proceedings caused widespread speculation as to motives and quite a lot of publicity. The case remains something of a mystery to those who do not understand Kansas divorce laws—and many of them are Kansas residents.

Unlike many states and the District of Columbia, Kansas does not have a separate residency waiting period. In the District, for example, a couple must live apart for at least one year, even in an uncontested divorce.

"You don't have to be separated at all," said Judge Adrian Allen, the Kansas judge who granted the Dole divorce. "Of course, to the court it might seem strange if you litigate by day and copulate by night," he added, with a leering laugh. At any rate, while there is a normal sixty-day waiting period between the time of filing and hearing, "emergency" divorce petitions can be filed in one day and the divorce can be granted that very day. "It's a peculiar law," admits the former Mrs. Dole's Washington lawyer, "but I got the impression it's done all the time out there. But both people have to be Kansas residents—it's not like Las Vegas."

The judge said the same thing. "Emergency divorces are as common as dandelions out here. My definition of an 'emergency' is far less than life and death. I granted it because it would work a hardship on the plaintiff—Mrs. Dole—to appear at a subsequent trial." It may be as common as dandelions but the former Mrs. Dole thought it surprising and local newspapers blared out headlines that "Judge Refuses to Reveal 'Emergency' in Dole Divorce."

All in all, the newspaper accounts added up to a picture of the Republican National Chairman railroading a quickie divorce through a friendly judge, who vehemently denied it. Dole's ex-wife's statements hardly helped. "It was at his urgent request, I had no choice. I didn't want to do it. I tried to stall. I wanted him to give me more time. I couldn't get anywhere with him. I had to do it." She said she had hoped for a reconciliation.

"I'm still trying to find a reason why he feels the way he does," she said at the time of the divorce. "Since spring there has been a change in him. I think he has been working too hard." Although she acknowledged her husband was away from their home much of the time that previous year—particularly in his new job as Republican chairman—she said, "We were not separated at all. I know he hasn't been here a lot, but he was here last week. He hasn't moved out—his clothes and belongings are here. He has not been living away from home."

She said her lawyer had explained the terms of the divorce, granted on the grounds of incompatibility, but she said, "I didn't think it would be instantaneous. Ten minutes after I walked in, the decree was granted. It's unbelievable. You can't go to Reno and do that. I'm still completely devastated by it, but I guess I'll live through it. Just this last week the whole thing was set up. It's obviously a new law in Kansas—instant divorce. I was not aware of it, and I did it at the urgent request of Senator Dole, which I stated in court—in front of the judge," Mrs. Dole recounted to reporters. "I didn't want to do it; but because of many things, including my daughter's emotional stability, I decided not to fight any longer. I didn't want to do it, but on the advice of my lawyer I went ahead with it."

The judge bristled at both her reaction and the newspaper accounts. "As for Mrs. Dole, I have no patience with someone who was here through the whole thing and then saying they don't understand." The Kansas City *Star* stories were "terrible," he said. "They weren't even true."

Dole was judged "politically astute" by some political observers. "Dole had a choice of judges and he picked a new *Democratic* judge. No one could say the judge was in favor of him. I think that's pretty shrewd," said Mrs. Dole's Washington lawyer.

No matter the protestations of the Kansas judge, in Washington the divorce story was generally recounted in this tone. "Dole was dreadful," said one former Senator's wife. "He managed to get his divorce immediately. Because of politics he wanted it to look as if *she* wanted it. He had the judge on his side; they told Phyllis she wouldn't get a thing and she just crumpled. These men are powerful and they gamble on their wives not making more of an issue of it than they do."

Dole did not amplify or illumine the reasons for his "urgent request" divorce except to add, "I think you have to make a decision sooner or later." I asked about his wife saying she was shocked and surprised at the divorce. "She did say that, but it was a long and frustrating thing. I don't want to get into all the gory details."

During his 1974 senatorial campaign, Dole took a poll, asking a series of questions that included what people thought of divorce. Although the survey reported less fallout regarding divorce than Dole imagined, he told me, "It still seemed to me it would be a major problem. I'd gotten a lot of divorces for peo-

ple as a lawyer, but I didn't know. Well, I found out most people aren't staying awake nights over it." Still, he noticed things
he had not noticed before—how his opponents always showed
up with their wives and children.

While there were rumors about Dole and other women—
especially following the "emergency divorce" publicity—he denied them all and remained unmarried for several years. One
paper reported that a former TWA stewardess and model
accompanied him on one political trip and reporters speculated
that his marriage had run amuck of his newfound national
prominence which "introduced him to all sorts of attractive
women." One article in the Kansas City *Star* said, "because he is
Republican National Chairman there is more than passing interest in the Senator and his personal life."

Dole's supposed new interest was reported at various times to
be someone on his staff, a secretary in the White House, a woman at the Republican National Committee, a model in Kansas
City, another woman in Topeka, still another in Russell, Kansas, and mystery women in Chicago and Florida. When Dole
went to Chicago, he received a telephone call from a gossip columnist who wanted to be "in on the ground floor" about the
blonde Dole had come to see. The "blonde" was three thousand
Lithuanian-American women, Dole joked. He gave a talk to
them.

While Dole at first tried to ignore the reports, he finally said
in an interview, "I have no plans to marry."

"I thought it would stop," Dole said. "How do you handle
something like this? You can't issue a statement of denial every
time a woman's name is mentioned."

More than a year and a half later, before his re-election in
1974 Dole was explaining to me one of the reasons he did not
remarry; he had to keep his "priorities" straight he said. By
"priorities" I thought he meant you just didn't marry for the
sake of marrying, that you had to find someone you cared
enough about. But no. What he meant, he said, was that "my
priority at this point is to be reelected." I was struck with the
cool pragmatism with which he regarded his private life, how
he talked of his divorce mainly in political rather than emotional terms. Now he had no time for such thoughts as remarriage.
"Getting reelected consumes all my thoughts."

One day during the waning months of Nixon's Administration, Dole absentmindedly twirled a paper clip and talked about his divorce. "The President sent me a book about Disraeli. I think what he was trying to tell me is that a politician can have a public and private life; that it made no difference."

And Senator Charles Percy clapped him on the back one day after his divorce and said, "I know you think your world has come to an end," but assured Dole that he should not let it be a problem.

But Dole knew the people of Kansas, and he was not so sure. Nor were they. His ex-wife voiced the prevailing view of many rural voters in a phone conversation with me: "My own feeling is if a man can't keep a marriage intact he has a heck of a nerve trying to keep the country in order."

Dole said he worried a great deal about that type of reaction. It was indeed a factor in his poor showing, even though he won. "You sorta think divorce must be a defect in somebody. You don't like it to happen, and then, you look at yourself as a politician. These things aren't *supposed* to happen to you. You're not *supposed* to be normal. You're not *supposed* to have problems." No matter how apathetically voters may regard politicians in general or how ineffective or weak they feel Congress has become, many feel a politician who is going to have some say about their lives ought to be a "fit" person; to some voters being fit is translated into having a perfect marriage.

His ex-wife feels that politics changed her husband and that something often does happen to politicians once they get attention. "After a while they don't even consider that a wife has any input." I asked her if there were always people around telling her husband he was marvelous and she answered tersely, "Yes." She did not think it was "totally true" that a political wife in Washington has no status of her own. "Many are active in their own right. I was vice-president of the Congressional Club at the time of the divorce and he didn't even know it." There was hurt in her voice. "They are not interested in their wives. They are only interested in their own gain."

For Dole there was an added dimension to the taint of leaving a wife of twenty-three years. The story of his marriage was legendary to the voters of Kansas. After all those years it still sounds like one of those World War II movie plots with Dana Andrews playing Dole's part and Teresa Wright playing the woman who nurses him back to health. We started talking at 3 P.M. in his office and the shadows of a rainy dusk gathered before I left four hours later. As Dole remembered his marriage, he said, "I felt people would say, 'Look at him, after she's done all these things, he doesn't need her anymore.' I became independent from a physical standpoint. It got so I could dress myself, do other things." His voice became soft. "But for some time I was very dependent."

There were several years when Phyllis Dole buttoned his shirts, sliced his meat, tied his shoelaces and ties, wrote his exams . . .

Dole's right arm hangs at his side, slack and useless, as if an invisible weight were holding it there. It is a tribute to World War II surgery that the arm and hand are there at all; they are formed from transplanted bone and muscle; a reminder forever of a hospital ordeal that lasted three years and three months. He lay in a plaster cast from knees to ears, both arms and both legs paralyzed, his neck vertebrae fractured and spinal cord damaged. Physicians didn't think he would live, far less ever walk again.

Born in 1923 in Russell, Kansas, a village then of three thousand, Dole, the son of a grain elevator operator, dreamed first of becoming a football or basketball star, then, maybe a country doctor. He is six foot one, tall enough for basketball in those days. He was a freshman pre-med student at the University of Kansas, waiting on tables and earning freshman numerals in basketball, football, and track when the war came along.

Dole was selected as officer material. In December 1944, he was a second lieutenant and platoon leader in Italy and the push across the Po Valley was about to begin.

A grenade sliver in his leg was his first wound and he later joked that it was "one of those things where they give you mercurochrome and the Purple Heart." A few days later, high-explosive shell fragments riddled his body. He lay for hours on the battlefield. "It was sort of a long day," he recalled. He was twenty-one, and for the next three years his homes were hospitals in Italy, Africa, Florida, Kansas, and eventually Percy Jones General Hospital in Battle Creek, Michigan. According to one story, Phyllis Holden, a young occupational therapist on the hospital staff, asked about Dole's chances. Doctors told her he could not possibly live. Dole wasted to 122 pounds from his original 194, and still paralyzed in all limbs, he developed blood clots in his lungs. He became a guinea pig for streptomycin, one of four patients in the entire country receiving the newest wonder drug on a trial basis. It worked.

Dole worked his way from bed to wheelchair to tentative first steps and, as the story went, he was assisted in the battle by the girl from Concord, New Hampshire.

At the time, Dole said, "You get the impression when you're paralyzed and immersed in plaster, that the other sex can't possibly be interested in you as a man. But she seemed interested in me as a human being more than as some poor soul. I got over feeling sorry for myself through her and also by seeing the plight of much worse cases than myself in the hospital.

"I was always something of a comedian as a kid and after a while, they were shifting me to wards where morale was low." He got his second Purple Heart, a Bronze Star with clusters and a "bedpan promotion" to Captain, but he needed specialized surgery to get back his right arm. In a series of then "miracle" operations, doctors transplanted bone and muscle from Dole's leg to his shoulder and arm, and wielded a magical scalpel on his hand and fingers. To shake hands, Dole usually holds something in his right hand as a prop and shakes with with his left. One endearing act of Nixon's, Dole said, is that he remembered Dole's affliction. "He always shook my hand with his left."

One month before Dole was discharged in June 1948, he married the girl he met in the hospital. The doctor who recreated his right arm, wired this marriage telegram: "Hope that arm I fixed will be used lovingly."

With that idyllic message, the Doles moved into a life many World War II veterans knew, college at a somewhat advanced age, past dreams lost because of injuries or a late start on life. Dole could not take notes but he used a recorder in his classes at Washburn University in Topeka, where he studied for a law degree.

In 1952, he passed his three-day Kansas bar exams by dictating the answers to his wife, who also helped him through school by working at the Topeka State Hospital. At the time of their divorce, Phyllis Dole recalled that the workaholic bent was in her husband even in college. "Even when we were in school, he

had to get all A's. He drove himself constantly. I would tell him
an A wasn't all that important, but he would not listen. He
couldn't stand to fail."

Dole makes light of his early political days and says he just
"sorta fell into politics." The politicians of Russell, Kansas,
came to him saying they felt it was imperative that young people get involved in government. At twenty-six, while still in law
school, Dole was elected to the Kansas legislature. After graduation from law school, he was elected county prosecutor for
four successive two-year terms. The salary was $248 a month.
The courthouse janitor's wages were more, but Dole used his
position to further himself politically. "Most politicians sorta do
an internship—go through Kiwanis and Red Cross, become
well known in the community, Boy Scouts, Chamber of Com-
merce," he said. Today, Dole feels he is probably the best-
known politician in his state. He says that with pride; it seems
damned important to him. He talked about how he loved campaigning. If you had a good night's sleep, he said, it was "an experience that never gets old." (I'd heard some people say the
same thing about sex, I recalled.)
    Dole, by his own admission, puts politics before everything
else in his life. He is the kind of politician who shows infinite patience with all those strangers whom he needs to vote him into
office. He often hangs around his office until 11:30 P.M., answering all kinds of calls. "Nixon's a jerk—why did you support
him?" "What's the energy crisis doing to us farmers?" "What
about inflation?"
    Did he think the family is used more and suffers more in po-
litics than any other life? "Oh, no doubt about it." At first, his
traveling was less frequent. "When you come to Congress from
a safe district, then you can go home once a month and you
don't do much speaking." Then the change comes. "Whether
you're driven by the excitement, or because you think you have
the ability, suddenly we let our lives be taken over by politics.
We find ourselves every weekend on an airplane when we
should be with our families. I don't care how strong a marriage
is, when you come in on Sunday night and the children are going to bed and you don't see them again until Thursday and
then only for a brief time before going out again, they literally
grow up without you knowing who they are. I don't see how po-

liticians with three and four children do it, how they have any time for family . . . Maybe the answer is more children," he said, as if musing about it. "At least somebody's at home."

We talked about how success-oriented men in other professions can also neglect their families, but Dole said, "It's just that extra dimension in politics. You find too often that you're making the choice that puts you back in the public eye and away from the family. If you become married to politics, something else is going to suffer."

Talking of his daughter, Dole said, "I don't think I really knew her well. I was there for the ceremonial things at school. But mostly they [his daughter and wife] were here and I was not. Sooner or later you have to make a decision—is the child going to be fatherless, or parentless too? But even when you leave the mother there, you're depriving the children. You need a father around. How can you discipline something that happened last Thursday? I don't think any Congressman can honestly say he had that contact with his children."

He feels closer to his daughter, Robin, now; she is in college in Virginia. They visit when they have the chance. He encouraged me to talk to her, something that few politicians and their families do. She sounded easygoing and forthright on the phone. "The one thing that is too bad about the divorce in politics is that your private life is made too public. I guess you can't get around it. I think the fishbowl existence was a sad situation . . . the only thing I ever disliked about him being Senator." Robin recalled the 3 A.M. phone calls from constituents— Dole refused to have an unlisted phone because he feels he has to be "on call." In some ways this adds to a politician's feelings of omniscience; that everyone turns to him in trouble. "I guess that's one sure way to break up the family," he said with a half smile. "You leave the phone listed—but you're away when the early-morning calls come." "Kansas is an hour later," his daughter said, "and anyone who calls at that hour is drunk. They can ramble on for an hour." She said she never hung up and was patient with the calls. "I usually am because I'm afraid not to be. There is this 'constituent' that runs through my mind—'should I hang up or play along?' "

"I have this horrible blank about my childhood," Robin recalls. "I really can't remember when he was there or not. I guess maybe right now, looking back on it, I wish I could have spent more time with him. But I learned to wait until he was there. And I might not have even noticed he was gone so much—except that it was brought up by him and mother. They'd talk about how it was too bad he didn't have enough time."

We talked about how difficult it was for a politician to meet the needs of constituent, wife, and family. "You tend to feel those close to you would understand and strangers won't, I guess. You give your life to strangers—maybe it should be the other way around."

There were never any "horrible fights or quarrels." As Dole said, he is somewhat skeptical of political couples who say they never quarrel and profess still to have an alive relationship. "I remember a story that said Senator Carlson [the Senator from Kansas who preceded him] and his wife lived together for years and never had a fight. Maybe his was a good marriage, but we weren't programmed for fights either. We didn't have *time*. Instead I was either on a plane or at the office. I often wondered what would have happened had I not been a politician. The marriage probably wouldn't have been a failure . . . but then I couldn't have been a judge and sat in that black robe all day, say. That really isn't exciting."

Robin sounds very much like a daughter who loves both her parents, does not want to be in the middle, and is happy that they seem to be doing what they want. She went to her mother's second wedding and thinks her mother is very happy now. "I never saw any personality clashes between my parents. I think maybe he was, um, maybe he . . . because he worked all day, when he would come home at night he was distant. The biggest thing they lacked was communication. Then, she would push something. The love just died. Maybe it was over for a long time. Both of them changed incredibly the last three or four years. The only thing that could have been a problem was that he didn't take her places—places she could have gone. I can't speak for her, but for myself, my first reaction would be rejection.

"There wasn't tension, but to me, it wasn't a perfect marriage for quite a while. I don't know anything about their private life together. He was home rarely, and when he was home he was tired and all that." As for the divorce, Robin says, "I really don't know the whole story behind it. They were very concerned about what would happen to me, about the publicity and what friends would say. But I didn't have any trouble at all. I think maybe the reason it went through so quickly was partially because they didn't want to hurt me. It didn't really upset me . . . but it sort of disgusted me. People insisted on calling, other divorced women, to talk to Mother. They'd phone her and tell her how horrible they felt . . . a lot of politicians' wives did."

Robin strikes one as apolitical. At Virginia Polytechnic Institute, she plans to be an occupational therapist like her mother. She says the majority of her friends "lean toward Republican" but the Watergate hearings were "no big deal" to them. She would not go into politics herself. "So many friends are amazed that my father can go at it so hard. The only thing I can think of is he loves it." She is uncertain about whether she'd marry a politician. "My boyfriend now has no interest in politics. If . . . I guess, if I loved a person enough I would."

She enjoyed the campaigning as a little girl—"I remember going from town to town distributing bumper stickers"—and says neither her father's being away from home nor the publicity and the divorce has soured her attitudes on marriage. "If I was asked, I'd probably get married tomorrow." She has no resentment of politics, but adds, "There is a big, big difference. Just the fact that I'm a daughter and not the wife of a politician, for example, you don't feel the same neglect."

The former Mrs. Dole was furious that her husband had given me permission to talk to their daughter. "It upset me a great deal. Such things should be joint decisions. I've tried to keep the relationship a good one," so as not to tarnish their daughter's feelings. "I've tried to be fair about him, but that is getting increasingly difficult." Then she said, "I'm happily remarried—fortunately. I don't want to discuss anything that has to do with him and I don't want anything to interfere with my present life."

Although she clung to the marriage, she now feels the divorce is the best thing that happened to her. "I didn't know what happiness was." She feels she could have continued her occupational therapy work as a Senator's wife although "I'm not sure how long it would have lasted with the demands. They were only at campaign time; there were no other requests . . . I began to live my own life. To have a life, I had to live one on my own. He often said I should work, that I didn't have enough to do, but I had a child to raise. I always feel there is one thing in this world you cannot do over, and that is children. It is an extra burden in politics because the children do not know their father."

Although Congressional Club wives had to pass a special ruling that allowed her to stay in the club after her divorce, she does not see the sad implications of the fact that these women are thrown together only through their husbands' work.

"They passed a special resolution asking me to stay. Had he remarried there might have been two Mrs. Doles. They went out on a limb for me. I was vice president and involved in all of our activities; the programs, teas, embassy functions at the time of the divorce. I worked on the First Ladies breakfast for years." It seemed almost barbaric that these women have so little outlet for themselves that when something happens to the marriage they also feel their own separate "ladies" social life goes with it.

Did she feel it was a hollow life? "Not at the time. . . . It was afterwards that I felt that."

She said flatly, "I do not think politics is good for a family but I agreed to go along with it."

There were many things the former Mrs. Dole went along with: the time away from home, the ego boosts that she feels so changed her husband. When he was elected to the Senate, she and Dole and their daughter posed for those wooden "at home" pictures that appear so artificial in newspaper write-ups. One such article said Mrs. Dole was making her inaugural gown out of coral-colored material she found on sale. This article carefully fit the Doles into the mold of a conservative, traditional political family. Mrs. Dole "enjoys campaigning and swears that no one can set a better tea table than Kansas women." She contends, however, "that voters would rather see him than her. 'He's the one making the decisions. He rarely discusses any issues with me.'"

So anonymous were they as a congressional couple for eight years that Mrs. Dole received very formal "Welcome to Washington" notes from other officials' wives who didn't know they had even been here before he won the Senate election.

Six years later, in 1974, divorced and living alone in an apartment, Dole is without close friends. "He dates some pretty good-looking women," one aide said, enviously. Dole does get calls from "girls who want to work for him" but he says with a smile "I think I can get home safely without a police escort." His work allows for no time for friends or sitting by fireplaces enjoying life. "Having a quiet dinner doesn't fit into my life." He recalls one Sunday when he had nothing to do. It was as exotic as a trip to the Taj Mahal for others—"I messed around the apartment, tossed stuff in the washing machine, piddled around doing nothing. I had been in the public eye three weeks. I was always in the public eye, always being scrutinized, always on my best behavior . . . that day, I walked around in my T-shirt all day long . . . "

Dole is quick to say that no one is holding a gun to his head to keep him in Congress. "This is not a sentence. I can quit any time I want to and there'll be a long line of people to take my place." He also admits there is no greater escape than politics for a man who wants to flee his own private demons. "I found myself taking more speaking engagements. [He made $33,050 in speeches in 1972 and over $30,000 in 1973.] I would find something to do in the office. Maybe I didn't want to face home. I could convince myself I was overwhelmed with all this work." As party chairman, he flew around the country four and five times a week, losing weight, getting rundown, loving it.

There are no close friends in Kansas, either. "There is no way to keep friendships going on a working basis. Anyone you see, well, it's all job-related." He does keep in touch with his parents, Methodists who believe marriage is forever and were upset by their son's divorce.

The sacrifices of home, family, friends, quiet moments of relaxation are clearly worth it all for Dole. True tragedy for him would be to get beaten. If that happened, he said, in a whistling-in-the-dark tone—it was clearly worrying him at the time—he would have to find a job. "Not everyone is in politics." Asked what he would miss, Dole replied, "You're back to the basic thing. I'd miss not being a leader in my state, not being able to do something." As for power? He smiled and said, "I've found only one Senator who didn't want to be President—and when I asked him for an affidavit, he declined. I think at one time or another we all think we're smart enough, but it probably isn't going to happen. If you are intelligent and have a good staff you can be a very good Senator." He paused. "And I don't want to leave."

14

"How Can You Be a First Lady When You're Not a Lady First?"

WHEN Maryland's Governor Marvin Mandel issued his Duke-of-Windsor-style pronouncement on July 3, 1973, that he was leaving his wife, Barbara, of thirty-two years to marry the woman he loved, Washington newspapers gave it equal billing with another couple who were somewhat well known and had split on the same day—Liz Taylor and Richard Burton. Mandel, unknown nationally except as Spiro T. Agnew's successor, rocked strangers and acquaintances alike with his startling emergence as lover of the year. In his mid-fifties, a sex symbol Mandel is not. Barely five feet six, Mandel is half a head shorter than his new wife, who is seventeen years younger. But this couple managed to drop a bomb that the world- and love-weary god and goddess of Hollywood never could. Things that developed after Mandel's announcement blazed new paths in the well-mapped world of marital politics.

If Mandel banked on a tearful but genteel disappearance from public life and into the divorce courts by his wife he was very wrong. Liz and Dick were quieter. Barbara, as garrulous as Molly Goldberg and as tough as Golda Meir, said what is this business about leaving the mansion? She refused to leave, which made it a trifle difficult on Marvin. There was just no way a fellow could establish residence in Las Vegas and remain governor of Maryland. He took himself to a hotel. Weeks went by and he moved into an apartment. It was costing him a bundle. One half year later, wife number one moved out declaring there was still only one First Lady and she was it. The governor moved back in. Shortly thereafter the woman he planned to marry moved into the mansion. In August of 1974 Mandel's divorce became final. Thirty minutes later he married wife number two, a divorcée with four children. They spent their honeymoon campaigning.

The Mandel split brought the sport of back-fence gossiping to new heights. Political officials and reporters participated, taking sides or chuckling at the first Mrs. Mandel's outbursts or weighing the political damage of the less than discreet handling of matters. Story after story kept readers abreast of the latest developments.

Wife number one, Barbara "Bootsie" Mandel, in her mid-fifties, has been characterized as vindictive and bitchy or brave and gutsy. Some saw her as a warm, bubbly, unpretentious Jewish grandmother who was rejected and injured; others viewed her as a tyrannical woman who knew the score for a long time but wasn't about to give up her mansion and title. Mandel was either an insensitive, calculating, and cold man or a caring, loving man who risked his political future for personal happiness.

Some argued that his lack of opposition made his act less a threat to his career than it appeared. His new wife was either an ambitious, domineering schemer who would not have looked twice at Mandel had he not been governor, or a woman wildly in love who admirably braved the "other woman" slurs. Everyone was talking and everyone had an opinion.

The person who had the most opinions was Bootsie. Her ideas tumbled out in rapid sentences, her little nuggets of philosophy falling here and there along with her explanations of what happened.

When a reporter told Bootsie the divorce decrees were final on August 13, 1974 at 9 A.M. and that the governor and his bride stood before a rabbi at 9:30 A.M., she said she was "shocked. No one bothered to let me know that I was even divorced, let alone that he had remarried. The governor would have shown better taste if he had waited a while. There should have been a common decency, which the governor lacks. They could have waited—the governor acts like an expectant father."

A few days later, Barbara Mandel answered the phone in her Baltimore apartment. I asked her about an article that stated she had made phone calls to Jeanne Dorsey Mandel when she was still the "other woman." Barbara retorted, "That's her story. How in the world could I make phone calls to her when I didn't know who she was or that it was taking place? Of course I heard the rumors just like everyone else and I went to him and asked him and he said, 'That's absolutely ridiculous.'" (Jeanne Dorsey Mandel's nine-year-old son was quoted as saying after the announcement, "That lady's weird. She keeps calling up our home to find out if her husband's there.")

Although many people contend that attitudes toward politicians' private lives are changing, an ex-wife, particularly one who has invested her entire life in her husband's career, invariably expresses one view held by some voters: that politicians ought to be above others and set an example of pristine private morality. The former Mrs. Mandel is hardly an exception. "Why she was living in the mansion with him after I left! There she was, committing adultery in front of her children. The press never wrote about that. Where are the morals of this world? Here's a governor—openly admitting he committed adultery." Her next sentence had the ring of a genuine classic in political folklore—"Now, I ask you—how can you be a First Lady if you're not a *lady* first?!"

Jeanne Dorsey Mandel maintains that she and the governor fell in love at first sight ten and a half years before their marriage. For at least five years residents of Leonardtown in St. Marys County, about seventy-two miles from the state capitol in Annapolis, were used to the governor visiting his love, who lived there with her four children by her previous marriage.

"We've been talking about that for years," exclaimed the wife of one of the commissioners in that small (population 1,400) rural county seat, when Mandel announced he would marry Mrs. Dorsey. A local newspaper editor said it was common knowledge. Mrs. Dorsey's pre-teenage son reportedly said he knew about it for four years. Such rumors nearly spilled into public domain in December of 1970 when Mandel's unmarked state police car collided with another car in Prince Georges County, a few minutes past midnight. A man in the other car was killed. Governor Mandel refused to say what he was doing out at that time in a chauffeur-driven unmarked police car. As rumors mounted and the press continued to probe, Mandel finally said he had been attending a "secret political" meeting. Despite his official explanation, his office was asked about persistent rumors that the governor was, in fact, returning from a visit to Mrs. Dorsey. His office denied this and just two weeks before Mandel's statement again denied that the governor and his wife were about to separate. During the previous year, Mandel's visits with Mrs. Dorsey were more blatant, including the time they appeared together in public at a festival sponsored by Leonardtown Junior Naval Academy, which was attended by one of her sons.

When Mandel's press aide Frank A. DeFilippo handed reporters the six-paragraph statement on July 3, he sounded
straight out of a 1940s movie when he cracked, "Here's your
firecracker for the Fourth of July." Mandel's coldly worded
statement indicated that he was aware Mrs. Mandel's public
reaction would be one of shocked surprise. He took away that
impact as well as her one political weapon, disclosure, by beating her to the punch and naming the other woman: "I am in
love with another woman, Mrs. Jeanne Dorsey, and I intend to
marry her. Mrs. Mandel and I have had numerous discussions
about this matter and she is completely aware of my feelings, of
my actions and of my intentions." The statement began, "I
would like to announce that I am separated from Mrs. Mandel
after thirty-two years of marriage. My decision and the separation are final and irrevocable, and I will take immediate action
to dissolve the marriage." He explained the announcement as
the duty of a public official to make his constituents "completely
aware" of his actions. "I fully realize that this is an intensely personal matter, but I also recognize that I am a public official
whose principal obligation is to the citizens of Maryland." He
asked to be judged "not by my personal actions, but my actions
as governor of Maryland." Acknowledging their two grown
children, Mandel did not throw his ex-wife one bone, not even
one line of compassion for a past shared life, as he continued,
"however, Mrs. Mandel and I no longer share mutual interests
nor are our lives mutually fulfilling."

Mrs. Mandel's reaction was a bombshell in itself, and included her highly quoted remark that "the governor crawled out of
my bed this morning. He has never slept anyplace but with
me." She said, innocently, "I'm surprised. Marvin has not discussed this with me. I don't know what in the world he's talking
about. The pressure of the job must have gotten to him. I think
he needs psychiatric help or something. With a little bit of help
and treatment he can get around to becoming himself again.
You don't take thirty-two years of married life and throw them
down the drain. I just can't believe it. I will remain in the governor's mansion until he comes to his senses completely. I intend
to remain Mrs. Marvin Mandel."

In the months to come, close friends of the governor said
Mandel had in reality asked her for a divorce two years before
and she had refused. Only one month before the separation

Mrs. Mandel left a governors' conference before the governor. He flew to San Francisco to be with Jeanne Dorsey. If hers was the face-saving refrain of an injured woman, Mrs. Mandel maintained it to the end. Defending herself to me more than a year later, even after his remarriage, she said, "He *did* crawl out of my bed that morning! We never slept apart in our entire life. There were fifty some rooms in that mansion, and twelve or fourteen bathrooms, and we still used the same bedroom and bathroom." While, she contends, the governor slept in her bed every night he was in Annapolis, she concedes it must have been another matter on the road. "If your husband says he has to be in Boston, well . . . I didn't check that out.

"But where does the press get the idea that I knew about it and refused to give him a divorce? We stood shoulder to shoulder in May of 1973 at a fund-raiser and *we* together collected thousands of dollars. Would I have done that if I had known my husband was in love with another woman?"

And then Mrs. Mandel, who is nothing if not frank, blurted out what a lot of people wondered but were afraid to ask. "Now she says she's been in love with the governor for ten and a half years. She has a child between seven and nine years of age and she was divorced only five and a half years ago. What would you say that makes her? Now I know the child is not his and I know it isn't a ten-and-one-half-year affair. If that were the case, why didn't she get a divorce right away? She didn't *want* just a member of the state legislature. She had married a state senator first. She waited until he got to be governor. There are just so many holes in this thing. Do you really think Marvin used me to campaign for him and everything and then left?"

Barbara Mandel s stance was in sharp contrast to the political activity that proceeded Mandel's announcement. For more than a year, the governor weighed his moves, sought spiritual advice from rabbis, hashed it out with friends. The political repercussions were discussed, the feelings of the children and all involved. Finally, sources told Washington *Post* reporter Richard Cohen, Mandel asked his wife for a divorce six months before his statement. She flatly refused and from then on, Mandel's friends said, the marriage ceased to exist. They played out their roles for the public and the press as governor and first lady. They smiled at the photographers and attended all the right affairs and did, as Mrs. Mandel said, stand shoulder to shoulder at his fund-raiser. In the meantime Mandel continued to see Mrs. Dorsey, twice meeting her in California.

When Mandel's long-kept secret hit the Maryland public it became the talk of Fourth of July picnics and parades. Politicians worried about his future and hoped the dust would soon settle.

When Mrs. Mandel barricaded herself in the 54 room, 104-year-old Georgian mansion, she continued to be an obvious presence. Some days she showed the real estate, to everyone who came in to tour. She put out ashtrays with her picture as first lady on them. She spoke at functions, was trailed by the press, and was cheered by matrons when she said she wasn't giving up the ship. Friends said she counted on public opinion driving the governor back. When that seemed hopeless, she hung on, they said, to get a better settlement. Her final statement—as she left with her eight wardrobe boxes of clothing and a love seat—was a masterpiece in describing a "lonely" vigil by a faithful wife: "Five and a half months have passed and our marriage has not returned to normal. Therefore, with deep regret, I am leaving the mansion." Even when it was all over Mrs. Mandel, once called the most politically oriented first lady ever to live in the mansion, professed to be unaware that her husband had the ability to lead a double life. Refuting the long-standing nature of Governor Mandel's love for his new wife, she told me, "Three years ago, right after the last election, I was asked to make a speech on the role of wives married to politicians, about how happy these marriages were. And he allowed me to make it. Does that sound like a man unhappy and ready to split?"

I asked her why she stayed on so long at the mansion. She is a fast talker and the words spurted forth. "The reason I did that—oh, it wasn't the fact of the settlement like they said—I stayed there for *me*. No one was going to push me out. No one was going to *make* me do it. It wasn't the governorship I was leaving, or any political position I was leaving. I was leaving a *marriage*. Even though he'd already left. I thought maybe he'd come back the next day. Maybe he had amnesia or was sick or something. Suddenly I said, 'There aren't any more excuses to make for this man.' In other words, I was not going to make a *rash* decision. I had to be ready *myself* to leave."

Jeanne Dorsey had the advantage of being seventeen years

younger and is an attractive blonde with a good figure. Interestingly, the governor's second wife has been described as just as determined, forceful, strong-minded, and politically attuned as the first Mrs. Mandel. "If Jeanne sets her aim high enough, watch out," said a longtime resident of her hometown in rural St. Marys County. Some people thought one of her attractions for Mandel was the fact that she comes from Southern Maryland lineage; hers is a well-known name in local history. "That may not sound like much to you," said one acquaintance of Mandel's, "but for the Baltimore son of a Jewish garment cutter it's something." As Mrs. Dorsey, she was also related to one of the most politically powerful families in the county. That marriage, to Walter B. Dorsey, who served in the state senate with Mandel from 1958 to 1962, was apparently rocky. Mrs. Dorsey was a politician in her own right, serving two terms as commissioner in charge of police in Leonardtown. During her tenure, she decided that state police should leave local enforcement to town authorities, despite the law which gives state police overriding jurisdiction. She informed state police of her decision and made it stick.

The first Mrs. Mandel said, "I understand she's bossy—but she only wheeled and dealed in a very small county. It's a tremendous thing for him, that a woman seventeen years younger comes along. Once he marries it'll be the same damn thing all over again. He may want someone twenty-five, what's the guarantee?"

One longtime observer of Maryland politics said, "I really like her, but Bootsie would drive me nuts if I were married to her. Too much the talker, the hair all done up and sprayed, it looks as if she hit her head she'd bounce. She's of an age and a type. Jeanne's got a good figure and a pretty face, although she looks older than her age. It could just be as simple as that; that he was tired of it all after thirty some years."

The new Mrs. Mandel talked about meeting the governor at a dinner party long ago. "This may sound corny but we both looked at each other and we knew immediately. What was it about him that attracted me? He was so kind, so considerate, the most unpretentious man I ever met in my life. You could just see it in his eyes. Marvin has the most expressive eyes of any man I've ever met. They broke the pattern with him."

The first Mrs. Mandel told me "power" had turned her husband into an Adonis. "As soon as he became governor she went for him. If they were so 'in love' all that time why didn't she go after him when he was in the state legislature? She didn't want him then. Let's face it, Marvin's not an attractive man. If I were to do it over, he wouldn't appeal to me, at his age. Let me tell you, when we were young he was very cute."

The Mandels were married at the age of twenty and his career desires quickly became hers. Mrs. Mandel is just repeating what others have said: "I helped him with everything! I put him through law school. And politics?! He couldn't shake a hand. But he had the brains. From the very beginning he was very shy. I was the one who was outgoing."

Mandel in 1973 and 1974 had other problems as well. Stories of financial hanky-panky moved close to him; some of his closest associates were indicted. Mandel protested his innocence, but the tawdry aroma of machine politics remained. This, coupled with the Watergate backlash and his divorce, could have hurt if he had any serious opponents. He did not. "Because he's 'flaunting' this woman isn't helping him," his first wife said. But she was clearly upset that there wasn't more outrage at his pre-divorce activities. Before the divorce was final, she exclaimed to me, "She stays there with her kids! Now what does that do? And my children? How do they feel? He's not your average man. He's the *governor*. She's in the mansion, and taken around by the state troopers, and the *people of Maryland are paying for that!* Look, I'm not saying they should just be playing pitty-pat. No one expects him to. But in Florida or somewhere else in Maryland or even Timbuktu—am I right? But not in the governor's mansion." By midsummer of 1975 Mandel's troubles deepened as federal prosecutors, probing Maryland political corruption, subpoenaed his personal tax records.

If one is impressed by the trappings of politics, it is easy to feel "important" as a governor or first lady. When you visit Mandel's office, outside the huge reception room, in the State Capitol there are gleaming chandeliers and a marble staircase, cool to the hand. There are school children in windbreakers on tour. It is in the spring, a few months before Mandel's divorce is final. On the first floor the legislature is in session; a lot of mingling, moving, yawning, talking. Upstairs, power is visible and tangible, a state trooper guards the ballroom-size reception room. Aides stride, filled to the brim with their self-importance, past the trooper. He leans down and flicks a buzzer and the door at the far end of the room opens for automatic admittance to the inner chambers. In the large and near empty room, the trooper reads *National Geographic* listlessly. I was scheduled for eleven-thirty. I had dashed, nearly parked illegally. At twenty to one I was told I could go in.

Mandel sits like the Godfather. Cuff links flash the state seal. He does not get up. He can't. His recently injured foot rests on a pillow. He is a small man and there seems to be an almost imperceptible gratitude on his part that he doesn't have to stand up. A fire is crackling in the fireplace, the Oriental rugs are thick. Mandel is a pipe collector. His zillions of pipes and footballs and baseballs surround us. There are dark circles under his eyes that seem customary. He studies you as you ask questions; he warms to you seldom. First two aides stay as protectors—and inhibitors. It is tough to have an intimate conversation with two clearly biased observers hanging around. One leaves, the other remains throughout, sort of as a "second." I think aides take a course in "hovering." No apologies are made for being more than one and a half hours late. This seems strange from someone who is so "shy," a man who says, "I was very shy, not aggressive at all." I always thought that shy people had a residual concern for others. His secretary asks him what he wants to eat. I—who sat through the lunch hour waiting—clench in my stomach muscles at the mention of food.

When she leaves with his order, Mandel tells me he is a fluke politician. How a couple of friends wanted him to run for Democratic State Central Committee and "I didn't even know what the hell they were talking about." There was considerable infighting over the position, and Mandel was the appeaser. "In order to solve the fight I ended up in the legislature." I ask about his father. The answer is terse. "He was a clothing cutter in Baltimore." I asked if being Jewish hampered him in Maryland politics; he was among the first. "It was never a problem." No great Yiddish stories, no small talk, warmth, or humor, no reminiscences about that childhood are going to come from this man.

I asked, what about all that's happened in your private life? "I don't know whether people want to know about it. I think it's more the curiosity of the press. I think the average person couldn't care less about my private time."

Mandel admits that in politics your "private life suffers considerably. One, I don't have the privacy I should have, and two, even more so, you really can't do what you want to do. You have to do what the job demands of you; first time I went way in three years was six days at Christmas—even when I get away . . . well, there is just no way. There isn't anyplace you can walk in Maryland without people coming up. I'm not being critical, they're all trying to be nice. Everyone wants to know why they can't get you on the phone—these are people I've known all my life, I work with, and yet it's impossible to take all the phone calls."

For all his protestations about no time for fun and games, Mandel found himself in hot water this year when the press discovered that the governor and his wife, Jeanne, jetted to Jamaica in a plane owned by an oil company that was seeking state and local government permission to build and operate an oil refinery in southern Maryland. In subsequent disclosures, Mandel admitted ten free trips in four years on private jets as the guest of friends who do extensive business with the state.

We finally get to the divorce. I ask how he made the decision. "I think you have to make a decision about what's more important as far as you're concerned. As far as I'm concerned I did what I felt was important to me—and that's my private life. I love being governor, and, oh, I knew what the political risks were. But I felt what I was doing personally was important to me; you have to run the political risks."

Did Mandel agonize over his decision? His face is impassive behind the cloud of smoke. "Once I make a decision, it's final. Once it's over, it's over." No more discussion. Interviewing Mandel is a study in fencing and rephrasing.

He shows no expression when I ask how the divorce and subsequent publicity affected his children. "Fortunately both are grown, but those adverse stories, it affects them." How did he feel when his wife stayed in the mansion? "I just went around doing my job as governor." Was it humiliating and difficult for him? Again an impassive face. "I just did what I thought I had to do."

Was politics a factor in breaking up his marriage? "I really can't answer that." A sign behind his desk states, "O Lord, Help my words to be gracious and tender today, for tomorrow I may have to eat them." He doesn't have anything to worry about. He doesn't say enough to get him into trouble. Once in a meeting with legislators Mandel made a joking reference to women—that you couldn't get along with them and you couldn't get along without them. Pauline Menes, a member of the legislature cracked, "If anyone should know, Governor, it should be you." Although several people in the room heard her, Mandel appeared as impassive as ever.

His new wife says "he talks to few people." He is stilted in conversation and wary. There is a reserve that wasn't relaxed even on their campaign trip, the second day after their marriage. His new wife, aboard their "Honeymoon Express" campaign camper, was holding her husband's hand, patting him, touching him, but the governor was unable to show affection himself.

Mostly, Mandel is a supercautious, hardnosed politician. One liberal Maryland legislator said, "Mandel is very able, but he is too reflective of big-city politics for my taste, He is foreign to my feelings." Two subjects Mandel can warm to are politics and sports. Our longest conversation was about sports. For a little man he was good. "I played every sport there is. You name it, I played it. I was pretty good, if I have to say so myself. There was a scout who wanted me to play in the Eastern Shore league. My father said, 'Look, go to college a couple of years, if you still want to play then, you can. I got hurt playing in college, but I still had aspirations. I played some semi-pro baseball. My mother—she was active in charitable things, always at the hospital helping—hated me to box." He kept his fights a secret. "She only knew it when I got my nose busted."

He seldom reads anything for pleasure and books mean little to him. Once at a governors conference Mandel was invited to hear the late Pablo Casals give a rare, private recital. Mandel asked an aide, "Who's this guy Casals?"

Mandel's positions on many things remain a mystery. His moves are calculated and without passion. Reporters have trouble trying to label him. Richard Cohen wrote of the former lawyer for strip joints on Baltimore's notorious block, "He has dedicated his life to politics but his politics is dedicated to no cause—unless it is survival." This is why so many were surprised by Mandel's separation. But, in fact, the timing was characteristically calculated to reduce risks. He had a fat campaign fund and virtually no opposition. By working things out so that he could remarry before the election, he all but ended the talk. During his first tour of the state with the new Mrs. Mandel, people who had tsk-tsked a year before were smiling and cooing their best wishes. "I don't like campaigning, I *love* campaigning," bubbled the new wife.

The one puzzle remaining, particularly to those who knew Mandel's traditional background and close-knit family, was how he could have lived two lives all those years. In reality, that may have been the reason for delay. His concern for family and children may have manifested itself in the concept of "sticking it out" for everyone's sake, at least at first. When Jeanne Dorsey met him, his two children were sixteen and nineteen.

Looking back, though, his relationship with Mrs. Dorsey does make a mockery of the homebody and politically close Mandels as portrayed in earlier interviews. He was clearly waited on at home, his wife turning on the TV set for him, getting him his pipe. A familiar figure in the gallery during legislative sessions, she talked to the interviewer about how she managed the public life. "My advice to wives," she smiled, eyes crinkling, "is to have patience. I like the political life. I campaign with him."

Once she moved out of the mansion and was back in Baltimore, her husband's old district, Mrs. Mandel considered running for the legislature. "I had lots of encouragement and I know I could do a good job. It's something I know well." (Reporters who had covered the legislature shared her view.) "But I decided not to because of the children. The press would have a field day with me in the legislature and Marvin as the governor." She briefly became a TV star, co-hosting a Baltimore program on election eve and, for a change, saying very little.

Mrs. Mandel told some of her close friends that, in many ways, she was a victim of the politics she loved so well. She bitterly said that she wished her husband had never become governor—feeling that women like Jeanne Dorsey would not have been attracted to him without his title. Also, much of her own sense of importance to her husband, she feels, vanished when he became governor. "I used to help him with his speeches. Now he has a speech writer. I used to drive him everywhere. Now he has a state trooper."

Her new life is going along "fine" she said. "He can't hurt me. He closed the door when he walked out. He can't hurt me—

now." Her upbeat tone changed. "But the day will come when no one is there to hold his coat. The state troopers won't be there. He will have to settle down with her. She will just be the little wife. He is fifty-four now. It will be very difficult for both of them."

The new Mrs. Mandel had no such thoughts. "The thing that's important is that we're both so happy. I'm thirty-seven and he's fifty-four and it sounds so corny, but if everybody could be as happy as we are it would be a great world. This marriage can stand anything because it has stood it all. It . . . is . . . forever."

15
The Ultimate in Discretion

IN contrast to the Mandels, team partners who split with the ultimate of characteristic discretion were Abigail and Eugene McCarthy. In Washington, nothing is so stale as yesterday's politician. A political star, mobbed a few years before, every utterance worth a thousand xeroxed copies and front-page stories, is dropped by the press and other politicians when he loses power. Though the politican may voice the same views, post-defeat, the value has gone from his words. What was puffing him up was not so much the brilliance of his thoughts or rhetoric but the importance of his position. This is, of course, the most fundamental lesson a politician learns, but it is still bitter fruit— especially when one has been a national hero.

For Eugene McCarthy, politics and his marriage died together in 1968. His wife, Abigail, went on to write a book about her life which established her as a professional writer. Their three-decade relationship endured a seven-year broken courtship. The future husband meanwhile pondered the priesthood. Their subsequent twenty-six-year marriage encompassed early years when they both taught, as well as his struggles as a young Congressman, a Senator, and finally a presidential hopeful. She relegated their marital end to a cryptic and in some ways chastising paragraph in her book *Private Faces—Public Places*. "Gene left our home in August of 1969. He had long since come to the conclusion that the concept of life-long fidelity and shared life come what may—'for richer, for poorer, for better, for worse, in sickness and in health until death do us part' to which we agreed in the church—was no longer valid."

Later she maintained they could have weathered the changes and strains experienced in any marriage had it not been for that 1968 presidential campaign. It was bitterly divisive, with a staff that conspired to keep her uninformed and invisible, she said. "I ran a valuable operation but it was taken for granted, almost as though I wasn't present. You don't have any status, you don't have any office. They resent you because you *have* to be present. So then you are sent off to some fund-raiser and if your husband does need you emotionally, you're not here because, for Heaven's sake, they've sent you to Peoria. It's a fantastic and ridiculous situation." The candidate's wife is, she said, often considered "excess baggage."

She recalled reading a magazine article that mentioned how Mamie Eisenhower was kept away from Eisenhower on the campaign train. Mamie roomed farther down the train, while Ike's advisers roomed near him. Divisiveness, separate lives, the changes in their marriage and personalities that national attention either brought or highlighted—were these the reasons for a lifetime together to disintegrate? Others held different views on the McCarthys. One longtime friend of both Eugene and Abigail said, "They are both very bright people who competed with one another for years. The competition between those two was always fierce. I'm not so sure they ever knew it."

Other political wives have known Mrs. McCarthy's experiences but that 1968 campaign was even more tense than usual. The family felt threatened by ugly moods, and the candidate's wife was picked apart as well as the candidate. Within the camp she was pictured by some as the ogre who competed for her husband's time and expected royal treatment. She said her interest was his health and well-being. This went counter to others who first and foremost wanted him to be President. Still others pictured her as the driving—and driven—force. It was said that she wanted political power more than he. And there were still others who felt that she was forced into playing the heavy because McCarthy was so vague and ambivalent as the campaign grew into a national movement.

Whatever views McCarthy has on his marriage remain unexpressed. In keeping with his image of the somewhat lofty intellectual and poet, McCarthy refused in the most detached and unemotional manner to shed light on his private life. "I'll be glad to talk to you, but not about 'that particular case' " was how he termed his marriage. He had not even read Abigail's book.

This was in the spring of 1974, when McCarthy was the subject of such condescending comments as, "What ever is he *doing* now?" In August of that year, McCarthy surfaced again. Like so many who can never give up once they've heard the applause, known the adulation, and/or felt a "calling," McCarthy was into a political comeback. He declared for the presidency. McCarthy stated that he would be a "deadly serious candidate for the White House in 1976," however many liberal Democrats groaned when they heard of the announcement. These were the people who felt that McCarthy never wanted the presidency, would not have enough clout anyway, and would simply siphon off the support of other candidates of similar philosophical and political persuasion in a personally gratifying intellectual gadfly exercise.

Before the announcement of McCarthy's once-again presidential quest, he lived rather obscurely in Georgetown, writing a book on the changes in politics within the last hundred years, giving speeches and poetry readings, commuting to teach and lecture at New York's New School for Social Research.

His apartment is rather spartan, a perfect setting for the contemplative. A black leather couch with a throw, classical music wafting from a Victorian dry sink that holds a stereo, a small portable TV sitting next to a large gray chair. A trumpet and violin rest on one table as a still life. Camus and James Dickey, *Esquire, Harper's,* a magazine on foreign policy are stacked near a chair. McCarthy stretches his long blue-jeaned legs straight in front of him as he scrunches down on the couch. His hair is almost a white silver now, the sun slants into his deep green eyes. One tends to forget how very good-looking McCarthy is and, equally, how very distant he seems. He has always been engaging, witty, pleasant, disdainfully aloof and detached; a private man in a very public business.

We talked about his running for some office again and he said, "I don't have anyplace from which to run." He mentioned a "handful" of people who showed interest in backing him for the presidency.

McCarthy, to many, has almost equal portions of brilliance

and pettiness. It is a startling combination—his fine mind can dip to the most ungenerous grudge bearing if he feels he has been in some way slurred. He has never forgiven the Humphrey faction or the Kennedy faction of 1968. He writes letters to magazines when members of the press have, he feels, inaccurate views of political events involving him. He defends his right to "correct" them and says drily, "It's not petty—I had a real *reason* to get even. It was an accumulation of these things." "What do you think of Senator Mondale in seventy-six?" I ask (this was before Mondale pulled out of the race). McCarthy said he judged Mondale by what he did in 1968. "Remember, he was co-chairman of the Hubert Humphrey drive. You'd think he [Mondale] was born after the war." Eight years before that, McCarthy was himself campaigning earnestly for his friend Hubert. But 1968 ended their relationship. In 1974, a friend spent a long lunch with McCarthy and said later, "I couldn't get over it. He knew how close I had been to Bob Kennedy, but he must have said about ten disparaging things about him. He can't forget 1968, and he's so bitter! Christ—in American politics, that's ages ago."

There are others who remember McCarthy's engaging, poet-loving side. One night in the 1968 campaign he sat in a hotel room with his gentle friend and poet Robert Lowell. A political confidant recalls a rambling discussion they had. One poet asked the other what sounds he liked to hear. The reply was "Have you ever heard the night dew as it dries and shrinks on a barn door in the morning sun?" They were off in a poetic reverie while the politico was getting ulcers. Reporters were waiting, there were statements to make. Impatient mutterings to himself—how about one sound *he* liked—the roar of the crowd? McCarthy and Lowell were unheeding.

When I talked with McCarthy he said he liked his privacy so much that he felt it was almost an intrusion the day the maid came, a sharp contrast to most politicians, who need people around.

For all his contemplative nature, McCarthy seems curiously lacking in reflection. A close relative once said that McCarthy was "so unphilosophical—except ten years later. He never probes why people do things." It is not so much a disdain for the human element—more that he is unresponsive to and uncomfortable with it. During our talk, he clearly disliked uttering generalities but he was not interested enough to verbalize many opinions or even tentative conclusions about politicians and a world he knew. Questions about the psyche of politicians, whether they made good fathers, the effect of politics on his family, would often be answered with a somewhat diffident and impersonal "Oh, I don't know." McCarthy feels it varies much with the individual, but he was disinterested in trying to find patterns of behavior.

I mentioned that his wife said they could have survived had there not been the ordeal of the 1968 campaign. McCarthy replied, "Oh, I don't know. It might have been in her case." McCarthy was interrupted by a telephone call for a request to speak. He negotiated for $1,000—"I sort of half live on these things."

McCarthy said it was political tradition to exploit the wives from earliest time."Today, you see the wives holding Bibles, the children standing by as someone is sworn in. Some argue that it gives the children a sense of history, but I see it as sort of exploitation of the family."

Abigail McCarthy spoke to me of the excitement, sense of involvement and participation a political wife can enjoy and the importance of an effective political wife. McCarthy hardly shared such enthusiasms. "At times, candidates probably prefer their wives not having as active a role as some wives want. The sort of thing where you have the whole family doing the running. Bobby had all his brood there when he announced. [Ethel, in fact, rated a separate story about how she controlled her pack of children at the ceremony.] I never did. I think that's exploiting the family, and not good for the family." The extended use of the family "confuses the political process," McCarthy feels. It's cosmetics, just as issues and political meaning are lost when the emphasis on looks and charm and the politician/actor increases.

How important are wives to a campaign? "I think it's sort of mixed. I don't really know. Once we begin 'expecting' them to appear it has some bearing on the campaign." He did not mention his wife's contribution.

McCarthy recalls one memorable incident in one of his early campaigns when the use of the wives was disproportionate to their worth and unsettling to some of the wives. "I think it was the League of Women Voters. They had the bright idea of having the wives of candidates make speeches, sort of debate. There were several wives—Humphrey's and mine, and the governor's wife, some others." He laughs. "It was just like women's wrestling. *We* came out all right" (again, the team connotation). Another wife broke down in tears, however. "She was a nervous wreck because she felt she had not done well by her husband. Whether the wife could or could not debate was *not* and should not have been the issue."

Some politicians and their wives share one view of McCarthy's: "The private life of politicians is public—and there is no reason why it should be. For the entertainer, the private life *is* his public life—getting their jet-set private life into print is what they *live* by, but the private life of a politician doesn't really bear on politics. What we get into is a Peeping Tom prying that doesn't have real justification."

McCarthy feels that publicity about the family also often points up to sensitive children that they have done nothing to deserve the recognition except be their father's children—which adds to their sense of personal inadequacy and competition. Although often not home for children events, McCarthy says he was not as pressured as those who ran from close districts. "I never had a close race. And I think I had as much time with my children as, say, most top-ranking military men." (Many wives of top-ranking military men would say that was nil.)

Like all politicians, McCarthy does not mind, on the other hand, *favorable* personal publicity and he certainly reads the gossip concerning him. *"Women's Wear Daily* listed me among the seven or eight men most in demand for New York parties. Most of the others were hairdressers or dress designers," he said with a laugh. "I'm big in New York."

There is some bitterness about politics but he says, "All in all it's not a bad life, it's better than getting caught up in the corporate structure. In politics you get the feeling there are things you can do that nobody else can do."

McCarthy's emotions are more revealed in his poetry than in conversation. I asked if he experienced a depression after defeat. "Oh, no, not really." But his wife said, "No one understands what it is to nurse a man through a defeat. There is a depression of cataclysmic proportions—a loss like a death in the family. He questions how 'wanted' he was. A friend, a newspaperman coming home off the campaign for a weekend, said he was so exhausted he slept for twenty-four hours. I said, 'Yes, but I have the children.' And nothing can be done for the *candidate* because he's still out there and is in worse shape. Then when it's over there is such a sense of defeat." We talked about the unwillingness of many politicians to express or examine their lives. "Part of the problem is their egos are so fragile; the arena in which they are personally tested is so constant that they can't bear to look at themselves. It's much easier to handle humanity than it is their home."

We talked of the often blatant rivalry for a politician by his wife and family and the relative newcomers in his life. "This is probably a very basic problem. You have a continuous view of your husband as a person from the time you first met him. I suppose what they see is the *image*—what you see is something else. It is not *less*, but what you're being protective about is something they're not aware of." The husband often responds all too happily to the new and fresh view of him as he moves into "something so heady—he is feeling so needed by everyone."

How did she cope with those first months after their widely publicized separation. "It is a testimony to how separate this life does become over the years when I tell you that, actually, my life hasn't changed too much—except of course the lack of companionship you have in marriage." She has the same friends. She never derived her social identity totally from being the wife of Gene McCarthy nor living the congressional wife life. Her considerable writing talent also set her apart from other separated political wives.

After years of having a staff at her disposal—"somebody brings you an airline ticket, makes arrangements for the hotel"—she had one problem. So used to being taken care of, she joked, "I practically didn't even know how to go out the door."

The McCarthys with their strong Catholic background remain separated rather than get a divorce. Her religious background conditioned Abigail McCarthy for the supportive role she would lead for much of her life—"it led me to believe the wife subordinated whatever there was to subordinate." To me, she seems a woman caught with conflicting emotions about the political-wife role. She does not see that this "subordinating" concept can make these wives uninteresting in the eyes of observers, or that by playing such a subordinate role the wives themselves help to maintain a negative image. Instead, Abigail McCarthy is defensive of the women. "I resent the Washington disdain for political wives, many of whom are effective women. No one ever bothers to document these women until their husbands suddenly emerge in the limelight and then people say, 'Why she is so interesting and bright!'" This is true, but one of the basic reasons is the wives have compounded the issue. It is rather a vicious circle with everyone "conditioning" everyone else. On the one hand, wives, even as intelligent as Mrs. McCarthy, admit they censor themselves, particularly "after being burned once or twice by the press." (Even as we talked she amended and softened her points of view.) Then at times the press truly does enter the picture. Some *will* take a comment out of context and cause additional trauma on the part of wives. And others have just given up trying to get anything real out of these same political wives who censor themselves to the point of dullness. The least industrious in the press quickly place the wives in what? Mrs. McCarthy's aforementioned subordinate position. The press then does its part in, as Mrs. McCarthy said, "forcing us into a sickly image. These women are superb managers of a very difficult life, but they get asked what their husbands like for breakfast. After one election the photographer came in and said, 'Get the children, put the dishes on the table, look as if you're cooking on the stove.'" Mrs. McCarthy could have added that the public concept, perhaps conditioned both by the press *and* the political wives, was equally one dimensional. For example, Mrs. McCarthy had folders full of letters requesting her recipes. For years the wives went along with that image—the standard book written by women about Washington wives until recently was a recipe book. Many wives have no one to blame for their icky image but themselves. Why has it taken political wives so long to rebel if they indeed resent their stereotype so much?

"It is strange we acquiesced so," she mused. "I guess there is a raised consciousness about the role today." Most intelligent wives resent the ambiguity and the put-downs. "The position becomes in a sense a career—but without the rewards. You are sneered at as only 'wives.' I feel most everyone has no idea what

political wives actually do. I don't think it's a frustration as long
as you get credit or appreciation for it. On a campaign you have
responsibility but no authority. The staff often despises you and
ascribes all kinds of arrogance to you." Sometimes the "bitch"
role is assumed by the wife because it is important for the husband to appear the good guy. "People said I got some staff
members fired. I'll admit there were some I didn't like."

As a team player Abigail McCarthy found her supporting
role rewarding. However, today she admits her own writing
gives her more of a sense of "adequacy," although she is realistic that her chance to be a nationally known writer would not
have come without the McCarthy name. "I had gotten used to
that over the years. But you can use this to a good purpose."
The accolades that followed were all hers. An educated woman
with a teaching career, she willingly chose her political-wife
role. "I was someone in my own right before I married Gene. I
chose not to work, but to have children. I always had an identity
in Washington and in our district." It was only during the national campaign that she felt any real problems and a lessening
of her own identity and her own worth.

Various cultural and regional differences mean dissimilar
ways of adapting to that happy political family role she knew
for so long. Mrs. McCarthy is from the upper-middle-west re-
gion that has a tradition of female activism. "The University of
Minnesota was coed in 1849—Harvard barely let in women
three years ago," she said. Younger women who remember
back only to the 1950s forget there were educated women,
post-suffrage, who did have careers. "In the thirties, you were
embarrassed to admit it if you wanted to get married. There
was only one girl collecting silver when I was in college. I was
president of our union when I was a teacher. We had it much
better than those of you in the fifties. We were much more
liberated. In our home states, we women all made speeches. We
operated in teams and this was simply taken for granted." It
was only in the political structure of Washington, Mrs.
McCarthy said, that she realized wives and women were given
the back-of-the-bus treatment by a male-dominated political
world. "Whether those men know it or not, it is built into their
psyches that women are thus and so." Mrs. McCarthy was also
caught in conflicting currents about the role of wives. "There
are whole sections of this country that don't bother with wives.

New England wives for the most part stay home and don't campaign. In New York machine politics, I don't think they know politicians *have* wives. There is a long history of Southern women 'coping' way back before the Civil War; they just do it differently. I remember one Southern political wife who said to me, 'You Northern girls, you just don't know how to do things. If someone gives you a compliment you say Thank you. *We* say, "Whay aren't you sweet to say thayat!"'

Like such women as Eleanor McGovern and Muriel Humphrey and Lady Bird Johnson, Abigail McCarthy had a strong sense of dedication, believed that any personal sacrifices were worthwhile for politics. They accepted without question that this included long absences and family separations. "They all do it—it's in the life. In the beginning you do it because you think you 'should' but as time goes on, I think the man and the staff just feel the personal considerations *should* be very secondary. I think the absences are very bad for the children. They can't help but suffer if their father can't be there repeatedly for the recital or the football game or what have you. But it never occurred to me or to many of us to question the life we were living."

It was only in retrospect that she questioned the family deprivation. Still, she feels the political family who copes shares something many families miss today. "Political life can be a salvation—there is a *need* for the family to stick together. It is similar to the reliance of the extended family on one another in days past. Politics is something you, the family, do together." When the husband couldn't make an appearance the wife would take his place. "At times you feel like interchangeable parts."

The headiness of the national campaign brought changes in her husband. "It was almost like being separated, you campaign so much apart." Nerves frayed with lack of sleep and exhausting public confrontations. As for the family, "There was no effort to 'save' us, to make things easier, to see that you arrived somewhere in time so you could take a minute to simply look decent." The intensity of campaign life is often a reward in itself. "Some people tend to live from one campaign to another. On the campaign trail conventions just go by the board. When I was young I was very much a part of the fun of earlier campaigns. As I got older I got more walled off."

During the 1968 campaign and after the McCarthy separation, there was talk about McCarthy and other women on the campaign. (In addition, two rather devoted female reporters were nicknamed "little sisters of the press" by some of the male press corps.) McCarthy said, "I could have denied all that if anyone had asked me because there wasn't any truth to any of it."

Mrs. McCarthy was not unaware of the rumors about McCarthy and other women. I asked how one learns to cope with such public whispering about your life. "I don't really know. I think I was numb. The campaign had been bad enough. My only thought was how do I make a center for the children." While most wives face the possibility that their husbands, as Mrs. McCarthy put it, "might have a weak moment" on the campaign, many say they do not, perhaps in self-defense, spend much time considering other women a serious threat. She says she disregarded the stories. "You hear these stories about politicians and women but how is the wife to know? You know you don't tell other people when *you* hear those stories. The bearer of bad news is the one who gets shot. And I am so naïve, I wonder if it's really true." (One reporter on that campaign said, "Don't kid yourself. We all still think something was going on and she knew about it. That's why she was so mad about everything at the end.")

She saw, however, changes in her husband. "A presidential campaign, especially one like the one Gene went through, is exhausting and devastating physically and mentally. He had to be against his party, against his home state, people, for a principle. It was a dividing point in his life—and he had to divide from so much to do it. He cut himself off from so many things that mattered." She denies that she wanted any power. "I didn't want to be First Lady. It's just that sense bred into us Catholic girls that it's your duty and you do it. Inherent in the political family is the ability to count" (votes, precincts, primaries). "I knew it was never going to happen but we would die trying. To me it was worth doing. I think Gene was heroic to do it."

At the end of the campaign Mrs. McCarthy says she wasn't mad, but ill and exhausted. Looking back at photos, she is startled to see how haggard she was. With her separation came a change in her appearance. The bun disappeared and her hair, cut and tinted, framed her face.

Despite the rocky moments, Abigail McCarthy still sees political wifedom as a fulfilling life and says she would have remained in her marriage had her husband wanted to. To her, it was an exciting life in which a wife could become involved in her husband's work. In addition to the pleasure she derives from her four now-grown children, Mrs. McCarthy notes that her own private life would have been far less rewarding had she remained single or had married someone else. Had this been the case, she thinks she would probably now be a dean of a small women's college. She also feels that Washington is a better place than most for her—there is greater freedom, more opportunity, and less restriction on a separated woman's social and professional life.

She has been asked to run for office herself but Abigail McCarthy says she has no desire to enter politics. "It's a very hard life for the person out front."

16

Portrait of a Workaholic

WHEN political team marriages end in divorce, other political couples and the public as well look on with some interest, if not concern, at the splintering of long-depicted idyllic unions. Among the most notable examples were Senator William Proxmire and his wife, Ellen, who used to be his campaign manager. They were separated for three years before reuniting last spring.

Senator Proxmire, by dint of the defeat of other Senators, seniority, and ceaseless work, has moved up to head the Banking, Housing and Urban Affairs Committee. One to strike fear into every corporate potentate, Proxmire thoroughly enjoys his reputation as the ethical causist who helped dump such biggies as the SST and fought the Alaska pipeline and defense contracts. "Why, he's a self-confessed maverick," exclaimed one banker with a shudder. He is praised as an incorruptible people's advocate and is highly respected for his tenacity and capability.

Proxmire, fifty-nine, is not unaware that he is also regarded as one of your wackier and weirdo Senators—with his health doneok.

fads, his constant jogging, his face-lift and hair transplants, his unflagging devotion to getting his name in the paper. "But he's crazy like a fox," said one Capitol Hill observer. "Proxmire is one of the five best known Senators in the country because he works at it and because of his antics."

Proxmire's spartan approach to life includes no alcohol, no excessive eating, plenty of exercise. Through sleet and snow and rain, he daily jogs in his electric-blue jogging togs to and from his fourteen-hour day.

Proxmire sounds like a man devoted only to causes when he takes on corporate heavies, but he can throw temper tantrums if he doesn't get enough personal publicity out of it. Proxmire will send out a hundred releases to get his name into two newspapers. So adroit is he at dredging up ways to appear in the paper that when he was mugged while jogging, the joke was that he must have planted the mugger.

A familiar Washington fixture, motorists wave at Proxmire along his regular jogging route to the Capitol. He once got roses from a motorist who passed him every day. Proxmire is also known as the Prince of the Plant Gates. This is a political ritual whereby a candidate with the constitution of an ox gets up early and arrives at factory gates to shake the hands and ask for the votes of blurry-eyed shoemakers, pencil makers, textile makers, doughnut and cookie makers, garment makers, automobile makers. Once in predawn darkness, doing an early jog before going on his way to the plant gates, Proxmire tripped and fell flat on his face, drew blood, and had to have stitches in his lip. He was back at it the next day.

Keeping Proxmire in office is quite simply the number-one effort in Proxmire's life. His son, Teddy, in his late twenties and a maverick in reverse (he works for Xerox and has a consuming ambition to make money) sees why a marriage to his father would have to break up. "I think it is very difficult for my father mentally to give of himself what a wife would like. I can't see any woman getting out of my father what she would give to him. He gives to politics and he gives to his children. A woman is third, so to speak."

Prox, as he is called, doesn't deviate from that concept of himself either. When I stopped by his office to talk to him, Proxmire's newly transplanted hair was in the sprouting stage. It looked like grass peeking through the ground during a spring thaw—or one of those ceramic heads always advertised in the back pages of magazines. According to directions, you water the top and soon "hair" (grass) will grow.

Proxmire's seedling hair was of considerable fascination and it was hard to pull the eyes down to conversation level. The rest of Proxmire is somewhat antiseptically energetic. He is, naturally, slim, and there is a bounce and eagerness. He could still play "tennis, anyone?" roles. One man recalls that "Proxmire once grabbed some skin on my side and said, 'If you can pinch an inch of skin, then you're too fat.' Can you imagine how skinny you'd have to be to pass that test?"

Proxmire was quickly talking about politics. "Personally I love it . . . but it's very unfair to your wife. I'm a workaholic. If it wasn't politics it would be something else, but politics really is tough. One year I was gone fifty consecutive weekends. I had absolutely no weekend with Ellen. Of course, there are counter-pressures to stay married. Obviously, a divorce is politically damaging. A lot do their best to stay together, but how many political marriages—how many marriages, for that matter—are happy? In the Senate there have been a number of divorces since I've been here. No one knocks it like they did before, but there is a 'subterranean' feeling about it. If you openly display your family, maybe you can pick up a few votes on that score. A good political wife can be an asset. Ellen was great with me. It finally just became too much for her."

Proxmire, like most Senators, has not been free of presidential or vice presidential aspirations. While he said it remains to be seen if a divorced man who had not remarried could make it to the presidency, he preferred to brush that part of the question aside as he recalled his thoughts. "Oh, yeah, I fooled around last year with the idea. I had a colossal flattering victory in Wisconsin. I carried every county in the state. Look what happens. Lindsay ruined his political career. Muskie? Look at him now. McGovern won the nomination and what did he get? Nixon, what's he got? He's worse off than anybody." Proxmire showed little introspection, and far more ease in talking about politics than in probing any meaning behind his way of life.

At one time in a long interview, his wife, then separated, shook her head and said, "Bill is very intelligent and I regard him as one of the five smartest and most capable men in the Senate, but that did not carry over to an ability to see what was happening in the family. The whole family could be emotional wrecks around him and he wouldn't be aware." Nothing was to interfere with the regime Proxmire set for himself not to miss a single roll call, no matter how insignificant, go back to Wisconsin every week, to hit those plant gates at 6 A.M.

A regimented, "sacrificial" drive was there from earliest times. He gave up ice cream sodas for one entire year just to prove to himself that he could do it. He was twelve years old. Proxmire seems an excessive example, but most men who seek public office more often than not seem driven to prove themselves. Almost pathetically underformed, Proxmire was the scrawny ninety-pound weakling who disciplined his body. "I think it was more competitiveness than ego," said Ellen Proxmire. "He just hated to lose." Proxmire was competing for—and, to his mind, failing to get—his father's affection. He was the middle child with an older, adored brother who must have seemed everything Proxmire was not. Handsome, debonair, a rogue, he was killed as a young man in a crash. The brother was "absolutely adored by Bill's father. Bill felt even before he was a teenager he had to discipline himself to do things that would assure his father's love for him," Ellen recalls. "His father was a wealthy Lake Forest, Illinois, doctor and Bill wanted to live up to his every possible expectation. He plugged away at sports he was too small for. He had to get straight A's, and had the highest average of anyone who went to his prep school at the time of his graduation. He constantly set impossible goals for himself."

With his kind of drive came a tenaciousness his wife would reckon with when she tried to separate. It took him a long time to agree to a separation. When he did, Proxmire walked up and down the street of their Cleveland Park neighborhood and knocked on doors. He asked the owners if they were interested in selling their home. He found a prospect—just a few doors from where Ellen and their young son, Douglas (twelve, in 1974), lived—and moved in. Although separated in 1971, the Proxmires never divorced. The Senator maintained an open-door policy, popping in to see his son when he felt like it. Like the politician he is, Proxmire showed no embarrassment if his wife was entertaining friends. He would bound in and quite sociably greet everyone, like someone out of a Neil Simon comedy. Like many a couple who have no definite plans to remarry, the Proxmires seemed to prefer the limbo of separation rather than divorce. The feeling in Washington was that Proxmire didn't want a divorce for political reasons, but both gave the impression at the time I interviewed them that it was simply easier for all concerned, including their son, to remain separated. When they reunited both emphasized they thought it the best move for their son.

Proxmire had his eye on politics long before he met Ellen. When he was a student at Yale, he walked into Sherman Billingsley's Stork Club and saw the famous being stared at and fawned over and recognized. He dreamed with envy of the day that would happen to him. "I vaguely recall the incident," he told me. "I guess I thought if I were a Senator that would happen to me. It's a very secure feeling to have that attention."

The dream came true, but it was a lastingly loathsome situation for his two children, Teddy and Cici. "The thing I hated most growing up was we'd go out to dinner in Wisconsin, and it would just drive me crazy," Teddy told me. "Right in the middle of making a point, people would come by and stop and he'd talk to them. He was looking for votes. I used to get frustrated. He'd get wrapped up for ten minutes and I'd get so angry. Cici and I would talk to each other. Then he'd sit down and forget what we had been talking about. It would go on all the time. Everything from 'I've got a bet with a friend at the bar that I can't go talk to the Senator' kind of people to those who wanted to get their kids out of service or had tax problems. They were voters so you just could not turn them away."

Proxmire had been to Yale and Harvard Business School and was back in New York after five years in the army when his father suggested that if he were going to marry someone, he might as well marry someone who was rich. Proxmire, at the age of thirty, did. She was Elsie Rockefeller, a second cousin of Nelson Rockefeller. Proxmire even carefully examined the states he felt might be the best ones in which to launch a political career. He settled on Wisconsin and started out as a newspaper reporter with an eye to politics.

"Politics is kind of a subtle thing to get into," he told me. "There isn't any way you can start at the bottom in politics and work up. Ninety-five percent of the people who want to go into politics are excluded. You can't really run and have a steady job—and with a family to support, you *need* to work hard at a regular job." One needs more independence than that for politics and Proxmire had it in his wife's money. He started on the Madison *Capital Times* and he lasted a lot longer as a politician than he did as a newspaperman. Proxmire was working one night when an incident about an AFL woman official caught in a hotel room with another woman's husband came up. "She was fully clothed—there was no indication of anything wrong. The AFL people naturally tried to kill it and I thought they were right. We agreed not to run it but the *Journal* [a competitor] broke their agreement. It was terrible. It ruined the poor woman and they put me on obits. But the real reason for being fired was that I was very active in the union." He laughed and said, "One of the reasons I was willing to be fired was I figured I'd better start pretty quickly to run." He spent all his time running for state assembly; in six months he covered virtually every house in the district. In 1949, Proxmire was thirty-three years old. He ran for governor of Wisconsin three times—1952, 1954, and 1956—and was beaten three times. Proxmire decided that the "action was all in Washington and that's where I wanted to be. There comes a point where you want to have power and authority. The Senate gives you a great opportunity to try to make things better and there is no question it's a nice ego bath. You give a speech and people applaud."

Many of the Wisconsin liberals of the forties and fifties jokingly refer to the "incestuous" camp of friendship and politics. The Democrats were trying to form a viable party. "When Bob LaFollette died, the Progressive Party died. All that existed was a young bunch of men—Bill, Gaylord Nelson, Pat Lucey," said Ellen. Her first husband, Warren Sawall, now working for Senator Gaylord Nelson, was a newspaperman before he became professional organizer of the state party. Sawall was a heavy drinker and their marriage had busted up. Meanwhile, Elsie had left the politically consumed Proxmire for her second husband, Miles McMillin, the editor of the Madison *Capital Times*. Ellen, as executive secretary of the Democratic Party, was one of the few paid employees in those days when they struggled to get the party going.

Proxmire was one of the pack and he and Ellen didn't exactly date. They were working sixty-hour weeks in politics and what time was left over she spent with her children. "Bill and I had known each other for years. We were not in love at all. I thought he had a fine intellect. We each had two children the same ages. We just sort of drifted, comfortable. I . . . uh, one reason I wanted to marry again was that I really wanted the children to have a good father. I was to find out later he resented my children extremely. I was so determined to make the marriage work that I would feed the kids before he got home. With them not there, it meant less tension."

Since she had known Proxmire for so long, couldn't she tell that his workaholic nature would have led them into a marriage that meant loneliness and a separate life for her? "He never knew how to relax. There was never a candlelight and wine dinner just for the two of us." She laughs. "But when we were first married, he wasn't running for anything. It was right after he lost the governorship for the third time and I figured it was all over. He was different. He was still very driven, had to be doing something all the time, but it was better."

Proxmire's winning streak began with the death of a man who had destroyed so many people during his witch hunts, Senator Joseph McCarthy. Proxmire, characterized by newspapers more conservative than the *Capital Times* as the "chronic candidate yet to win statewide office," decided to run in a special election in August 1957 for McCarthy's seat. Proxmire was considered a "sideshow," a Yalie divorced from a Rockefeller who had identified with the common people so assiduously that he stayed in $2.50-a-night hotel rooms and wrote speeches on a typewriter in the back seat of his Chevy campaign car. His wife said that was no campaign gimmick. The support of four children and Proxmire's ever-constant pursuit of office had diminished their funds. Those hotels were all they could afford.

Proxmire decided to capitalize on what he was—a loser. One of his speeches went, "I'll take the losers. I'll take those who've lost in love, or baseball or in business. I'll take the Milwaukee Braves. The next Senator from Wisconsin should be one who has known defeat."

Proxmire won. "For the first time in our lives, we had a police escort, reporters trailing us and hangers-on who seemed to materialize from the night," wrote Ellen in her book, *One Foot in Washington*, published in 1963.

All American politicians were eyeing that election because of McCarthy's vast notoriety. The calls came in—Adlai Stevenson,

Lyndon Johnson, Estes Kefauver. There were parties and songs and confetti. At 1 A.M. they retreated to their hotel room. Reporters camped outside, telegrams poured in, the phone rang constantly. They had four hours' sleep. Proxmire was keyed up and more than a little lost. For the first time in months he had no campaign literature to hand out, no hands to shake.

The next day marked the beginning of a life-style over which Ellen Proxmire had little control. A flight had been booked for 4:30 that afternoon. Proxmire had to be sworn in in Washington. There was a momentary flood of tears. Ellen had no time to pack or buy clothes. She would not even have time to go home and say goodbye to her small children before they left. In her book, there was but one brief sentence about that sorrow. After all, winning was a "climax of years of hope and effort"— or at least that was how Ellen Proxmire said it then in her breathless prose that extolled the excitement, the joys, the political maneuverings of her life.

I did not know the woman who wrote that book—which is important in retrospect for what it did *not* say. It was a rosy and glorified picture of politics. Much of it Ellen Proxmire may have meant, but there was very little introspection, and only fleeting attention to the human problems. The following summer, 1958, the Proxmires' first son was born on July third and named William Wayne. He died the next day. Ellen wrote only one sentence about the incident. It was "a tragic blow to both of us and to the older children, but there was little time for sorrow and disappointment." Ellen was soon back campaigning and had set up a desk in her husband's Senate office. What she did not mention in the book was that her husband took off for an important convention in Wisconsin soon after the baby's death. She recalls it as two or three days later; he recalls it as a few weeks later.

Proxmire remembers that "it was years later before I knew she resented my leaving. She felt lost and alone. She had her two children and mine to care for and she was depressed." He feels his decision to leave at that particular time was not peculiar to a politician. "It's the kind of thing that might happen to a businessman or a newspaper reporter. It's a human thing. Of course, any husband could have said to hell with it, and not left, and I think I might have done that today. While that may be a poignant, dramatic example of what political families have to give up, there are other examples constantly in day-to-day life. The wearying and wearing thing is to go home to the state every weekend. It was very, very difficult for Ellen. I had two children and she had two, ranging from nine to thirteen and they required parental support. I was gone."

Still, Ellen pictured herself as the joyous young wife who faces with a smile three hours of sleep and the fishbowl existence and campaign days when you can't remember what town you're in.

Deeply into the helpmate role, she wrote in those days, "The greatest asset a politician can have is a loving wife whose encouragement and enlightened companionship mean much." Ellen Proxmire today appears to me much deeper, more sensitive and real. In her late forties, she is slim, young-looking, and attractive. In slacks and tennis dresses, her brown hair pulled into a ponytail, she has a sporty girl-next-door look. She has an infectious laugh, and although she was a capable political organizer and now runs her own wedding consultant business, there is no hard, charging aspect to her personality. As we talked about her life, there was some uncertainty about the future as well as some sorrow about the past. In many ways it was as if she had become a successful businesswoman and organizer almost in spite of herself. While she clearly enjoys it and has an independence about her, she was of a generation geared for marriage and feels that there is something missing without marriage. She would like a companionship she never had in either marriage.

Unlike her book's gung-ho accounts of fun on the campaign trail, Ellen Proxmire now recalls much of that time as an "extreme nightmare." Because Proxmire won in a special election in 1957, to fill the remainder of McCarthy's term, they had to go through the same ground all over again in 1958. Recounting her baby's death in a straightforward but soft way, she frequently punctuated her sentences with the phrase "Oh, it was just awful." It was in the hot days of July and she was frantically working on a shoestring as Proxmire's campaign manager. "It was all just a nightmare. I stayed in the hospital two days and then I had to get back to the campaign." Proxmire's leaving for Wisconsin was a "low blow for me. I was very depressed; I really wanted that baby."

Then it was November and the election had been won. Ellen

was pregnant again. "Saturday after the election, Bill insisted we all go to a football game out of town. I was so exhausted." She started feeling ill. "On the way back I literally had a miscarriage in a garage." She admits she did not take care of her health. "I've done some really dumb things. Part of it is so hard to put into words—there was just so much momentum, so many children, so much to do , always so much to do . . . you just go and do and don't sit and think why."

Their son, Douglas, was born in 1961. In 1958, Ellen thought "six beautiful years" but Proxmire "quickly announced that sixty-four would be an even tougher year and that 'I can't let up a bit.' We went four and one half years without a vacation—even a weekend."

The 1964 campaign was "heavy duty" time for her again. Hers was not just the handshaking sessions Lyndon Johnson once described as "coffee, doughnuts, and bullshit."

A few weeks before the election, Ellen argued that they had done as much as they could. "I remember I said, 'Bill—relax. Don't get up at five-thirty A.M. and do plant gates.' He said, 'I guess you're right. I should simmer down.'" When she got up, he was gone anyway.

She recalls the "incredible fatigue that sets in." The weariness in the bones, the inability to sleep well because the mind is on all that must be done the next day, day after campaign day.

"I was responsible for raising a quarter of a million dollars and handled fund-raising events in New York, Washington, Chicago; banquets in Milwaukee. After it was over, I was really physically ill. I remember collapsing in the back of a car." Coupled with the actual physical stress was a great deal of emotional strain of a mother who had to leave her children so often. "It was just so terrible. I'd feel shredded anytime I'd leave. We never had full-time help. We simply couldn't afford it. The four oldest were either in prep school or college. I never got any help from my first husband for child support." Proxmire was making in those days, first $22,500 and then $30,000. He was not well enough known to be asked to speak but later he subtantially supplanted his income by talking. "Bill inherited some money but it was for education costs and never for anything else."

Douglas was a toddler who felt lost and alone unless his older sister, then fifteen, was there. Ellen praises her daughter and says she took on a lot of responsibilities a fifteen-year-old "should not have had." Douglas was a "very dependent, needing child, particularly with Bill gone." When she would back out of the driveway to go on a campaign trip, Douglas would stand in the driveway and scream. His voice would echo in her mind long after she was in the airplane on the way to Wisconsin. "Everyday I used to wonder how we'd get through."

She had finally persuaded Proxmire that they needed a vacation after the election. "We were all set to go to Antigua and Bill said, 'I'm not going. I've got to go around the state and thank everybody.' I said, 'Well, I'm going.' He finally went, but even then his stress on constant activity wrecked it. There was six A.M. jogging, swimming laps. "It was not my idea of vacation. I'd want to sleep till noon, have a leisurely swim, eat dinner at eleven at night." As she sat there on the sand, Ellen Proxmire took time to reflect on her life and it was then that they decided to go more separate ways; with her dropping out of the world she had joined so actively to be with her husband.

She said she had done her last campaign. "I said, 'This is it, this is all I have to give, I'm out of it.' That's when Bill gave me a tennis racket and it changed my life."

For a woman who started the game then, when she was forty, she did very well. She also used her organizational abilities to plan tournaments and got so good that she plays tournament club tennis in and around Washington. The tennis group became her first real friends in a long time, almost since they left Madison. (Proxmire had been far too busy to socialize.) The tennis group knew each other by first names and many didn't even know she was the wife of a Senator, an anonymity she also enjoyed.

Although Ellen Proxmire is highly praised as an effective political organizer—her husband says, "She's smart as a whip at politics and I always said she should have run"—she says, "I'm not a public person. I found it very hard to make public appearances." In those days, no women's liberation movement was there to help anyone into rebellion if they were on the verge. "I accepted the role carved out, the helpmate role," says Ellen Proxmire. The aspect of "flakking" her husband and not having an identity of her own "really didn't bother me at all. I really viewed myself in a tertiary capacity, without any resentment about that part of it. The fact was, I just didn't want to do it at *all* in the first place. It's physically exhausting. Day after day on the treadmill—no fun, no joy, no gaiety." When the Proxmires were in Wisconsin they never were together. For maximum exposure they were busy hustling different parts of the state. Her schedule would sometimes hold five to ten coffees, teas, and luncheons a day. The only fun and "gaiety" was what the wives created for themselves.

One night in 1974, I was at a party given for Pat Lucey, the governor of Wisconsin, and his wife, Jean, who were in Washington for a governors' conference. Jean Lucey is a dark-eyed, dark-haired woman as tempestuous as her Greek heritage. She recalled a 1964 campaign in which Proxmire was running for Senator, Lucey was running for lieutenant governor, and the husband of another friend, Patty Reynolds, was running for governor. She and Ellen laughed as they reminisced about the three candidates' wives zipping across the state in a car with a campaign sign on the top that would blow off everytime they got past fifty miles an hour.

"We were speaking in a border town so Republican that they wouldn't let us three Democratic 'ladies' speak," said Mrs. Lucey. Since the hotel would not give them a hall for their meeting, the women refused to stay there. After their appearance in another meeting hall, they went across the river to an Iowa town to find a motel. They wandered into what they thought was a roadside restaurant but was more of a roadside tavern, The Pink Elephant. The men in the bar were more than mildly curious about these well-dressed women and moved in for a little conversation. They asked what the women were doing. Governor Lucey's wife took over. She pointed to Ellen and said, "This one sings," and then she pointed to the other woman, "and this one dances, and I manage them and we're on our way to Hollywood." After eating greasy hamburgers and rolling out their story as long as they could, the women left for a motel—only to find they were being followed by some of the men from the tavern. Finally the women told them who they were—and the men fled as if attacked. Only later did the candidates' wives stop to think of the adverse publicity their "Hollywood" story might have caused. As they told the story, it was punctuated by laughter. As Pat Lucey walked in from another room he said in mock boredom—"Ohhh no! Don't tell me we're back at the Pink Elephant bar."

* * *

Once in the Senate, the Proxmires found that entertaining was for business reasons, although this could be very stimulating. As a Senator's wife, she gave six dinner parties a year, mixing and matching those people important to her husband.

"We saw all the great minds, especially during the Kennedy years. One night we had the greatest party. John and Jackie Kennedy came and Chester Bowles and I can't remember everyone but it was just fantastic conversation." Such evenings were still "prepared entertainment. Everyone arrives at eight and leaves at eleven. It's never, ever, that 'let's have a good time and go get Chinese food' sort of fun. We didn't have friends like we did in Madison."

When her husband was out of town, Ellen Proxmire did not feel like going to parties alone. Proxmire is a man of few friends. He will not relax enough for that. In fact, Proxmire was in many ways prepackaged for the political life. His personality was perfectly suited for the heightened demands of politics. Ellen Proxmire contends, as do many, that politicians have an "'emotional shallowness.' They create a life so packed with things to do that are more 'important' or 'justifiable' than giving of themselves emotionally." This is one reason many of them are so good at the nonintimate darting in and out of people's lives that comes with campaigning. I asked Ellen how it felt when Proxmire was always appearing solicitous to voters. "That does grind at you some. I used to think about it when he'd go to county fairs. He'd shake hands with a thousand people—but he'd never have time to go to a PTA meeting or, for example, the fiftieth wedding anniversary party I gave at this house for my parents."

Her own sheltered, close-knit family with an ever-present father made it difficult for Ellen to adjust to her own marriage. Hers was a middle-class existence, growing up in Washington, D.C., pre-World War II when it was a sleepy small town. It was an old-fashioned life. You saw Grandma on Sunday and there was dinner every night with the family. There was a very disciplined, rigid mother—a member of Women's Christian Temperance Union—and there was not so much as a drop of wine in the house. "You didn't 'entertain.' What you did was 'have over' your aunts and uncles and 'family.'" Ellen Proxmire's voice trails off. "Life was so simple in those days." But it was also depression time. Her mother was a schoolteacher and her father was a graduate engineer from Cornell. During the depression, engineers were dispensable. Her father "walked the streets for months." He took a job at the age of forty in the patent office and went to law school at night, taking five years to graduate. Her father "never had the nerve" to put his legal knowledge into private practice and stayed in the patent office.

In a way she feels her family life was "almost too close-knit" for her own good. "When I did go to college I had never been away from home. Although my mother was a schoolteacher she was 'very domestic.' I still prefer to be home than anyplace else. Everytime I would end up in a hotel room in Hurley, Wisconsin, I'd think, 'What am I doing here?'

"Once a year we went to Glen Echo amusement park. Once my older brother saved up money and took me to see Rachmaninoff. Going to see him was a luxury." The work ethic was planted early. She went to Westhampton College for Girls at the University of Richmond, graduated with honors, and was president of the junior class. In her senior year she met her first husband at a dance, one of the many men returning from the war. They got married in her senior year and she transferred to the University of Wisconsin.

Raising five children, mostly by herself, was far from easy, and it was compounded by the feeling on the part of the children and herself that Proxmire openly favored his own children over her two daughters. Teddy said, "If he had time left over it sort of went to Cici and me first." While he could not give of time or emotions, Proxmire gave money and saw that the children went to the right schools.

One problem was that Proxmire was so competitive he never had any fun with them. "If he played ping-pong he not only wanted to win but he just had to demolish them," said Ellen. None of the older children is married except Ellen's daughter, Jan. Her other daughter is divorced. The child who came out of it best was Douglas, a handsome young boy who is described as the politician in the family. He idolizes his father, loves to campaign, and was handing out campaign buttons before he was three. He is engaging and likes sports and Proxmire now has the time to spend with him that he didn't have in his climbing days. "One of Bill's books talks about how you should relax and be gentle with everyone. That's not him unless he's taken a 180-degree turn. He didn't have a bad temper, he was just unbelievably demanding. Why, he's a horrible driver because he's so competitive!" said Ellen.

Interestingly, Proxmire does not see the same things that his wife, or even his oldest son, Teddy, see when they talk of the family. "We're lucky as the dickens. The kids are just marvelous. I never indicated one bit of difference in anything I've ever done for any of them. Little Douglas was elected to the student council at Landon. He's the politician. The oldest don't want anything to do with it." He adds, hastily, "But they're good, decent, fine kids. They have entirely different value judgments. Ted has no strong social values, he never wanted to get into politics. He likes to make money. My daughter, Cici, is very feminine and not interested in a career. Douglas is the real jock. We saw the Chicago Cubs play four days straight on our vacation."

Ellen recalls that "those long years when Bill was gone had their effect on Teddy. The impact of politics on your life is that it is constant. Even a reporter knows he can let up at times. Then, when Bill did have the kids he crammed unrealistic activity into every moment—eating out, sports events."

Teddy was a classic example of a son who rebelled against his father's way of life. He did not campaign, he became an "unbelievably nonmotivated teenager," said his stepmother, who now has a good relationship with Teddy. A hell-raiser, fun-loving, easy-going, carousing Teddy couldn't have been more opposite to his father. Immensely likable today, he and I had a long lunch-hour conversation. Like his stepmother, he often talks of his father with affection, as if he is some distant character who is so vastly different that it intrigues him. Teddy is also very loyal to him.

"Your first year or two away from home in college, so much hits you in the face and you sometimes find it difficult. With me, I got to know myself as Ted Proxmire, period. Not Ted Proxmire, son of Bill Proxmire, the Senator." One important factor is that political children whose fathers are respected acquire a sense of well-being. There are not the psychological scars that come if their father is unpopular or vilified. "Madison was an extremely Democratic ward and Father was very, very popular. Had I grown up a Republican I guess it might have been different. And when I went to school there he was well respected and looked up to by my peers." There were two problems: no matter what scrapes he got in, Teddy worried about it reflecting on his father—"You gotta watch out. If you do something at all controversial you gotta do it smart and not get caught." The second problem was that Teddy "grew to be skeptical of people. Because of the position of my father, I wondered if people were interested in Ted Proxmire because of myself or because of my father. Maybe I have a cynical view. . . . My father's very different from me. He really doesn't have cronies. I understand in his earlier life he never had anyone close to him."

For all their differences, Proxmire did not foist his own way of life on his son. "I was sort of wild. I once got picked up for juvenile drinking and I was so worried it would hurt his chances for reelection. He wasn't concerned about that." Teddy defined "juvenile drinking" as the kind of thing you do when you "want to be accepted by your peers. I was sixteen or seventeen; if you had three beers, you were pretty drunk." Being protective of his father, Ted said, "Even though he was gone all the time, he always called home every night. I was able to talk to him. If I had a problem he would ask if it could wait until he got home. And my stepdad in Madison is terrific. If I couldn't get my own dad I could always talk to him. In my senior year I got kicked out of boarding school for drinking. It was a bad year. I know this took a great deal of time out of my father's own life—helping me to adjust, helping me get into another private school." As he recalls the incident, it was "basically a beer party. A little vodka. I can't remember how we got caught. Two of us were kicked out to make examples of the situation. The other boy was president of the senior class." His own friends tried to protect him. "They said they'd take some of the blame because they knew Dad was a Senator and they didn't want to get him involved."

Ted recalls, " When I was a kid I was forced to read an hour a day." He adds with an engaging grin, "I would spend seven hours thinking about ways to get out of it." He laughs at how different he turned out than his father. "When I was eighteen or nineteen, I'd be coming in at the time he'd be getting up to jog. He knew I wasn't out stealing hubcaps or anything but a favorite quote of his was 'How in hell can you be out doing anything *constructive* until six in the morning?' I'd have some guys over and we'd be playing cards and we'd let out some four-letter words. Dad would come down and watch us and ask us, 'How much you guys playing for?' He seemed to want to talk to us. In a way I probably reminded him of his brother and he might have thought these are some of the things he missed. There are only so many hours in a day and my father's biggest enemy is time. I really admire the way he gets it on. He works fourteen or sixteen hours a day." He defends his father: "Pleasure to one person is not to another. Pleasure to him is working. His idea of pleasure is having a coat and tie on on Sunday, poring over what he's doing. Working sixteen hours a day, that's the way he gets off, so to speak. When some fat slob goes on about my father's jogging, I feel like saying, 'Buddy, the shape you're in, you could use it yourself,' but you have to be diplomatic."

Ted consciously turned away from politics. When he was young "it was just more fun playing baseball and screwing around with my friends than going on some political thing. He never really placed any demands on me. I think I tried to divorce myself from politics. To be perfectly honest, I don't give a damn. My life is my life. I don't want to be compared with him. No one serves his constituents better than my father does, but when I was in my teens I sometimes wished he'd get out of politics, basically for selfish reasons. I used to be somewhat ticked that he wouldn't use his position in any way like others would do, say to get Redskins tickets or something I wanted to do. He always said it was too controversial. I respected him for that, but I would think, 'This one time, can't he make this one sacrifice?'

"I definitely tried not to emulate him. I think I realized at an early age—well, I look at it like a ball game. If I went into politics, there is no way I would get a victory or even a tie game. I would definitely come out the loser. I don't want to be a loser. I just couldn't compete with him and win, and I chose a completely different path. I am much more money-oriented. To me, my goal in life is to be a very rich man and to be self-made. All I'm interested in is developing myself." This means a different pace than his father's—"I own my own home, I party quite a bit, I date quite a bit. I work hard at times, but I have fun."

There were very special pressures growing up as the son of a well-known politician—"When he came to the school in Wisconsin he was never 'just a father.' And I can remember when he was defeated in 1956 for governor. I was nine and all my friends were saying what fun I was going to have living in the mansion. I can remember how bad I felt when I saw the headline that said he was beaten." But there was also extreme pride in his father, Ted says. While his father's travel and interest in his own work meant they were "never super close," Ted no longer sees that as a minus. "I was given a lot of freedom to be me."

Proxmire's hair transplant and face-lift came as a surprise to his wife. This is the man who gets lost in his work rather than women. (When I interviewed him, his compliment was as male-politico obligatory as it was corny: "I really enjoyed talking with you—you're one cute dish.") "Having to be youthful doesn't fit with his aesthetics. He never cared about clothes. He'd just as soon eat a bowl of cornflakes as a gourmet meal. Nothing in his life reflects a need for glamor—especially to go through the pain and the expense," said Ellen. Proxmire's reason for the hair transplant was he didn't like the image he saw of himself on TV. His son said, "I think it was for purely political reasons. When he watched himself on a taped TV show he'd be very upset about the way the light glowed on his head. He said it made him look ten years older than he felt. Let's face it, no one wants to look old."

In 1967, Ellen took a plunge that would carry the Proxmires farther apart. She started, along with some other women, Wonderful Weddings, Inc. Despite the counterculture, there are many young people who want weddings and, consequently, guidance on them. "The wedding business is steadily growing in terms of money spent—there are two million brides a year. No matter if they have lived together three years and wear blue jeans all the time, when they want to get married, they want a nice party and families still need help. It's a very emotional time." Out of her first project grew another business, called Washington Whirl-Around. Ellen Proxmire's latest venture is planning sight-seeing programs for the families who attend conventions. "The forgotten quotient of conventions is basically the wife and children."

After years of a "separate" marriage, Ellen Proxmire decided it was ridiculous to keep it going, but her words couldn't really impress her husband with the urgency of her feelings. In reality, they had long ceased to be a couple and Ellen finally wrote him a fifty-page treatise, examining the quality of their life together, and gave it to him one morning. At first, Proxmire agreed to leave, then later in the day changed his mind. One lawyer, who charged a retainer of $1,500, suggested that since she had no grounds, she should make life so uncomfortable that the Senator would *have* to move out. That seemed distasteful and petty and juvenile to Ellen. She couldn't do that, so for another six months they were living together. It was pretty much of a standoff with little resolved.

So used was Proxmire to his way of life that he apparently made little attempt to change during those six months. Then one night he came bounding in from an appearance on the Dick Cavett show, full of his performance and acting as if everything was the same. Ellen Proxmire's pent-up frustrations did not stay pent up for long. Picking up an ashtray, she threw it and it smashed into a million pieces on a coffee table. It was the first thing she had ever done that made Proxmire realize how she felt.

When they were living their separate lives—with just a few houses separating them—Mrs. Proxmire reflected on divorce and separation. "I really didn't realize how hard it would be." She felt her name hampered some men interested in dating her. "It's not like going out with Suzie Glutz, although it should be." She made more friends than when they were living together and went on ski trips with a woman friend. Many attractive women past thirty-five face the grim fact that few men in Washington are available. If unmarried, they usually have problems or don't like women, and if divorced there is an inclination to date younger women. Many shy from the responsibility of handling a woman and children. It is not difficult to be spoiled by the availability of women if you are a Washington male. And to complete the circle, a large number of "successful" Washington men are overachievers not unlike her husband, who have little time for the women in their lives. Ellen was frankly shocked at how difficult it was for her to have a rewarding social life after their separation. "This is just a terrible town for older divorced or separated women. I say to myself, 'You're lucky, you're healthy, you have wonderful children, friends.' I'm interested in and get satisfaction from my work—but still, life is not full unless you have someone really in your life to share it."

And the Senator? His is more tunnel vision. The troubles of Watergate don't make him introspective about politics, nor does his less than rosy private life. "Do I ever wonder about the life I picked? Oh, no, no, no, no. Not me. Being a U.S. Senator from Wisconsin is just the best job on earth. I am helping to change things. There was the enactment of the truth in lending act, stopping the SST, the consumer credit bill. A lot can be done. No, I'm not disillusioned in the slightest. I wake up every morning just as excited as I can be."

After they were back living together, Ellen admitted that Proxmire had learned no lessons in those three years. Asked if he had changed; slowed down politically and taken more interest in her and the joys of togetherness, she laughed and said, "Are you kidding? You know Bill." Had she found someone else to share her life with in those three years, the ending might have been different. But now she seems to have accepted the fact that her life is a compromise. She said with a barely perceptible sigh, "Maybe this is simply all there is."

17

"This Profession Is Terrible Competition for the Wife"

WHEN husbands leave their wives of long standing, much is said about the "other woman." Many political marriages break up over other women who work in politics. In that respect, politicians are not unlike men in other professions who find companionship with female co-workers—except that there is more publicity involved—and more opportunity to find women interested in their power position. While young secretaries and receptionists are often attractive diversions, when it comes to leaving home and remarrying, the woman is many times an aide who knows that a way to man's heart is through the latest bill he's introducing. She sometimes is almost as serious about her job as she is about her boss.

Governor Mandel's new wife was a county commissioner in Maryland; former Maryland Congressman Lawrence Hogan, who ran unsuccessfully for the governorship in 1974, married his administrative aide when he divorced his wife of twenty-five years. Al Ullman, who moved up to head the House Ways and Means Committee following Wilbur Mills's disastrous episode with "another woman," was in his late fifties when he divorced his wife of twenty-eight years and married an office worker. Both Michigan Congressmen Don Riegle and William Ford met their second wives on the Hill. Some second wives, such as the wives of Senators Russell Long and Fritz Hollings, are considered decided pluses. Many in Washington retain the view that the first wife was, after all, a person who just couldn't keep up with her husband's life . . .

Don Riegle was a young Michigan Congressman who made a quick name for himself in the early seventies as a Republican maverick. Older conservative Congressmen joked about his long hair. He was on the side of the antiwar protestors and in his office there is still a picture of him shaking hands with then President Lyndon Johnson. The President, like a senior professor chiding a young pupil, inscribed his "hope" that Riegle would think better of him "with age." Riegle felt he could do little to change the Republican Party and moved across the aisle to join the Democrats.

Along the way, Riegle wrote a journal about his congressional life entitled *O Congress*. It was billed as a trenchant look at Congress but this personalized account by a newcomer was viewed by many on the Hill as a lightweight effort. Among those unhappy with the book was Riegle's former wife, Nancy. The breakup of their sixteen-year marriage was given a few paragraphs. Nancy also felt that the references to her husband's secretary and girlfriend, who became his second wife, were disturbing to the Riegles' three children.

At one point Nancy Riegle spoke freely, if bitterly, about what politics does to marriages. In one interview she said that her husband's ego was the cause of their problems. Because the husband rationalizes his devotion to "causes"—when "all they want to do is see their name in the paper"—the wife is left to "raise the kids alone. She takes care of fallen trees and the shopping and broken cars. In the long run, it's a lot easier for her to make her own decisions than wait for some stranger who comes in every two weeks," she said. "These men would sell anything down the river to get ahead. Good people just go to the dogs to get money to stay in power. And they wind up using so much, there's hardly any left for kids' shoes and food. Sure, they raise funds, but something always happens, like a brochure doesn't get out in time because the funds have run out. So rather than not have the brochure come out, you shell out a few thousand dollars to pay for the printing. Don began to be more and more anxious for power. He got caught up with the 'who I am and what I can be' syndrome. He began to believe what he read in the papers about himself. He relished the applause and the acclaim. All politicians start off with a bad case of ego. Who else would put themselves in a popularity contest every two years?" Nancy said they went to a marriage counselor who said the problem was basically her husband's. According to Nancy, the counselor said, "He is an extremely selfish individual who always puts himself first. He has to be constantly adored. And until he faces up to the fact that he's just another man, he'll go from one secretary to another, from one wife to another."

More than a year later, Nancy said, "I blush every time I think of that interview. It sounds so terribly strident. I really want to put my life with Riegle behind me now. And yet I think people should know what politicians are like to their families; but how can you explain what politics does to a marriage without sounding like some shrew?" She would not elaborate, on the record, except through a written statement.

One friend said, "It's the darndest thing—I like Don, Nancy, and Meredith [his second wife]. I can see where Meredith is suited to Don; Meredith is quiet and calming. Nancy is just a different person, but she's equally as nice." A child psychiatrist who worked with both Don and Nancy said, "I think it was a personality conflict between Don and Nancy. To get them in the same room at the same time was a problem. But they were both very concerned about their children and worked together concerning them. And they were both very attractive people individually."

Nancy, a pretty, fresh-faced blond in her mid-thirties, has a dynamic, excitable personality. She has gotten involved in art classes since her divorce and says of the political life, "There's a big world out there—and yet they all think it all begins and ends on Capitol Hill. It's all so kind of silly—you get so caught up in politics. We were just like so many people up there. We took ourselves so seriously."

She handed me the note she had carefully composed. It was a more controlled comment, but an indictment nevertheless. "Political marriages certainly are very difficult, since these men are so involved with their jobs. Although this is also true of doctors, professional men, and salesmen, life in Washington brings out the ego and drive for power in a unique way. Politicians often rearrange traditional priorities and let their families slip into the background." So "consumed" by their ambitions and causes, Nancy wrote, politicians "lose their sensitivity to people—so they're nearly impossible to live with happily." The character and maturity of everyone involved is "important," she noted. "In my own situation, political life certainly aggravated an existing problem. I doubt if our marriage would have survived regardless, because my ex-husband is basically a 'user' of people and displayed the cruel capacity to distort truth and facts to serve his ends—regardless of the consequences—for his personal gain. It makes me frightened and sad to think of the power invested and misused, and the potential wasted, in politics today. There are some politicians you can respect, however, and so there's always hope—although I prefer not even to think about it anymore. I've found so much contentment in my new life, that it's depressing to look back at my former marriage with such a selfish person. Politics is a natural arena for his type, I'm afraid."

Riegle, however, thinks of himself as a "sensitive" man. He talked about his former wife's description of him. "Most people who know me don't think that's true." The Riegles were only in their teens when they married. Don admits that he was "driven to accomplish things," and that he also went through a long period of "introspection." He spoke often about "rebalancing" his life and "getting in touch with yourself." He recalled his attempt to enter the business world (as a junior executive at IBM) as "very upwardly mobile." He spoke about how it was invaluable that new attitudes were helping people to "break out of those role stereotypes we got loaded up with in the fifties." Riegle said he and his new wife were sensitive to the roles foisted on political couples, admitting that he did not think "much about such things in the past." His new wife, in her late twenties, was "just that much younger that she won't be forced into any roles, including probably having three kids with anyone. We're very sensitive to this role thing. She feels very strongly that she has to do her own things. She's a full-time editor at

Smithsonian magazine, and Meredith makes a conscious effort to make sure her own identity doesn't get lost or swallowed up in being a Congressman's wife."

Riegle reiterated the common complaint of politicians: "There is never enough time to do what you want to do. You have to *force* a balance in your life. I try to spend Sunday with the kids. I found I had to build in time into my schedule for the kids. But in these eight years in this job, I think I've managed to get more in touch with myself. The divorce troubled me at first, but then I realized these things don't happen to you or your kids in a vacuum. Others go through it, too."

One of the conflicts of politics with one's private life, Riegle said, is that a politician is vulnerable to the daily public examples of defeat. "You get beaten on publicly every day and if you're sensitive, you have to put up a protective shield just to see that you don't get obliterated. This makes it much harder to be in touch with someone else or yourself." Speaking of the demands of constituents, Riegle said, "It's as if you, a reporter, had 450,000 editors, each one with different requirements, demanding that you meet them. And then, on top of it, you have to miss your child's birthday to give a speech. Every day it's an enormous juggling act. I think what happens is that the tension ends up internalized. The anxiety gets bottled in. Everybody has a different tolerance level. Some try to cope too much." (One Congressman told me of a colleague who was so conditioned to his own "nice guy" image that he couldn't explode in front of anyone, including his staff. To relieve tension, he would go in his office bathroom, shut the door, turn on the water, flush the toilet and scream.) Riegle was considered a man of considerable gall when he said, as a freshman Congressman, that he wouldn't mind becoming President. He now looks on it as a "miserable job" that attracts, among others, men who do not mind giving up the "human" aspects of life. "We've got to reorder what we consider important so that decent, sensitive men can become President."

The "other woman" lingers in the minds of many wives who thought their marriages were secure in the past, if for no other reason than the stigma of a political divorce. For example, one grandmother in her late fifties still seems shattered by the actions of her Congressman husband. He left her for a "younger woman"—of fifty.

Since his divorce, he has moved into one of the most powerful positions on the Hill. His ex-wife is a well-kept woman, slim,
her hair slightly tinted red. There is nothing easygoing in her
manner, in the way she sits ramrod straight at the dining room
table. It is a spotless home, filled with grandfather clocks, oriental rugs, bric-a-brac collected on her husband's European junkets, and the floating treacle of Muzak. Her children are grown
and the woman seems quite alone with her memories. She
keeps track of every political divorce she reads about in the papers. Clips them, files them, refers to them.

She tells her story in whiny, long-suffering tones; altogether a
dreary woman who, at the end of a long afternoon, weeps as
she says goodbye. Her only identity had been through her husband, and she has not readjusted her life, although it had been
more than four years since he left home and nearly three since
he remarried.

"I have to go on, even after I am rejected by the one I loved
and trusted. I had been crushed to the point where I couldn't
talk to anybody. But I don't hate. I thank God every day for this
difficulty. It's taught me to become strong." She does not believe in psychiatrists, and feels they need more help than their
patients. She is from the far west and she pictures Capitol Hill
as a Sodom and Gomorrah unfit for Bible-reading people like
herself. "The divorces you read about in the papers are only
the half of it. So many of those Congressmen are quite open
about living a 'double life' with the girlfriend and then having
the wife and family too. If the family isn't worth anything, then
the nation is going to fall—you mark my words. They're carrying on this double life. You know Carl Albert's always dashin'
around."

The former wife said that a "loosening of morals kind of
started in the Kennedy and Johnson days. Money is the root of
all evil, but so is power. These men go berserk. Rockefeller
thought his wife wasn't a showpiece like Jackie was, so he
dumped her. If Mandel can leave, they all think 'Why can't we
leave our wives?' The nation's leaders set an example for everyone. In fact, that's what one Congressman said as an excuse to
his wife when she found out he was playing around. He said,
'Everybody's doing it.'"

I had talked to the woman a year before and she was still on
the one-note theme she had begun with me at that time, although she says, "I'm not as shook up as I was then. Everyone

says I look more beautiful and I feel a lot better. I'm not a religious nut, but I go to meetings with a group and it's been my
salvation."

The former wife sees the real casualties of politics as the
wives who "knew their husbands when." She dabs at her eyes
and then gets angry. "Most all of these men were brought up
with patches on their pants. Then when they get higher up they
don't want the wife around. These men just become power-
hungry. There was a real change in my husband once he started to move on the Hill. And then they go berserk over a secretary who in turn becomes more powerful. She has the key to his
door and everyone knows it. She travels with him. The wife's
not welcome. You've got the children and he says you've got to
stay home with them and you believe him. And yet you're the
one who struggled hard to get him here because that was his
dream. . . ."

During World War II she lived with her family and took care
of their children while he was in the Navy. "After the war I
scrimped and saved a thousand dollars and economized on
meals so he could run. Why, you go back to the state and all the
older people will say he wouldn't be in Congress if it weren't for
me and my family. When he got up in the clouds so high, he
forgot who helped 'way back.' Why, back home he can't even
look some people in the eye who got him elected. He's forgotten those good friends. He's in a bigger ball game now.

"His days as a family man ended when he came to Washington. From then on it was his 'fishing trips with the lobbyists.'
Oh, there were the oil companies who flew him to Hudson Bay
and on another committee trip they all went to Paris on the taxpayers' money and had a good time. DuPont, Chase Manhattan, the timber and oil people—they are all nice to you when
you get on an important committee."

Her husband had a girlfriend for many years before the wife
knew about it, she said. Like so many of these women who profess surprise at the break-up of their marriages, one has to wonder whether there was a purposeful putting on of blinders or
whether the amorphous "duties" of a politician's job are such
that he truly can, as one wife suggested, "easily live two different lives." This wife also contends that with so many factors all
designed to insulate the politician from his family, it is easy.

"A lot of 'em take the attitude that 'What I do in Washington is my business. If I want to wheel and deal I can, because here is where I am.' The people back home, three thousand miles away, don't know. Back home they will not flirt with waitresses, get drunk and act silly. Why, Dingell, who is so outrageous, when he's back in Michigan he's holy as a preacher." (She was referring to Congressman Dingell, who left his wife of many years. When I asked the former Mrs. Dingell if she wanted to talk to me, she said no. "I am sick of politics and everything about it. My husband acted unbelievably. He's just an abomination! Why anyone would want him as their representative, I wouldn't know!")

The ex-wife continued, "I can't tell you the number of women I've helped who are just left around this town. Politics is all rigged against the wives. It affects the children. They don't want any part of government. And in nearly every case it's a secretary. I had a college degree; *she* just barely got through high school. Why, I know dozens of those men who are 'playing double.' Their wives are under tremendous strain. I just say, if they're 'too busy' to come home, watch out. If they've got time for a secretary and lunch and cocktails, they've got time for a wife."

This axiom of hers was something she never heeded until it was too late. "That romance of his went on four years and I was the last to know. The children noticed it. They'd say, 'Dad isn't very nice to Mom.' I thought he was sick. He came from a fine family and he comes to Congress and falls in love with this woman from Maryland. She was ambitious and she moved fast. She came in as a clerk-typist, just a little clerk-typist doing the dirty work in the back room. She had a husband but she unloaded him fast. She just wanted to marry a title. She moved up the ladder pretty fast. Became a receptionist on her 'personality.' Couldn't even write a good letter! They'd have office parties and there she was at those office parties with the banjo music and the drinking. When the staff gave him a present, she made sure he was aware that she went out and got it. As I say, I was the last to know about her. The staff works against the wife and family. They just build up a wall. I held out for over a year after George [not his real name] left home—I didn't know about her until then. She got some of the old staff people fired and they told me about her. She is tough and pushy and she got them out of there. She didn't want to be reminded of the past."

She remembers the day her husband walked out as if it were yesterday, although it was four years ago. "He was here the night before, and then, in the morning, without so much as saying anything to me, he walks to the school bus stop with our son—he was sixteen at the time and the last one at home—and he tells our son, 'I'm going to leave.' Then he came back in the house. I heard the door close. I had on my pink robe, combed my hair, and had put on a little lipstick. I walked into the kitchen and then he told me right then and there that he had told our son he was going to leave. I started crying and said, 'We need you, we love you,' and I kept asking him what was wrong. He wouldn't give me an answer. It was snowing and he wanted me to follow him in my car to see the lawyer. Just like that. I said I couldn't drive or see the lawyer, that I'd cry." Recalling the incident, the woman started to cry. "He said that if I couldn't drive, we'd get in his car. He kept insisting his lawyer was a nice old guy who would help. He insisted he only wanted a separation, not a divorce. I didn't know if you sign a separation, everything—all the terms—for a divorce are pretty much agreed to. I guess he thought that I was in such an emotional state that I would agree, but I didn't. He left that morning and hasn't been back. He took his clothes and his fishing pole. He called a few times after that, but I guess he felt guilty. After that, we communicated through lawyers."

Listening to her story, I was reminded of the smallness of life of most politicians. They are little people struggling with their own problems, and yet they and society have superimposed on their often meager reservoirs of strength and understanding the job of being responsible for thousands of others. When their marriages and private lives break up, their stories are as cliché-filled as any soap opera. I was thinking of her ex-husband and the pride he takes in his position, which was gained by virtue of seniority, and how squirmingly embarrassed he was at any discussion of his personal life. This is a man who doesn't sell out in any high-living way, a man unknown by most in Washington; a man considered politically quick but of mediocre talents; characterized by one Capitol Hill reporter as "buyable." He lards his conversation with those phrases about loving to be of service to his country.

I wondered what they had ever been like as a couple. She continued in her one-sided story of a wronged woman. "I was twenty-six years old and had gone with plenty of young fellows when we met. I wasn't in a hurry to marry. Well, he was poor and I worked with him and for him. I taught school." Her story parallels that of any number of housewives, except that she had a patina of sorts, the wife of a man who was at least a political figure in his own district, and she took satisfaction from that. By the time he became a force in Congress, she was out of his life. Probably as parasitical as some suggest most political wives are, at the time I interviewed her she seemed narrow and unable to do much but reweave the small events that led to her being alone; a lost woman who clearly thought her life had been set forever. For her, politics had to be the ogre. "Oh God, he just got hit by the bug. The job ruins the man. When he came here, my husband was the world's sweetest guy. He learned, like all the others, that you've got to be ruthless. Once he became ruthless in committee, he learned to practice it on me. He was always ashamed afterward. I really feel sorry for these men. By the time they get any power they are into booze, women, ego, and pride. Everybody's busy scrambling—and then all of a sudden home doesn't look good anymore." At the end of her long soliloquy on the ruination of family through politics, she dissolved into self-pity and said, "No one gives a darn about ex-wives.

"One thing that helps these congressional romances—they can use the money from their staff budget to have these secretaries go to their home state. Why, that woman in his office had hardly been on a plane before. I remember one campaign when *I* took her back to the district to help in the campaign. She bought herself a wardrobe fit for a queen. She had money to dress fancy and look good because she was working! And here I thought she was just a simple girl in his office. Well, I could see right then and there it was stars in her eyes."

The ex-wife puts a lot down to designing females, and male menopause. "Like all men, he needed to build the ego from about age forty-eight on. They want to become popular. It kind of goes back to high school days. They want the 'fraternity' of the Hill. The wife doesn't hold any glamor after twenty-eight years." For a woman who spells out "bad" words and says the Bible and the church saw her through her trials, she was surprisingly candid about sex. Indeed, sex was a problem—but the way she tells it, the problem was his, not hers. "He had more than he could handle in his own bedroom," she said with a solemn shake of her head. "My doctor said that age forty-eight to fifty-two is the dangerous age for men. They fear impotence and wonder if they can make it. My doctor said they often feel the need to recharge their batteries with someone new. A politician can do that because other women get interested in them." The wife tinted her hair, went to a health spa, prided herself on being a good dancer.

For all her "surprise" at his girlfriend, there was every indication that the wife, as well as her husband, tiptoed around a confrontation. "These men will wear you down. Weeks and months would go by. He'd come home and stare at his briefcase, or the television or that clock on the wall. You'd start conversation or talk about doing something and he'd say, 'I don't care.'"

Her "wearing down" of the wife theory is reiterated by other ex-political wives, who will tell you the men want the wife to file for divorce to take the onus off them. "He deserted *me* and then he tried to force me into filing for divorce so he could show his constituents that he was a fine fellow—that *I* just wanted out. They all have some cockeyed pattern, but I didn't go along. I laid low for the kill. He would have foxed me into signing those papers like Bob Dole did to Phyllis Dole. First of all, those men have the feeling the law can't get at them. Nixon's not the only one who feels he's immune. My husband gets caught going sixty miles an hour and all he does is show the policeman his card."

The woman said, "I could have ruined him. He was moving up in the power structure at the time. Many don't know he's divorced to this day, he kept it so quiet. He was scared to death of publicity. He may be taking her back home now, but for a while he kept her real quiet back there, too. Heavens, he ought to know I wouldn't have told it to the newspapers like some of those women. I'm not going to fight and scrap like that out in public. I wouldn't want my children having people coming up to them and saying, 'Look at your mother. She sure is loud.'"

The woman's former husband is a study in black and white— black suit, black-and-white wide tie of Countess Mara vogue, black-and-white hair. He looks younger than he is, but there is more of an air of the all-purpose Congressman than the dynamism some politicians project, or at least hope to project. He was more comfortable talking about the specifics of his role on his committee than anything else. Asked why politics was his choice for a long-standing career, he said, "I haven't analyzed it. Well, as . . . because . . . it's uh, it's uh . . . it gives me the opportunity to become totally involved in the whole—the, well, the, in the process of the country." Once the clichés were in place, the sentences were more sure.

"I have some capacity to change and mold direction and resolve the problems of our country. And then there is the contact with people. It is the people thing. There are multitudinous contacts. There are all kinds of great human beings all along the way." I asked him how he got along with people who were diametrically opposed to him in Congress. "I don't have time to analyze people's motives. I look upon every other member of Congress as a great friend."

We started to discuss the role of the family in the life of a Congressman. He said he felt the wife's role was akin to that of a corporate executive's. He spoke proudly of his wife. "I try to go on trips only when I can take the wife." He said, "My wife enjoys campaigning. She's just a natural-born politician. A great asset. You know, there's a problem of getting out of the office here at a set time at night, and it's a problem most wives don't understand too well. The fact that I have an understanding wife makes it all possible." The Congressman was giving every impression that this was a long-standing marriage. When I asked him if politics contributed to the break-up of his *first* marriage, he looked startled, then winced. "Well, uh, I'd rather not discuss that. I wouldn't attribute my unhappy situation to just the congressional thing. But this kind of public life accentuates personal differences, difficulties, emotional problems. And I think some Congressmen overdo it, by overplaying the family, although the wife should appear often enough so that your constituents know she's part of the team. When the kids are growing up there's no question there's a problem. Then when they're older, the wife feels frustration. While there are those who say this is a profession in which the wife can join, by the time the kids are grown, some wives are left out of it."

Still feeling uncomfortable about his divorce, the Congressman said, "I'd, well, really appreciate it if you didn't write about it. The reason I didn't do it earlier, well, divorce just gets so *accentuated* in public life. At the time, I wondered personally if I could go on. I was going through the emotional travail and of course I was in the public eye, on trial more or less, all that time."

Now, he said, "I'm tremendously happy, and it has an enormous effect on my ability to work more decisively. I couldn't be doing the difficult stuff I'm doing now. This has been the most significant difference. There is a *personal* incentive to go in public life now. Having love at home is so terribly important. Here you have pressures all the time. People in public life are living in a glass house. It is *so* important to have a base to operate from. I know there are unhappy marriages that are deeply affecting some of my colleagues." (His first wife sniffed and said of his "happy" second marriage, "He'd have to say all that. He couldn't admit he flopped at anything.")

The Congressman would not speak of his first wife at all, except to say that had she had a career, "it might have been an answer to our problem. When a woman can't do that, she funnels all her frustration through her husband."

After her husband left home, the first wife said, "I was in a state of shock for several months." She stayed in the house for many weeks. "I finally decided I had to be out and busy. I walked a mile and looked at the sky and kept saying, 'I am a person who is going to be positive.'" She went to Europe with her sister and to the Orient. She went to church and she started to see her friends again. They were women with whom she went to meetings and worked on cookbooks and talked.

Who were her friends? "Oh, just the wives—the ladies of fifteen years on the Hill."

The wife who chooses to stay in her home state rather than move to Washington may feel she is doing the best thing for her children. Sometimes the marriage survives—any number of congressional "commuters" have lasting marriages. For others, the separation can be the final admission that there isn't much left.

"My wife wasn't ever particularly interested in what I did. My kids were raised to hate politics by my wife. She stayed at home a couple of terms—but I finally forced her to come down here."

Congressman William Ford from Michigan was talking. His eyes look directly at you when he talks, the politician's trademark of sincerity that becomes reflexive after years of practice. Now in his mid-forties, Ford was a Michigan state senator for two years and has been a U.S. Congressman since 1964. He is divorced and since remarried. Although Ford at first defended the politician as being no different from any other professional man who gets involved in his work, the Congressman later acknowledged differences and ended by saying, "It's an impossible life—married or single."

"I know of no other elected public official who has to constantly fight for his life like a Congressman. You're on trial every day. You're thinking from the moment you get here about doing the right thing to get reelected in two years. There's constant and unrelenting pressure. Speeches here, speeches back home, meetings, late nights, never being home. During those early years, when you are getting known politically, there is a constant strain on your marriage. This profession is terrible competition for the wife. Sex is simply out the window half the time. You don't have *time* to romance someone else and you don't have time to romance your wife. There is so much talk about politicians having affairs. If it's anything, it's just a quick thing. There is no time to devote to a true, honest relationship."

Ford has memories of being poor, of seeing people suffering. He came from that Detroit world of asphalt where a drifting, meaningless life for many young people went unexamined; escape was found in the restless, aimless motion of just getting in the car and going somewhere—anywhere. But Ford had feistiness, pride and a self-admitted what-makes-Sammy-run drive that took him from the motor company assembly line to Washington. Still, he thinks often of that world of factories in which his father died.

"My father was overcome by smoke in a factory fire, at the age of forty-six. When he left us I was twenty. There were three of us and my mother. I had the political bug and a central drive to get through law school. I worked in the factory at Kaiser-Frazer one summer on the assembly line. Then I sold anything there was to sell—from encyclopedias to burial insurance. I finally got a reasonable job working at an insurance agency and going to school full-time. My mother was working at everything she could find."

He has a haunting understanding of the problems of the blue-collar workers in his district and a conflict at times between his goals and theirs. "You fight for a poverty program and that's not anything the blue-collar factory worker can identify with." His voice softens. "One thing you have to understand about people who work in factories." We talked about the stupefying monotony, the oppressiveness of the work. "The problem is so immense in the auto industry that nobody's got a handle on it. Young people won't go into it. My contemporaries I saw aging much faster than I, despite the fact I was living with a great deal more mental tension. I drink too much, but that's 'socially approved' drinking. They drink in a more corrosive way. The 'Polish martini'—the shot and beer at eleven A.M. The younger blue-collar workers who are on drugs are more devastated than college drug users. It's not like the college crowd; blue-collar workers are doing it as a real escape. All this is what makes people in my area put so much emphasis on education. Nobody wants his kid to follow him into the factory. There is no pride in having your son follow you into the shop, as there once was in the craft unions. Hell, the only way I could survive one *summer* on the assembly line was I knew I was going back to school. I still drop in the neighborhood bars and I see some of the men who went into the factory with me that summer. They make pretty good money, but they're really old men. They're forty-five and really old men."

Ford married at twenty-one. As he was clawing his way, he followed the normal route, using law as a stepping stone to politics. "The bulk of people in politics have a tremendous amount of personal drive. Oh, you have some 'accidents' and some pretty boys with a lot of money, but most are driven." He feels there are many like him who worked their way to Congress with little money.

Defending politicians as family men, Ford said, "Take a doctor—he gets the adulation from everybody who works with him. The wife is home raising the kids. When he comes home, he doesn't want to be involved with playing the whole ball game over for her again. And his unusual hours are an added pressure."

But Ford agreed that there is more privacy and less uncertainty to that life. "There is an enormous pull just to accept all those speeches. Before I got remarried, I got a request to speak in San Francisco. I wanted to do it, primarily because it gave me the opportunity to kick the hell out of Nixon's education policy. You could go on and on with those engagements. When I got married I had to stop and think about it more. Sure, you get more adulation but you also catch more hell than most people. We went through the crazy busing thing in Michigan. It's a scary feeling to have people turn on you. A man I'd known for years grabbed me by the lapels and started shouting at me when I went to one function. I wanted to get him outside so he wouldn't disturb the other people. And he had been a client! I know someone else who lost to a crazy John Bircher who had no qualifications at all. That kind of uncertainty is involved. You never quite know what the hell you're going to get into.

"Then when you get home, how does a wife handle the difference between the way you treat her and constituents? There you are, less accommodating to her than the other guys in the neighborhood are to their wives—and yet, she sees you being nice to people you don't even *want* to be nice to. Someone screams and hollers at you about your stand on, say, busing, and then who do you scream and yell at? Her. Everybody else gets the attention, the concern, the adjustment from you, and she doesn't.

"My wife spent a lot of money on psychiatrists. And I knew B's wife [another Congressman] years ago. She was a real, alive woman. Now there's something vicious, almost nuts, about her since their divorce. I'm sure my marriage would have terminated earlier had it not been for political pressure. It was considered damaging to your career, and that causes you to take a lot more crap."

We talked about the effects of divorce on politicians today. "People in public life have very little private life, and divorce strips away the last of your private life. It usually makes the papers. If the wife takes a whack at you publicly because you're separated, that's bad stuff. People feel there is something of the playboy syndrome involved. And then there are always those who still have the old attitude that only those who are irresponsible get divorces, and that can go against you."

After Ford "forced," as he said, his wife to come to Washington, things were better between him and his children, if not between him and his wife. "The one advantage of her coming here was that I did see the children a little more. I think politicians feel guilty about the amount of time spent away from their children. You tend to overcompensate and give them too much attention when you're with them." He shook his head, as if remembering.

One added problem of his profession is that his children "took a lot of heat" at times from other children. "My son was stoned by a mob and came home all bloodied. I was a local judge at the time and I had made an unpopular decision on a touchy case. On one hand, here was a widow whose only subsistence came from payments from a family who rented a house from her. The family never paid the rent, and they were evicted. There were four or five kids in the family and they told everyone in John's school that I was the daddy who forced them out of the house. It was really rough for him.

"When I was state senator and my daughter was a high school sophomore she had a government teacher who had a habit of singling her out. The teacher would say, 'Well, since your daddy's a state senator, you must know the answer.' She had as much interest in government as any high school sophomore girl—which meant she *didn't* know a lot of times. She got the impression she was a dummy and she was picked on. The move to Washington relieved them of the tremendous heat they took back home. Here they blended in with a lot of other kids whose dads are in politics."

Ford was divorced for five years. A short man, he is not unattractive, and he displays that type of energy drive that some women find interesting. As a divorced Congressman his work kept him from developing lasting relationships. His dates were on a "part-time" basis. "I definitely couldn't make plans ahead of time. Suddenly my schedule would change and I'd call a girl and say, 'Can you go out tonight?' A lot weren't too appreciative if you called at the last minute."

Although Ford's own children were "raised to hate politics," his son, in his early twenties, is now interested in politics. "I think he may run. He's got all the looks and charm. He's the kind that young people identify with and old women give all the brownies to when the tea party's over." Ford said it with obvious pride, but when I asked him if he wants his son to become a politician, Ford hesitated. He said he supposed so, but added, "Like I said, it's an impossible job, married or single. The constant complaint you hear in the cloak room is 'I'm going to cut this crap out.' The reason given most often when someone decides not to run again is, 'So I can start living a normal life.'"

This view has not exactly gripped Ford. Now that he is remarried, he still has little time at home. A vacation was coming up at the time I interviewed him. I asked him what his plans were for the vacation. "Attending lunches, dinners, meetings, going to schools and dances and giving speeches and what-have-you in between. Every damn thing I can get."

Although Ford's second wife worked for one of the committees on the Hill, Ford says, "She knew practically nothing about all this." He jokingly adds, "That's why she got married. She's Peruvian—only been an American citizen a few years." He adds casually, "She's being molded in my attitude." As for a second marriage, Ford says he "tries harder. I'm a little more aware of the kind of things in my personality that make me impossible to live with." He still did not seem terribly aware of some of the problems that might occur. I asked how his wife felt about his irregular hours and time away from home. "She's working, and she has a little boy by another marriage. She has plenty to keep her busy." He added, "While I'm gone."

One of the easiest, least publicized, and often convenient dodges for politicians is the political "separation," a practice of long standing which is shrouded in ambiguity. The wife stays in the home district with the family, and the politician—ostensibly sometimes, at other times quite accurately—goes home to them on weekends.

Sometimes there is open speculation as to whether the marriage is one in name only. No one can recall Senator Edward Brooke's Italian-born wife showing up at a Washington function. At one White House luncheon for Senate wives, Brooke was represented by his mother. A warm and open woman, the Senator's mother joked that she kept her sunglasses on while she was inside in order to hide her bags. "People will think this is all Edward can get to represent him!" One former aide said, "It's my impression that the marriage was over in the real sense a long time ago, and that they stay married for political purposes. It also affords the Senator a certain mobility. No one expects him to make a commitment to anyone else while he is still married."

Some separations are innocent extensions of the political life. Others, if not the initial problem, precipitate a final falling out. And then some separations go on for years, with the wife some shadowy figure back home and the girlfriend much in evidence in Washington—making it difficult to get an actual body count on the number of political marital splits.

For example, one of the most irascible, least-liked members of Congress quietly separated from his wife in the 1970s. Over the years the Congressman, Wayne Hays, has been accused of having a number of choice secretaries in his life, but most of his colleagues assume he still lives with his wife when he returns to the district. "We, ah, have been separated for some time now, but I wouldn't like you to necessarily write that, though," he mumbled. "Nawww, we're not going to get a divorce."

A number of older men on the Hill could qualify for the lecher of the year award, but Hays has consistently been written up as a prime candidate. Marshal Frady reported in a *Playboy* article that an agitated Hays, reading his profile in the 1972 Nader congressional report, yelled, "That son of a bitch! He put in there that I sleep with five different girls every week. I called over to that place and told those jerks that if they didn't take that out, I'd be getting every cent of Mr. Nader's GM suit money. That son of a bitch. If you want to know the sorriest gang in the world, it's a bunch of Jew boys led by an A-rab." There are various stories regarding what Hays actually did about the Nader report. One of Nader's profile writers told me, "I heard he called up here and said that he was flattered that they would say that about those girls at his age, but that he would be the laughingstock of his colleagues—because everyone knew he couldn't get it up that much!"

Hays, noted for his raw "one-of-the-boys" talk around males, was more than shy in discussing this story with a woman. He muttered to me that Nader had a "bunch of punks over there." He said he called Nader's office and did threaten him. The report deleted any reference to his sleeping-around prowess, but it did keep in a 1967 *Wall Street Journal* article that pointed up an ironic blind spot in Hays. Hays "took his 26-year-old secretary to Bermuda for an informal meeting with British parliamentarians," the article stated. "He chose the same young lady to join another Hays-headed delegation for 20 days in Europe. Then, having spent $6,589—enough to make him congressional travel champ—Mr. Hays came home to head a House subcommittee that investigated and denounced Adam Clayton Powell's female-accompanied private pleasure jaunts at taxpayer expense."

Despite such disclosures, Hays flourished and continued to travel, so much so that former Ohio Senator Stephen Young nicknamed Hays "the Marco Polo of the Ohio delegation." Young said Hays's "personal fact-finding missions" in Europe at taxpayers' expense consumed thirty-four days in 1970 and twenty-six in 1971. Solemnly, Hays explained to me that the "press of business" was the reason he was unable to see his wife and adopted daughter, Geeta, enough to make the marriage work.

For all his reputed bombast and name-calling, Hays bent over backward to appear, well, courtly, when we had lunch in his lavishly furnished office. He so eagerly tried to impress that he was a man of taste, despite his dingy beginning in a little mountain junction. Only occasionally would he slip. Talking about one article written about him, his eyes narrowed as he spoke of the author. "The guy was a 'switch hitter.' You know? One of *them*. A fairy. Wouldn't have talked to him if I'd known. I'm just a simple country boy."

There is little "simple country boy" innocence in Hays's cruel and vitriol-filled attacks on the Hill that make him feared as well as despised. Speaking of Fulbright, Hays reportedly said he'd heard that Fulbright was crafty enough to have "something up his sleeve." Pausing, Hays threw out, "All I got to say is, if he doesn't have any more up his sleeve than he's got in his head, he's a goddamn paraplegic." He nicknamed John Gardner of Common Cause "common crook." One television commentator who criticized Hays was called a "slimy little jerk." Don Riegle was named a "potato head." Indiana Congressman Andy Jacobs said, "One thing you can say about Wayne Hays— he never kicks a man when he's *up*."

Known as a "bully" who cows waiters and elevator operators, Hays is feared because he is one of the half dozen most influential members of the House as chairman of its administration committee, chairman of the joint committee on printing, chairman of the Democratic congressional campaign committee, and a high-ranking member of the foreign affairs committee. The administration committee provides Hays with most of his power, wrote Robert Walters in the Washington *Star-News* in 1974. This committee has almost total control over every dollar spent in the House. Hays, hardly reticent about asserting his authority, is an interesting study because he points up the insular preoccupation with cloakroom politics that engulfs many Congressmen. Hays has turned his petty duties into a position of ponderous power and is so abrasive that he is given a wide berth by other members. He controls a wide array of services upon which House members depend—the carpenters, plumbers, barbers, and electricians come under his jurisdiction. His major coup was to put the House restaurant on a sound financial basis—but in so doing Hays can easily take the time to bawl out an elderly employee who used a paper napkin, rather than cloth. Like some modern-day Uriah Heep, he also approves House expense vouchers. He once vindictively fired an aide hired by Representative Donald M. Fraser because, Hays claimed, he was "meddling with my subcommittee." Hays backed down three weeks later when Fraser threatened to take the matter to the House floor.

Still, some on the Hill have a soft spot for Hays. "Underneath it all, he can be very generous once he realizes he can't push you around," said one colleague.

Hays's devotion to niggling details makes him perfect for his committee assignment—and earns him the contempt of young and impatient House members who see in him the embodiment of "this endless inside game of ego, absolutely detached from what is actually happening to the people out there. So much of this goddamn place is countless hours of the most incredible and deadening crap," said one. "If you have hopes of counting for anything around here, you have to atrophy into the system."

When we had lunch and Hays told me of his troubled marriage, his grasping for political power, his pathetic pride in the trappings of power with which he surrounds himself, he seemed to shrink in size. A man with small eyes, pointed nose, thin mouth, and the insignificant countenance of a CPA, Hays looked old and unimportant.

Today Hays eyes his acquisitions like a small boy taking stock of his Christmas booty. He showed off his refurbished Capitol Building digs, a suite tucked off in a corner of winding corridors. There are paintings and antiques and Oriental rugs and a $1,500 crystal chandelier. Hays said he had to do something with the GSA green walls and explained that the old lighting fixture was "sorta early Mussolini in style." He did not keep track of the cost of his interior decorating. "The American people who foot the bill can be proud of these rooms," he reportedly said.

I listened with ultimate disbelief as he said, pointing to his Oriental rug, "The Shah of Iran saw this rug and said that seeing it was the high point of his visit to Washington." I looked at him for a possible flicker of humor, a smile to indicate that he was poking fun at himself. He was completely serious.

Hays talked with more warmth about his possessions than his wife, once described by a reporter as a "quiet, thin, blonde, somewhat harried-looking lady." With vague indifference, he recalled, "We lived all our lives only eight miles apart. I think I met her at a dance." Although a former teacher, Hays has long been in politics—first as mayor of Flushing, Ohio, then a state senator and county commissioner. For more than a quarter of a century he has been in the House. "My wife knew what she was getting into," Hays said, rather defensively, "although she really never wanted me in politics. But she worked behind the scenes very hard. She's rather a private person and managed to have her private life."

Hays wanted to get into politics so he could become "somebody." This man who is a shouter and turns on people with vicious personal attacks is still mostly at war with one person. Himself. "I had a tremendous inferiority complex as a child. Used to walk across the street to avoid people. I was bashful and stammered badly as a child. My mother put me through a rather rigorous training course." She would encourage him to talk and repeat words and sentences. "By the time I got to school it wasn't so bad." Instead of Hays's own personal problem developing his compassion for others, it only made him ever on the alert to get the other guy before he got him. He said there was no question that he went into politics to "overcompensate" for his shyness, but he is quite unable to speculate as to why he felt so inferior or lacked self-confidence. Hays says proudly as a grown man, "I got where I am because people feared me. Politics really gives you something to feel about yourself." That politics also messed up his family life he acknowledges as a flat matter of fact and with no apparent sorrow. "Washington and politics are very rough on marriages. I think more than other professions. I see a lot of lawyers who are home on weekends, and those corporate boys get out to play golf. Neither my wife nor daughter, Geeta, liked politics. Geeta wouldn't go to a political meeting if her life depended on it. She's got a bashful side." Childless, Hays and his wife "set out to find us a baby" and adopted Geeta in Germany.

Clearly uncomfortable talking about his wife, Hays switched abruptly to his daughter. "I feel very badly about Geeta," he said. One of the great selling jobs Congressmen do is to convince themselves how terribly vital it is that their every waking moment be spent in Congress, as if that lumbering institution would somehow creak to its final collapse without their presence. Hays is no exception. "We used to plan things. Geeta would want me to go to some school function. I just couldn't. I had to be here."

For a while his daughter attended one semester of school in Ohio and one in Washington. "She got almost straight A's in both places," Hays said proudly. I asked him how old his daughter was. "I can't think—she's a junior at Ohio State—has to be nineteen or twenty. You know, it's not easy, having to be in the district on weekends. For years I haven't had a chance to spend weekends with my family. I think it's very difficult on a child. I don't think you ever get close. When you're home, even if you don't keep office hours, constituents come to your house. They're hammering on the front door."

Hays's daughter "flatly refused" to go to high school in Washington. "She said she wanted to be with her friends out there. I said, 'Look, your father's job is here.' She said, 'Daddy, I'm not trying to be troublesome,' but she just wouldn't stay. She and her mom moved back to Ohio and that's been over six years ago." He mused, "When you're in Congress you really have no time to yourself." His eyes did not even blink as he said, "You have no chance to take the family on vacation. I was able to take Geeta on vacation only once really. She was three years old. If I'm absent from here I feel uncomfortable, guilty."

I asked him why he didn't take his family on those much-publicized European congressional trips. "Ohhh, that usually gets written up in the papers. My wife didn't want to get exposed to that business about taxpayers picking up the cost.

They said I took the House waiter over once. I paid his way out of my own pocket. The only thing he ever got from the taxpayer was a seat on the plane."

Hays says the subject of sex and politicians is overrated. "In fact, there's a built-in caution if you're a politician. Too many people watching. You get a girl pregnant, that's a story."

Still, the stories persist. His receptionist is short and squatty but voluptuous in a Lillian Russell sort of way; her waist so compressed by a belt that one admired her ability to breathe. She reminded me of one story I'd read about Hays. One male visitor reported in an article that Hays said, "I want you to come with me for a second. I'm gonna show you something that'll knock your eyes out." Tilting his head into the doorway of one of his committee offices, Hays motioned forth a spectacularly buxom female, the visitor recalled. After a few words, Hays dismissed her, then asked, "Now what do you think of that? Any of the other fellows around here got anything you've seen that can beat that?" Hays also reportedly joked, in that clubby male way, that his greatest ambition was to "be ninety-nine years old—and shot by a jealous husband."

But Hays denied it all and only repeated, "Politics certainly is not easy on the family. As I said, I never really ever had much of a home life."

18

"Congress Is a Perilous Place for Marriages"

SOME wives of politicians get fed up with what they consider a life of neglect and walk away. The most celebrated of these wives is Mieke Tunney. Her ex-husband, Senator John Tunney, had little difficulty getting back in circulation. He was seen in the company of starlets shortly after the divorce, and one national magazine quickly listed him as one of the ten most "eligible bachelors" in the United States. To outsiders, the Tunney split looked more like a Beautiful People disintegration; the aftereffect of a too glamorous life. Mieke, however, says the trouble was strictly politics. As she was telling John goodbye, a more anonymous couple was divorcing in an interesting way. The wife of Indiana's then-Representative William Hudnut sued the Congressman and preacher for divorce in 1973, three weeks after he led a White House Sunday service.

And California Representative Pete McCloskey found that the headiness of his 1972 quite hopeless quest for the presidency cost him his wife, "Cubby." A close friend of McCloskey's said, "Cubby just had enough of it. The story is that she smiled all through one of his speeches for the photographers, walked off the platform, and said she was through. When she left, Pete was heartbroken. He came over to our house and we drank wine and sat up and talked. He didn't know what hit him."

Kandy Stroud reported in *Women's Wear Daily*, shortly after his wife of twenty-three years left in the summer of 1972, that McCloskey sobbed and said that he would "resign from Congress tomorrow if I knew it would bring her back." Until his wife walked out, McCloskey was unable to comprehend what his career was doing to their marriage, particularly that challenge to the President that took him all over the country and into the snows of New Hampshire for the first primary of 1972.

"I've been crying myself to sleep every night," said McCloskey. "We spent years building a life together. It was a wonderful marriage, but she was right to leave me. Politics is a grueling business. You get so involved, and there is such an artificial environment. It's all those goddamn cocktail parties where you do half your business. It's the demeaning bit of begging for money to sell yourself. It's the tendency to try and absorb more and more information so that you can do a better and bigger job. You know, a friend once said about me, 'Pete's a great guy. He'll do anything for his country, his friends, and his family— in that order, which is not very good for his family.' He was right. I put Cubby second. I took her for granted. When I decided to challenge the President on the war, I was gone 207 out of 365 days. I thought Cubby would put up with it. She never asked for much except that I'd put her first when she needed it. But I didn't even do that, and I've learned now that the price was too high. All I can say is that every single productive Congressman I know has a lovely wife solidly behind him. It's the key to all strength. And I'm going to try and regain it. I've got to reorder my priorities. I know I'm a hard guy to live with but I know I can go back to being a quiet, hard-working Congressman who comes home every night, not one who gives ninety percent to the cause and only ten percent to my wife."

No one thought those were crocodile tears, but a number of colleagues and wives of Congressmen felt that McCloskey's rather obvious ego would never allow him to "reorder his priorities." Another former wife of a Congressman, Nancy Riegle, spoke bitterly at the time. Her husband, Don, was a pal of McCloskey's and she feels that in both cases ego was the problem. "These guys think what they're doing is so important that they lose perspective. They think they're being unselfish worrying about the kids in Vietnam and the poor in the ghettos, but that's a bunch of crap. All they want to do is see their name in the paper. It's all for their own aggrandizement. When it comes to being a daddy or husband, they don't have time. They're off taking care of their 'causes.'"

One California political consultant recalled, "I remember one of their anniversaries. They rented a summer cottage across the street from ours. On their anniversary, Pete somehow got stuck out of town. There are just so many times you can say to an aide, 'Send her a dozen roses.'"

Another friend said, "Cubby is just a great woman. In his fight against Shirley Temple [when he ran for Congress in 1966], she had more fans than McCloskey." Now in real estate, the former Mrs. McCloskey refused to comment on her divorce except to say that politics is "unreal." Her ex-husband said there is a tendency to "put all our time into politics—there's no limit to what you can do if you want to put in the time." Politics is also one of the more rootless existences. McCloskey said that they had created a "lovely" life in the Portola Valley. "Then you ask your wife to uproot. We had to sell the home, bring the children to Washington, get accepted in a new environment. Then the children go away. A woman turns to some need for her own identity, her own self-respect. I took her for granted."

There is more than a little evidence that McCloskey—a man I termed an "unreconstructed Marine" after a disastrous dinner date we once had—has trouble accepting women as equals. I sensed an incredible hostility to me. Three male friends of his agreed that McCloskey can be "that way toward women." One male friend said, "His basic attitude toward women for a long time is defensive. McCloskey can fight with anyone. We've had some beautiful fights, but he takes it from me because I'm a guy." I tossed out my Marine image. His friend laughed. "You're so right. Pete has this incredible machismo thing. I remember him speaking to a group of feminists about abortion reform laws. He kept referring to women as 'girls' and 'ladies.' One got up and said, 'We're *women*.' Well, Pete adhered to that for three lines of his speech and then he slipped right back into 'As you girls know . . . '"

In pictures, McCloskey looks freer and more easygoing than he is in reality. His mouth is thin and belies a tenseness hidden in a boyish face.While the rest of his hair is closely cut, the front sweeps up, giving the appearance of a cowlick. One night the two of us demolished a nice woman's hopes for a fine evening when she decided that we'd be dinner partners. At the table he asked me what views I had formed on political marriages. I said it was sad to me that in so many cases it seemed to be an "either-or" proposition. If you wanted to get big marks as a major political leader, you had to expend so much time that you gave up your family life. I had just interviewed a Senator who makes an effort to find time for his family. I mentioned how he was regarded as "lazy" by some people because he refused to put his work first. McCloskey, who had not been looking at me, but who I presumed was listening, whirled at me and said, "What do you mean it's 'sad' to be a Senator, or that Senator —— is 'lazy'? Who are you to say he or anyone who is in the Senate is sad or lazy?" I said that's not at all what I had said. As I tried to rephrase it, McCloskey cut me off with, "Well, I hope you write better than you talk—I haven't been able to make any sense out of anything you said." My next sentence was explicitly clear. I called him a complete ass. Luckily for all concerned, this was around dessert time. The host then followed a social ritual that I understand even Joe Alsop stopped years ago; he separated the men and women for brandy after dinner. Congressman William Cohen from Maine stayed with the women and started talking gently about how his entry into politics had troubled him for the very thing I mentioned: What do you do about politics versus the family?

As we were all leaving, I was beginning to get the remorses. I told McCloskey, "We were both rude. Let's finish with a drink." He said stiffly that he was in a hurry to leave. There was no offer to walk me to my car and I had to laugh. The incident reminded me of a line attributed to Barbara Howar: "Sex in Washington is the White House car slowing down to thirty-five miles an hour to let you out at the door."

The next time I saw McCloskey, I was with his friend Bella Abzug. He was all smiles and he said, "Do you know this girl called me an ass?" He gave me a kiss. I said we had both been pretty silly and I was sorry he hadn't understood what I had tried to say. He agreed, then added, "But after we men fight all day, we like our dinner partners to be cute and cuddly." I groaned, "Oh, no!" McCloskey backed away in mock helplessness and smiled and said, "Yes, I'm a male chauvinist pig." With him was a very pretty young woman who looked adoringly at him.

Politicians can get so caught up in themselves and power that they expect an automatic reverence from the opposite sex. McCloskey is not unaware of what can happen to political couples, as his quotes indicate, but even his allusions are jocko-macho when he talks of political power: "It's like the tiger. He's satisfied with milk until he tastes blood. There is a heady atmosphere in Washington. You're at the center of power. The decision-making process. All of us love the power."

Power was a lure for William Hudnut, a tall and gawky man, who is remembered as being one of your better pulpit men when he preached at the first Presbyterian Church of Annapolis. But except for his basketball height (six feet five), Hudnut was no towering presence among his 435 colleagues in the House of Representatives. In fact, the ordained minister surfaced only once spectacularly during his first and only term in Congress—when his wife walked out on him three weeks after he led a White House Sunday service.

Hudnut, who voted to the right of Genghis Khan until he was defeated by Andy Jacobs in 1974, is open, seems naïve, is as enthusiastic as a Great Dane puppy, and gives you one of those politician's handshakes guaranteed to crush a few bones. "I can remember taking him into the press gallery back when he was a minister," recalled an Indiana newspaperman. "All I can remember him saying was, 'All this power.' He was very awed by it all. I kept thinking, 'Jesus, you stupid son of a bitch, what power?'" (When I interviewed Hudnut I asked whether he felt he had any power as a Congressman. "I'm not out for power,"

302 CANDIDATES FOR DIVORCE

he told me solemnly, "I'm out for the opportunity to serve people.") His newspaper acquaintance continued: "He really doesn't have too much depth and he can be really politically naïve, to the point of being embarrassing. I remember he was giving some award to some Indiana group and he was shocked and dismayed that we didn't show up to cover it. It was something very inconsequential."

Hudnut had to explain his domestic decisions to a public audience not once, but twice in his life. As a minister marrying a divorcée with three children he gave an impassioned speech to his congregation about marrying the woman he loved. Thirteen years later, as a Congressman, he issued a statement about his divorce. He later told me, "Congress is a perilous place for marriages."

According to acquaintances, as well as her former husband, Ann Hudnut felt more suited to the relative regalness of a posh Indianapolis parish than she did to politics. "I remember her saying she didn't like politics because it took us out of 'our' side of town," Hudnut recalled one afternoon during an interview.

Hudnut classified himself as a "typical P. K." when he was growing up. "A typical what?" I asked. "P.K.—Preacher's Kid. Kind of a brat. Always in a little trouble. Shooting off at the mouth. Life was in a goldfish bowl, although that never bothered me too much." He went to an all-boys prep school and an all-male college. "I never saw girls except at Christmas holidays until I was twenty-five." Was he popular? "I doubt it." Hudnut's family was one of the oldest ministerial families in the country and he grew up in a household where the father was "very authoritarian" and the mother was "very subservient."

It was not unnatural to him to have his private life scrutinized when he too followed the family tradition and became a minister. He had his flashy red car painted blue, a properly muted shade for a man of the cloth. He didn't drink. When he was twenty-seven and his wife twenty-six, "I guess I fell in love with her. She thinks I'm excessively romantic."

When he married Anne, Hudnut said, "She didn't have any comprehension what the demands were on her. She wasn't that comfortable as a minister's wife, but things got worse in politics. She didn't go to college. I'm a charger—I go a lot—and it's hard to keep up. She hated the limelight of politics. She hated me being gone so much, the phone always ringing." He was in Washington and she stayed in Indiana. "When I was over here, some other fellow moved in. She was vulnerable." His face took on a look of pious sincerity, somewhat altered by his disconcerting habit of chewing on his tongue. "I've learned a lot by experience. I went through that book, *Creative Divorce*. I learned a lot about myself, relationships with children, women. Now take her. She's forty and he's fifty-eight. Eighteen years older! But he has a lot of time for her. He's in insurance. He gave her a lot of attention. And then he's a director of one of the banks, belongs to a country club. This is what she craved."

He really did talk as if he had indeed read all those cliché-ridden books on marriage and divorce and love: "There was a deficiency on my part, a failure to make her feel needed, to share a dialogue about some of the serious things on her mind." While some politicians do not want a wife who might shine on her own, Hudnut protests, "I'd be tickled to death to have a wife who was a woman in her own right. I knew she was sensitive about being known as Bill Hudnut's wife. Some guys don't get the message, but as the announcer says, 'I got the message.' I tried to encourage her to do needlepoint!"

Unlike many politicians, who view getting help as a sign of weakness and are too worried about their political image to seek out psychiatrists, Hudnut said, "I do not have hangups about psychiatrists. I went during our trauma. I hoped for a reconciliation." Sex was among their problems. "Annie never gave the impression she wanted or needed me. She underverbalizes the sex problem. She's a pro at hiding her feelings. It prevented a meaningful dialogue." He asks eagerly, "Have you read Erich Fromm's *The Art of Loving*? He talks about how love is respect. How you should respect the 'otherness' of the beloved. I think she felt I never respected her personhood. She used to say, 'You want me barefoot and pregnant.'

"I asked the psychiatrist for help, but there was no way. Her heart had turned to stone. She just did not give a damn about me. She said I was weak; that I could make no decisions on my own, but hell, I am not omniscient. You have to learn to keep your own counsel, but when you need help you have to know enough to get it." Hudnut said he felt no bitterness and then, with a magnanimous look, added, "To understand is to forgive."

While they were married, Hudnut said, "My anger was repressed, submerged. My wife did feel I was constantly craving ego reinforcement, which she resented. I know she talked to the psychiatrist about all the praise lavished on me. I remember when we were going to the White House she said caustically, 'We've all come to town to watch Superstar perform.'"

When Hudnut decided to go into politics, he was well along in what he calls the "hatch, match, and dispatch" profession—in other words, baptism, marriage, and funerals. He left behind a huge Presbyterian church with four ministers, a half-million-dollar budget and "an elevated class of people."

"People ask me why I left the church. I just feel life comes to us in stages. I had been there ten years. People around the Hill always ask each other, 'What did you do back in *real* life?'" Whatever fantasy there may be about the life, Hudnut insists there are also some cold, hard facts. Politicians are not treated with the same "way up there" social acceptance accorded those in the ministry. "Some thought I was even forsaking God when I became a politician. I don't feel that way—you go where you're called. And there's lots more camaraderie on the Hill than in the church."

Hudnut said that the stress on his marriage was caused not only by absences but financial problems as well. "I only said it half in jest when I once said everyone in Congress should be a bachelor and a millionaire. There are heavy expenses, always having to raise money for personal expenses when you're running. I had five kids to support and a wife. Until we split up I had heavy mortgage payments on the house back there and an apartment here. A lot of guys in politics who are married are hard up."

After Hudnut came to Washington, his wife's frustrations at the separated life only exacerbated existing problems. "I think she had the idea that life was a great romance in Washington; that I was out all night at parties, with other women. I think she was suffering from cabin fever. So she'd call and say, 'Do you mind if I go out with Jack?' Now that's a tough question. If I say 'Yes, I mind' then in her eyes I'll be a bastard, still trying to dominate, while I'm out having fun. If I say 'No, I don't mind' then in her eyes that would mean I don't care."

So Mrs. Hudnut, according to her former husband, found solace with an insurance man eighteen years older, who had the time to give her what he did not.

While Hudnut's divorce got national publicity at the time, there were no lasting political effects. His 1974 successful opponent, Congressman Andy Jacobs—who incidentally had the congressional seat before it was redistricted and Hudnut beat him in 1972—is himself divorced.

We talked about whether politicians were too inherently selfish or absorbed in their own interests to give of themselves to a family. "I'm sure my former wife would say so. Politics takes strong ego and self-confidence. I'm in it because I love people."

Hudnut had no desire to return to the church. "I've been that route. And besides, I'm not really a very marketable commodity—a divorced minister and defeated Congressman."

Hudnut, after losing his congressional seat in November of 1974, was back running like mad in a few months—this time for the office of mayor of Indianapolis. He also married an Indianapolis real estate saleswoman. He is finding his new life "awfully hard on marriage. I've been out every night since the party endorsed me two months ago." He thought for a minute and said, "I guess more of us ought to learn about the power of love instead of the love of power."

It was 10 A.M. and I was rushing for an interview with Mieke Tunney, the former wife of California Senator John Tunney. Her son, Teddy, a handsome, blond twelve-year-old she calls Tedsy, opened the door. I asked if his mother was there, that she was expecting me. Just then a good-looking young man in slacks and a crew-neck sweater and loafers came down the stairs. "Is my mother here?" her son asked. The man, who referred to himself as "a friend," took over. "She'll be down in a few minutes." He seemed interested. "So you're doing a book on political families?" "Yes. Are you in politics?" He said "No," and there was a finality to the tone that said he wasn't going to offer up much else as to who he was.

Next to the Kennedys, the Tunneys possessed more glamor in their married days than any other senatorial couple. Everything about them shouted the phrases coined in the sixties to replace the 1930s café society—jet-setters, beautiful people. They were close friends of Joan and Ted Kennedy. She was exotic. Other political wives came from Grand Rapids, Michigan, or Kennebunkport, Maine, or Little Rock, but Mieke was European and sexy. This was not a Senator's wife to roll bandages with the Senate Ladies. In the sixties the Tunneys went to all the swinging parties that the oil-rich Arabian embassies lavished on Washington before it was unchic to spend all that money. Even before they became a congressional couple, because of Tunney's association with Ted Kennedy, they were JFK's White House guests.

And her husband had a rich childhood. He is the son of famous world heavyweight champion Gene Tunney, who fought his way out of New York City's Irish ghetto, married into a wealthy Greenwich, Connecticut, family, became a self-educated addict of poetry and enjoyed the company of such literary greats as George Bernard Shaw. Young John Tunney knew a Zelda and Scott Fitzgerald existence—with the children alternately shipped off to private boarding schools in an attempt to protect them from a "lionized life," and then being taken out from school for a vacation with Mary and Ernest Hemingway in Cuba. His sister, the only girl of four children in a male-oriented world, was not as much a survivor of that life as John. She murdered her husband in 1970 and has since been confined in a mental institution.

Although his former wife recalls that John in later years did not consciously seem to have to prove himself as the son of a famous man, he nevertheless absorbed a competitive spirit from his prizefighting father. Tunney insists his identity crisis—"I found it difficult to find out who I was"—actually was eased by his father. "If it hadn't been for my father being famous, it would have been devastating." Still, there were deep problems. He learned to box at Westminster School in Simsbury, Connecticut, and gave infrequent exhibitions until he realized that "my father was so good that people would expect me to be equally good." His father's impact was a "very deep psychological thing," which intensified the Senator's drive for success and his striving to be the best at anything he did. In a rather chilling comment, his brother, Jay, once said, "We were trained to battle each other." This planned competitiveness was not only in sports. His father would offer money to the son who could most quickly memorize a poem he selected. Tunney is still a poetry spouter from memory. (His younger brother, Jay, learned early that there are some sacrificial rites to politics. Tunney was known mostly as Varick, his middle name, when he first ran for office. A poll showed that more than 60 percent of his prospective constituents thought the name Varick was either Communistic or Russian. From that moment, Tunney decided to use his first name, John. To avoid confusion, his brother, whose first name was the similar Jonathan, was forced to call himself Jay.)

With success came a tamping down of Tunney's youthful candor. It was replaced by surface mannerisms that come off as consummately insincere. New acquaintances stare in wonder as old Tunney friends say, "He can be very introspective about himself if he cares to be." Tunney said that "baring my soul got me into a lot of trouble."

Tunney's Kennedyesque voice and mannerisms are easily, and often, imitated, particularly that drawn-out "Nice to meet youah." One politician said, "He's like that. He's the kind that would go home, see his own kid, put out the hand and say, 'Hi, Teddy, howah youah.' He's always onstage." There are many Tunney jokes. One that made the rounds in 1972 is that George McGovern wanted Tunney as his vice presidential running mate. McGovern urges and urges Tunney to take the position but Tunney protests that he simply could not—"the divorce and everything, George." McGovern then says he thinks the country is ready to handle divorce and that they could be a viable team. The kicker to the joke is that Tunney, then baring all those teeth to the sun in a beaming smile, says, "But, George, you don't understand. Mieke gets custody of the *teeth!*"

In reality, Mieke got custody of a happier life, she says. "I've gone from high pressure to zero pressure. Those years of continual scheduling are over." An admitted "dilettante," Mieke has written articles since her divorce and in 1974 was "thinking about getting a degree in economics," but had no specified career goals. "I am free to unleash all my interests; there is no confinement anymore."

Tunney steadfastly retreated from comment at the time of his divorce—except to say that being a Senator "is such a terrible life. Mieke just couldn't take it." His wife, however, did not. Mieke Tunney became a hit from coast to coast on the disillusioned political wives' circuit, giving interviews and appearing on talk shows. Tunney winced at her phrases—"All politicians have jumbo egos" and are men who can't allow their wives to share the limelight. He took polls to see if the divorce had hurt his political future, was assured it had not, and was soon living

up to his newfound "bachelor" title, squiring very young things
around.

Mieke Tunney was one of the first political wives to break the
mold. Until the early 1970s, former political wives chose either
to weep on each other's shoulders or to fade stoically from
sight. Mieke spoke out, not with revenge in mind, but as a way
to expose the hypocrisy of an American political system that she
feels ruins marriages.

To be sure, it was also a chance to expose herself. Mieke Tunney frankly admits she needs her own ego massaged, and although her pursuits have a distinct "dabbler" quality to them,
she did try as a Senator's wife to be her own person. She cut a
widely unknown rock 'n' roll record, "Habit of Love," and half
finished an ecology book on California. Her duties as a Senator's wife hindered completion of the book, and she now says,
"One of the tragedies of my life was not finishing that book."
She considered designing clothes and renewed her considerable talent as a photographer.

The morning I interviewed her, Mieke Tunney came down
the stairs in gray slacks and black turtleneck sweater, hugging
her arms in the chill of a house where thermostats were lowered as a concession to the energy crisis. Her blond hair is thin
and long and she stroked it back with her hand and pulled it up
behind her head in a rather constant gesture as she talked.
Mieke Tunney has wide-set green eyes and a long-limbed sexi-
ness. She is intelligent and pleasant, but there is no easy
warmth, no attempt at instant palsmanship.

The signal radiates: it is not her job to set you at ease; you are
there to extract what you can about her and her life and then
leave. At first, the manner seems to border on a cool arrogance,
but after continued talks with her, I realized it was more a di-
rectness. Frank and honest in her opinions, she is contemptuous and distrustful of those who employ artifice ("I don't have
much time, so let's go straight to the point and ask me what you
want"). As a reporter, I find this a welcome and admirable quality, but it was one of her big problems as a politician's wife. "I
didn't like being so intimate with so many people. You have
nothing in common, yet you must be forced into acting as if you
are close—as if you've known them all your life." She shakes
her head. "Spending nights in strange people's homes night after night!" She explained that during Tunney's early cam-

paigns, they would spend the night in the homes of local political chairmen. "Local chairmen are flattered by that. I was naïve
enough then to go along." Mieke likes solitude and feels everyone should. After such constant lack of privacy, "I felt I had
nothing left of myself." Born and raised in Holland, Mieke's
voice is still markedly accented. "I am very European. I am very
slow making friends, but they are forever. If I don't like someone, I know it right away and don't bother. If I do, it still takes a
long time to get to the layers of intimacy and trust. I'm not as
outgoing as the average American."

Mieke and I talked about the resistance and hostility generat-
ed when someone speaks critically of the political life. It is as if
an examination of one segment of society is an imminent threat
to an anti-family way of life germane to all overachievers; a way
of life that "good" wives should "learn" to accept. Mieke said,
"People used to tell me John was just a hard-driving man who
would be no different in business, and that I should just learn
to understand it. But I think there is a difference. What politicians have is an enormous drive to prove something to themselves. It stems from a basic sense of inferiority—a much deeper rooted sense of insecurity than most." Hence the constant
need for reassurance.

"At first I couldn't understand why I couldn't manage that
particular aspect. I loved my husband very much and I wanted
to accommodate. After a while I realized I was chasing a wind-
mill. Politicians are out to charm you—but it is really like looking in a mirror, hoping to catch a reflection of themselves. They
hear the long applause."

Mieke felt her needs were not being fulfilled. She went to a
psychiatrist for some time, read psychology books in an attempt
to understand her husband's personality and her own, and
finally realized she was helpless to do much about it. "If a man
has a truly frustrated ego, it comes from lack of self-love. He
has to get other people to applaud. One of my friends used to
say, 'Oh, John, you're having a birthday party every day,' and
that's just what it is. I have a lot to give. When you love, it is easy
to be generous, but after a while you run dry."

Her husband had no understanding at the time. "It was like
talking to a blank wall: 'Why don't you see a psychiatrist, go do
something of your own? You're jealous of my success.' I was
only trying to say, 'I am a person. Please me, too.'"

Tunney learned the Kennedy ploy of self-deprecating humor and on occasion can poke fun at his own vanity. Speaking to a group of women, Tunney told how he would pass out photographs of himself to travelers who recognized him in airports. After one stewardess began to praise him profusely, Tunney told her she was embarrassing him. Tunney recalled, for the benefit of his audience, the comment of an observer of the airport scene: "How can you embarrass a man who carries around 8-by-10 glossy pictures of himself?"

Today, Mieke quickly denounces the appendage role she played, but at the time she didn't mind it. "For a European that was all right. I was trained to please a man. Women's lib didn't fit at all in my life. I learned such things as how to light a man's cigar. I learned about wine because that was my father's big interest." She adds there were important differences in attitude. "European men were *also* educated to deal with it. Even though ladies went through a subservient routine, there was no true subjugation. They were truly very strong and got what they wanted."

When politics shoved her into more of a secondary role than she wanted, Mieke was unable to make the accommodations. After her divorce she said, "As a political wife, either you join in totally or you lose your identity and become a doormat, which I was." The political wife is the antithesis of the liberated woman, Mieke said. "She is not a master of her own time or her own mind." Although she was urged to do something on her own, the staff set up a schedule for her that left her with no time. "As a good political wife you always have to stifle your identity and play second fiddle." The adaptation to inferior roles leads to wives who "become a cliché, uttering all those cliché phrases in those 'canned voices' with the automated smile—or else they stay in the background trying not to be provocative one way or the other."

Such thoughts were far from Mieke's mind when she met Tunney. She was well educated—to catch a man. Her father was a well-to-do businessman who encouraged his three daughters and one son to have an education. Mieke, the oldest girl, knew a sheltered life of private boarding schools and close family ties. Although she was educated, "There was no way I could get a job. He would have approved only of my becoming a doctor, because that serves mankind." She was studying journalism and photography in Holland and Tunney was studying international law at The Hague. "It was really ideal. Very dreamy. We had a great time. I was twenty-one and he was twenty-three. By the end of the summer, without any intention of falling in love, we were both hooked. It took about a year and a half for everything to work out and we were married."

Politics was not in their future at that time. "We never even discussed it," she said, with a rueful smile. "John was going into the import-export business." While she admits that an ambitious streak was part of Tunney's innate personality, she feels he would have been different in some field other than politics. "I wouldn't have looked at him two seconds if he had been the same person back then as now. In business, you are competing with money; but in politics, other *people* are your competition. It is very insidious."

When the Tunneys were young and in love, John was family-oriented and attracted to the secure solidity of Mieke's home life. She just naturally thought their own life together would be much the same. However, when she was twenty-six and Tunney was first running for office, she was "rudely awakened" to just how much politics would control their lives. When her husband announced his candidacy, Mieke, then pregnant with their second child, was visiting her family in Europe with her baby son, then one year old. Returning to Los Angeles with the child and a nurse, Mieke recalls, "I expected a loving husband. John arrived an hour and forty-five minutes late. He brought with him a man I'd never seen in my whole life. I had to listen to that man talk politics in the car and that annoyed me no end. When we got home, John dumped me and the bags in the hall and was gone. I cried that whole first week. All your basic needs go straight out the window when politics comes in."

Mieke expressed a common complaint of many political wives—that she got little appreciation for what she did do. "They would sit around and rave about some prime advertising spot they had to pay money for, and there I would be, on a prime news program, reaching thousands of people, talking about how wonderful John Tunney is. No one would say anything! My secretary, who traveled with me, would be the only one singing my praises. They barely acknowledged all that free publicity. I have my own pride and I don't think I was an egomaniac just because I wanted John or someone to say 'That was a job well done.'" The problem is often the husband's insecurity. "The husbands don't like their wives to shine too much. A wife must be careful not to steal attention away from her husband. Do you know any Senator who has a wife as famous as he is? Any wife whose life is as illustrious? Yet a lot of these wives have enormous talent they never get full credit for. Either the husband or the staff takes credit."

Tunney told a friend when he was first elected to Congress in 1964 that he was thinking of the Senate, which he decided to run for after his third congressional victory in 1968. Mieke encouraged him. "I felt if he had *that*, then he'd come home. And it would be six years instead of campaigning every other year." It changed things all right, but not for the better. It meant more notoriety, more adulation, more work, more absences. John's brother, Jay, once mentioned how politics was therapy for his brother. "Politics is like getting into the ring, or being a gladiator. John has tremendous energy. It's therapeutic for him to be on the move a lot. It's like a shot, it's like taking dope in a way—it relieves the internal pressures, the nervousness. Greenwich Country Club is no antidote for this kind of nervous energy."

One major problem was common to many political wives. They experience a lack of self-worth that stems from the characteristically anti-wife quality of political life. "It is very frustrating for a wife to realize you don't really count. Even those who genuinely like you as a couple—well, after a while you convince yourself the only reason you're invited is because you are 'Mr. and Mrs. Senator.' You feel you're being used and cultivated. Something about fame is very peculiar. I got a deathly fear people were acting out a part in front of me. I really got starved for real people. On trips, I found myself asking my secretary how people treated her. If they were nice to her, I figured they were okay, but if I found out that they were rude or ignored her or put her at the other end of the table or in general gave her the 'kitchen treatment' as opposed to the way they treated me, that was it for them. That's how suspicious you get."

Tunney earned a swordsman's reputation. Unlike some women who either dissolve over or endure a husband's infidelity, Mieke is confident enough to feel "I don't think I need to compete with any woman for a man. If I have to, I'd just as soon go my own way. My Dutch pride taught me that. There's always another man." When I phoned her for approval of her quotes, she was protective of her husband and amended some sentences that might have cast him in a bad light. Therefore I was surprised when Mieke added candidly, "And you can say that I have never quite forgiven John for some of his love affairs. He had a raging affair when we were married and I said I wanted him to stop seeing her. He said he would, but he didn't. Something like that causes permanent damage."

The lure of a man with power is equal to the fascination on the man's part with a woman who is willing to be adoring. "Even the politicians' love affairs are ego trips. The girl provides the ego massage. The wife has lost hope. She puts up with a frustrating campaign and his being wedded to his career and then along comes a fresh young beauty who has no children and nothing else to do but wait for his phone call. It's not like home, which is a melting pot of frustrations." What's in it for the girl? "He flashes her around at famous restaurants and he gets asked for his autograph."

I asked, "But isn't that all just fairy dust and the illusion of power?" "No, it's not the illusion—it *is* power. Don't kid yourself; that's the real thing. A Senator's casting his vote one way or another on an important issue means wielding a lot of power, and this power is played upon by various lobbyists. The flattery is unbelievable. There is a lot of raw power there, and the girl-friend feels she is going to find reflected glory. Sooner or later, she finds it's truly 'reflected.'"

Political wives say that women openly flirting with their husbands is a spinoff of the "anything goes" aspect of today's "new morality." Mieke laughs as she talks about one such incident. "I remember once we were in a plane to California. I thought, 'Here we are *strapped* into a plane with our seatbelts. I will finally have him to myself, to talk to him for four hours.' And then, on this long airplane ride, the stewardess sat on the arm of his chair for hours. It would take her twenty minutes to give him his Bloody Mary, and of *course* he had to pay attention to some little blond babe. He has to be charming: 'Where are you from? who are your mother and father?' the whole routine. Who knows how many votes that means?"

As neglect turned into separate interests and separate friends, Tunney still thought, according to Mieke, that "surely I would not leave him! When he saw I was serious I felt that I might have been able to talk him into giving up the Senate if I had wanted to. But by that time it was too late." The uncertainty and the pondering were over for her. "I only had to make the decision and I cheered up enormously." At the time, the press publicized the fact that Tunney got a court order for her to bring back the children following her flight to Europe with them. She explained that she could not get an attorney to handle her case. "A famous California lawyer stalled for the longest time and then said he couldn't take it and he couldn't find anyone else. He was planning to run for attorney general and he feared my husband's political influence. In desperation I got on a plane and flew to Holland." Mieke feared a custody battle and a reduced settlement unless she got a good lawyer to handle her cause. She finally did get an interested lawyer and in the light of unpleasantness and publicity, Tunney did not contest the divorce.

Mieke hoots at the idea of ever marrying again—"I couldn't bear going through a divorce again." She also thinks that with no signed agreements and the door open for both parties, there is a healthier exchange of true feelings. "You have the feeling you can always get out when you want to. It keeps everyone on his toes." She has had a steady relationship with a man slightly younger than herself since her divorce, and enjoys being a private person totally out of the political limelight in Washington.

I asked her if she retained many friends and she said, "Many of those I got to know through politics have stuck with John. I don't go to California the way I used to."

Because of the swinging life-style image the Tunneys projected, many political wives scoffed at Mieke's criticism of a life they feel she never knew. Mieke sometimes attended some of those "duty" functions, but most of her time was taken up with a more international social life, Tunney's campaigns, and her three children. "There would be hours and hours of just getting organized. You'd get a call from the office—'Get his black tie ready'—and the next call—'No, take out the black evening dress; plans have been changed.' John was using our house like a hotel, and all I was doing was hanging in there. It was a real pain.

"And for this 'fantastically important' job he gets $42,500, and we were trying to live like the president of ITT. When there is a budget crisis to solve, it comes back to the wife. I made a budget and showed it John, to show where everything was going, and the only thing he could think of to take off was the forty-seven dollars a year to have the windows washed."

Mieke said her children are proud of their father's being a Senator. "It would have been a terrible shock if he had lost, but now that he is in, they feel very secure." The competitiveness fostered by Tunney's father carried over to his attitude with his own children, two boys and a girl. "He is competitive with his own sons," Mieke said, and pushes them to work "better and harder," impressing on them the importance of amounting to something. One year they were having some school problems with one son. His teacher was criticizing the fact that because they were away a lot and the children were left with foreign help, he wasn't getting correct guidance in English. When they got to the car, Tunney turned to Mieke and said, "Why don't *you* read with *your* children?" In their home, phone calls were coming in at the rate of thirty a day. Mieke finally switched off the phone after school hours. "I just couldn't be all that—wife, and mother, and socializing, and the whole bit."

She recalled that Teddy, now thirteen, once told her, "I would *never* be a politician." His mother asked him why. He replied, "Because I would never see my children." She adds, "but that was when he was young. I think he's changed his mind now."

She recalled the nights when both she and Tunney made an effort to keep the children up until he came home. "The office would phone all the time and say he would be there in half an hour. Then another half an hour. I would keep the children up. An hour and a half later he'd come in. They're exhausted. And then the phone would ring and it would be for him. He'd be on it for an hour."

There was a basic psychological frustration. "There seemed to be such superdemands on your husband and so you would feel, 'How can I compete with such world-shattering, important pressures?' A businessman can get away from it if he wants to, a politician says he can't. I'm not saying those marriages don't disintegrate. Yes, many of them do, but for different reasons. When you are in public life there is an enormous pressure to always be out front. The family is always coming last. When you are running a statewide campaign in a state like California, you build up an enormous deficit. The wife is up against it. She says, 'Please stay home, it's our son's birthday and he'll be *so* disappointed,' and he says, 'But Joe Doe is giving me a $100,000 fund-raiser and we have this enormous deficit.' So obviously he won't be there for the birthday." Other times, Mieke said she would ask that he be home and her husband, so used to being on the go, would ask, "For what reason?" Her answer was, "For no better reason than I *need* you. I need your attention." Often that would end with "some man getting in from Ohio to testify or some such thing, and then it's out to dinner with him."

Mieke thinks her marriage would have survived under different conditions. The first is if they had not been in politics. She still thinks it might have lasted if her husband had appreciated her role more, or if American political attitudes changed regarding the role of the wife.

The woman should either be left to her own life or be allowed in as a full partner. Had she been treated less like an ornamental doll Mieke thinks a feeling of usefulness might have countered her dislike of such a public existence and a diminished home life. "There was a lack of belonging—one day the staff keeps you out, the next they decide they need you for some appearance; you're hauled in and hauled out—and yet you're making all the sacrifices." Mieke thinks a Senator's wife should be treated like an ambassador's wife. "She's very much an official part of his life and she gets the credit and as such preserves her own dignity and self-respect." Realizing that every Senator's wife would approach the role differently, Mieke said, "I know it couldn't be a specified *role*, but it should have specified *respect*. Being a Senator's wife should be regarded as an office." Within this partnership role should be the freedom to speak her own mind. Either that, or the "wife should be allowed to have her own career with time and breathing space to have it. As it is you have to walk such a thin line on what is right and wrong, so as not to antagonize anyone." Consequently some wives exist without "spunk" or "fire" and become "rather narrow-minded." That life was "role playing, and I hate it."

Mieke says that in her new life, "I miss mobility more than anything. I've chosen to be home with my children. During my marriage, after a while of sitting home and saying, 'Please, John, don't go,' I was also gone. John would leave me all the time and so I'd toot off for Europe. I had excellent help then and the children were loved to death by their nurse. There was always a friend to visit. The children were used to my travels then. Now I'm home much more and they are upset when I leave." Like many divorced parents, Mieke says she feels "much more responsible" for the children even though their constantly traveling father is, ironically, no more absent from their lives than he was during their marriage.

There is a certain acceptance that in Washington she will be remembered as the former wife of Tunney so long as he remains a Senator, despite Mieke's attempts at a separate identity. "I just stay here for the time being," Mieke said. She paused as she thought of her future. "I'll be traveling when the children get older."

Part III

The Man Behind the Woman

19

Male Spouses: Mr. Anonymous

MENTION Congresswoman Bella Abzug's husband in a casual conversation in Washington and there will often be a surprised reaction. "Does *Bella* have a husband?" Most people are content to think of the Manhattan Congresswoman in one-dimensional terms—battling Bella who knows those words that need no translation for truck drivers; shouting Bella who tries to railroad her way through the established way of doing things on the Hill and doesn't care whom she antagonizes. But there is another side—Bella the mother, who waited to try for Congress until her two daughters were older; Bella the wife whose face lights up when complimented on her choice of husbands. "Isn't he a great guy?" she responds in that husky voice.

Martin Abzug, a stockbroker, and Conrad Chisholm, a former city investigator who now works mostly for his Congresswoman wife, Shirley, are not exactly household words anywhere. Like most political husbands, when they are known they are often subject to initial ribbing. Just as political wives are often dismissed as stereotypically bland appendages, political husbands are on the whole dismissed as being weak and demeaned. This is usually a sight-unseen judgment. These men are as much victims of the myths perpetuated by male-dominated politics as are the wives of politicians and the women politicians themselves.

It was not too long ago that John Lindsay bounded up the City Hall steps as a woman television reporter asked him, "Why aren't there more women commissioners in your administration?" The mayor's eyes twinkled as he tossed out this line for TV consumption: "Honey, whatever women do, they do best after dark."

That's just one of the countless cracks that typify the macho-locker-room aura of American politics. Women on all political levels find that the bourbon and branch-water rites, the smoke-filled room, the all-night poker session are closed to them. "Not that I give a damn for the partying," one gray-haired female state legislator told me, "but they do get important things done there that you aren't privy to." The not-so-subtle sexist remarks in the political arena often leave a woman politician defensive—and defenseless. The double standard prevails. She is more often the target of innuendos about her sex life—if she is not getting a frosty "Why aren't you home with your children?" Until recently, money, supporters, and voters were hard to come by.

When Frances (Sissy) Farenthold, running for governor of Texas, ducked into a beauty parlor, they took pictures of her getting her hair washed. What male candidate gets his picture taken when he ducks into a barber shop? When she *didn't* take the time and she looked a mess, she was criticized for being sloppy. Some anonymous donors snidely sent her a cheap wig.

When Congresswoman Pat Schroeder, Colorado liberal and antiwar proponent, fought hard to get on the Armed Services Committee, she had to face the over-seventy-year-old Eddie Hébert, the former chairman and a strong advocate of our military might. During one argument that she lost, Pat Schroeder supposedly said, "You only went against me because I have a vagina." Hébert then supposedly said, "If you had used *that* more than your mouth, you might have gotten somewhere." Hébert cackles with glee at the story. Pat, an attractive and outspoken brunette, said it isn't true. Although she won the respect of many male colleagues, she often gets such comments as "I'll always think of you as a sex symbol."

In 1971, when Pauline Menes of the Maryland legislature fought for a seat on that legislature's "privy" council, the former speaker of the house, Thomas Lowe, presented her with a mink toilet seat as a fitting token of his esteem to the first woman to serve on the "privy" council. "But that little act backfired," said Mrs. Menes. "In fact, that broke things open. There were 143 members, eight of them women. A number of men made it known to us that they were disgusted. He lost clout. It was a price he paid." In eight years in office, Mrs. Menes has seen a change. There were no women's groups like the National Women's Political Caucus to push women candidates. "You used to knock on doors with your literature and housewives would say, 'I don' know, I'll discuss this with my husband tonight.' I don't see that anymore. They're reading the issues and they're not apologetic and mealymouthed." When Speaker Lowe tried to place her in a position of ridicule, Mrs. Menes was bolstered by her husband, an accountant. "He's the first one to buoy me up when I'm exhausted, disgusted, or beaten. He says, 'Tomorrow you'll win one.' His ego and self-confidence are very much intact. He's a tax accountant and when I'm the busiest, *he's* busiest. I'm sure if he were alone at night during the session it would get to him, but he's busy too."

It is hard to make generalities about male spouses of politicians because there are so few women politicians. As of January 1974, there were 7,584 state legislators in the country. Only 450 of them were women, or 6 percent of the total. (After the 1974 election women state legislators increased by 26 percent. The now 591 women members make up 8 percent of the state legislators.) Women represent 53 percent of the national vote, but they lack even token representation on the national level. There is not one female U.S. Senator, and only eighteen women are in the House, one less than the high of nineteen during 1961–63.

As incredible as it may seem to those who have not stopped to look at political officeholders, fifty-five-year-old Ella Grasso in 1974 became the first woman ever elected governor in her own right. (Three other women governors—Alabama's Lurleen Wallace, Texas' Miriam "Ma" Ferguson, and Wyoming's Nellie Taylor Ross—followed their husbands into office.) As the governor of Connecticut, Mrs. Grasso is now the highest-ranking woman official in the country and the *only* female governor. She preferred to play down these facts, fearing a backlash because of the "woman" aspect. (She winced at the joke, before she was taken seriously, that Connecticut was too old for a governess.) She doesn't want to be labeled a women's lib product or pigeonholed in any other way. She is no spokeswoman for the movement, although she is careful to accept their help. Although an aggressive campaigner, she is essentially a pragmatic politician whose innate caution keeps her firmly in the middle on all controversial issues. One exception is abortion, and her firm stance is counter to that of the women's movement. A Catholic, Mrs. Grasso opposes legalized abortion but says she is "sworn to uphold it as a constitutional officer."

Ella Grasso has something going for her that was vastly appealing in 1974—an image of an honest politician. Honesty, of course, was the battle cry of female candidates in 1974. Spurred on by the feminist movement and post-Watergate disillusionment, more than three thousand women offered themselves as viable alternatives for local, state, and federal office—*triple* the number that ran in 1972.

They were indeed aided by Watergate. No one could call them back-room or establishment pols, and so they were not victims of the anti-politician mood that prevailed. Pollster Peter Hart said, "Every time we ask who's more honest, men or women, a plurality will say women."

Some women candidates may object to being referred to in a collective bloc, but it is progress of a sort. For the first time they were around in enough numbers even to be noticed. "We're at a threshold year—this is the beginning," said Jane McMichael, executive director of the National Women's Political Caucus, the largest women's political group. In some states, parties decided to throw influence and money behind serious women candidates instead of giving them token support.

The women represented a wide variety, from lawyers and experienced politicians to housewives. One nun ran for a Tennessee congressional seat, and a self-declared lesbian, Elaine Noble, won a seat in the state legislature from a Boston district. "The important thing," said one male reporter, "is that the lesbian thing was never made an issue."

Women were still subject, however, to such out-of-it paternalism as a Washington *Star-News* editorial entitled "Don't Ignore 'Em." The opening line went "It was Ladies Day" in Maryland primary politics. And the "Will power corrupt women?"— if and when they ever get it—question was inevitably raised. ("You bet power will *change* women," said Mary Anne Krupsak, the first woman lieutenant governor of New York, "because power gives you confidence!")

Despite the token representation on a national level, women scored several firsts on state levels. Joan Growe was elected Minnesota's first woman Secretary of State, and March Fong became the first woman Secretary of State for California. North Carolina elected Susie Sharp as the first woman in the country to hold the office of Chief Justice of a State Supreme Court. In all, out of fifty-one women candidates who ran, thirty-one were elected to statewide posts.

More women in office, while still a very small percentage of elected politicians, will no doubt help to ease the extra burdens a woman officeholder experiences that her male counterpart does not. (While politicians frequently have mistresses, one 1972 winner of a New York post said she guessed she'd have to marry her boyfriend; that living together as they had been would not go with her new job.)

Not only does the female politician battle for a toehold in the inner sanctum of politics. The demands on her time if she is a wife and a mother, particularly the latter, impose emotional as well as physical obstacles. Women with young children are almost invisible on a national level. U.S. Congresswoman Pat Schroeder, with her two elementary-school-age children, was the only female House member to have young children until Yvonne Burke became the first member of the House, as the joke goes, to give birth to a baby in the cloakroom (she gave birth during her first term in office in 1973). New York's Liz Holtzman and Texas's Barbara Jordan, both impressive members of the Judiciary Committee, are unmarried. Shirley Chisholm and Martha Griffiths, who retired in 1974, are childless and both say they could not have run for office if they were mothers.

"It's been my observation that women over the years, especially in politics, have to do things twice as well in order to get credit," President Ford said in 1974. "We've got to change that." (One male political adviser, conditioned to the stereotype of femininity, said, "Most of them have made it thus far at a great loss to their femininity. Look at how tough Bella and Shirley are.")

The male spouse of a woman politician cannot easily be lumped into some category. In families where the wife is the politician, the husband's role is usually closer to that of the husband in any two-career family than to that of the stereotypical political wife. And because so very few women politicians have made it to the top, the husbands have been, for the most part, extraordinarily supportive and/or participatory. Sometimes the male gets fed up with his role. Representative Edith Green's former husband, a shadowy man in Washington, finally packed up and went home.

Even for a husband who enjoys the role, it is not without hazards. Because she is constantly seen in the mostly male company of advisers and colleagues, there have been rumors about the marriage of Republican Congresswoman Margaret Heckler of Massachusetts for some time. Her husband, John, an investment executive, is not unbothered by the talk. At parties he also has trouble staying out of the wives' corner. "If we had a party where we invited all members of Congress," said Heckler, "they would all talk shop and I would end up with ten or twelve wives who really weren't interested in talking about finance. If we invited a group of my clients, they would all gravitate toward Margaret to find out what she thinks Congress will do; again I would end up with the wives."

Pat Schroeder's husband, Jim, a lawyer, does not usually experience this problem because he is active in her campaigns (he ran unsuccessfully before she did). Also, recognizing the long-standing male attitudes, Schroeder said he often initially gets singled out at political functions because men can't imagine his young and pretty wife really being the one who knows what's going on. In Washington, where name recognition is most important socially, Schroeder does have to sometimes put up with blank stares and indifference when introduced. He was talking with me at a newspaper fund-raising party when another couple I knew came into the group. I introduced him simply as Jim Schroeder. No reaction beyond a polite hello. Schroeder had just purchased a "Trust in God, *She* Will Provide" T-shirt and he said he was going off to show it to his wife. "Pat will get a kick out of it." At that point, the light bulb glowed over the other couple's heads. "Oh, you're *Pat* Schroeder's husband!"

Male politicians have a hard time understanding males who accept a back seat to an elected wife. Even former Senator Fred Harris, whose wife is a well-known human rights activist, said, "Hell, I could take everything—until they started calling La-Donna 'Senator.' That's where the liberation stuff just stops."

But most male spouses do not feel as threatened or have as great an identity loss as do many of their female counterparts. For one thing, they have careers of their own. They often have an upper hand most wives of politicians do not: the money they earn enables their wives to run for office. Their own egos are massaged within their own professional circles, bringing a separate identity and separate sense of security. Also, if they choose to go the campaign manager route, it is not unlike being the manager of a movie star or singer, or an editor who marries a writer. It is a strong and independent role, respected by other politicians—one on which the wife politician is often very dependent. He can be as strong and important as she is, the only difference being that he is not in the limelight. And still another reason is that society does not put these men in the same self-diminishing "helpmate appendage prop role." They may be treated like curiosities, but that beats being ignored. They have to endure jokes but, as one husband said, "At no time does anyone *expect* me to go to a tea, or sit on the platform smiling rapturously as my wife speaks, or stand in front of a supermarket and say 'Vote for my wife.'"

After Lindy Boggs was elected to fill her dead husband's congressional seat, her friend Lady Bird Johnson quipped, "And to think you did all this—without a *wife*." Everybody got the point.

Last, but not least, is that what sacrifices these men make are usually paid back in the undying gratitude of their wives. We are not so far along the road to equality that many women mates can take this supportive assistance as casually as most men do from their wives. Women are conditioned to be much more aware of family demands and sacrifices; when they neglect their home, they feel both guilty and immeasurably grateful to their husbands who do take over for them. Even if the couple in any dual-career family is fairly loose about their arrangements, they are forever told by well-meaning friends, "Isn't it wonderful that your husband does so much for you?" How many people say this to a male politician or male careerist about his wife?

Shirley Chisholm, the bantamweight who endured endless slurs when she ran for the presidency in 1972 (there were, after all, more ridiculous candidates—Wilbur Mills and Sam Yorty, for example) and battled for women's rights, sounded out of character when she said of her husband, "I thank Conrad every day for *giving* me this chance to do this."

I enjoyed the male spouses of women politicians I talked to. There was an innate respect for working women and so little of the battling for supremacy that occurs with men who are threatened by such women. Their attitude immediately translated into an easy and nonthreatening encounter for both parties. To me, instead of being weak or subservient, the mates of female politicians seemed, although often unspectacular in personality, secure in their manhood, far more so than some of the power-obsessed, up-front male colleagues of their wives.

On his rare visits to Washington, Martin Abzug becomes the favorite male of many women at social functions. His whole demeanor exudes the feeling that not only does he like women, they are co-equals. He and Bella dance at such gatherings in obvious enjoyment. Abzug is a tall, distinguished-looking man with gray hair and glasses.

I first talked to him in 1971, after his wife was first elected. He sat in his Wall Street stockbroker's office, an affable island in a sea of blandness. Everyone else wore conservative suits, white shirts, and narrow ties, but Abzug was in the mod dress of the moment—bright blue shirt, fat tie, flowing sideburns. A product of the garment center, Abzug is more street smart than Harvard. His immigrant father was a garment cutter. Abzug was one, too, and then a salesman. In 1947 he wrote a novel about the pink jungle, *Seventh Avenue Story*, and in 1950 he wrote a war novel, *Spearhead*. He became interested in selling stocks after editing an economist's newsletter. The woes of his profession cast an understandably doom-and-gloom spell over another conversation in 1974, but at that first encounter Abzug was his usual upbeat self. Talking to a client on the phone, the garment center in him emerged. "I had to get an extension, the whole megillah, so listen, either pay up or take your account the hell out of here. Look, I'm giving it to you flat cuz I want you to understand."

After a few more "pleasantries," he hung up and began talking about what it's like to be married to Bella. "By the way," he said with a laugh, "I'm *not* looking for a mother." It seems his mother wasn't exactly looking for Bella as a daughter-in-law when Martin and Bella wed in 1944. "She was opposed. She kept saying, 'Martin, why do you want to marry a lawyer?' My father took the intelligent approach. He said, 'So what do you want him to marry? A pot?' " (As in kitchen, not marijuana.)

Although Abzug feels most men are "very threatened" by liberated females, he is not and feels it's a popular fallacy that two strong people can't make it in a marriage. Three years later we talked more about his own background and how he could so easily embrace an egalitarian marriage. His attitude was shaped by rebellion from domineering parents who imposed their will on him. Abzug wanted to go to college, but as the oldest of their family he was constantly being lectured about going into the retail dress business with his father. "I had to sacrifice everything. I left school early on, thirteen practically." He remembers his battling parents, and a mother who thought women should stay in the home. "All the fighting made me liberal. Because I was imposed upon, I didn't want anyone in my family imposed upon. I was the fall guy because I was the oldest, and had to give up everything to help out. It's rather a switch, but that made me very much liberated about any wife I would marry or children I would have. They could do what they wanted professionally." Did you like your mother? "Who knows? I suppose. But she didn't like Bella." Bella was equally insistent that Martin should do what he wanted and he said there was "never a career problem from the beginning. The key is maturity."

What makes him bristle, though, are jokes he considers cheap. "Like one women's dinner [when Bella first came to town]. They introduced wives of new Congressmen and they all stood up. When they got to me they said 'and Mrs. Martin Abzug.' I didn't stand up. I didn't see the joke in that." He also slammed the phone down when a customer called up to invite him to dinner, then launched into "What kind of life is this that you lead? That's no kind of life alone. Couples should be together." Abzug added, "That guy, by the way, is divorced."

The Abzugs' daughters are now out of the home. Isobel (Liz) is studying law in Boston and Eve is in the art field. Life has not changed for Abzug much since the first year his wife was in Congress. "It's the same bit, the Monday to Thursday thing. We've adjusted pretty well. There's always action." With the economic crunch, he said, "We can't make up our minds whether to move down there. The apartment in New York is damned expensive. Our income has been cut by our problem." The Abzugs had more time together when Bella was a practicing lawyer for twenty-three years. "We took more vacations—we don't do that anymore—and we had weekends pretty much free." Now there's always something she has to attend. When Bella is in Washington, Abzug goes to movies, plays, visits friends. "I don't have affairs, nothing like that. We have mutual friends that go back a long time, and I see them. Yeah, I get lonely. That's natural and it's very easy to solve—I read books, watch TV. I'm a big sports fan." When they're together they talk politics. "She tries to—I go to sleep. Oh, we talk quite a bit. That's because I listen. She calls me every day, usually around midnight. Sometimes she's still working at that hour. It's a thirty year marriage; it's nothing new, you know."

Abzug is all for more women in politics, but he sees a "helluva problem" when the woman is a mother with young children. "It's practically insoluble in our society. It boils down to money.

Years ago we gave our housekeeper one hundred dollars a week. She was essential."

That was when Bella had a career that allowed for more time at home. "One reason she didn't run for Congress until later was that she didn't want to leave the kids that much. I always had more time, even when she was a lawyer, to be with the kids. I simply pitched in on that." The daughters have inherited their mother's outspokenness, friends say. Liz has a degree in psychology, a green belt in karate, and a reputation as a fierce tennis player. When someone asked her what she had learned from her mother, Liz gave a quick answer that indicated she was a little tired of being regarded as Bella's daughter. "You might ask," she replied, "what did Bella learn from her daughters."

Many Congressmen have the reputation of being impossible to work for and have difficulty keeping a staff, but Bella is always accused of this. Frances Cash, who became a flagwoman on a Capitol Hill construction site after six months as private secretary to Bella, sounded off on her old job. "It was unbearable—spending all that time listening to Bella screaming and calling everyone 'dum-dum.'" The woman continued her broadside; her headaches disappeared, she was feeling good and losing weight. "At Bella's I never got any fresh air from 8 A.M. to midnight, and I had headaches from all the screaming. I couldn't take another Congressman—the excitement of politics is beat out of me. Six months with Bella scrambled my brains." An aide to Abzug said, "Frances is flaky."

Bella has a formidable manner, but when she's enjoying herself she exudes warmth. One night she plowed through a sea of communication workers at one of their cocktail parties. Women in silver spiked heels, with blond bouffant hairdos and overdressed in chiffon, greeted her with the news that they were getting off switchboards. They were working as linesmen, in the service department, running for office in the union. Bella would shake their hands vigorously. She was mobbed by both men and women and she loved it all. Some men came up to her and said they were all for the new women's caucus of their union. She smiled and nodded at all they were saying, then, in an aside, whispered as we left, "Wait'll those women start taking over—then they won't think it's so cute." Although a big woman, Bella has a soft face and dark eyes and is far more feminine than the stereotype image projected of her. She is sensitive and has been known to cry when people make fun of her girth. "Bella does come on strong," said her husband, "but a lot of her impatience arises from being loaded with work. She always has to push herself. She's totally committed—on impeachment, the war, whatever. She's fantastic." He is continually one of her most vocal supporters. "People assume now, because of the money situation, that I am not making as much as she is. I don't feel inferior. You dig? But I know my limitations. If we compare, I don't have the brains she has or her ability or her drive."

For all her celebrity status, Bella is not considered that effective on the Hill. "She's learning how to play the game and is more respected now," says one New England male colleague. "But a few years ago, the kiss of death was to have Bella introduce a bill."

Abzug is not overly interested in politics. "I don't attend those functions. That's not my bag. What have I got to do at the women's caucus? How can I compare what happens to wives of politicians? I've never been a wife. Naw, I don't get bored when people ask me about that. Bella's so unusual they don't know it's happening in all walks of society, although real equality is a long and subtle process." Abzug is resigned to the comments about his marriage. "I get this thing all the time: 'You must be a great man to be married to her, to be able to take it.' People don't know me think I'm some kinda martyr. But whaddaya say? I usually don't say anything. I know who I am, so that's okay."

Their marriage is not without disagreements. "We disagree on almost everything—but we had them aired before marriage." Such disagreements included whether or not Bella should finish school during World War II or take time out to work in a shipbuilding factory. She wanted to finish school and Abzug thought she should contribute to the war effort. She contributed to the war effort. Their biggest disagreement was about her running for Congress. "I thought she didn't have a chance, that it would be a wasted effort," he said with a shrug. "Listen, when I haven't listened to her I've suffered, including in the stock market. I'm stubborn, and I suppose it was partly because I wanted to assert myself. I didn't want to be dominated—but believe me, I suffered."

Abzug is annoyed at knee-jerk definitions of feminine. "So she has a low voice. Would you say someone who has a low voice like Lauren Bacall is not feminine? Like I say, Bella comes on strong but she's not domineering. She's very gentle and very sensitive."

Abzug said he fell in love with Bella Savitzky immediately, when she was a college girl on vacation in Florida and he was going into the army. He is four years older than Bella, who is in her early fifties. "But she doesn't look it, does she? She's got a great face." He recalls "I picked her up on a bus after we had both been to a Yehudi Menuhin concert. I spoke in free verse. Some guy wanted to give her a ride in his convertible, but she took the bus instead with me."

A 1945 graduate of Columbia Law School, Bella went to Mississippi in 1950 to argue the appeal of a black man, Willie McGee, convicted of raping a white woman. Editorials talked of lynching McGee and his "white lady lawyer." Her husband said softly, "She was seven or eight months pregnant. She was followed by some local detectives, got worried, and spent the whole night in the bus station; slept sitting up. She's got a lot of guts, that woman, more guts than the whole damn army."

20

Unthreatened and Unperturbed

"THAT Conrad Chisholm is remarkable. He's wrapped up in her life—lives for her alone; he's the total extreme," said Martin Abzug. Conrad Chisholm is indeed unusual among the husbands of female politicians. He has given his total life over to the care and feeding of Shirley Chisholm. "My life is devoted to her," he says.

In her book *Unbought and Unbossed,* the first black woman elected to Congress wrote of her husband: "Probably few men could have stayed happily married to me for more than twenty years. I don't think Conrad has ever had a moment of insecurity or jealousy over the fact that I have always been a public figure. Thoughtless people have suggested that my husband would have to be a weak man who enjoys having me dominate him. They are wrong on both counts. Conrad is a strong, self-sufficient personality and I do not dominate him. As a matter of fact, a weak man's feelings of insecurity would long since have wrecked a marriage like ours. Conrad is able to let me have the limelight without a thought; I thrive in it and he doesn't care for it."

Chisholm, in his late fifties, looks younger. He is a jolly, serene, pipe-smoking man who speaks in the lilting voice of his native Jamaica. He seems unthreatened, undaunted, and unperturbed that anyone would consider him so self-effacing as to be weak. "Of course there are certain sacrifices you have to make, but they are nothing new to me. My wife was in the state assembly for four years; before that she was always at meetings and working. I make these sacrifices graciously. I'm happy to help."

Congresswoman Shirley Chisholm, a feisty little woman with ramrod posture, fought all the odds when she ran for the presidency in 1972—and brought cheering Black Caucus members to their feet when she told them, "I'm the only one among you who has the balls to run for President." Shirley Chisholm is cocky, self-assured, messianically driven. When the political strain is heavy, Conrad sees his role as "giving her the moral support she dearly needs. The shoulder to cry on." She was kissed off as a member of the lunatic fringe when she announced her candidacy in 1972, and both voters and other politicians narrowly viewed her only as a woman's or black candidate. She was not a "symbolic" candidate but a serious one, she said, and when she was overlooked by the press, Shirley Chisholm successfully sued the TV networks for equal time with her male opponents. At the same time, her candidacy was hampered by the internal hassles of her minority-group followers, and she was criticized by other blacks, women, and liberals for not dropping out and supporting George McGovern's candidacy. Black men, sensitive about female domination, ran her down as a "would-be matriarch."

She doubts she will try again in 1976: "The American people will not raise money for a black woman for President. The inherent racism and sexism is imbedded so deep. The silent white majority will not vote for Shirley Chisholm."

When Shirley Chisholm entered Congress in 1968 she rattled the time-honored tradition of freshman acquiescence. She had been assigned to the House Agriculture Subcommittees on Forestry and Rural Development and Family Farms and, attacking the seniority system, she defied her Agriculture Committee placement. "All the gentlemen know about Brooklyn is that a tree grew there" became her well-known one-liner. She received nationwide coverage and was reassigned to the Veterans' Affairs Committee.

Six years later, Shirley Chisholm looked back on her years in Congress. Her difficulties stemmed not so much from her being a woman. "It's just that the congressional system is not conducive to progressive-minded legislators." She has been under attack by her people for some of her positions. A strong advocate of the repeal of anti-abortion laws, Congresswoman Chisholm was attacked by black militants who see abortion as the white man's attempt to practice black genocide. Chisholm points out that those who raise that issue are black *men*, not black women. In her view, the genocide argument works in reverse, since nonwhites die more often than whites under present abortion laws. More blacks are among the poor who seek low-cost, "quack," or self-induced abortions. "In maternity-related deaths in one year in New York, abortion was the cause of death for 25 percent of white women and 59 percent of nonwhite women," she points out.

Her life is mostly her work. "I'm a lonely woman. I'm misunderstood quite a bit. Of course, a person who is assertive and has tremendous confidence and who feels she must operate from a basis of her own convictions has to be a lonely person in this political business," she said one morning in her office. "But the Speaker of the House told me I was one of the most respected women on both sides of the aisle. Even those who don't agree with me say I'm a lady." She feels Bella Abzug, in fact, would accomplish more if she "didn't come on so strong and do this"—Chisholm sticks her hand out and starts shaking her finger. "She's a very hard worker and very bright; it's just her manner. You *have* to compromise in politics. Compromise is the highest of all arts."

Chisholm knows that strong and aggressive black women have a special problem with black American males, who have felt threatened by a white male-dominated society. Her husband's Jamaican childhood may have contributed to his serene acceptance of his supportive role, she feels. And Conrad says, "You know, I'm from a country which is inclined to give a woman her role, whatever it is."

Chisholm is strong in her praise of her husband. "I wonder now, if I were not married to Conrad, if I would ever have moved up like I have. His ego is secure—he's a lovable kind of person who realizes his wife is talented and people want her. So long as I use the talent I have to help people, it's not going to make me unhappy." Conrad says he has no desire to play a more active political role. "I can't accomplish as much as she. First, I haven't got her aggressiveness and talents. I give her all the assistance necessary to carry on in this very important role. She's made great strides and it's catching on now. More women have an interest in politics."

Conrad sees himself as a reassuring force for his wife, whom he describes as "a thin bundle of nerves." "With the tension she has to go through, the brickbats from outside, when she comes home she has to have a shoulder to cry on." Both Conrad and his wife emphasize she was born with an abundance of self-confidence, but the Congresswoman does not hold the view of feminists who consider men their enemies. She is bandbox neat, wears perfume, earrings—almost as if to offset any unfavorable "tough" image. "I don't care how versatile she is, how she's adulated, how many satisfactions she might have, if a woman's human she needs affection and companionship. Every woman needs companionship to satisfy her needs. I enjoy men . . . I love to be around men. I constantly look forward to the times with my husband, even though I don't have enough time to enjoy him as much as I would like. Sometimes I have a guilty feeling, but thank God, he understands. The women politicians for the most part seem to have been able to develop some kind of understanding relationship with their husbands although they are away most of the time." Chisholm felt this was not the same with many of her male colleagues. "Is it because women politicians are more aware of the needs of a husband? I don't know if male politicians make that same effort. There is this ingrained attitude in society toward women—that they belong in the home and bearing children—until one day the wife has had it and then—snap—she decides she's not an appendage anymore."

Shirley Chisholm wonders what she would have done if she had been a mother. "If I had children, I just don't know about politics. But I must be honest. I probably would have done it anyhow. I'm a woman driven to do what I feel I must. I would have found a way. Still, my own feeling about young children is that they need you. I tell women, 'If you have *young* children please don't [run].' I know the movement will say I'm crazy or that I'm stifling them, but it's so hard." She works from 8 A.M. to 9 P.M. many days, drops off at parties she feels are important to attend. "I don't have to go home and make sure my husband eats his dinner. I'm alone in Washington and I live in an apartment by myself. It's easier for me. But a woman of Congress here with her husband and child—I wonder what kind of satisfactory arrangements can be made."

Chisholm was concerned that her colleague Yvonne Burke wouldn't be able to carry the load when she had her baby. Yvonne Burke's husband, William, a health care consultant, stayed in Los Angeles and his wife keeps the baby with her, crisscrossing the country as many weekends as possible.

Some of the women in Congress felt an empathetic pang for Congresswoman Burke when they would see her, anxiety and tension on her face, rushing home in time to bundle up her daughter, Autumn, and make it to Dulles Airport. And one day, in the male-dominated cloakroom, Chisholm was having a motherly conversation with Yvonne Burke. Chisholm worried about the effect of all that flying on the baby's ears. (By the time Autumn was four months old, she had logged 30,000 miles.) Thinking of her colleague's various roles, Chisholm said, "I don't think I could do it."

So strongly did Conrad feel he was needed in a back-up role, that he took a leave of absence from his job (an investigator for the City Bureau of Medical Services) when his wife took office so that he could be with her more often. He helps out in her Bedford-Stuyvesant district office; acts as a clipping service, cutting out stories of interest for her, sometimes discussing speeches with her. He sometimes tries to get her to slow down her frenetic pace, but seldom gets into discussions of issues. "She does her thing and I do my thing."

A few years ago we sat in her Manhattan district office and Conrad explained that one of his responsibilities is to make sure she doesn't travel alone, which she sometimes wants to do. "I tell her she must not, for her safety." The Chisholm entourage has been "very security conscious" and she has guards that protect her when she speaks. "In this country, when one is too outspoken . . . " Chisholm didn't finish the sentence. (Shirley Chisholm says she is recognized everywhere she goes, even in Japan and Europe.)

When Conrad first came to the United States he started as a cook. (He does most of the cooking when the Chisholms are together, and *McCall's* asked *him* for his recipe for red peas and rice; another specialty is curried goat.) Later, Conrad got into the field he "loves," investigative work. "I did negligence claims for insurance companies. That's not dangerous investigating. It's the type of investigation having to do with *matrimony* that's dangerous," he said with a knowing look.

"If the woman is dominant and strong, why should she take a back role? My wife's most aggressive. If we're to get on an even keel, America needs its best brains—whether it be man or woman, black or white."

Conrad learned his helpful and disciplined role early in life, as one of thirteen children. "My mother had so many of us she whipped us to make sure we'd put everything in its place. Whipping? That's just discipline, back home. And I have grown up in politics all my life. My father was a councilman there. He did everything for the community. I played the same role I'm playing now. When Father would go out and speak, I was kind of his secretary."

Shirley Chisholm's life was one of early struggles, two different cultures, discipline, and strong family ties. Born in 1924 in Brooklyn of Barbadian parents, Shirley St. Hill returned with her seamstress mother and two sisters to Barbados in 1928. Her father remained behind in Brooklyn to work as a baker's helper and factory hand, trying to save enough money to bring the family together again in the United States. "I grew up in the British system and that kind of strict training prepares you for many things in life. I was very disciplined in mind and body." This meant exercise as well as studies. "I excel in roller skating and ice skating, swimming. I love the outdoors. And I do a lot of what you call meditation all by myself."

Shirley returned to Brownsville, New York, in time for the depression in 1934. The family was together again, but in an unheated, cold-water apartment, and movies became Shirley's pleasure escape. Graduating cum laude from Brooklyn College, Shirley first worked as a teacher's aide at Mt. Calvary Child Care Center in Harlem. After college, Shirley joined one of the old-time political clubs in New York and formed a life-long resolve to get women and blacks into active, mainstream political roles. One task given her by the club was to decorate cigar boxes to be used in an annual fund-raising event—the only activity run by the women of the club (most of whom were wives of members).

From decorating cigar boxes in a Manhattan precinct to becoming the first black woman in Congress to run for the presidency is a long way, and Shirley sincerely doubts she could have done it without her husband's support. He seems supremely content. "If you know your role and play it to the hilt, you'll be far better off. Not everyone is as bright as my wife—including some of the men who ridicule me."

The new wave of feminism has found younger men and women examining their views on marriage and stereotyped male and female roles. Many younger men profess a working knowledge of the kitchen stove and the diaper today. That wives will have major careers is an accepted fact among those in college. Interestingly, however, the husbands of those few women in Congress have been quietly managing supportive, egalitarian marriages for many years. Martin Abzug, Conrad Chisholm, and Thomas Grasso are in their late fifties. And Hicks Griffiths, the "totally liberated" husband of Martha Griffiths, is in his late sixties.

Griffiths, whose wife retired in 1974 after twenty years as a Democratic Congresswoman from Michigan, continued his Detroit law practice all those years, although it meant some professional sacrifice. He would not handle cases involving federal agencies. (In a few cases, political husbands enjoy unforeseen rewards from their wives' careers. When Patsy Mink was elected to Congress from Hawaii in 1964, her husband John quit his job as a hydrologist with the Honolulu Board of Water Supply, won a fellowship to Johns Hopkins University, and later joined a Washington-based scientific consulting firm that regularly sent him to the Pacific basin.)

One afternoon Hicks Griffiths sat in his wife's Capitol Hill office and discussed how he escaped male chauvinism all his life. Hicks had long been his wife's campaign manager, but they have actually been a team ever since college. He has been the dominant force in her career, insisting she go to law school and then into politics. He wanted her to go on to the Senate but she said no. "I knew if I did, I would never see Hicks again. As the only Democratic woman in the Senate, I would have had to go to every darn state. My private life would have been lost." Now that she's retired, their joint partnership in Griffiths and Griffiths law firm has been resumed for their sunset years. Still, if Griffiths had his way, his wife would be the first woman on the Supreme Court. "She'd be such a great asset." He recalled how some friends who admired his wife were still dubious when she first ran for Congress. "Then by the time she announced her retirement they said, 'Let's run Martha for President.' A woman President is going to happen, but probably not in our lifetime," her husband predicted.

Martha Griffiths speaks with some wonder, even after all these years, that she found Hicks. "He was the man who really did everything for me. I must say he had more judgment than anybody that age. Imagine, here is a kid twenty-three years old in 1927 with his sort of views! I remember him saying 'Martha, you're not going to stay at home. You would go crazy staying at home.'"

Hicks Griffiths seems equally mystified at how he reached his views on women. "I don't know. I never thought much about it until you asked the question. I can't account for my attitude except that every time I ever noticed discrimination I didn't like it. One of the real problems today is that men are afraid of competition that women will give. I just say to companies and law firms that we need the best talent we can get." Perhaps the key to Hicks Griffiths's ability to enjoy his role is that it *is* so subconsciously a part of him. His attitude on women was nothing with which he ever had to struggle. "It's a matter of self-assurance, or our kind of marriage is not ever going to work out. If you've got to dominate the situation, then in that case you ought to marry some stupid woman who won't challenge you. I can sense that a lot of people are trying to go along with the idea of women having equal opportunity in careers and business and politics, but they're awfully nervous about it. Some sort of sidle up to me—they're very careful—and say, 'Do you *really* think a woman belongs in politics?'"

In addition to the personal security of his own career, Griffiths had another self-fulfilling and gratifying position as his wife's campaign manager. "We would have discussions, but she followed my ideas and that was it. I was in charge of the campaign. She had a lot of confidence in me. I'm a perfectionist. Everything I do I want absolutely right. Martha will tell you I can get more effort out of people." Griffiths is a slow-speaking, somewhat pedantic, calm and solid person, with no flights of fancy in his talk and an easy manner of praising his wife. During her congressional years he worried about her not getting enough rest and had to calm her during a campaign; she always ran scared.

"I felt that some people were, you know, threatened, when she started in Congress. They thought I'd probably come up here and she'd support me. But it was different in our situation. I had been active—gone from precinct to district to state chairman in politics, and I was a probate judge and I have a very nice practice. There is no reason to feel inferior, and I didn't care about the attitude of some people. Martha will be a great loss to Congress—she has such great integrity and ability."

Martha Griffiths said, "I really doubt I could have done it with children. Politics is perhaps the most demanding of professions. But one thing that happened is that I simply would not go along with it all. At one time Hicks would call and say, 'Will I see you on Thursday night or Friday?' and I wouldn't know. Then it got to be the 5:30 plane, then the 7:30, then the 9 P.M. I finally made up my mind that I had my own life." Like other women in Congress with husbands, Martha Griffiths seemed to worry more about her home life than did her male colleagues. "Men are preconditioned, and then they don't make that effort. When you don't, what you're really saying to your family and spouse is 'My life is so important—you can wait.' Second, when I got home, I didn't surround myself with staff and politicians. We go to that farm. Maybe I'll make a speech Thursday or Friday night, but it's not that business of speeches all weekend, or going to the office or down to the closest bar to see people. That's totally unnecessary. You can sell yourself too much."

An attractive woman with light brown hair who looks younger than she is, Representative Griffiths was one of the most respected and knowledgeable members of Congress. She was able to fight for such woman-oriented issues as the Equal Rights Amendment and still be considered one of the regulars. She has decried the blatant discrimination she sees in job practices and inequitable laws, but when other women were getting the feminist headlines she was relatively nonpublicized. Her husband said, "I never did think she got enough credit for what she did."

And Martha Griffiths exploded, "It doesn't bother me when

they say I'm not militant enough, but how could anyone say I'm 'not with' today? What do they mean? I *made* today."

Representative Griffiths's family goes back to the Revolutionary War—"one relative fought with Washington"—and her parents were Missouri pioneers. Her father was a mail carrier and her mother was a substitute carrier. "They would deliver the mail with a team of four horses, hitched two and two. Mother would drive those horses.

"I never expected in my life to marry and simply stay at home and be supported. One reason, I'm sure, was because my mother never did. But in those days all you could do was be a nurse or teacher. I taught for one year and said, 'This is not for me. I'm not going to sit here with these idiots!' I was nineteen and most of the kids were the younger brothers and sisters of my friends. Oh, it was hideous. I hated it!" she said with a deep laugh. "All those kids coming around and crying. I could hardly wait to push them out the door." Going to college was unique for a woman, but Martha Griffiths made up her mind she would go. Money was scarce but she went to the University of Missouri on a scholarship. Hicks Griffiths entered her life through a political science class; the two of them were the smartest in the class and often debated one another. "I was absolutely mad about him. He was very handsome. Besides, a man who says 'You are the smartest person in the whole university' is naturally so enchanting," she said with another laugh.

At first, Martha thought she would work while Hicks went to law school, but he insisted she go to law school too, although it meant giving up his own plan to go to Harvard. "I found out Harvard Law wouldn't accept women," he said, "so we went to the University of Michigan." Then, when they got out of law school, Hicks said, "I noticed discrimination against women immediately, and it was close to home." They got equal jobs but Hicks was given higher pay. "That was 1940—and it's still happening."

Of the three thousand women who ran for office in 1974, Representative Ella Grasso of Connecticut was the only one given a good chance of capturing a top government post. Her husband, Thomas, a retired school principal, was very much in the background during her twenty-year political career, until it began to look as though she would be the first woman elected governor in her own right.

Ella Grasso said she didn't think Connecticut was ready for a woman governor four years ago, but that the women's movement has changed that. "I may have lots of problems, but being a female won't be one of them."

And the newspapers have changed. She was described in 1974 as "gubernatorial candidate" or "Congresswoman," and no longer as "Ella Grasso, mother and housewife." As with any "first," Representative Grasso's life-style was duly examined and people were trying to find out what Thomas Grasso was like. His wife was regarded as an effective, intelligent, hardworking pol, but her husband was asked those Prince Consort type of questions, such as how he would like to live in his wife's mansion. Mr. Grasso replied as nicely as possible to the type of press treatment many candidates' wives get. "I anticipate it will be very thrilling living in the governor's mansion." Then he indicated that he was getting tired of it all. "It's a bit of a nuisance being Ella's husband when one is tired and wishes rest. The newness wears off."

Grasso once described his wife as a "worrywart of a mother who constantly wants to know where her children are, a very pleasant woman, very cheerful, seldom relaxed. I think she's happy." When asked if he was happy, there was a long silence at the other end of the phone. "Well," Grasso said quietly, "most of the time."

Governor Grasso cannot say enough about her husband, who backed her all these years. She talked about their meeting in a trilling voice. "I thought he was the most wonderful man. He was so handsome and he wrote the most beautiful poetry. I began chasing him and I finally caught him." Ella was fourteen and he was eighteen and a half when they first met during a summer at the shore. Her chase was "subliminal," she said with a laugh. "He spent two summers building a boat on a lot opposite us and I spent the two summers sitting on the veranda, watching him." They married in the summer of 1942 after Ella graduated from Mt. Holyoke. Her husband is her "best friend" and "constant companion," she said. "I talk to him two or three times a day when I'm in Washington. He can make judgments on things. He knows all the people I work with. So it's almost like having another self." Grasso is less enthusiastic about the importance of his role and said, "I'm very happy that Ella is doing what she wants to do."

She has been in politics since her early League of Women Voters days. "I went into my first primary when Jimmy was nine months old." At times, family considerations have held her back from making national moves. Approached by a group of interested Democrats about running for the U.S. Senate in the late sixties, when she was Connecticut's secretary of state (long a feminine preserve in Connecticut), Ella Grasso declined, among other reasons, because her husband was not well at the time. (She ran for Congress in 1970.)

Ella Tambussi Grasso, now in her mid-fifties, was the only child of Italian immigrants ("My father pretended he could read and write") and a product of a Catholic parochial school. "It took me years to learn 'youse' is not the plural of 'you.'" Extremely close to her parents, Ella was bereft when both of them died in their eighties a few years ago. "I tell you," she said, "There is nothing so pathetic as a fifty-year-old orphan." Her father was a baker and her mother worked in a mill. Ambitious for her one daughter, Mrs. Tambussi sent Ella to posh Chaffee prep school at a time when comparatively few Italian-Americans of either sex were receiving higher education. Attending school with the rich never bothered Ella Grasso. "They accepted a batch of us on the basis of our grades. I was scared and I never worked so hard in my life before or since. It was a perfect experience. Perfect!" She announced that half her graduating class worked in her campaign, adding characteristically, "Of course, there was only sixteen in the class."

After Chaffee, Holyoke was "easy" and she made Phi Beta Kappa in her junior year, then went on to earn an M.A. in sociology and economics.

She is generally regarded as a moderate liberal who is astutely cautious. "She's skillful at doing her good deeds quietly so that the conservative element in the party remains unoffended," said one Connecticut backer. Her enemies call her a machine hack, but Grasso, as co-chairman of the resolutions committee at the 1968 Democratic national convention, pushed through an anti-Vietnam War minority report, then left the convention (over the objection of machine politicians) in protest of the action of Chicago police.

After the election, Governor Grasso and her husband maintained a low profile in the governor's mansion.

During the closing weeks of the 1974 campaign, Colorado Congresswoman Pat Schroeder was back home fighting her opponent, described by Pat's husband as the "male Louise Day Hicks of Denver." A superintendent of schools, he was putting the fear of busing into his campaign. "We're running very hard and scared," said Jim Schroeder. Part of his job was to "hold down the fort" in their Virginia suburban home while the Schroeders' two children, ages four and eight, stayed in school, he told me, after having cut out of his law firm to be home at 5:30 P.M. in time to have dinner with them.

The efforts of Jim Schroeder to help keep his wife in office have been considerable since she was elected in 1972, but her private life wasn't a campaign issue the second time around. The first time, however, "that really was a problem for the voters," Schroeder said. "They would ask, 'What are you as a young mother of two small children going to do?' 'What's going to happen to your children?' 'What's your husband going to do?'"

When Pat's mother, Bernice Scott, went doorbell ringing in 1972 she was told by one woman that "I wouldn't vote for that Pat Schroeder. Any mother who would run and leave her kids." Pat's mother, a distinguished, gray-haired woman, calmly said she couldn't criticize the woman for her feelings, but added, "I was one of those bad mothers who worked, too." The two women talked about raising children, and the housewife was curious about how Mrs. Scott's two children had turned out. Mrs. Scott replied that her two children were both lawyers. She paused and added "and my *daughter* is Pat Schroeder." The astounded woman thought that with a mother like that, Pat Schroeder couldn't be so bad after all.

Once Pat was elected, the Schroeders made the decision that they would move as a family to Washington, with Schroeder getting a job there. The ensuing years were kind of like skiing—"With one ski in Denver and one in Washington," Schroeder remarked.

While job hunting, he had to candidly tell prospective employers that if his wife lost her position, they would be moving back to Colorado. He had to take a pay cut, had to refuse such tempting offers as Common Cause because of conflict of interest with his wife's job, had to find a boss who would understand that he would want time off to campaign and that if the kids got sick at school, Jim would be the one to leave the office and go home. Schroeder doesn't believe in "equality" in a dual-career marriage when there are young children; at one stage or another one partner must surface with the predominant career. "When there are two careers in the family, one career has to be able to compromise and give more than the other. When we started off and were getting a family going, my career was obviously predominant. In most cases in America today, the husband's career is the primary one, and so it's the woman that's expected to make adjustments. But with Pat's election, her career became the important one. My position is secondary in terms of career levels and time decisions and so forth."

An easygoing, deliberate, pipe-smoking man who has a round face and the remains of a somewhat "preppy," tweedy look, Schroeder takes it all with considerable equanimity. "First of all, what alternative do you have? You really can't sit around after you've won and say, 'My gosh, I didn't think we'd win and now I don't think I'll live in Washington.' I think I can appreciate the problems of her job—it has enough prestige and income that I can make the sacrifice, if you want to call it a sacrifice. If your spouse wanted to, say, go off and start a pottery factory and it was going to cost you twenty thousand dollars and maybe you might make a few bucks—now *that's* a sacrifice.

"As for the children, what I find is you tend to compensate. Pat does a wonderful job of making quality time," he told me one day at lunch. "She's leaving for Denver tonight and won't be back until Sunday. But yesterday she took our son Scotty's class and gave him a birthday party in the dining room of the Capitol. They had a clown and they just had a ball. Probably no other member of Congress thinks of his kid's birthday like that. Okay, so I'm here with the kids this weekend. I probably spend a lot more time with my children than the ordinary father, which is probably good. I see a lot of McDonald's and Arby's," he added with a laugh. "And breakfast is no problem—you get the cereal boxes out."

When things go smoothly everyone manages, although, Schroeder said, "It is a never-ending hectic pace. Somebody's always leaving or coming; it's a day-to-day existence." When

Schroeder was in general practice, he handled divorce cases and he saw the high incidence of family problems. "The family problems in our society are all probably magnified in the political and public family. We're on a very tight schedule, and the least little thing becomes a crisis. Those political pressures heighten the two-career family pressures. When one of the kids gets sick it's really a problem. When the school called, I went to get our child. Pat couldn't; she was busy on the floor."

Pat Schroeder, in her early thirties, talks in the easy vernacular of a younger generation and has had to face the leers as well as the hostility of threatened older male colleagues used to a more traditional breed of Congresswoman. Slim and attractive, with blue eyes, brunette hair, and high cheekbones, she looks more like a model than a member of Congress. Her real sacrifice was having to give up her blue jeans to go to work on the Hill. "But I felt it just wasn't worth the hassle," she said, sprawled on the living room floor with one of her children in the work clothes that she had not had time to change—a modest shirtwaist dress and nylons, shoes off.

It is too early to see if their congressional experiment has worked totally with the children, but the Schroeders feel they have adapted very well. On that one late afternoon I visited, the children seemed to be the typical products of permissive households; perhaps a shade more kinetic. The youngest was riding a pony stick through the middle of our conversation, ceaselessly commanding her mother to watch. Pat may have been overcompensating, but the child went unchecked. Her mother's absences may have taken their toll, or it may have been a stage, but at one point the girl went halfway up the stairs and began to cry. Her mother swooped her up with big hugs and asked, "Where does it hurt?" She answered petulantly, "Just the big people have the fun; the little people don't have fun." Her mother said, "Come here and let me love you." The son, very aware of his mother's job, was mad at her when she voted to cut the space program, Pat said with a laugh.

As a pretty, young, anti-establishment liberal female, Pat Schroeder could not, and did not, blend with the majority of her Hill colleagues. On one level she was caustically amused by the eighth-grade antics of many; on another level she was deeply concerned that they were so out of touch with many of the people in America. The Schroeders' "real" friends are various congressional aides, newspaper and TV correspondents, a handful of her colleagues, people they knew before, some in Jim's Washington law firm. "They're the ones we do things with—you know, you get pizza and sit on the floor, the same floor where the kids' bubble gum is embedded—that so-called 'glamorous' life of a politician," she joked. The friends among her colleagues are "outside the establishment." "I just don't have that other kind of value system. The psyche of traditional politicians and their needs just frightens me no end. Waiting ten years to get an 'important' room with a window on the Hill. Whoopee. And there is this most incredibly outgoing, friendly air, and yet they are competing like mad and are out to knife each other. Sometimes I just call long distance to some friends from the cloakroom; I just have to find someone 'real' out there. This job is the biggest thing that happened to so many of these guys. They're so afraid they're going to lose it, they will sell out on anything. Some I'm very close to and admire, but a lot see themselves as the biggest sexual objects in the world. The banter never lets up. One of the women in Congress is sort of uptight and unbending, so after we have two cups of coffee, they want to know if she is homosexual. They're like eighth-grade boys. They probably have 'slam' books."

In her easygoing way, Pat Schroeder gave what is referred to as a "fairly famous talk" at a congressional prayer breakfast. She thought it was going to be a nice little group so she addressed herself to one of the things that bothered her, the congressional treatment of one another, and ended up adding a less-than-pious commandment to the scriptures: "Thou shalt not bullshit thy colleagues." Some said it was the most honest address ever heard at their prayer breakfast, others were stunned into silence.

Her husband feels that Pat's open and warm personality "creates a remarkable rapport with all kinds of people. She can speak out and be respected for her position and yet she never scares anybody. I've seen her talk to hard-nosed union groups and Rotary clubs and they become her grudging supporters." Schroeder feels that he gets better treatment than most political wives, although he sometimes thinks the fact that they can give more full-time help to a campaign and the family is an asset. "I worry because I'm working that I can't give Pat all the assistance she needs." One asset he has that most women spouses do not is that he has been in politics. He sometimes writes her speeches, researches the issues, and gives speches for her outlining their shared views on issues. And because of the maleness of politics, union leaders and more conservative males will often talk to Schroeder before his wife. It's an unfortunate fact, but he goes along with it in order to give his wife more mileage. Schroeder himself ran for the Colorado house in 1970 and lost—by only forty-two votes. "Had I won, Pat wouldn't have been in politics. It's as simple as that. But I think she's the better one up front."

Facing the frustrations of a new and maverick member of Congress, Pat Schroeder at times wondered if it was worth it to run for a second term. However, her husband urged her on. It was important that those willing to critically examine the institution make it into office, he told her. As a woman with young children she spoke for a nationwide constituency heretofore unrepresented in Congress; an increasingly active constituency. It was important she remain in Congress to give them a model, but it meant an added burden. She got three thousand letters per day, many from women all over the country.

Among the many things that disturbed Pat was the lack of concern for family that so many of her colleagues expressed. She tried in her own way to make a dent in their feelings. "The family pictures are something else. When one guy's father died, the campaign director couldn't stop thinking of the funeral— what a great time to get a picture of the whole family for the brochure! I don't know what it is. The family is like a possession. The minute the session is over, I try to split and get home. We limit extra activities at most to twice a week. We cut below that if we can. We've cut all those awful, awful receptions—given by the American Mousetrap Manufacturers and the Clay Pipe Association of America. I have more fun playing in the sandbox with the kids. I find it a great release. And those stag things! I say, 'If Jim can't come, I won't come.' Some of the men say, 'I couldn't say or do that.' They have a feeling they'll be considered sissies or something if they said they won't go without their wives. The incredible thing about Jim is he has such ego strength none of it bothers him—and he loves to pull their chains."

Talking about the Congressmen who are never home, Pat

Schroeder said, "It's almost as if they're proud of it." As for those extracurricular activities they feel are so important, she adds, "I just feel an awful lot of what they do is 'make work.' Maybe I'm just kidding myself, but I think I've done as much legislatively as any other newer member. If those damn receptions and meetings mean anything, then I'm in trouble. And this business of keeping up contacts. I'm not too sure. I think it's a justification. When we were all invited to the White House prayer breakfast I said I would go if I could bring my children and husband. Everyone said, 'You can't bring your children to this!' and I said, 'Well, is this a *worship* service or a political service?'"

For the time being, Schroeder is content for his wife to have the dominant career. For one reason, the demands of her job would make it impossible for them to live any other way. And one final reason, he said with a grin, is "I don't think the public is ready for a husband and wife in public life at the same time."

So convinced is he of her importance in Congress that one night in her first year as a freshman member of Congress he sat down and typed a supportive letter. It sounded more like something written from an admiring colleague than a husband. At that moment, Schroeder felt that was what she needed from him more than anything else.

In part, he wrote:

"You won a tough, uphill, very close election in November 1972. You need that ten-day Thanksgiving recess in the district—your staff has scheduled you for numerous important public appearances; and you're concerned about keeping in close touch with your constituents.

"You're also tired—it's been a tough fall, you need a break Besides, there are those two small ones—3 and 7—who you fee you don't see enough; and you've promised them a vacation back in Denver with their grandparents and friends.

"But you're also a member of the House Armed Service Committee. You fought to end U.S. involvement in Southeas Asia, and have been a tenacious and outspoken critic of Penta gon spending. Your chairman has wrongfully attacked you for your lack of knowledge on military matters. Thus, when a special subcommittee is formed to visit the Middle East war zone during the recess, your staff (and husband) feel it's essentia that you go. Your committee will soon be asked to authorize over 2 billion for new Israeli arms, and over 4 billion for new U.S. weapons. The Middle East is a powder keg, which affects U.S. oil supplies and economy; and you keep remembering 'On the Beach,' a popular novel and movie of the late 1950s, which begins with the end of WW III—which starts in the Middle East.

"10 days and almost 30,000 miles of flying—many hours on planes and buses with 20 'colleagues'—your elder, male, more conservative fellows, who love to criticize you (if they aren't trying to get you into bed).

"So, you decide to go. It will be the first time an official U.S. congressional party will visit Cairo in years. You went to Athens the day of the military coup. You went into the war zone at Suez. The trip was about the issues of war and peace, the possible expenditure of over 6 billion dollars. What could be more important in November of 1973? (Although none of the other half-dozen dissenting voices on the committee decided to make the trip.)

"It was an important trip. You talked to Mrs. Meir and Moshe Dayan. You inspected the status of the Israeli army. You flew in Israeli helicopters to the west bank of the Suez. You met President Sadat and visited with the speaker and members of the Egyptian parliament; and then met with the Egyptian 2nd army troops on the east bank of the Suez. You visited Port Said, and saw the death and destruction caused by U.S. fragmentation bombs. Your picture with President Sadat appeared on the front page of the Cairo newspaper. On the way back, your views and opinions were carefully respected by the subcommittee chairman, and hopefully, will influence the subcommittee's report.

"You returned home—tired, and with a cold, and to two sick children. But, the trip was worth it. Or was it?

"—One Denver paper (the one that endorsed you in 1972) carried a prominent article, attacking the trip because of the amount of jet fuel being used by the Air Force 707 that carried that committee.

"—Although news media had followed and photographed the committee for 10 days, the only footage that appeared on one national TV network showed several of the members (including you) enjoying an Egyptian horse show and riding camels—the one 'tourist' event of the entire trip (and sponsored by your Egyptian hosts, at that).

"—The other Denver newspaper highlighted your view that the U.S. should proceed with 'caution' in resupplying Israel with arms. This served to touch off an immediate adverse reaction from many of your friends and supporters in Denver's Jewish community.

"Well, ironically, your trip occurred the weekend of the 10th anniversary of John F. Kennedy's assassination. Kennedy loved Robert Frost, as you do. Frost wrote those memorable lines about two paths crossing in the woods: 'and I—I took the one less traveled by, and that has made all the difference.'

"You were in Cambridge on November 22, 1963. A classmate at Harvard Law wrote in your yearbook:

'For a brief time our generation has had its hand upon the rudder of national destiny. For a moment it appeared as though our venerable institutions and conventional mythology were to be reexamined and revitalized. Perhaps we shall, like the generation which followed Lincoln, turn away from paths illumined by the late President, turn inward in pursuit of private future or backward in conformity to comfortable, if hardly serviceable, ideas.'

"Well, keep on your path, Patricia—the one less traveled—the one illumined by courage and marked by critical examination of our institutions and mythology."

21

It's Not All Roses

AT the 1972 Democratic convention, Frances "Sissy" Farenthold, a moving force in the relatively minuscule Texas reform politics, was nominated for the vice presidency. Women were at that convention in record numbers and there were loud cheers for the woman who had battled the establishment and came close to becoming governor of Texas in 1972. The cheers also came not only from women but from men such as John Kenneth Galbraith, who seconded the nomination.

Back home in Texas, Sissy's husband, George, heard the announcement on the radio. "I just thought it was another one of her whims," he recounted. With dead honesty, the Farentholds make no attempt to paint a rosy picture of togetherness about their twenty-four-year marriage. There have been too many separations—and too many separate paths—for that. Sissy steadily became a strong force in the National Women's Political Caucus and before the push for women's rights was a spokesman for liberal causes in the Texas state legislature, where that took more than a little courage. Her husband continued to make money in the Texas oil business (his company sells oil pipelines to foreign countries; "My business is steel—not s-t-e-a-l but s-t-e-e-l," he spells with a wink). He also remained more conservative than his wife politically and stayed clear of her political activities. Throughout a two-hour conversation in their Houston home, George Farenthold seemed anxious to prove that he was the boss of the house and of his life. While most husbands of women who have made it as far as national politics are highly supportive, he is a surprising sort of husband for Sissy. Of Belgian nobility (some Texans called him a "Belch"), he seems to find her independence unsettling. Although he said the "positive" side of his wife's political involvement was her inspirational leadership—"If I had to choose tomorrow between a gal who is in the Junior League and plays tennis all day or a woman who really is doing something for others, there is no question. Why, she's had nationwide attention. She gives women something to shoot for. She's doing great things"—most of his comments were more defensive. "I think Sissy's got a great advantage right now. It's the time of the woman. She would never have got as far as she has had she been a *man*," he said. At another point, Farenthold described the Capital Club where the more establishment politicians, judges, editors, and some businessmen gather. "I find they don't pay much attention to Sissy. *I'm* part of the group. She's not. It's a funny thing—they like Sissy but they don't usually have too much truck with her. I have an upper hand there," he said with a chuckle. "It's amazing to all of us. Who would have ever thought Sissy would do what she did?"

At one time George urged her to get out of politics but when I was with them in November of 1973 he said, "I think it's gone so far that she can't stop." (A few months later she tried again, unsuccessfully, for the governorship of Texas.) He admitted, "We have separate lives, different friends. Sissy's been good about it—I've had to make my own friends and I do. She's gone fifty percent of the time." How do the two of them get along? "We tolerate each other's friends."

Even to her friends, Sissy Farenthold has remained something of a mystery, a woman admired in that same awed way as Eleanor Roosevelt. I had seen her at the 1972 convention, weary and overextended. More than a year later, serving dinner for friends in her own home, she was relaxed and more open but there remained a mysterious, almost melancholic quality to her. She is a handsome woman, tall with brunette hair and large eyes, brilliant, an unswerving follower of her own causes. She seems to have a great capacity for inner sorrow. There is little of the ego tripping evident in many politicians' personalities, and no artifice. One friend, John Henry Faulk, said, "The key to her personality and what has made me love her is she is one of the few legislators who has the capacity to be *outraged* by injustice. She'd take on those crooks in the Texas legislature [she led a band of mavericks called the "dirty dozen" who would not go along with Texas politics as usual and helped end a corrupt machine] and they'd go white with rage. You don't understand the courage that took. She has complete and total integrity. Yet, on the other hand, I think she has a certain reserve in intimate relationships. She's more one of these public people, truly motivated by the desire to see society improved."

Another Texan critical of Sissy's rather pessimistic seriousness said, "She is never one who just lets go and has a wild time."

Sissy seems hard on herself regarding the family sacrifices for politics. "One of the greatest political myths is the 'Happy American Political Family.' How can it be? Maybe the myth is the happy home life, period, but politics does cut into your time together. Everybody goes his own way. When I started in politics I purposely took the children with me. I was raised the same way by my father; from the time I was eight or nine I went places with him. And yet, I know the people in my family are sick of politics, I'd say about half of the time."

Despite what seem insurmountable ideological differences, Sissy appears simply to ignore her husband's political attitudes and vice versa. Her children have also been allowed to express their own political views, which are more in alignment with their mother's than their father's, although they are not in total agreement with her. In 1968 Sissy was going to a reception for Hubert Humphrey and her daughter, Emily, now at Vassar, was a teenager marching with Gene McCarthy supporters— who were boycotting the reception. "She's lost interest in politics now," said Sissy. Jimmy was seventeen in 1972 and he was "fascinated by Wallace. He watched him every time he could. I didn't say anything and after two months he'd had it. We've never had a clash in politics. To me, everyone's choice is so personal. I've never been able to ask for anyone's vote."

Sissy is one of the leaders of the women's political movement who does not think women are any less concerned with power than male politicians. "I was on a panel with other political women and I was the only one who said, 'Look, what we're about is *power*.' I say repeatedly that I don't attribute all political virtue to women. Just the use of that elected office means power. The night I went out of office [in the state legislature] I got one last call from a constituent. A woman whose son was in prison for years as an addict. She wanted to get him into some sort of program. George and I were having a late supper and I wept. George was touched at my reaction and I said, 'Yes, I was touched by that woman, but I was also weeping for my *powerlessness*—not to be able to do anything.' People can argue that you want it for good causes, but it's still the *use* of power." She talked about the injustice of one incident she had read of that day in the papers, Mexicans who had been kept in prison fifteen years. Her hand clenched. "Maybe I might not have been able to do much [if still in office], but I would have called some characters. It's the use of power, no question about it. That power was supposed to be for the people; it's for just about everything else," she said pessimistically. What about politicians who say their life is no different from that of overachieving executives? "They're lying to themselves. Number one, in politics you have a public life. You can be an overachieving executive of a corporation and not have all those problems of being a public figure. You're not in public life."

In their home, Sissy is an almost retiring person, and is in sharp contrast to her public person—the one who was quoted across the country as a leader in reform politics and the women's political movement, praising the strides women made in the 1974 elections. She was busily clearing the table, deferring to her husband. One of her friends said, "George is 'Le Baron' and he wants everyone to think of him that way." Farenthold said of his wife, "When it comes down to it, she is very feminine in that way. She has more or less catered to me, deferred to me. The first thing she does in a campaign is introduce her husband. She doesn't believe in 'Ms.' as a name. She says, 'I'm Mrs. George Farenthold.' She's just that much a woman and a wife. She's said many times she hates that 'Ms.' "

That she could be at all compatible with George Farenthold might puzzle her sisters across the nation, but it was certainly in keeping with her Texas upbringing. And, although a foreigner, Farenthold was not so different from the Texas men she would have known as a young girl. As John Bainbridge described Texas women in *The Super-Americans* in the early sixties, They would be the last to shuck off a time-honored "feminine" role: "Chivalry in contemporary Texas, as in the olden times, makes few demands on women, but the few it makes are strict. The first is an at least ostensible acknowledgment of male superiority." The dogma to remember was, as put by one Texas woman to Bainbridge, "For a woman to act as if she thinks she's as bright as a man—that's fatal." The writer allowed that many business and professional women in Texas agitated for the equal rights amendment to the state constitution, but "few other Texas women would think of bringing up this subject or any other so potentially displeasing to a male."

Bainbridge continued that, at that time, "There are few women anywhere in the country who have the daring to pursue a contrary course in public, but whereas implied deference to men is, to a certain extent, voluntary elsewhere, in Texas it seems to have the oppressive status of law."

How does Farenthold feel about his wife's political activities? "It doesn't bother me a damn bit. I just turn it off. I go to bed at nine o'clock; I get up fairly early in the morning. I don't answer the phone for her. I am able to divorce myself. If she became President of the United States I'm going to keep my way. I travel as much as she does—to Europe and Africa."

George Farenthold pretends to hold a startlingly patronizing and opposing view of social concerns—perhaps in part to maintain his own individuality; difficult to do when living with such a symbol of social reform. "I'm much more conservative. I don't believe certain people Sissy is trying to do things for are actually

ready or educated for them. You can do just so much for
minorities. I think responsibility comes with education, and I
firmly believe children of Mexican Americans and Negroes
don't get enough food when they are babies. The families have
to work and leave them without proper care in the first years of
their life. They are handicapped the rest of their lives."

Farenthold hardly had a democratic background. Cooking
steaks at an outdoor grill near their swimming pool, Farenthold, who looked like a burly stevedore, with a thick neck and
balding gray hair, took great pride in revealing his European
background. "I was raised with princes. I was raised in Spain
and Belgium and I had a title. I was a baron—there were lots of
princes but very few barons. I came to the United States when I
was nineteen—I had my valet who had taken care of me since I
was fourteen. He and I came here. From the time I was four I
had tutors."

Their home is filled with antiques, tapestry, old paintings, an
ornate and ancient gilt mirror from his ancestors. Growing
more expansive as he talked about himself, Farenthold said, "I
was one of the fastest downhill racers when I was young." He
jumped up and brought back a picture. "Look how handsome I
was then. I am in front of the stables of a prince." There is a
picture of a young man, bronzed arms, in his short-shirted polo
outfit. During a visit to Texas, Farenthold married the daughter of a rich Texan. After their marriage, Farenthold said he
had intended to return to Europe to finish medical school but
his new wife said, "If you do, I won't be with you." He decided
to come back to Texas. "I went to work in the oil business." Farenthold described himself at that time as "very much on the
fascist side—I was a fascist in those days. Basically I didn't want
to go back to Europe. I just wanted to get away from that whole
mess. I didn't want to face reality, what was going on in Europe.
I remember going back on the boat just before 1939, and I met
a very attractive Italian guy. I was just a young guy of twenty-
two and I popped off. It was one of the worst things that ever
happened to me. I said I didn't believe what Hitler was supposed to be doing and certainly there was nothing wrong with
what he was doing to the Jews." Farenthold noticed the startled
look on his audience's face. "This Italian guy said, 'I'm Jewish.'
I was just a kid, I didn't know any better. I was a fascist," he said
by way of explanation. Farenthold took his first wife to Europe

on their honeymoon, and that is when their troubles began. "If you have enough wealth in Texas you can build an empire. She thought if you have enough money they would accept you. In Europe it is more based on family. I think she never got the acceptance she expected. We were just kids with a lot of problems. The only problem we didn't have was money."

Before they divorced, Farenthold and his first wife had one son. During Sissy's 1972 campaign, tragedy of the most violent sort touched their lives. George's enormously wealthy son by his first marriage was murdered, tied and cemented, and thrown into a Texas river. The unsolved murder was linked to organized gambling, although the motive has remained vague.

From the very beginning of the Sissy and George Farenthold marriage, she was active in the background of politics. "Dad wanted me to go to every country election and I would drag George along." George, in fact, was involved in politics as a campaign manager for an unsuccessful candidate for U.S. Senator.

When she got to the state legislature Sissy found that the infighting took its toll. "In a place like Texas, if you make your peace you can go awfully far. When it comes to legislating bills on oil and gas you can say to yourself, 'How much easier just to rationalize this.' I don't like to be a constant critic, but that climate had to be constantly fought. I guess the fighting took more out of me as a person than anything. At the time I went up to the capitol you just weren't 'with it' if you weren't profiteering—or is it profiting?"

The emoluments can be corrupting, she acknowledged. "I know, for example, it's a lot easier traveling with a retinue in a statewide race than barreling around the country by yourself. I miss these things, no question. And if you *cherish* the office holding, you develop certain traits. Incumbency breeds cautiousness. I saw it happen. The 'being there' was the thing. I've lost track of the times people would say, 'If you'd just stay out of other people's business, you wouldn't have any opposition.' I've seen votes walk away when I wouldn't say the reassuring thing people wanted me to."

Sissy and George were married when she was twenty-three and he considerably older. (Sissy had decided she would not marry a lawyer because there were too many in the family.) She admits that the ego of a husband of a politician can be easily bruised. "I probably don't do as much as I should do, but I have a sense of obligation about that." How does she bolster his ego? "I've tried to do what I could, but maybe I did not do all that I could have done. There were times during the governor's campaign when I wasn't given a minute to call. I'd have someone else call. I remember trying to place a call from the floor of the national convention. He was offended if I didn't call. It was always on my mind."

There were conflicting signals for Sissy Farenthold, the product of a genteel, cultured "first family" of Texas. Her grandfather was on what is now the supreme court of Texas. From her youngest days her father encouraged her to have a law career. A brilliant student, she was a rarity in her time, one of the few females in the University of Texas law school. She ended up practicing in her father's law firm. "It was very definitely unlike what most women did. You know, my mother had a totally different kind of life, but they were always pushing me to go on." Things might have been different for Sissy had her brother, one year older, lived. "He died when I was two; he was three. They used to call me the 'two-in-one' child. I was to more or less follow what the oldest boy had done. I also had another difficult role. Mother was sick a great part of the time. People told me I *ran* that household. I was a little girl, seven or eight, and I was running the servants. I must have been a horrible pain! People told me that when the caterers came for a party, I would show them where the silver and crystal were. . . . I remember mother in the hospital nearly one whole year when I was eleven."

Sissy was expected to carry on for the oldest son, follow in her father's steps as a lawyer interested in social reform, and yet, as a well-bred woman from a Catholic background, raise a family. And then, a tragedy in her own life pushed her farther into politics as an escape from sorrow. "I've been prodded in many, many ways." One of her children, a twin brother of her youngest son, Jimmy, nineteen, died in 1960 at the age of four. The family had a history of hemophilia and when her son had an accident, his blood would not coagulate. "Sometimes it works, if you can exert pressure on the wound, but his was internal. . . . It was so terrible, but I just couldn't dwell on it. My own experience with my little brother—I knew what the loss was to my parents. They never got over it." Sissy threw herself into politics in an attempt to forget.

"I gave myself ten years to do something in politics and then get out: politics is so dehumanizing. It's hardest for the spouse of an officeholder and the children, I feel. One of my four who was having the most problems went to a child psychiatrist and told the doctor that no one could understand the pressures he got from his peers." Did she know the origins of that comment? "Of course it was privileged information, so I never knew." Hers was a rather dispassionate analysis of her personal life and she seemed reluctant to probe her children's problems; partly because her civil libertarian feelings make it difficult for her to interfere unless the other person asks her help. When one child was picked up for possession of marijuana it received publicity because of who she was. Her identity, she thinks, "has always worried them, has been a burden on them." She paused. "The children protected me." They did not reveal what had been said to her. Did she ever probe? "Oh, sometimes, other times not." Her battling in the state legislature made her family both more vulnerable and visible. "Had I stayed with what we call 'women's issues'—education, tax advantages for garden clubs— we'd have had a 'niche' and would have been left alone." I asked why she did not pursue the children's problems. "Sometimes I tried to put it in perspective. Perhaps it is just the price we pay in public office," she said, sounding neither unconcerned nor indifferent, but resigned to the problems her position created. But then she said more harshly, "Where a woman feels particularly vulnerable is with the children and the things that happen to them. It makes your blood run cold." Her war with the speaker of the house in Texas led to the man zeroing in on Sissy's son. "He ordered the House photographer to take pictures of our oldest son, who was long-haired. He was going to use it against me as having a 'hippie' son. I went to the speaker and he denied it. It's difficult enough to raise children not to have this going on. Your home is where you're most vulnerable. The double standard is difficult for women politicians, who often face rumors about sex. Rumors were always spread about me in the campaign, usually about sex or the family. Throughout west Texas they kept saying I had four husbands, so I just spoke up and said, 'There's been some confusion—I have four *children* and *one* husband.'" Her husband did not make it a practice to campaign with her but spent the last week of both the primary and the runoff with Sissy because of the rumors about her marriage.

Most women Sissy Farenthold's age have been conditioned to feel guilty about anything that seems like neglect of children. It is particularly intense among those with careers, while women who play bridge all day somehow do not often feel the same torn and conflicting feelings. "I've seen kids with lots of problems with full-time mothers at home," said Sissy. "At least I tried not to put too much emphasis on that. Maybe I'm just being defensive. And yet I feel, as a female politician, that men in politics don't get quite as uptight about their kids. As a mother you feel they are essentially your obligation; that's the way you were brought up, and I lived through a lot of pain over that. Younger men and women feel both have a responsibility; I think they are completely different and it is less a strain on women."

Reflecting on what politics cost her personally, Sissy said softly, "You try to hold on to the family thing, and you probably fail. So much of that simply goes. But what goes before the family is friends. When people were in the hospital, I used to go see them. I can do that now only once in a blue moon. I used to be deeply interested in the extended family, but not anymore. The erosion within the immediate family is very subtle. As I said, my kids were always with me. When I went to Austin [for the legislative session] they'd pack up and travel with me. But I do think you come to them with depleted physical resources. I'd get back home and I'd not be fit to talk to." What about after a defeat, such as that tough 1968 governor's race? "It is an incredible letdown. It took me quite a long time to live through it. You'd be going down a highway and you'd remember being there . . . the questions asked, the people. It becomes a personal part of you. At the convention, someone repeated a quote I had said, and I didn't even remember saying it. There are such forces of change."

There was "an awful lot of juggling" to manage her private life. "It was very, very difficult, there is no getting around that. I remember one year one of the boys wasn't doing well on the school bus and it was imperative he be picked up at 3:30 P.M. [She did not elaborate except to say there were behavioral problems.] Things were so difficult I just don't even like to dredge it up. One of the most difficult times was when I was in the legislature. The youngest and the oldest sons didn't get along." She would ask an aide, "Can you possibly go out to the apartment?" She explained, "I couldn't leave; I had a commitment to go up and vote. I made a point never to miss a vote in those two sessions."

Close friends, however, protest that Sissy's view of herself as a mother is incorrect and harsh. "She is terribly concerned about her kids and they know it. They are enormously proud of what she's done and they are all gung ho for her politics. All their peer groups are working for Sissy," said one. While there is more of a generation gap with George, this friend chuckled and said that George, even, was not entirely what he seemed. "He plays a role but the wonderful thing about his 'authoritarianism' is he's not all that authoritarian. Sissy and the kids take it as a joke. He plays a role but George is actually a very sweet and good natured guy. And Sissy has given him a status he could never have had."

Sissy Farenthold seems unable to totally enjoy any of the political advancements she, as a woman, has gained in recent years. It is as if she must keep reminding herself to tamp down the effects of both public adulation and public hatred.

"Here's how I debilitate my political ego," she said with a laugh. An oil picture of her, the original of a campaign poster, was hung above the washing machine in the laundry room. "I just felt it was good to put it here and not somewhere else in the house."

Is she disillusioned with politics? "No, I'm not, or I'd stop, I guess."

When I talked with the Farentholds it was after her term of office and before her second unsuccessful attempt for the governorship, but her nationwide speeches and his international business kept them as much apart as they had been while she was in office. It seemed to be simply a reconciled marriage of two very different people. "We don't see that much of each other now," said George Farenthold. "But we've been married twenty-four years—you don't have to be in bed all the time. It's not that important for couples to be together all the time. We're not kids anymore."

Part IV

Patterns: Scenes from
Political Marriages

WE have now examined the hazards of public power—the hidden price that some politicians have paid in broken marriages and alienated families. We have heard from the divorced and from that still relatively rare species, the political husband.

The picture would be incomplete without the views of a variety of political couples on how they have coped with public life. Some have already expressed their feelings in previous chapters. In the following portraits, some wives and families detail their rebellion against, while others defend, the outside forces that have come to bear on their private lives. As much as possible, I have tried to let them tell in their own words how they see themselves and political life.

22

"Birch Is My Career"

ONE'S first impression of Marvella Bayh is decidedly deceptive. She of the Ipana smile, the soft fluff of blond hair, the slender body, and gushing, almost babyish voice. The look is 1950s cheerleader, but it masks a quick and ambitious mind. That voice can move with compulsive, autocratic efficiency. One day, she tried to phone me at the Washington *Post*. I wasn't there and when she reached me two days later, she complained that no one on the switchboard had answered her call "for the *longest* time. In *our* office we certainly tell somebody if something goes wrong. I *really* think you should notify someone." She was calling to tell me she had an incredibly heavy schedule, would have to postpone the interview for three weeks, emphasizing that when we did reschedule "I will have only one hour."

When I arrived at her house I got an extremely pleasant smile, and an introduction to her maid, who was waxing the hall floor. She talked to the maid with a lot of "honeys" and very sweetly asked, conveying an order nevertheless, "If you put too much polish, won't it take the wax off?" She also asked that the woman not make too much noise because we were going to be talking in the living room.

The living room was one of those unlived-in living rooms; the Bayhs prefer the downstairs red, white, and blue rec room; in a $100,000-plus town house built in the 1960s, in northwest Washington near the Shoreham Hotel. The living room is non-intimate: pale blue rug, gold and beige furniture—French provincial style, four birch logs stacked in a fireplace which looks as if it had never been introduced to a match.

We started to talk but she was quickly distracted by the noise of the waxer in the hall. "Let's go up to my office, although I'm afraid it's *just* a mess." It was immaculate. A small pleasant room with two floral chintz chairs and a desk. The only possible disarray was a neat stack of letters for her to answer. On the walls hung the memorabilia that pertained to her; not unlike the usual Washington trophy room, filled with heads of politicians, and constant reminders of one's importance. Hers are

365

signed pictures of Lyndon and Lady Bird; a letter to her from Lyndon wishing her well after her 1971 cancer operation; a picture from Bayh "to my Marvella, the girl of my dreams, with all my love, forever and ever." And a note from him: "Welcome home to the one who makes home worth coming to." There was a framed laudatory column about her husband giving up his bid for presidency to be near his wife after her operation. Also hanging up was the Pride of the Plainsmen Award given to her by her home town of Enid, Oklahoma, when she was the 1950 President of Girls' Nation.

She sat down and said, "I'm a perfectionist—and I don't say that as a compliment." She talked for a few minutes, then stopped in midsentence. "As I'm sitting here talking to you I realize for the first time those two doors behind you are not the same height. That will just drive me *crazy*."

Marvella Bayh at forty is a woman who does not seem either vain or self-conscious about her looks. She casually put on glasses when she had to read something. As she moved into talking about herself and her life she did it with a certain amount of reflection that was not there before her 1971 cancer operation; there are more wonderings about where the Bayhs are and where they are going. Following her mastectomy her husband faced the TV lights and newspapermen and in a choked voice and with tears in his eyes moved out of the race for the presidency. While there has been no recurrence, Mrs. Bayh explained, "they don't call you cured for five years. Every two months I go for a checkup."

Marvella Bayh's life is one shaped by tragedy and success; enormous highs and lows. Her mother was ill all her life, her father, whom she had worshipped as a child, became an alcoholic after her mother's death, remarried, and then one night shot and killed her stepmother and then himself. Marvella was in a car accident while in college which left her with double vision for months. Both Marvella and the Senator were in a plane crash with Ted Kennedy, an accident that killed two people. In Washington Marvella is often regarded as brighter than her husband, as the driving, ambitious force behind him. Much of her drive stems from a recently unmasked desire to do something on her own, and a pent-up frustration at not having been able to do so. She tells friends that Birch couldn't have gotten elected without her. She would have preferred the presidency herself, it has been said.

Being a Senator's wife is a "full-time job" she says, "I've always been a career-minded type of person. That's unusual to say, in a way, because I've never had one. I finally finished my degree after Evan was born. *We* were elected that year to the Senate." Without a smile, she adds, "Birch is my career. I never had a paying job as such. It is a thorn. If something happened to my life tomorrow there would be deep regret that I never tried, somewhere, sometime, all alone to paddle my own canoe." The appendage and supportive role can get to a person, she says—"you do begin to feel like you've done nothing concrete. I worked like a dog last year, but here it is [she flings her arm out at the pile of letters on the desk]. Birch is smart enough. He always makes me feel that I'm truly important. But the frustration is that if I worked I'd have something to show for it—'here's the paycheck.' Sometimes I feel like a college-educated flunky." Marvella has changed dramatically from a gung-ho to a relatively reluctant team player. Some months after she complained about her non-career status, she started free-lancing for women's magazines and took her first paid job as the weekly "Bicentennial reporter" for the NBC-TV affiliate in Washington. "Now I'm not just some wife and mother," she said, "I'm me."

She worries about her husband's health and told me that *"personally* I'd be the winner, if he lost. I'd have him home more often. I wouldn't have to share him with thousands of people." Just before her operation there was the beginning of a rude awakening about their "joint" effort. "If something happened to him," she told the Washington *Post's* Sally Quinn, "not only would I lose a husband, a best friend and a breadwinner—but my own career."

When Bayh's ambitions, at least on the surface, were concerned with returning to the Senate from his conservative and rural state and not with presidential dreams, he called himself a Hoosier and a farmer, although he spent much of his childhood in Washington while his father was superintendent of District schools. Fortunately for his political biography, he returned to Indiana in time to become Indiana's Tomato Growing Champion and to graduate from Sherkyville High. When he came to Washington, as one friend said, he was "so naïve." Now, she said, "The façade is still naïve, but inside he's damn tough." He is thought of as everything from an idealist to a not-too-bright Boy Scout to a supremely political opportunist. An ex-aide, making a distinction between "intelligence" and "brightness," refused the first adjective and said Bayh is "bright, quick, and smart."

This year an ex-aide who left politics because "I didn't like what it was doing to me" recalled a conference he had with Bayh, Marvella, and a couple of other staff members in the hospital following Bayh's airplane crash with Ted Kennedy in 1966.

The Bayhs shared a room, which meant that Marvella was in the next bed while he conducted business with his aides. "That was the only time I can remember in my five years with the Senator that there was a rush of human reaction from Marvella. Her hands flew up and she kissed me. It was the only time she treated me as a human being."

The aides were discussing whether Bayh should hold a press conference. "He was bruised and banged up. I remember we had to hold him up to urinate, his legs were so weak. Well, during the discussion, there was his wife, and particularly since it was *her*, he did ask her opinions. He was genuinely in pain, but I remember telling him not to forget to grimace. Remember, the actor has to have proper stage directions," the aide added sarcastically. "He did it beautifully. At one point during the press conference he shifted his weight during his answer and grimaced, just fine. I guess I'm just cynical but they're all such actors."

Bayh says his wife is one of the best political advisers he has, sides with her through the clashes she has with his staff, some of whom end up quitting from battle fatigue. Most of her Washington detractors admit she's invaluable back in Indiana where her nickname of "Marvelous Marvella" originated.

An ex-secretary said, "A lot of people in the office thought she was a bitch and there were lots of times when I did, too. On the other hand, she is a perfectionist. She demands perfection on anything she's working on. She's more like a caged woman. She was an integral part of his campaigns and I argued she should have had an office during the presidential campaign. The recognition she got would have been a positive move for the whole operation. Her bit really is speaking, but on the other hand she had some good ideas. She wanted to be a part of it. To feel as though she were important."

One of the typical stories in the Bayh office is the day she asked someone to drive her to the White House. It was snowing and her fear of driving, the legacy of her old accident, was on her mind. One aide came into the office and everyone was giggling. One of the girls said, "Mrs. Bayh wanted someone to drive her to the White House for a tea with Lady Bird, wait for her, and drive her home. Since you weren't here, we elected you." At first the aide thought they were joking but then he realized they weren't. His reply was that he couldn't; he had guests for dinner that night. No one wanted to make the phone call. When he did, he recounted, Mrs. Bayh went into a tirade and told him that she "represented the office just as much as my husband does; in these kinds of cases you work for me just as much as him." He explained about his own guests and offered to get her a taxi but she said taxis were not to be trusted to be there on time.

The former aide recalled that Marvella said, "I'm going to call the Senator about this." One observer said, "She tracked him down in Indiana and he got on the phone and said in a weary voice for the aide to "do this for me. Do *me* a favor." The aide did.

When I mentioned to Marvella that some people thought of her as the ambitious—and sometimes bitchy—member of the duo, her smile stayed in one big crescent shape and her eyes widened and her voice was touched with wonderment. "You're right—so many feel that!" she said, shaking her head that anyone could think that of her. "I *did urge* him to leave the farm. And I urged him to get a law degree [he flunked the bar the first time] just so we could *afford* to lose, if that should happen. I *was* eager for him to run for the Senate the first time. For me it was absolutely the greatest office in the whole world. I . . . well, perhaps I will brag just a little." She paused. "In a campaign-type situation, you know your worth. Then, in the years in between, while *he's* getting *personal* satisfaction from the legislation that he gets through, you're no longer as much a part of it." Marvella did play a part in some legislation—"ones with which I closely identify, like efforts to abolish the electoral college system." She also urged him to speak out against President Nixon's intervention in the Calley case, even though Bayh's mail was 1,000 to 1 against that stand.

One afternoon Bayh sat in his office, chewing on some ice left over from a glass of Fresca, and talked about his wife and politics. Although he regards Marvella as a "full partner—in every respect," he admits that what she does for him "is not the kind of thing that's hers alone. I do everything possible to get her involved, but it's still really Senator Bayh—not Senator and Mrs. Bayh. It's *me* instead of *us*. We're trying to figure out what to do to create an opportunity for her to do something very much on her own. She can climb a mountain barefoot if she wants to, once we get this election over. It's a tough, mean, nasty election. If a career means that much to her, it's important for her to do it." Bayh adds, a trifle defensively, that if she decides on a career (Marvella said she was interested in one now that their one child, Evan, is in college) she's going to have to decide how to spread her time around. He hints that there may be a lessening of closeness. "Now, I don't make a major decision without getting her input and we spend our personal time bringing her up to date on my work. She's going to have to be willing to forgo this control. There's only so much time you can take out of public life for other things. She's going to have to determine her own life, where to draw the line. I've been telling her she's not as strong physically as I am. Mentally, she's probably stronger than I am, in her resolve and determination."

This is not just a simple little argument, apparently, but a deepening dissatisfaction. "Marvella has been very concerned about the future. She's fed up with some of the pure crap you have to put up with, but she doesn't want to blow it for me. Marvella's a charger and I am a charger. How she did so much, I don't know. I was the kind that always tore up the barn and I'm never going to be content working an eight-hour day. But now she's ready to put it in second gear—and I've still got it in overdrive. And, by gosh, if people like Marvella and Birch Bayh are not willing to put up with some inconvenience and personal abuse we in politics have to put up with, who is? I really like people to an excess. These people have been an invasion of our personal life to the point where she gets fed up." The re-

alization of this is genuine but there is no indication that Bayh
wants or intends to change.

The introspection that came after her serious cancer operation is a far cry from the early days in the Senate when Marvella
and Birch pursued a relentless campaign to become important
and powerful. Their style was somewhat studied cornball.
Their ambition and drive for power was raw; almost likable to
some because they were less sophisticated than others in Washington about hiding it. One Senator's wife, who came to Washington about the same time, contrasted their modest life-style
with the Bayhs'. "They were giving those parties, with everyone
a title—you know, one of this and one of that—an Ambassador
and another Senator and all of that—and they'd stop *exactly* at
eleven P.M. Even Muriel [Humphrey], who never says anything
bad about anybody, wondered how they could afford it."

One former aide, whose remarks are no doubt tinged with
the jealousy that can come between competitive people involved in the same person's career, said, "One night they had
this green stuff for dessert. As they were bringing it around, I
asked her what it was. 'It's soufflé,' she said. Then, as if talking
to a child she hissed in a whisper, 'You take the doily off your
plate and the waiter will put some on your plate—and you-eat-
it-with-a-spoon." The aide was so angry that he leaned over and
with a little smile said, "My, how did a little girl from Enid,
Oklahoma, ever learn about things like that?" He recalls, with a
laugh, "My fortunes began to decline rapidly after that."

Her own experience turned Marvella into a leader in the cancer crusade and she shows more genuine emotion for cancer victims than many acquaintances could have guessed in those earlier days of ambitious Marvella. Much of her correspondence is
from other women who have had breast cancer surgery. When
Mrs. Ford was so suddenly stricken, Mrs. Bayh went on television and frankly admitted the deep psychological concerns she
and other women had at the time of their operations. There is
the fear of the future but another psychological problem also
emerges. The fear of losing your attractiveness can be a terrible
blow, she admitted.

Marvella praised the Reach to Recovery program, in which a
woman volunteer who has also undergone a mastectomy visits
the patient in the hospital several days after surgery. The visi-

tor talks about her own postsurgical experiences. "The woman who came to my room really helped me. She wore a figure-revealing jersey blouse, midiskirt and boots. I just couldn't believe it; she could have been a model. My husband and friends had been terrific, of course, but I had all these girlie questions to ask her and they just came bubbling out."

Today, what does she not like about political life? "Really, I see the long hours, the hate mail, the hate phone calls until we got an unlisted phone." She had wanted one for a long time but Bayh felt they shouldn't until one day Eric Sevareid praised him on TV as another JFK, for his leadership in the Carswell defeat; "Evan answered the phone and heard a threatening voice saying 'if Bayh becomes a midwestern JFK then I'm going to be another Lee Harvey Oswald,'" Mrs. Bayh recalls. "Of course Evan began to cry and I was emotionally spent and burst into tears. Birch walked into that scene and said, 'Okay, we get an unlisted phone.' What used to disgust me is he'd spend sixteen hours at the office and then on the few nights he was home, the phone would ring."

Few nonpolitical people realize that campaigning can be a constant pressure. "There are so many pressures. It isn't only during campaign year. Being a Democrat in Indiana you have to campaign all the time. I look at some of my friends from the Deep South, unless you pull some *horrible* mistake you're in forever, you don't have to kill yourself the way *we* do. And it's an enormous financial drain. Two places, living beyond your means, all my traveling. The travel allowance isn't enough, the telephone allowance isn't enough. You always have to supplement it with your own money. You call a plumber and they recognize your name and say, 'Oh, the Senator?' and I can just see the price rise! You're allowed twelve trips per year; he sometimes makes four a week! The campaign deficit is always hanging over your head."

She is not easy with her "winging it" life and is nervous about the uncertainty, not knowing when they will adjourn. "I can adjust to anything if I know what to adjust to." She was alone on Thanksgiving. "He *had* to be in California." Doing what? I asked. "Taping the *Dean Martin Show*." (Bayh has made $68,000 on speeches a year; she says much of it is poured back into campaign costs.)

"He's almost never here in a crisis; it's like a military family.

But when he's here he has so many things on his mind he usually just says, 'Do what makes you happy.' I pay all our domestic bills and get the man to fix the basement—plus this desk," she said, waving at her mail. "And I don't get any salary."

We talked about the uncertainty of the profession. "One day you have a job and then that night you see the roulette wheel go and if it comes up that the other guy has more votes than you— well, if that happens it's just one more paycheck and you're out. There's absolutely no security there."

Had she not married Bayh when she was nineteen, Marvella feels that she no doubt would have gone into politics. But, she adds, "I'm not a women's libber. I think the connotation grown up about the movement is wrong, but I'm for equal work and equal pay." She pushed her husband to support the Equal Rights Amendment. "I can remember arguing with Birch with tears streaming down my face six years ago, maybe five, trying to explain to him *why* a woman would need to feel fulfilled in her own right. He would say, 'What do you want that I am not able to give you?' He'd say, 'Don't you have more now than you ever did in your life?' I would say, 'Supposing I was able to support you—that I was rich and you could lie on the French Riviera, sip wine, do whatever you pleased. Would you feel your life is being utilized to the fullest?' It took me a year of explaining, trying to bring him around, to understand that."

Although she married young, she was determined to finish college, but then her "most personal, lasting tragedy" occurred.

"This is something most people don't even know about. That was in 1954 when we were in a very serious head-on auto wreck. It completely incapacitated me for almost three weeks. It left me with complete and total double vision for almost three years. I still see double when I get too tired." She carries a special pillow for her neck wherever she goes, carting it through those intensive campaign trips. College was halted. She couldn't read for a long time. "It took me a long, hard time to get through college because of the wreck." Her attempts at a career were thwarted when her husband won his Senate seat and she became his partner. "I had to work hard. I finally graduated the year after Evan was born."

This upset came to a woman who from early days had a need and a flair to excel in the farm world of Enid, Oklahoma. Some of her high points seem to be those golden days before her marriage when she was full of promise. "I was one of two chosen from Oklahoma for Girls' Nation. It was the summer of 1950 and I was seventeen and a half. And then I was *really* lucky and was elected *president* of Girls' Nation. I went to the White House to meet President Truman; he met with us in the rose garden and we were *so* excited. We all brought gloves to wear for the occasion. I presented him with a citation and, oh, do you remember how they had the 'News of the Week' at movie houses? When I went back to Oklahoma and I went to the movies with a date and they ran the newsreel, there I *was* on the film in the rose garden. When our theater manager found out, he gave me a bunch of free tickets. Enid was such an ideal town in which to rear a child. When I came home from Girls' Nation they had a big parade for me to welcome me back home. If I had lived in a big city like Detroit or Chicago or Washington, D.C., that never would have happened."

Her skyscrapers were the huge grain elevators in this town of about 40,000. Marvella lived on a farm until she was ten when they moved into town because of her mother's failing health.

"My father was a hard-working, plain dirt farmer. I had an experience growing up Birch didn't. Indiana was a state one hundred years before Oklahoma—and I had the experience of living on a frontier. I was about seven and I was just so excited. We were getting electricity. With that we got an electric pump for *cold* water that we had to heat on the stove. We never had running water in the house. No indoor bathroom facilities." She went to a one-room school and recalls it idealistically. As an only child she was considered "both their daughter and their son" and this shaped her sense of self-sufficiency. "At harvest I would drive the tractor, and drive the truck and haul the wheat. Even when we moved, I'd go back from town in the summer."

Her mother's spine was ruptured when Marvella was born and her mother's health grew increasingly worse. When Marvella was ten, her mother was told she would never walk again. After surgery at the Mayo Clinic she could walk, "but from then on she had a heart condition and a nervous condition. She was orphaned when she was seven and had a rough childhood. She didn't get proper nutrition."

Though ill, Marvella's mother "did a lot for me." At three,

Marvella was already taking elocution lessons. She was entering speech contests when she was four. Her mother had to teach her the readings, because she could not yet read.

"I never got the feeling I was being driven, but my parents always made me feel I could accomplish everything anyone else could. I was never 'just a girl.' I was their boy and girl together. I grew up thinking it was more exciting being boys. When I was first elected president of the student body it was even more of a thrill because it had never been an office held by a girl before."

Enid was proud of her when, as a senior in high school, she beat another student named Birch Bayh in a national debate. (Bayh says often, "She won the contest, but I won the girl.")

"Mother died ten years ago. She saw Birch elected to the Senate and she was so thrilled." Then, she started talking about her father. "Three years ago, no, I guess it'll be four years ago; how time flies, well . . . Daddy, when I was growing up, was a fantastic teetotaler. He never even had a bottle of beer in the house. But shortly after I married, he became a total alcoholic, then he remarried very quickly after Mother's death. Too quickly. It was a bad match. [Her stepmother was, in fact, younger than Marvella.] After about five or six years of that his mind went. He shot her and himself on the last night in March. They found them on April first."

She says, "To lose the closeness with my father, that was worse than the death. Mother kept his drinking from me. She kept thinking he'd get over this. She knew we had a beautiful relationship and she didn't want to destroy it. Then after she was gone, all the plugs came out. I called him one day. Birch had a speech in Oklahoma and I said I would fly out with him to see my dad. He went on a big drunk the whole time I was there. I never did get to see him. I called once just to phone and he was totally out of it."

An acquaintance said that Marvella in her father's latter days was ashamed of him and fearful that he might come to Washington someday to disrupt her public life and the Washington acquaintances she had carefully nurtured. She spoke of him calmly to me, although there still seemed to be some bitterness, guilt, and resentment that things turned out the way they did.

"I had done *everything* to help him. As Birch said to him, 'You are taking the most beautiful relationship I have ever seen be-

tween a father and a daughter and just throwing it away.' He
and I were so close, but for the sake of my own health and family I got to a place where I put him out of my heart. It was just
hell going through it. That was 1964. Mother died and within
two weeks of that I found out his complete and total situation. I
was at a dinner party when they called and told me Mother had
died. Six weeks after her death he remarried. Within nine
weeks of Mother's death Birch and I were in the plane crash. I
had all that." She adapted to the death of her father better than
to his problems. "Death is something so final; you have to learn
to accept it. The situation with Daddy was like a wound that
would start to heal and then you'd rub the scab off again." Sixty-four was not a good year. "Dad would call me on the phone,
drunk. My heart was racing, just racing. It would wake me up
at night; I felt as if it were going to jump out of my chest. I went
to the doctor and he asked if I had any personal problems, and
I burst into tears."

The doctor urged her to get help. "I went to a psychiatrist"—
adding quickly—"*just* four times. He put everything in perspective; I got to see Daddy as just sick. When I spoke at his funeral
I said the man people knew for the last seven years was not the
real man they knew. If there was a shut-in on the block, an old
man, he'd be the one cutting his hair, shaving him. He was always the one driving the kids to school things. He never missed
any of my performances. When I was a little girl every vehicle
on the farm—the combine, mower, trailer—every one had a little seat on it for me."

In April 1970 Mrs. Bayh was in Monaco, where she had gone
with her husband to attend an interparliamentary conference
when she was notified of her father's suicide. Bayh had already
returned to Washington to work up support to defeat Supreme
Court nominee G. Harrold Carswell. She dazedly started the
long trip home. When the plane landed in Boston, newspapers
were brought on board. There were the glaring headlines.
Again, political prominence provides no shelter from a public
accounting of private disasters: "Bayh's Father-In-Law Kills
Wife, Then Himself."

"The body of Delbert M. Hern, 60, was found sitting upright
in a living room chair. His wife, Patricia, 35, was found
sprawled on the dining room floor. She was killed by a gunshot

in the ear," the story read. There was no indication of a struggle and Marvella's stepmother was shot from a distance of a foot or two away, an assistant district attorney stated. It looked to police as if they had just finished dinner. The gun was found in her father's hand.

Marvella had taken sleeping pills and there had been hours of thinking time on that plane. She landed a dazed and emotional wreck. She recounts without bitterness that "because of the Carswell debate, Birch couldn't come to meet me. The staff people met me and brought me home. I waited four hours before he could come home."

After her father's funeral, Marvella sat in the Senate gallery, her eyes swollen and puffy from crying, and watched the Carswell defeat. "*We* didn't think we'd win that one." Some political observers are skeptical of Bayh's avowed altruism in the leadership role he played in the Carswell fight. It was said at the time that his decision was dictated by labor leaders, and Bayh, from both an industrial and rural state, has been criticized for being too cozy with labor. But Bayh declared he was motivated by the distress among civil rights leaders who feared Southerner Carswell.

Bayh recalls that their "presidential disagreements" created much dissension in 1972. But by 1975 neither denied that he might join the crowded field of Democratic contenders.

Marvella who had been opposed to his running from the start recalls, "His dropping out of the presidential race was the greatest gift he could have given me. He was scheduled to be out of Washington for two entire months." That was when she was getting radium and chemotherapy treatments, which often leave patients nauseous and depressed. "He didn't drive me to the treatments or anything like that—but he was able to come home and be there in the evening. Chemotherapy was nothing like the radium treatments, which leave you so nauseous. I'd be low and weepy and he'd be there." Marvella says an understanding husband is the most important security for a woman who worries about her loss of feminine appeal after a breast operation.

"He was marvelous and terrific. After I learned I had cancer I was crying and said to him, 'I'm only thirty-eight years old, and I'm going to go through the rest of my life with only one breast.' He said, 'I'm five years older than you are, and I've gone through my life without any.' He let me know that he married *me* and loved *me*—the me that no bodily amputation can change."

The obvious expressions of devotion between the Bayhs bring snickers to those who read gossip pages or listen to Capitol Hill gossip about the Senator. He has, as they used to say in less liberated days, a "reputation." Bayh scoffs, with the rejoinder, "I get all this credit for all these beds I'm supposed to get in and out of and it's not so. The damn thing is so ridiculous." Speculation mounted when one magazine printed flatly that Bayh was supposed to be the Senator in Barbara Howar's autobiography *Laughing All the Way.* A Senator who, by the way, backed out of her life when it might threaten his political career. Barbara laughed. "That always amazes me why people were so troubled by who that was. I didn't write that to tell who it was but to reveal to what lengths people in power would go. I didn't say who it was then and I'm not going to say so now."

I asked Marvella how it feels to read such articles about your husband. "Oh, why, I'm just as sure as the sun comes up that he's just one hundred percent faithful to me—as I am to him. I just don't think a *thing* about it. Besides," she adds with one of her wide smiles, "he's just too busy! Women come up to me and say, 'Oh I just *love* your husband.' Some school wanted an old sock of his for some bazaar."

How can you live with a man from whom people want an old sock?

A former aide said, "Women throw themselves at him all the time. I arranged a meeting once between Bayh and a woman who was at a party in Indiana and who clearly wanted to see him. He knew she was interested and I set it up. For all I know they just had drinks. But it's an unavoidable attraction." Marvella insists that sort of adulation doesn't bother her. As for Bayh, he said he was dancing with a woman once who asked if the Howar-Bayh story was really true. "I just told her she was crazy." Did you deny it? "Of course." Bayh acknowledges that political mystique, which includes the sexual attraction, "is part of the appeal of a candidate. It's the kind of thing that makes people walk that extra mile for you. But I've not found it diffi-

cult to handle. Probably the greatest compliment my wife paid
me is that it doesn't seem to work on me."

Mrs. Bayh is relieved they have only one son. "I'm the kind of
perfectionist that I'm not sure I could have handled it all with
more than one child. I'm the kind of mother who was first in
line for the measles shots and everything. I wanted to be sure I
could give him my time." There were a few politically induced
crises in Evan's life—the fear of threats on his father's life, being taunted by schoolmates who chanted, "Birch Bayh is a rat,
because he is a Democrat," some insecurity about the possibility
of losing and having to change schools. "When he was sixteen,
in 1972, Evan didn't want Birch to be President because he felt
he couldn't be normal with the Secret Service around. He also
said he wouldn't have to share Birch with tens of thousands of
people all the time."

Bayh said, "I'd like to have two dozen like him." The public
official's plight of not having enough time is countered by talking "religiously" on the phone, leaving notes, having an inviolate week of skiing alone with his son. When asked to give the
commencement address at Evan's school, St. Albans, Bayh
checked it out first with his son. "That was the most important
speech in my life. Evan was apprehensive—sat pretty far back,
but after, when some of his friends said they thought his old
man did a pretty good job, he was fine."

Evan, tall and handsome, was home on college vacation during our interview. As our conversation was winding down, Mrs.
Bayh got a phone call. Talking to the mother of one of Evan's
friends, Marvella's voice was as soft and sweet as honey. "I am
fine and I want to *thank* you for that delicious bread. Home-
made bread is one of my weaknesses and I have *never* eaten any
as good as yours. Oh, I think you could sell it. A delicatessen or
caterer would be *thrilled* with it.

"Now, I'm going to send you three cans of corn for popping.
This is the bestest corn—it's from Indiana. Now I'm going to
make sure Evan gives that popping corn to your son." Marvella
repeats, as if doing a commercial, "It's just the bestest corn—it's
from Indiana."

As I reached the door, Mrs. Bayh had a look of minor apprehension on her face. "Now, in what we said about the presidency? I don't want you to get the impression that I thought Birch

would not make an outstanding President." She smiled. "Why, I think he would make an *excellent* President!"

23

Mavericks

GAYLORD NELSON is one of those politicians who feels he ought to be able to make it on his own. He has been in politics for thirty years and his wife will freely tell you she hates politics. "Now, what is this book about?" she said on the phone. "I hate politics so much, I just don't want to make an ass of my-self."

The stories are legendary about Carrie Lee Nelson—and her husband relishes every one of them. Was he ever embarrassed by her frankness? "No, I always got a big kick out of it—besides most of what she said they couldn't print anyway."

He wants Carrie Lee to do what she wants. For her, a former nurse, that's mainly providing a home for the two teenage and youngest of their three children, and being a close companion to Nelson. It hardly ever means campaigning.

Riding on the subway from his office to the Capitol, Nelson brushed off the "useful" political wife. "It's okay if she wants to do that stuff, but I've always thought this business of impressed servitude of the wife participating in *your* campaign was a lot of bullshit. The few times Carrie Lee did it she was damn good. When she appears at some women's group I hear about it for years, but she doesn't like it so it's her business. If I can't get here on my own, I hadn't ought to be here." How would he feel if he had an ambitious, eager political helpmate? "It would drive me right out of my cage."

Carrie Lee loathes campaigning and appearances because she is basically shy—a fact that stuns friends who have seen her reel off amusing anecdotes and talk with hilarious easygoing candor about nearly anything. But she enjoys a low public profile and was uncomfortable when her husband was gover-nor of Wisconsin and she would go to the grocery store only to hear women whisper, "What on *earth* is the governor's wife do-ing her own shopping for?" "I didn't like being first lady of a state," she said. "Here I'm just me and fairly anonymous." Carrie Lee is happiest when she can make people laugh and when she can hide her feelings behind humor. This quality fails her in a political crowd of strangers, "I really do loathe politics and campaigning. It really frightens me to dislike something so much. I'm unable to cope with crowds.

"This may be a reflection on me, which is all right, but I don't think Gaylord needs me to be any role. He doesn't need me propping him up." Unlike some political wives who puff themselves up with the importance of their own campaigning, Carrie Lee says, "I've probably *lost* him votes." I started to laugh and she said, "Now that's not meant to be smartass . . . it is intended to be very serious. I can't remember when I ever won him a single vote—even when I tried. Nothing I ever said or did ever gained him a goddamned vote." I asked her when she ever tried. She rolls her eyes. "In 1968. It was pretty gross." She can't explain her vast difference, in public and private. "I don't know why." There were a lot of childhood insecurities and when she met Gaylord she was in awe of his articulateness and intelligence. "When we met I was not well read, I was not politically aware, I never even voted. I'm sure I developed a reticence, feeling I had nothing to say; just a little Southern hillbilly born back in the mountains of Virginia." More politically oriented wives feel she should study up on how to campaign. "They'll say, 'Why don't you go study public speaking?' and I say, 'Because I don't *want* to.' I want to do a lot of things but public speaking isn't one of them."

She feels it is a waste, and wives who think otherwise are fooling themselves. "Gaylord is unbelievably understanding. He hasn't expected anything. Once only in all these years—and we've been in one campaign or another since 1948—did he say, 'You've got to do something; I need a lot of help. I really need you.' It was when he was running the second time for the Senate [1968]. I said, 'You know I hate it; but I'll do anything to help.' At the time, I meant it. The next day, of course, I didn't. Well, I went out for a week of coffee hours—a solid week of six to seven days, running from six A.M. to ten P.M. in all those neighborhoods." She stops for emphasis. "I *never, ever,* so far as I know, met anybody who wasn't already committed to Gaylord. The few who weren't were definite possibilities. They then convinced me to go into ghetto areas with this kind of whore who took me in this tavern and drank double Chivas Regals at three dollars a pop while I was supposed to talk to the bartender and tell him to vote for Gaylord. Just how the hell do you make a dent in a vote with some old chick up there drinking away and me standing there feeling like a fool? When I got back, I said, 'My god, I got screwed out of fifteen dollars' worth of booze on her and didn't get a vote!' "

Carrie Lee's responses are unpredictable, to say the least. She is rather like Dom Pérignon after Gallo for those writers who must scribble the ever-cautious quotes of most political wives. Stories about her are legendary. One man swears he overheard her talking with a particularly obnoxious man. After several blunt questions, he finally asked, "If you hate politics so much, why did you marry Gaylord." Carrie Lee was supposed to have replied, "He knocked me up." When I asked her, she laughed. "I don't remember that one. Oh, so much has been said about me. You can't imagine what I was supposed to have said to some national politician who came to Wisconsin and kept raving over how great our local Democratic setup was. He was supposedly boring me and I finally couldn't stand it and said, 'Oh, fuck that noise.' " She paused and said she knows she never said that. Her eyes got a little dreamy. "Although it *is* a marvelous expression."

I asked her if it was true that her mother, depicted as a Mammy Yokum type, really did bring her own bourbon in Mason Jars to parties at the Wisconsin mansion when Nelson was governor. "Now, where in *hell* did you get that story?" She paused. "It wasn't bourbon—it was white lightnin'. My uncle used to make the best white lightnin' around until they sent him to jail for it."

Carrie Lee calls herself a "hillbilly" and some of the twang is there for evidence. Hers is the handsome face of Elizabethan English portraits—so many hill people carry those traces of the English, Scots and Irish who migrated and settled there. She is fair with reddish blond hair, a flat-bridged nose, wide-set eyes, a high forehead, and noticeable cheekbones. While she swears often for exclamatory value it is neither harsh nor contrived to shock. There is a simple naturalness about it. Her inflection seldom changes, which is, in part, what makes her wry stories funnier. Her delivery is deadpan and she is thoroughly genuine, warm, and likable; a former nurse who cares deeply for her friends and cossets them when they're ill, she has absolutely no use for the phonier aspects of Washington life. She is tall with slim legs, an ample bust, square and broad shoulders.

Her manner is also, I suspect, a part of personal survival. She is a loving person who needs love to erase some far-off memories of poverty and family separations. "Dad died when I was three. I was the ninth out of ten and we were very poor hill people. He was a shoemaker and county clerk. Now let's see, there were eight living children. Two died in infancy. He had no money and left us nothing, but he was a thirty-third degree Mason and there was this place called the Masonic Home in Richmond, Virginia. Children of Masons who were so poor they couldn't care for them went there. First, my two brothers went and then I think I went in the fall of 'thirty-two. I was not quite eight and somehow they talked me into going with the other two. All I remember is how sad it was. Mother was just a poor country woman who wasn't emotionally able to handle it all, with no money. When I was little my clothes and underpants were made of flour sacks. We were not just 'rural.' It was an 'up the creek and down from the holler' kind of existence." I mentioned my coal miner grandfather in Southern Indiana, who in the late forties still had no indoor plumbing and only an outhouse. She laughed and said, "You were *rich*—we were so poor we didn't have an outhouse. We'd take the slop jars and deposit them down a hole, past the corn crib."

She talked about meeting Gaylord. "I'm sure he didn't know how frumpy and hillbilly I felt. Here he was, from this gorgeous unknown state of Wisconsin. I was very shy. I didn't come with fun and humor at that time. I had none. I listened to him and was fascinated. He was filled with an interest in all kinds of things, politics even then. He was kind of a man's man—had marvelous rowdy relationships with his college pals and their wives. His father was a small-town doctor, his mother was a nurse. They were *the* prominent family in town."

They met during World War II at one camp, had a few dates, and then rediscovered each other on Okinawa. "Two days after I arrived there was a knock on my quonset hut and this soldier said, 'Lieutenant, there is a General Nelson to see you.' Well, he was fooling about the General, but standing there in those old combat boots and fatigues was this darling, handsome bird. I always said he was at a disadvantage; there were a hundred women and five *thousand* men. Well, we began a courtship the likes of which Okinawa hadn't seen before or since. We were much in love by the following spring."

They were married in 1947 and he was elected to the Wisconsin legislature in 1948 and remained there until he was elected governor of Wisconsin in 1958. He was reelected in 1960 and has been in the Senate since his first election in 1962. The Nelsons are popular in Wisconsin liberal Democratic circles despite her aversion to politics. When he was being considered for the vice presidency in 1972, Carrie Lee threatened to leave him. "But she didn't mean it," her husband says. Carrie Lee says Gaylord is not "nationally ambitious" despite those ever-suspicious Washington observers who think he, like most Senators, at one time wanted the presidency. I asked her if she felt he deliberately ruled it out because of her attitude and feelings. "If he has, I don't know it. You feel as if you know his heart and mind when you live together as close as we do. We share long evenings of talking, boozing, reminiscing, and I sure don't get that feeling."

As for reactions to her stories she said, "People are so stunned that anyone in public life would say anything." She says matter-of-factly, rather than defensively, "There are some people who are going to say, 'Gaylord Nelson's wife is pretty profane.' If they're going to be concerned about my calling somebody an ass, then they're not going to vote for him for almost *any* reason. Anybody who's got his head screwed on right is not going to hold a loud-mouth female against him."

She remembers only one time that he got mad at her for speaking out. Her child had fallen against a radiator and needed stitches. A nurse, yes, but she was still a mother, about to rush her child to the hospital. The phone rings. The housekeeper says it is an urgent long-distance call. She tears into the house, only to hear a *Life* reporter inquiring about their dog. It is one of those ever-constant stupid "at home" stories about politicians and their dogs that have been ingrained into editors' minds since Falla and FDR. "They want to know something about our poodle. They need a sharp tight caption. 'Does the dog campaign with the governor?' I answered, 'No!' 'Does the dog go to work with him?' I'm saying 'No, of course not.'" Her child is crying and she is trying to be polite but gets silent in her exasperation as he asks, "Does the dog do anything interesting?" Finally the reporter asks what the governor says about rural farmers who think he should have more of a "he man" dog rather than a poodle. Carrie Lee answers crisply, "He says bullshit." There is a pause and the reporter says, "This *is* the governor's wife, isn't it?" They both laugh and he says, "Mrs. Nelson, could you say something I could *quote?*" She remembers, "The reporter and I later became good friends, but for some reason Gaylord was livid."

But, "Gaylord doesn't give a damn what Washington thinks of me. We're not programmed for the national scene. People who are social climbing and looking for the newest luminary on the national horizon aren't sitting around in Georgetown saying, 'Hey, let's have the Nelsons!'" Carrie loves to entertain and does so often. If they are politicians or reporters, they are there strictly as friends. "Gaylord says, 'I spend all day with those birds, I don't want to spend all night with them.'" At one time he was intrigued with what made Senator Eastland tick, a man often considered venal and racist but cultivated by many, including the Kennedys, for his political power in the South. Gaylord happened to mention that if Eastland did come to dinner, Carrie Lee "would have to bear in mind that he might use the word 'nigger' from time to time." Her answer was, "Do you mean I'm supposed to sit through a whole dinner with someone using the word 'nigger' and not do something about it?" They didn't have the Eastlands for dinner.

When the Nelsons first came to Washington, he was called by Betty Beale, one of the haughtier society chroniclers, who started telling him that he *should* make a customary speech at an important congressional night party given by the all-women press group. Nelson resented her manner, commanding rather than telling him when to arrive, when to give his speech, and that he would be her guest. An aide protested that she was a very important woman in Washington and that as a new Senator he could not turn down the invitation. Nelson thought for one second and said, "Does she vote for me?" The aide said no. "Does she have any family in Wisconsin?" The answer was no. Nelson said, "Then to hell with it, I'm not going." He didn't.

Nelson is torn between his love and fascination for politics and an intense dislike for the time-consuming aspects of it. "It's the most consuming occupation of any I know. Doctors even get some time off. Politicians worry about what they're going to have to say and think about some issue, even when they're home. You worry about money, the time you have to spend traveling. People need some 'alone' time and you don't get much. It's always back to the state. Even when you speak there is a double duty; you've got to *listen* as well. We listen more than you know. You *have* to listen to find out what people think. Take the energy crisis—now that hurts farmers and they want to talk to you about it. If an issue is up front and you're going fifteen different places, you'll be asked exactly the same question and you get damn sick of it. Last year, I received 175,000 letters. They don't want form replies. *One* person wrote *one* letter. They're entitled to get a response. Reelection is always on your mind, whether or not you admit it." The incredible pace in a very tough race would be too grueling, Nelson feels. He is lucky to be a favorite in his state. "I just wouldn't spend all that time running around. If I had to do what some of these other guys do I just would forget it. I want time of my own. The goddamn pace some of these guys set—yet everybody admires it and I get attacked for being 'lazy.' You have to make up your mind whether you're going to be a full-time political automaton or whether you will have time to yourself. I think it's important to do some goddamn reading and have some time for yourself."

Gaylord has a deep sorrow that he did not spend enough time with his first son and goes to some lengths to be with his teenage son and daughter. He remembers his days as governor as an "incredible strain on the family. You get out of the habit of being with the kids. The kids were little; we just couldn't go that route again. It was too demanding. I think there's a higher percentage of political children deprived of a father-son or father-daughter close relationship than those of fathers in any other business I know. I have to be in Wisconsin three solid weekends in a row. Who in the hell has 'kiddie time' when you get through? I want 'Gaylord Nelson time.' I want to read, to go to a restaurant and get a bottle of beer and a pizza. I want no phone and I want to be left alone."

Politics was in Gaylord's blood early. He remembers his father taking him to hear Bob LaFollette when he was only nine years old. He remembers sitting on his dad's shoulders. "I was thrilled to see him. His blue serge coat fell off the railing and it was stepped on. I thought his mother was sure going to give him a whacking, I couldn't imagine letting that happen to my one Sunday suit. Dad asked if I wanted to be a politician. I said I wanted to but that Bob LaFollette would have solved all the problems before I got a chance." Thirty-five years later, LaFollette was dying and Gaylord, then a candidate for governor and by then a friend, went to see him in the hospital. He will never forget LaFollette's words—"Well, Gaylord, do you think old Bob LaFollette left enough problems for you to solve?"

Nelson stops to think. "If there was one more life, as much as I love this, I'd like to be that country lawyer in northern Wisconsin. My twenty-year-old . . . he just went right on by me. He loves me and I love him, but the time spent together, well, I'm ashamed of myself. I took him camping once." His guilts make him think about what he's missing, but not enough to give up politics. (His daughter, Tia, works for him part-time and although she dislikes Washington and will go to college in Wisconsin, she beams when she talks about her father. "I'm very proud of him. I think he's just one of the best politicians. He cares about people." His second son and he have a good relationship. One night during a dinner party, Nelson went upstairs—at his son's request—for a talk before they went to bed. "We all sit around on the bed and watch TV and talk and rub backs," Nelson said.

Carrie Lee says, "He loves them dearly and they know it, but he's not the type to spend hours playing Daddy even if he had the time." She feels their children would probably have turned out the same, whatever Gaylord did. People remark that they are very unspoiled for politician's children and Nelson says, "That's a tribute to their mother." She remarks, "If Gaylord were a lawyer he'd still be a rather self-centered, self-interested kind of person."

Their only real sorrow is in the handling of Gaylord (Happy) Nelson, Jr. He felt the loss keenly when his father was governor. He was five when Nelson was elected. Two years later he was asked, "Wouldn't it be fun if your daddy got reelected?" Happy replied that he guessed it would be all right—"but I *never* see my daddy anymore." Carrie Lee says, "It was such a plaintive little voice. Even Gaylord got misty-eyed. Happy never did like politics, never showed any interest. He reluctantly participated in Gaylord's 1968 election." They feel some of the pressure would have been off their son if he had not carried the unusual name of the Senator.

Happy got busted in a bizarre pot incident. Nelson feels the judge was harder on him than the law of the state requires and thinks he would not have been fined if he was not the son of a Senator. "If you're a first offender and a minor, which Happy was, you usually get off with a suspended sentence. If nothing happens in a year it's not even a matter of record."

Carrie Lee says, "Happy was going through his 'rite of manhood' at the height of dissidence about the war and the height of drug use and abuse. He was into it as much as many kids were. He was picked up carrying a shirt full of grass. They were out west and had picked it—growing wild along a railroad track. It was green and unprocessed. I know he thought the publicity and treatment were unfair. If they hadn't recognized his name he would have been treated the way the rest were. Then, as they asked his name, he ran. I know he was scared and thinking, 'Oh, Poppa's going to have to go through all this.' The stories wrote it up as an 'escape.'" Carrie Lee pauses, looks sad, and says, "You know how you blank out things you don't want to know? He left that station and hitchhiked to the nearest airport and called us. We told him to go right back, and we got a lawyer to meet him at the police station. He got the fallout in the newspapers."

Carrie Lee is warm and easy with her two youngest, filled with pride for seventeen-year-old Tia, who is pretty, articulate, and interested in politics. Her twelve-year-old, Paul, she described as "sweet and pliable." He walked in later with a friend. A good-looking and pleasant boy, he gave her an easy and unself-conscious hug—then asked for money to go ice skating. She got the money out of her purse, laughed ruefully, and said, "See?"

Carrie Lee said, "I think possibly one of the reasons my kids haven't found it so difficult through all the years Gaylord's been in politics is because of my nature and the way I was raised. Even when he was governor and we had lots of help, I made it a practice—well, I just wanted to be home by three P.M."

She went back to nursing briefly after twenty years but says she is now home by choice. "It felt really great at first." She worked as a volunteer—few people knew she was a Senator's wife—at a clinic. "Then when I began to see some of these young girls turning up their rumps for those VD shots for the second time, girls under sixteen, hand holding some little pimply-faced boy, I had had enough. Occasionally you see some young child of a family acquaintance. It was just so depressing."

Nelson is the opposite of most politicians. Instead of being turned on by campaigning, Carrie Lee says, "He's in a funk before, during, and after a campaign. He gets cross and resentful because he has no private time. Sometimes I have to jack him up and say, 'This is a job *you* want. A lot of people are fighting right hard and using up a helluva lot of money and time for you.'" He also has two faces—but unlike some public men, the best one is reserved for the family. "The Senator part is, at times, totally different. Those who know him only as a candidate and Senator can hardly believe the difference when they spend a relaxed evening with us. I have what a lot of wives don't have. When he's home, he's totally home. And when he's gone, it's a good gone. I work in the garden, have in old friends who bore the hell out of Gaylord and vice versa."

Nelson is at times addicted to the sound of his own voice and his own interests, but he is entertaining and fun and he does listen to others. Despite her surface calm and genuine unconcern for politics, Carrie Lee knows it's her husband's life and so she worries about reelection. "I'm always filled with apprehension, I always feel Gaylord's going to lose, no matter how marvelous he is."

People in Washington spend some time trying to figure out politicians. You find one who is an ultimate egomaniac and you think that explains his drive. You find one who is insecure and trying to prove to himself and the world what he can do and that explains his drive. Carrie Lee thinks it's a combination of both ego and insecurity. "I really do feel Gaylord's less so than most, although he has those tendencies. I suppose you'd be shocked at how many times a combination of insecurity and ego does play a part in everything they do."

When Mrs. Robert Eckhardt moved back to Houston, Texas, some Washington friends wondered if that signaled something wrong with their free-wheeling marriage. The only thing "wrong" was that the Texas Congressman and his wife, Nadine, were trying one more household arrangement in a struggle with what he calls an "impossible" life.

If Nadine stays in Washington he sees her at night during the week, tired and preoccupied, and is back home in Texas on weekends. If she stays in Texas, they have more relaxed weekends and no time together during the week. "You can't win either way," Eckhardt, chairman of the House Democratic Study Group, says. Expenses were also a problem. They had to keep their Texas home anyway and it was cheaper for the family to move out of Washington and for him to get a small apartment. A year later, Nadine returned to Washington more and more frequently.

And besides, Nadine, a native and liberal Texan, was getting a bit bored with Washington.

"Every stage of life is really scary," says Nadine, a good-looking woman in her early forties. She admits there is "a great deal of hostility on my part" about a life molded to an extent by the public, and she rebels by running away from it with her friends. Back home in Texas, she said, "I'm sure people say I've run from Washington but I never felt I had to compete in all that status stuff. I knew it was such a pile of shit anyway. I really had access to anyone I ever wanted. Bob is not one of those ambitious politicians so I don't feel the pressure to have this or that one over. None of that so-called big-time Washington social life had any basis in reality. It was hard to find real people. A political wife has to struggle to find her own emotional sustenance. Some can't handle Washington. I never felt that way, I just wanted out for awhile. Much of the congressional business 'socializing' is nil," she says. "You sit between some little gray men who talk about how they miss their golf course or how important they are on some damn inconsequential committee. Who wants to hear that? Besides, maybe it's that I know how much grass-roots politics is important to Bob, but I feel more important politically in Texas. I'm doing it for myself, too. I may end up taking his place someday and I'm building up real good ties. And my own ego structure gets stroked well enough. I prefer the little leaders of little locals to some head of the shoe-clerk international you meet in Washington. The telephone rings all day with problems and I can get back to Bob with them. It makes me feel good. You're damn right you need your ego massaged. I'm giving a speech to some Young Democrats this week and I'm going to talk about the American people not getting the right information. Congress can't even make a good judgment; no wonder we're so fucked up." Nadine feels a lot of political wives are still in the nineteenth century. "Those wives don't even realize their egos are suffering. It's a kick to have people say, 'What a speech you gave,' instead of, 'Oh, I think your husband's wonderful.' I answer that I think he is too, but I also feel, holy hell, so am I.

"I don't see any advantage to politics for the political wife unless she's got something going for herself. She's got to like it. And if you don't have much between you, you're in deep trouble. We still have enough stuff going that we can go to those dumb receptions and have a good laugh about it later. Bob's a bigger man than most politicians and nothing I do or say would freak him out—most politicians are all cripples, compensating for something. Most of them have deep insecurities from when they were young. I would not have liked my husband when he was a young man. They became leaders to prove something to themselves."

We were having a late-afternoon talk before I had to get a plane back to Washington. It had been a weekend of Texas conviviality, intense as well as hilarious conversations about politics—Nixon, Watergate, Congress, those "other" Texans (the rich and conservative ones). Their good friend and raconteur John Henry Faulk had been there to speak of Eckhardt at a fish-fry fund-raiser. Later he said admiringly of Nadine, "She's unlike most political wives. She takes nothing from anybody. She's a solid citizen who says, 'I'll pitch in and help keep this thing going—but I'm still me.'"

Their home is outside Houston in a cluster of scrub pine. It is very rustic and casual—cathedral-ceiling living room, big fireplace, bedrooms reached from a long outdoor porch. There are a couple of horses that Eckhardt rides. For those who have a stereotype of Texans, the Eckhardts fit it not at all. Shelves in the living room have books jammed every which way—many old and well worn. The taste is eclectic—volumes of Shakespeare and Longfellow, *Translations from the Chinese* next to *History of Texas*. Commager's *The American Mind* is beside *Famous Plays of the Restoration and 18th Century*. Eckhardt has a far-reaching mind to match his reading tastes and a quiet humor.

When someone said he was an ultraliberal he smiled, touched his big Texas hat, and broadened his accent. "How kin innyone who wears a hat like this and talks like this be a Comminist?"

Several of us were sitting around after a dinner of chili—Nadine defrosted a tubful that she had frozen earlier. Eckhardt smoked a long and crooked cigar. A big, sprawling man given to bow ties with his suits in Washington, Eckhardt was in the oldest of faded blue jeans and muddy boots.

He accepts the frustrations of politics as part of the game; he seems to have little desire to try for the Senate and enjoys being a technician who knows how to write good legislation and guide it through the House to completion. He has been criticized for spreading himself too thin, following too many interests and issues at one time. His wife argues the same thing. "I like the challenge," he says. "I've been able to write stuff into legislation that permits citizens to be participants, like the product safety bill." Eckhardt works quietly and often shuns publicity if it could threaten a bill. "We had an 'undercover' fight when we got the consumer class action bill going. It would have virtually been destroyed by the business lobbyists who could go to the subcommittee and build up enough votes to defeat it."

The talk shifted to political wives; he interjected his humor into the subject. "Politicians have such vacuous wives that many use the work as an excuse to get away from home. Ah know ah would," he drawled. He added, "I shouldn't be making a judgment because I don't know enough political wives, but my general impression and my own observation is many live on the periphery." He jokes that the best campaigners are those who are "simply not engaged in helping the opposition. I'm inclined to think a man alone in a campaign would be better." Surprisingly to his audience, he said that a nice, warm, friendly wife with no ambition or ideological bent can often make the best political wife.

Nadine was sitting quietly, but hardly containing herself. She is a strong personality, vivacious, and with a strong ideological bent, reads politics avidly, discusses it avidly, and has an avid opinion. When Eckhardt mentioned one "perfect" wife who "loved" politics and fit the pattern he had just described, Nadine asked with a shade of innocence, "Why is she perfect?" "Because she does it so well." She replied, "Well, 'good, supportive' wives are not necessarily happy."

He seemed somewhat perplexed at the interjection of the word "happy" into the conversation. "I didn't *say* they were *happy*—I said they were tremendous assets." She said, "I don't think they are really assets. Did you ever see her *really* smile? Did you ever see her happy?" He said, "I'm not talking about happy, honey, but about *assets.*"

The women at the table started in—didn't he think it takes some happiness in order to be a true asset? He said, "You're ganging up on me."

Eckhardt started categorizing wives: (1) those who have too much personal ambition and are not necessarily assets; (2) those who are not instinctively politicians but still push their husbands to higher office, like B. A. Bentsen; (3) wives who have no personal ambition or even personal conviction—"Now Pat Nixon is a perfect politician's wife," he allowed. Several women at the table made faces. By this time Nadine was in the kitchen getting something for him. "And fourth"—he spoke up loudly—"the best of these classes are the Nadines . . . You *hear* that, baby?" He described her as a "woman ideologically motivated in accord with her husband, and not merely an alter ego but an influence. She has her own views and she gives them." He laughed. "She's not necessarily the kind that gets him *elected*—but she's more fun."

He classified the worst as those that "don't do a goddamn thing. They just essentially resent it, but they take the emoluments and love it, like most of the Texas wives." He feels they are probably an "impediment. One's husband's been in so long she thinks she's Queen Victoria."

He said there is "no question politics brings tremendous pressure on the family, particularly when you have young children. It's an old-man's profession."

Eckhardt talked about the politicians who "live on the margin." They are insecure about getting reelected. "To them, that's everything—so they don't do anything to rock the boat." He said most politicians "have nothing left for family, for themselves, for contemplation . . . for just *being.*" Nadine announced that "every congressional wife should get a pension." He groaned, "Oh, my God." He asked why they should have one any more than the wife of anyone else. "Because we do a lot of work that's not on the payroll. Think of the money I'd make if I went into business. But I have to be a full-time wife and mother."

Nadine added, "And Congressmen make the worst Daddies in the world. Hell, they abdicated as fathers years ago. You can't find one wife who doesn't bitch. I knew one Congressman who seemed like a good Daddy. He was defeated.

"Take Sarah." (Eckhardt described her as nine—going on twenty-eight.) "She gets on you all the time about being gone," Nadine said. Her husband replied, "That's because she's your alter ego—Sarah is Mommy's 'little deputy.'" Even though this conversation is more than half meant, it is without venom. It is a healthier exchange than many political-family conversations.

I asked Eckhardt when was the last time he spent some time with Sarah. "Well, let's see, this afternoon she was riding her bicycle and I was on my horse . . . What did we talk about? I don't remember." Everyone at the table laughed. So he started in again, in a teasing voice. "Well, I remember I said, 'Sarah, be careful, that car might hit you.' I adequately expressed concern for her safety." Then, more seriously, "I haven't been home in several days. Last night I dug up a couple of books she was interested in reading, an old book I had on Huck Finn and *Ole Yeller.*" We talked about whether he had any inability to get along with the kids. He said, "Not much." His wife snorted, "How can he say that? He doesn't know what being a father's *like.* Congress is an advantage—you don't have to be a father." With a soft smile, he said, "You're bitter, baby." She said, with another soft smile, "Well, who the hell raised these kids?"

Her son by a previous marriage, Willy, is a good-looking boy in his late teens. He seems to be frighteningly cool, but that reflects, in part, a shyness. He didn't go to his father's fund-raisers. "I don't like that political stuff at all." He's at an age of rebellion from his parents' way of life. They regard it as natural and made nothing of the fact he didn't go. "I like to write, but I don't have that big a vocabulary," he said. He was impressed as anything by an older friend who "interviewed Robert Redford." His father is author William Brammer, who wrote a novel about LBJ's Texas, *The Gay Place.* Eckhardt has a tendency to withdraw, Willy said. "Yeah, very much . . . nothing else can move in . . . the whole Eckhardt family tend to forget about other people and other things." His bright and dark-haired nine-year-old sister was in ballet costume, sitting on a kitchen table. She piped up, "They're forgetful, period." Willy tucked his face into the fur of the cat he was holding and tenderly touched it. He said Eckhardt was responsible for making him like politics the little that he does. He does not want to go into politics and "do the comparison thing" and compete with Eckhardt. Sarah laughed and said, with awe of her father, "I don't think I'd have a chance." His answer was, "Poppa's pretty good, huh?"

There are some advantages to having a political father. Willy was in a car accident. Eckhardt gave him advice as a lawyer. There was also a built-in reference for classes like civics and government. The minuses? "Like what we've been talking about . . . the status thing and how he can't be too close to the family." Sarah said, "Sometimes you can't depend on him." It is just a flat statement of fact. Willy added, "There are a lot of pressures on Mom, she has to tend to a lot of things, when mail comes here she has to answer it." They are much happier in Texas than in Washington. "The people are more friendly; it's slower here. In Washington it was all real quick, everyone rushing around. Here, people are nicer. The air is nicer." Willy felt a lot of "unreality in life in Washington. I think a lot of kids take advantage of their fathers' being this and that. People just ride on status. Mom went somewhere and people said, 'What do you do?' and she said, 'I'm just a housewife.' It blew their minds." "The kids are nicer here, they're not out to hurt anybody. In Washington they're consumed by status. Kids say, 'My dad's a Senator . . .' It wouldn't be the *first* thing they said, but you'd get the message after awhile." He paused and said, "It's almost as if they don't have time to be nice."

Nadine makes "allies" out of Eckhardt's staff, and he jokes that they are in league against him. She jokes back, "I tell the staff I want a xerox copy of everything that goes on down there." When she is in Washington, they have Mexican lunches and wine in his office. She persuaded him to hire women in major positions. "The insecure wives throw their weight around. I don't ask the staff to do anything I wouldn't do. Sometimes I go do some of the shit work, like opening the mail, to make life easier for them."

Eckhardt is essentially a loner, and his "closest" friends say they do not know him. Nadine, his second wife and several years younger, feels she knows him better than most, but politics still gets in the way of their "close" times. When she came up to Washington for a visit, she joked that she was "shacking up with my old man. I guess it's good I moved back to Texas—he really missed me.

"As I said, we've got a lot going. Too bad I don't always get the feedback I need from Eckhardt and therefore have to live my own life with my own friends, too, but, hell, no marriage is perfect."

24

"Mr. and Mrs. Perfect"

LLOYD BENTSEN and his wife, B. A. (for Beryl Ann), are very attractive, very rich, and very Neiman-Marcusy. Nothing is overstated, nothing is understated. The Texas Senator's office is Paris on the Potomac; the French-Provincial furnishings look straight out of a Paris drawing room.

The Bentsens' showcase apartment in the Shoreham West has a *Better Homes & Gardens* interior-decorated precision to it; elegance and vivid Van Gogh colors. A bright orange wall is a backdrop for glass shelves, full of pre-Columbian art, Middle Eastern artifacts from 1500 B.C., and rare Venetian glass. A twelve-foot-long white sofa and a thick white area rug contrast with deeply polished walnut floors. A silver coffee service gleams on the coffee table, a priceless French clock sits in one corner. There are lots of good paintings and expensive Chinese vases. Art collecting is practically a sickness in Texas, and Bentsen looks pleased that I like his clock. He points out that it is French and tells a story about how he found it in Mexico but thought it was too expensive. Engaging the owner in conversation, Bentsen dropped the invaluable nugget of information that he was once decorated by the Mexican government. The owner was sufficiently impressed. "I made him an offer and he took it." There lingers the smile of a man who maneuvered a deal. Like many a millionaire, Bentsen loves his art for business-minded reasons as well as for the beauty. He spoke of how he started collecting many of his pieces; a group of nine businessmen gave black-tie dinners and spent money on paintings and rotated them in their homes and would sometimes buy out of the arrangement.

But there is no nouveau to Bentsen, certainly, by Texas standards. He is second-generation rich; his father, Texans say, "owns" the Rio Grande. There is also very little of Texas in

Bentsen. He looks more like a Senator than Henry Fonda does—early fifties, hair graying at the temples, a crinkly-wrinkly smile. But there is something disconcerting about Bentsen. The crinkly-wrinkles look painted on. Each facial expression seems well tested in advance. He tries to downplay his wealthy childhood. "I was born and reared in ranch country in the southern tip of Texas, the Rio Grande. I went to a small school made up of Anglos and Mexican-Americans and learned to speak Mexican as soon as I did English." What he didn't mentioned was that his "Daddy" (no one has a father in Texas) and his uncle "owned" that valley. His father's reputation for shady real estate deals and cheap wages to wetbacks lingers in the minds of those who know Texas business and politics. "You would not believe how Byzantine border politics is," said one Texas reporter. "When Bentsen was growing up there were discriminatory laws passed with literary tests in English wiping out all non-English-speaking Mexicans. The 'good' Mexicans were told how to mark the in-English ballots. It was all part of an amazing political machine that makes Daley look like a piker. Bentsen's daddy and unkie were perfect bastards; they were *patrones* who ruled that land."

Bentsen pictured himself as a struggling Congressman with three young children back in the fifties. "I got no urging from my family; they were ranchers and in real estate and they thought politics was too tough and mean a life for me. I think the money had gotten up to $12,500 a year when I was in Congress. You just can't make it with three children. Those who think $42,500 is a lot for a Senator just don't know." I asked him what he thought of those who lived on that salary alone and he said, "Good grief."

"It's just another pressure on a fellow in this business. I decided I needed financial independence to stay in politics. My dad had money, but that's different. So I went back and started a business. A life insurance company. I built it into a pretty good size life insurance company." He is being modest. Seventeen years later his business interests included banking, insurance, farming, and defense contracting, according to the *Texas Observer*, a liberal paper that consistently gores establishment Texas politics. Bentsen admits that members of his family "participated in, and invested in" his business. In 1970, his father, "Big Lloyd," was chairman of the board of Bentsen's holding company, Lincoln Consolidated. Touchy about questions trying to pin down his financial holdings (estimated at as much as $20 million), Bentsen said he would not disclose his worth until elected. This was one of the things he has against public office. "It was pretty rough having to file a financial statement when I came up here. I don't like doing that. It's really giving up your privacy." (His statement said he was worth $2.3 million.)

It is a Saturday morning and Bentsen is in a gray herringbone sports jacket, white shirt faintly striped with blue, rep tie, Gucci loafers. Mrs. Bentsen is in her Guccis, wool houndstooth-check slacks suit, a gold ball dangles from a necklace chain. Tall and willowy, her hair is a frosted brown and she has on brown eye shadow and what look like false eyelashes. It is 10:30 A.M. I had been warned about the eyelashes. "Are they for real?" "We all think they're false—find out" was the curious and catty remark of an otherwise charitable wife of another Senator. "We old country girls can hardly believe her." She looks like the model she once was; the kind of awesomely put together woman that makes you more aware of your ragged fingernails, hastily combed hair, uneven hem, and, as ever, inexpert mascara job.

Later, I was made even more aware that I must have been cluttering up their tasteful view when one Senator's wife recalled an evening with the Bentsens. "We went to a dinner there—once. We walked in and Lloyd took one look at my husband. He had on this little old bow tie, nothing much, but it surely didn't bother us. Well, Bentsen couldn't stand it; we didn't blend enough with the decor. He took my husband into the bedroom and pulled out a case full of evening bow ties, selected one of those stylishly fat ones with a blue lining to match my husband's shirt, and insisted it would look terrific on him. I was surprised, but he went ahead and changed. After, my husband said, 'What was I supposed to do? I was his guest and if it meant all that much to him I figured I'd go along.' I can assure you we are not what you'd call bosom buddies with the Bentsens."

The aura transmitted by the Bentsens is one of narcissistic joy in one another. They are an interlocking team. Instead of opposites, it is rather like looking in the mirror and finding the same image and being highly pleased by it. Her voice is very controlled, almost of the clenched-teeth school, and well modulated. She has just a trace of a Southern accent (her husband has virtually none) but there will be no Fanny Flagg in her future if this Texas woman were to become as prominent as Lady Bird. Neither she nor her husband could possibly be so easily lampooned. Bentsen's whole demeanor is that of a man with champagne taste who would be offended by beer—any beer— but certainly Texas's Pearls beer.

Bentsen made two separate political journeys to Washington. In the fifties he was a Congressman who quit to make money. Before he left Washington, however, one of Bentsen's principal contributions to statesmanship was to advocate dropping an A-bomb on North Korea. He came back to the Senate in 1970, worth several million dollars more than when he left, and with a not too subtle drive to be President of the United States. During his Senate campaign he was asked about his A-bomb suggestion, unsupported by many others in Congress. "This was a time when we had great nuclear superiority," Bentsen answered. "I thought the threat itself would be enough . . ."

In 1970 Bentsen defeated Ralph Yarborough, whom Texas liberals reflexively refer to as "good ole Yarborough." Yarborough had all the liberal heavies in his corner. Harold Hughes said Yarborough "either sponsored or cosponsored every major piece of legislation in my public career." There was a lot of name calling. A reporter for the *Texas Observer* said, "Bentsen conducted a brilliantly choreographed and vicious smear of Yarborough." Referring to Bentsen's former connection with Lockheed Aircraft (he was a director and owned 1,000 shares of stock), Yarborough asked, "Have the war profits you've put in your pockets for years so warped your judgment that you can't support the constitutional guarantees of free speech?" (referring to antiwar demonstrators). Yarborough charged that Bentsen was a "big tax dodger" and that Bentsen's company, Lincoln Liberty Life (which became part of Lincoln Consolidated in 1967), paid "not one red cent in federal income tax from 1964 to 1968." Championing larger income tax exemptions for the poor, Yarborough blamed the laws permitting corporations to pay little or no income tax for Bentsen's enviable tax position.

Bentsen looked hurt when I asked him about that. "I would prefer not to have that kind of race. But Yarborough got tough on me and I got tough on him," he said, proudly. A Texan like Bentsen knows the value of a Communist scare. After the U.S. Senate censured Joseph McCarthy, the Corpus Christi *Caller* in 1954 quoted Bentsen as not exactly condemning McCarthy. He said only that the Wisconsin Senator's tactics were to indict groups instead of individuals—the kind of attack that undermines public confidence. Bentsen continued with the view that it was our job, the paper stated, "to increase our efforts to ferret out 'the reds.'" Slashing at Yarborough, Bentsen took out after Yarborough's denouncement of the Vietnam War, wanting to align in the minds of voters the elderly Yarborough with "them hippies" who supported moratoriums. He consistently harped on Yarborough's endorsement of moratoriums, implying that Yarborough would advocate violent overthrow of the country. Yarborough, Bentsen said, "cannot escape the fact that demonstrations against the war might begin as peaceful dissent but rarely stay that way. The next step is invariably a riot, the next step is planned violence, and the next step is anarchy!"

Bentsen was a bitter pill to swallow for the Texas liberals who knew him when. They pictured the Bentsen millions, aligned with big-money interests and "the state's economic royalists," as the *Texas Observer* named them, taking over Yarborough's seat. Still Bentsen was an unfamiliar man to many in Washington when he returned here and they were willing to view him with impartial curiosity. Bentsen knew he was suspect to some and an unknown quantity to most and so he hired a staff who helped package and promote him into a "new" Lloyd Bentsen. Many viewed his avowed interest in the presidency as an audacious case of Potomac Fever—and an excellent example of the kind of exalted opinion one can suddenly acquire of himself when he gets "enshrined" in marble in those Senate chambers. But by January 1975 Bentsen had more than a million dollars squirreled away for a presidential campaign collected before the campaign fund reforms went into effect.

When Ted Kennedy bowed out of the Democratic presidential race, Bentsen was being named repeatedly as a centrist contender for the spot. Bentsen has been described as smart, slick, smooth. I never for one moment thought I got past the gloss in a two-hour interview. During his campaign, John Connally, his close friend (who later was indicted in a money scandal but acquitted), spoke of Bentsen as a "good sound conservative boy."

But once outside of Texas and playing for national stakes, Bentsen shucked that image. He soon became known as a brainy team player. Once in office he shocked his aerospace constituents by opposing the SST.

One Texas politician and longtime LBJ confidant said of Bentsen, "He pursues the limelight with an eagerness; it's like something stuck in an ostrich's throat—it just won't go down. I don't think anyone could get very close to him, except those people admitted into his confidence—the same type as he is. Smooth, attractive, well-to-do people like the John Connally crowd. I can't say as I like him. I like touches that reveal some vulnerability in people. I don't feel any vulnerability in Bentsen like, say, Hubie is vulnerable. But do not discount him. I think he's got a lot of stuff there."

Bentsen's face grew studious. "Let me give you an example, Myra, of how I vote." (This last sentence is an example of what I call the "comma-name-comma" school of familiarity and sincerity. Politicians often employ it when talking to reporters, apparently to show that they are good fellows and they know who you are, even when they don't. It is designed to flatter. Unfortunately it works all too often, even when carried to an extreme. Senator Charles Percy once comma-name-commaed me for five sentences out of ten.)

"You see, Myra," Bentsen continued, "my pension bill, *my* bill on pension regulations came out of the finance committee. Most places are equitable, but there are enough horror stories. A month before a person qualifies for a pension, they fire him, you see?" He looks sincere. "Those are the goats I'm out for. Now here's where the ego of being a politician comes in. I don't think the pension bill would have gotten through without me. I was on a TV panel and one newspaperman said, 'It seems to me that what you're seeking is power.' I said, 'I never thought of it that way. Guess that's true. But how you use it when you obtain it is the thing.'"

Mrs. Bentsen had been sitting patiently through the political talk and I thought I should ask about her role in politics. Her husband says she is a vital team member and he couldn't do without her. She says she is happy to be just his team partner—"I happen to have no talent." He protests, "Now, B. A., that's not *true* . . ."

B. A. says, "I campaigned for one year, almost every day."
Bentsen interjects with a wide smile, "She did a great job." She
continues, "My role was not giving speeches but more or less
getting people to recognize Lloyd's name, to see us as a family—a good and happy family." Does she mind the appendage
role? "I do not feel frustrated in any way." I mentioned how
Eleanor McGovern, for one, expressed her own views when
asked about issues. "Oh, I think that's amazing! I don't think I
could express myself to that degree." She walks out to the kitch-
en to get more coffee and as she passes her husband's chair,
Mrs. Bentsen smiles down and says, "I'd rather let you make
the statements." Although we had been talking about the presidency, Mrs. Bentsen seemed surprised when I asked her if she
would mind being First Lady. "Why," she said with a laugh,
"that never occurred to me! I enjoy being a Senator's wife. But
that's hard to answer. I certainly go along if he wants to run for
the presidency."

Bentsen is a man who clearly follows corporate practice on
judging wives. "When I hire a man in business I always want to
meet his wife. Sometimes you can read a man better through
his wife. I agree with you that a man develops a veneer and you
can get behind it better if you know his wife." Both Bentsens
felt without question that a politician's wife who had a reputation for drinking too much or was too outspoken could hurt
her husband. We discussed the Jane Muskie incident when a
few innocent remarks were taken out of context during the
1972 New Hampshire primary. "That's why I stop before I say
anything." Does that do anything to her own psyche, always
curbing what she says. She seemed surprised at the question
and asked, "Don't you do that for your husband?" I said no, but
added that I had not married either a businessman or politician. They both looked at me as if I was rather strange. Bentsen
considered his wife's attitude a "definite asset."

Despite her lack of expressed views, his wife did not escape
political controversy in any event. A picture showing Mrs. Bentsen, Mrs. Allan Shivers, and Mrs. John Connally at a campaign
coffee honoring Mrs. Bentsen was used to point out that Connally had publicly endorsed Bentsen and had talked him into
running. Shivers was the boss of the business-politics machine
that ran Texas in the 1950s.

Did Bentsen feel that a divorce would make much of a difference to his constituents these days? "Well, it would make a helluva lot of difference to me," he says, beaming at his wife.

Their children are grown and the Bentsens have a heavy social life. "We put limitations on how much we go out—but we are out, say, four or five nights a week," he said. "I generally campaign on weekends, make speeches." How have things changed since their corporate entertaining days? "I go to a lot more public functions. We do a lot of private dinners for twelve. That means you can have a conversation." Who does Bentsen mix with, I wondered. "Well, let's see, who are we having Tuesday night . . . we'll have Mike Mansfield, Leon Jaworski [fellow Texan and Watergate prosecutor who was very hot at that particular moment during the Watergate trial] and John Tunney—he's a friend of mine. We'll have columnist Rollie Evans and Joe Kraft and then we'll have other Senators. We had Ben Bradlee and Kay Graham" (she is the publisher of the Washington *Post*). Bentsen had not mentioned one person who wasn't potentially influential for him. "We like to get people with diverse views. One night we had Peter Flanigan [Nixon's former controversial White House aide] and Ted Kennedy. That damn Rollie," Bentsen says with proprietary affection, "he's supposed to stay *out* of those debates!" (Evans is the other half of the Evans-Novak column.) "Well, Rollie interrupts with a four-letter word and Kay is in the other room and says, 'Oh-oh, that's Rollie.'" Bentsen hastens to add, "We don't publicize these dinners in any way."

Are there any little old improptu evenings at home? "It really doesn't happen. We were here alone last night, but we weren't expecting to be. A trip was canceled. We're constantly moving."

This does not faze Mrs. Bentsen. "I'm organized to the point of sterility. Still, I'll get somewhere and will have left all my belts to my dresses at home."

When there are free moments they play tennis. "We love paddle tennis—we'll go to play out at the Chevy Chase Club" (Washington's bastion of Waspdom, which periodically gets taken to task for its long-standing policy prohibiting membership for Jews, a policy club officers repeatedly publicly deny).

Do the Bentsens have any plain old-shoe-type friends? "We have, and we cherish them. They're back home." We talked about the surface socializing inherent in the structure of Washington political society. Bentsen looks puzzled that surface socializing might be considered a minus to some people. "When you're politically oriented you just like to meet people." His wife adds, "The more people I meet the happier I am." He comments, "Here's a big point about this girl I live with." (He smiles and looks across to her. She looks back and smiles.) "She loves to go, and I want her to go. We keep our suitcases pretty well packed all the time."

Did she travel when the children were small? "Oh, yes, I always managed to travel." Did they feel it was healthier for their children not being raised in the limelight of politics? She said, "Of course, in Houston where we lived, you were a prominent, outstanding person, Lloyd. You made the graduating speech to the high school." All of Houston knowing you was a little different, he protested. "I think it is a problem for prominent politicians' children, much like it is for movie star and sports figures. I think it would have been a problem for us had we stayed in politics while they were young."

I was waiting for that old cliché, spoken by so many parents, but I was not prepared for the way in which Bentsen made it sound as if he had just invented the thought. "*We* feel it's the quality of time you spend with kids, not the quantity," he said with a profound look. "We'll go somewhere *together* where no one's competing for their or our attention. We've been on floating trips down the Amazon, hunting and fishing in Alaska. Oh, we've had some great trips."

Ignoring one salient fact—the extraordinary amount of cash it takes to live that way—Bentsen said that as a political family, "You've got to have places to retreat to where you can have that quality of attention. Now we go down to this little place in the country—our place. It's got a tennis court and a lake and the children come down to spend some weekends with us. They're now businessmen and busy themselves."

Mrs. Bentsen feels her husband's background in business serves him well as a politician. "One of the reasons he's able to do a good job in the Senate—and I must say he does a good job"—he smiles and says, as an aside, "I like those 'objective' criticisms"—she smiles back and continues—"is because he's a businessman. Most politicians began in the state legislature, not a business background, and . . ." He interrupts in a chiding tone, "B.A., that's not enough, hon. I've known good businessmen who were great failures as politicians. You have to have the ability to relate, to have empathy." I asked if that meant the ability to sell yourself. "That's right! And that's not the situation in business. You get a mandate. Here you have to sell your viewpoint, you have to sell yourself to the American people." Mrs. Bentsen persists, "But you know when you're in the finance committee and the chairman will say something extremely important and . . ." Her husband stops her with a warning. "Now, B.A. . . ." as if she might reveal something said in committee. She finishes with, "The chairman *will* ask your advice, he'll say, 'Lloyd, now *you* understand business, what would you do?'" Bentsen looks modest.

Why do men who have all the money in the world choose a political life? "Well, I don't know of any better place for someone to leave his footprints somewhere. Everyone seeks a little bit of immortality. I think the place to do it is in public service." And what about this running for the presidency? Bentsen was running hard and early, trying to get his name known around the country. He gave me his most supersincere serious look. "If you're going to try to leave that footprint I spoke about, there is no question you can do it in the presidency. The second-best place is where I am." We talked about wrestling with one's conscience and having to vote certain ways because it is politically expedient. "Sure, I've made some votes I wasn't totally happy with. The man who tells you differently . . ." I supplied an end to the sentence: ". . . is not in office?" He laughed, politely, and said, ". . . is not telling you the truth. But on the big issues, I try to bite the bullet."

Talking about the pressures of political life compared to business, Bentsen said, "Let me draw a sharp distinction. The pressures while in business were equal to what I had in the House, but not what I have in the Senate. There's a great difference representing a very large populist state and representing a congressional district. I have twenty-four times as many constituents as any House member from Texas." Does Bentsen subscribe to the late Sam Rayburn's axiom that "to get along, go along"? Bentsen said no. He did not elaborate. How does he handle people he doesn't get along with? "Very gently." He smiled at his joke, then continued, "Sure, you disagree, but you don't have to be disagreeable." What about some of the Nean-derthal types? "Some can be very *helpful* to you," he stressed. "I've been able to get along. To be successful, a politician has to, of necessity, be pragmatic. Of course there are degrees of prag-matism, but I don't think you can be a total idealist." Bentsen seemed mystified at the loners who get into politics. "It seems like such a contradiction, but they are there. Hughes used to sit there in his quiet rage and you wonder what he's thinking. McGovern stays away from the group."

Whatever Bentsen's philosophy, it's pretty well disguised. How would things be different if Bentsen were President, I asked. I was thinking about the social ills that so beset us today but I must have worded my question ambiguously, because Bentsen moved into a discussion of the job *techniques*. "I'd par-ticipate in management decisions. I wouldn't delegate it all through the staff. I'd participate and when I had a tough deci-sion, I wouldn't isolate myself like Nixon. I would face it in the open."

On a personal basis, one of the rewards in politics is "you meet so many interesting people. How else would I have met King Hussein or President Sadat?" he said. She interjected, "Or Marshal Tito on his island?"

Mrs. Bentsen said she does not keep abreast of politics through her husband as much as she does "from reading the papers. The nights we don't go out he has an armful of papers he sits down to read. We don't have much time to talk. I may ask who he had lunch with and that's about it. You know, when he's away and I'm alone I'm never miserable. I read a great deal. What have we just finished reading? What have we . . ." she asks. He said, "Arthur Schlesinger, *The Imperial Presidency.*" She said, "I love political novels, like *Facing the Lions.* I have just opened *The Imperial Presidency.* I rather gather it's a legal tome."

I asked if Bentsen saw enough women entering politics to change it. "I see a trend, no question." But Bentsen completely ignores any discussion or examples on the Hill and comes up with the exceptional woman. "I went to see Sadat and King Hussein and Golda Meir all in a period of two weeks—and I de-cided those fellows were overmatched," he said with a smile. (Bentsen is better than many Senators about hiring women, he said. A woman with her doctorate, who speaks three languages, advises him on foreign affairs.)

His wife has no desire for politics. "I have no talent, as I said." Their idyllic union astounds Mrs. Bentsen when she thinks of the chances they took in their marriage. "We had six dates and we got married." Her husband joked, "It takes us a long time to make up our minds." They beam at each other. "We've just had our thirtieth anniversary."

B. A. Bentsen, an only child, had more personal tragedy from the age of six to twelve than most people do in a lifetime. Her mother died of tuberculosis when she was six, her father two years later, a grandfather two years after that and a grandmother when she was twelve. "An old maid aunt came to live with me," she recalls. "It was a lonely life," she said, but it was so far in the background that she could say that without emotion. "I always had a lot of friends and you learn to deal with it." At sixteen she went to Texas State University for Women. She decided to go to New York and soon found a job modeling with the now-defunct but then well-known Harry Conover agency. B. A. and Lloyd had met once at the University of Texas. Lloyd, then in the service, remembered her when he went through New York at six o'clock in the morning on his way to combat intelligence school. "I called her and she joined me for breakfast at that ungodly hour. I thought, 'Gee, how marvelous. How could anyone be so cheerful at this time of day? I've just got to get to know her.'" He adds the kicker to the story; it sounds as if he has told it often, "It was years later that I realized she was just coming in from a date!" Like many World War II couples, they were married just before he went overseas. "I wasn't going to give her any time to think." She recalls, "We didn't talk about politics—we didn't talk about *anything*. It's amazing how fortunate we've been. I could have died of fright meeting new people, for example, but it was not that way."

At the door of their apartment, she stands with her arms around his waist as they say goodbye. Bentsen comments once again on what a perfect political couple they are. "She gives me that needle." He punctuates the air with three jabs of his right fist as he says "go-go-go." I said I wanted to know the secret of the political wife's ability to look rapturously at her husband during speeches as if she'd never heard the subject before. She smiled serenely. "I really do enjoy hearing him speak. He's just so good."

He smiled and said, "Aw, B. A."

25

More Mavericks: Southern, Northern, and Oklahoma Style

IT is six o'clock in the morning, and late for Herman Talmadge. It seems miserably early for an interview, but Talmadge had already been out jogging. He rarely gives an interview after working hours. In fact, he rarely goes anywhere but home after work. He saves himself for those 4 A.M. wakeups.

His wife, Betty, in a robe, her short, curly hair somewhat touseled, is warm and friendly and sympathetic about the hour as she offers a cup of coffee. At that point, a visitor would think Mrs. Talmadge, the wife of the Senator from Georgia, is Southern woman personified. "Oh, I've *never* entered into political discussions. I've shaken some hands but I don't make speeches. I sort of just follow along." But wait. The interview is not over.

Enter Herman Talmadge, early sixties and looking younger. A trim testimonial to jogging. I tell him he looks like Walter Matthau and am not original. Lots of those people who saw him on the Watergate hearings thought the same. He smiles. "He's a great actor, but not very sexy."

Talmadge settles into a favorite chair in the den of their Washington apartment, chews on a cigar, every now and then spitting into the spittoon at the side of the chair. He takes charge of the conversation, which is at that point about them. "Betty was only eighteen, I was twenty-eight when we got married." He was elected governor seven years later "in nineteen hundred and forty-eight." Did she campaign? "Not as a rule. Most of the Southern wives don't take to the stump on behalf of their husbands like they do in some other parts of the country. They may go to socials but not discuss issues." We talked about his wife's ham business that she had parlayed into a $3-million-a-year venture. There was no praise forthcoming and little interest. "A woman's primary responsibility is as a homemaker to look after her husband and children." Betty shoots him an impassive look and says nothing. While her place is in the home, Talmadge feels the wife of a politician should take as a matter of course an invasion of privacy in that home. "Any politician forgoes his privacy. To begin with, you don't have any. I've got collect calls clear from Guam. The phone rings constantly at home, all hours of the night or day. It's just the price you have to pay."

Herman learned politics at his Daddy's knee, as they say. He started "stumpin'" for his father, the legendary Eugene Herman Talmadge, governor of Georgia and ardent segregationist. Upon his father's death in 1947, Herman was elected by the state legislature to replace his father and served for sixty-seven days, then vacated the office because of a decision of the state supreme court. He was elected then by the people of Georgia to fill the unexpired term. He remained governor of that state until 1955. He has been in the U.S. Senate since 1957.

He remembers the "best political advice" he ever got. It is cagey, wary, and shrewd: "Remember to whom you speak, of whom you speak. When and where and how. Treat your enemy of today as though he would be your friend of tomorrow and your friend of today as though he'd be your enemy tomorrow."

He inherited two political factions—the pro-Talmadge and the anti-Talmadge—with not a great deal of people in the middle ground. But unlike his father, Herman chose to work with his enemies. He is a pragmatic politician who says "Not everyone can have the same views" (although later in the interview he referred to Adam Clayton Powell as being the "biggest racist in town when he was alive"). The last time Talmadge lost his temper politically was almost thirty years ago when an "ultra ultra super liberal asked some damn irrelevant, impertinent question. I dressed him down in good fashion." He says proudly that ultraliberals and blacks are now among his supporters. "I don't know how much I attribute to Watergate [he was considered one of the most intelligent members of that committee], how much to my own accommodation, and how much to their accepting reality instead of theory."

Talmadge has no illusions about possessing any Olympian authority—"the most influential member of the Senate has very little to say about how the country is run." He likes the work, and the attention he gets, however. The national exposure dur-

ing the Watergate hearings made him an instant celebrity and it
is said he puffed and preened most happily when people recognized him in airports around the country. He coolly appraises
the social ills of the country with more than a little contempt for
many of the poor. "People think that the government spending
for programs is the only way poverty will be eliminated. It depends on the individual involved. All you can do is give them
the opportunity. So many think if you pass a law it will make everyone healthy, wealthy, and wise. Some, who are thrifty and
productive, do benefit. But you can pass laws for the next hundred years to eliminate poverty and you won't eliminate a one.
Give 'em a penny and they'll be broke before dark."

One longtime acquaintance of Talmadge said that his façade
is nearly impenetrable. "It wasn't socially elite to be a Talmadge
supporter when his Daddy was running things. Early in his
childhood, Herman built a wall. Sometimes I can't even pene-
trate that shell."

Talmadge talked about his childhood slightly. "My family operated a twelve-horse farm and I worked on that farm." Mrs.
Talmadge chuckles. "That's the last work you ever did, Herman." He darts a look at her and does not laugh. "We didn't
live flashy lives." He was popular and elected president of this
and that in high school and was on the debate team in college,
but he "wasn't the social type. I never did dance until I went to
college. I never dated a great deal."

Betty said she "came out of the real Bible belt, where you almost bowed down and said your prayers." When she met Talmadge she said her heart was "all a-flutter" and clasped her
hands in a knowing parody of the sweet little ole Southern girl.

Talmadge said that a political marriage brings its special tensions; the husband traveling and the wife at home and the
phones ringing and the fishbowl life, but he clearly has no interest in the subject. His wife often attends functions with her
female friends because Talmadge will not change his long-
standing pattern of coming home and going to bed early.

When Talmadge left for the office, his wife and I suddenly
moved into an animated and open conversation. She turned
out to be one of the most delightful political wives I had met.
She's not sure either the state of Georgia or her husband is
quite ready for her, so she plays the game, with some resentment and increasingly more public fire.

This woman who never gave a political speech in her life is a witty, forceful, and popular speaker in her own right as she talks about her business enterprise to women's groups across the country. She admits, "I've done one thing all my life—and that's stop and think what the political impact will be. But my mind's made up. I see no reason to subjugate my entire life to his political ambitions. I don't want to take his thunder—because I can't. But if there is some of my own, I want to get it."

She says, "It's a man's world and it's their rules and we've been fool enough to play it their way." She worries if that is saying too much. She emphasizes she does not come from a Southern generation that was a hotbed of feminism. An ever-growing person, she is appalled by the "white only" doctrines of her past. "And to think we accepted it." Her manner of independence is not through words—"that only gets their backs up." "I don't *say*—I go out and *do!*"

She feels with her two sons grown that her husband respects her more now that she's working, "he wouldn't admit it though." It has given Mrs. Talmadge a new sense of herself: "I've decided I've done about as well as anyone else, I've made it in the business community, and I've taught men who are supposed to have all the wisdom. My dear, the greatest pleasure in life is when you've accomplished a tough job. Everyone talks about women staying in the home. Children grow up and the husband drops dead and what happens? Everyone is so sorry for her—for six months, and then that's that." She admits her husband doesn't understand her, but then they're even. "I don't understand him."

There is a lovely mansion for Betty to recline in back home—it was used as Tara in the Hollywood epic *Gone With the Wind*—but she is having none of it.

People who don't know Betty Talmadge assume that the ham business is in reality her husband's and that she was more or less given it to dabble with. While she admits the name opens a few doors for her, "Once they're open, you've got to have something to show."

She is a natural businesswoman, shrewd without being tough, and thoroughly genuine behind the Southern-lady mask—which slips rather quickly when she is talking with women who are also into careers. Her speeches started a couple of years ago when she got a letter from a Memphis, Tennessee, marketing association. They wrote, "What would be your fee, *if any?*" "I

talked to Liz [her friend Liz Carpenter, former press aide to
Lady Bird Johnson and an indefatigable and witty speaker] and
she said, 'Go, and charge 'em a thousand dollars.' I said, 'Oh,
Liz, what for, to tell them about my experiences?' Well, I wrote
and told them and son-of-a-gun if they didn't say yes."

Speaking to the National Women's Council of Realtors in Atlanta, Mrs. Talmadge started out in Southern cornpone. Her
husband was the "speaker of the house." She was "flattered"
that they wanted her to talk. But she quickly moved into:
"There is no reason why women shouldn't get more involved in
business . . . and more involved in *life.* You can't enjoy life
and profit from it by sitting on the sidelines as a spectator."

She then poked fun at her husband. "Herman would be the
first to admit that he had become a national celebrity," she said.
In a "little ole me" vein, she said she "sort of backed into" her
career, then "eighteen years and millions of hams later" she was
"suddenly" running a business with $3-1/2 million annual sales.
Her husband started the business in 1951 when he was governor and too busy. His wife had a few stocks and bonds and he
asked her if she wanted to invest in his new venture. She did
and "when *my* money became involved—so did I!" Once involved, she couldn't get out—"you don't own a business, the
business owns you." Her "instinct" for knowing who to listen to
and who to take advice from and her interest in people were
her qualifications. She didn't know a debit from a credit; she
said she had more courage than sense.

Once in, she got overextended financially. "I had payrolls to
meet and I had to sell those hams." She thought of ways to plug
the business. When her husband was asked on television what
he was going to have for breakfast he said, "Eggs." "I was ready
to kill him, because he could have said 'Talmadge Ham.'"

She started with a small concrete-block building with a three-
ton refrigeration unit and a room that would hold 1,500 hams.
The first time she looked at it she thought she had cornered all
the hams in the world. "To show you how your perspective can
change, we do more ham business than that in one day now." It
was a struggle, though. Her highest-paid employee for the first
four years made $37.50 per week. Her "titles" at the time were
president, secretary, treasurer, salesman, bookkeeper, manager, employee, and janitor. Without salary.

One time a vice president of Armour & Co. came down to

handle her complaint that a shipment of hams from them was poorly trimmed. She was performing the menial but necessary job of rubbing hams, up to her elbows in grease and salt, trying to get the curing process started. The man looked in disbelief and said, *"You're* Mrs. Talmadge?" She drawled, "After I had shown him the poor job his company had done and then handed him a knife so that he could help me properly trim the hams—he *knew* I was Mrs. Talmadge."

Then she told a story on the Senator. A prosperous banker saw him on the street and said he was so glad the business was doing so well. Talmadge asked him how he knew that and the man said, "Because you've stopped calling it *Betty's* business and started calling it *our* business."

Mrs. Talmadge said she thinks women's liberation has done a great deal of good "but it has also alienated a lot of people that we ought to have on our side. Certainly it is understandable how women can be angry. But being mad will not win the battle. We don't want to win the argument and lose the customer." She was asked once whether she wanted to be listed as Ms., Mrs. Herman Talmadge or Betty Talmadge. Her reply was, if women can get the jobs they want for equal pay, "they can call me *Mister* if they want to." In 1974, she started a new venture, a food brokerage business, called Betty Talmadge and Associates. "After four months we were in the black."

She feels she may have neglected her home to some extent and that it was a struggle to achieve a balance. But she adds, "Women must be able to determine for *themselves* what they want to do. That includes being homemakers, having careers or any combination of the two. The point is freedom of *choice*. No longer can women be stereotyped and assigned to a particular station in life"—she looked determined—"and *kept* there forever."

Jane Hart, the woman who flies planes, goes around town on motorcycles, and plans sailing trips around the world; the woman who got sentenced for marching and dissenting against the war, refused to pay her income tax, and made a trip to Hanoi with POW families. But Jane Hart is still, after all, a wife and mother of eight. Some people wonder how much marriage is really there. It is a marriage and family unit of extreme independence at this stage with, as a friend said, "everybody off doing his or her own thing." Her family money more than helps—as does an "assistant mother" who has run the household for ages, both the Senator from Michigan and Mrs. Hart are quick to say.

A close friend said, "Although Phil and Jane are separated a lot that doesn't mean they have one of those 'convenience' things. There is deep respect there."

The Harts have never spun their wheels in Washington's social circuit. They care, as they said, "not at all" for the social scene. In their home, near the Shoreham hotel, there is an easygoing rapport. She is a slim, athletic woman with short blond-gray hair. His handsome face is partially hidden by a beard that makes him look older. He started wearing it because of a war protest bet he made with his children and kept. They do not find "togetherness" the epitome of life and were practicing an open marriage long before it was called that. He doesn't fly a plane or pilot a boat or ride or breed horses. Hondas? A quick smile—"I don't fly one of those either." He likes to read, has had his share of father-son games of catch and touch football, enjoys long conversations with his family and close friends. At one time, an off-hours project, he said wryly, was "attempting to find a herbicide not dangerous but effective against crabgrass. That'd do more good than anything I could ever do in the Senate." A soft-spoken but staunch fighter who emerged as a spokesman for the Senate's liberal Democratic bloc in 1970, Hart was unimpressed with jockeying for national power positions. A title "means nothing. We're very disorganized. The hallmark of the liberals is to march in nine different directions at the same time."

A gentleman to the core, Hart does not "use" his Senate title. When an airline was bumping people from an overbooked flight, Hart made no protest when he went unrecognized. Instead, he sat with a family who had also been bumped, and talked about kids, and waited for another plane. (One Michigan staffer said, "I've been bumped by Lenore and George Romney more than I want to say.") The man waiting with Hart was so astounded when he finally realized who he was talking to that he wrote a letter to a newspaper commending Hart.

The Senator has a quiet putdown for those who say he isn't forceful enough. "In the Senate, they call the roll and you make your decision known or you absent yourself. I have a very good attendance record." He added softly, "I sometimes envy the man who thinks he knows the answers for everything. The point is the problems that confront us are so complex that the sane man can't be that decisive."

During an interview with me a few years ago, Mrs. Hart said her husband was "incredible. I don't see how he copes with the world every day. He never blows his cool, but that doesn't mean he's a bland person." Talking of the Senate, she said, "He seems to understand the reasons why they say and do the things they do—somehow." She does not, and added, "We have beautiful fights." (Her husband nodded agreement.) "We have fights about whether the whole system has survivability built into it. I read the news and I say, 'Ye gods, we're not giving anything to the kids—anything they can even *correct*.' Then I scream that it's all his fault. He's the 'institution' and he should fix it." To which the Senator added, affectionately, "By tomorrow." Hart will retire at the end of this term.

Hart learned about issues early. His father, the local town banker (Bryn Mawr, Pennsylvania), was also the "local town Democrat—what would you expect from an Irishman?" His seventeenth birthday gift from his father was a membership card in the NAACP. He says with pride that "Janie was a dove way ahead of time," but he also adds, "I marched in the 1930s campus protests."

Mrs. Hart comes from such wealth—her businessman father, Walter O. Briggs, once owned the Detroit Tigers, and Briggs Stadium is named after him—that one wonders where both her sense of social consciousness and money values come from. She sold her airplane and boat when all the children went off to college or private schools. "It's too costly." Although she said things had gotten pretty "cruddy" in their home, she had decorated it only once in twelve years. "It's just too costly."

Mrs. Hart's father, the son of a railroad engineer, quit school at fourteen to go to work, drifted into Detroit's automobile business, and became the largest independent automobile parts manufacturer in the world. She was stung early by the difference in her life and others. "During the depression, I was nine or ten, and I can remember seeing people in Detroit . . . long lines of people . . . and I was not one of them. I remember the contrast." Hers was a childhood of debutante balls (about which she now makes a face) and the exclusive Catholic girls

school, Manhattanville College. She quit college to drive a Red
Cross truck in the war but she dismisses that "as a very upper-
middle-class thing to do." Her parents planted the seed that led
to involvement in liberal causes and her feelings were heightened when she met and married Phil Hart, her brother's room-
mate at Georgetown University.

As a Catholic, Mrs. Hart admits it was a difficult decision to
go against beliefs taught in childhood, but she feels that birth
control is necessary and right. "If I were to start now I wouldn't
have had such a large family. One of our girls said she wanted
twelve children. I said fine—but have a couple and adopt the
rest—regardless of background or race. There are too many
people consuming up the world. I think perhaps the only use
for moon travel is it would be a great place to lob our trash."

Such an offhand remark about the space race didn't keep
Mrs. Hart from battling for female American astronauts. She
took the physical tests and passed easily, but said, "The bias still
exists." If they ever stay on the moon for months, "Well, then
they'll need a cook—so *she'll* probably be *black.*"

A proponent of the women's movement, naturally, Senator
Hart said, "If anyone doesn't understand that this culture, if
that's what it is, has lost enormously in contributions of women,
he's hopeless." He is also a civil libertarian who puts his wife's
right to act in her own conscience before his reelection. She
was, in fact, more shocked and alarmed than he that her actions
received widespread publicity. Some were predicting that she
had done him irreparable harm. In his 1970 acceptance speech,
the Senator movingly spoke off the cuff about his wife. He considered his victory an indication that the people knew what she
was doing, understood her reasons, and liked her for it, although they may have disagreed with her tactics. The Harts are
also astute politicians who have an innate ability to turn what on
the surface seems a great detraction into an advantage by being
very open and honest. Part of her program at that time was to
talk to people about her actions and it paid off. A very active
campaigner, Mrs. Hart acknowledges the fact that some on her
husband's staff might fervently wish she would get laryngitis before participating in his campaigns, because she always speaks
on issues. During the fuel crisis and pollution concern, she said
her Honda should be "respectable" now. "It's a much smaller

polluter than cars." But then she had to add, "But of course, *Detroit* doesn't make Hondas."

Mrs. Hart studied anthropology in the seventies and has thought of teaching on the college level when she gets through her sailing venture.

There is such an air of security about Hart that he once said it is a great thing that his wife's money allowed him to pursue a political career. It is a "blatant fact," she said, that with such a large family politics would have been beyond them without her money.

Decrying the expense of campaigning and the whole political system she said, "Just think how many really brilliant people are lost to public service because they can't afford it."

Hart is also secure enough to let Jane Hart be completely herself. "Phil actually seems to enjoy it. Mrs. Roosevelt, whom I always admired, was given a free and clear head to say what was right in her conscience. That's the way it is with Phil." Then, she added, "You know, we really do like each other."

When Fred Harris married LaDonna Crawford, half-Comanche and raised in a home where Comanche was the primary language, no one much approved. Harris was about as poor white as you could get in Oklahoma, which didn't set well with her parents. He was embarrassed that his father had to sign for their marriage license, because they were teenagers. "There was this woman laughing at this little feller who was going to get married," he recalled.

He joked that he was intent on a career as a bootlegger until LaDonna "straightened me out in my senior year of high school." Harris tells jokes with a manic gleam in his eye and makes nearly everything sound funny. He was born in 1930 and was soon to become a firsthand student of the great depression, as the son of a poor Oklahoma sharecropper. Other politicians are given to larding childhood experiences with pious meaning, but Harris reared back his head and said, "When I was five years old I was a little bitty feller driving those huge mules that weigh hundreds of pounds." He received ten cents a day for riding them around from daylight to dark to power an old-fashioned hay baler. "I used to whip and yell and people couldn't even see where this voice was comin' from I was so small. I'd be yellin,' 'You old son of a bitch, move it!' and 'Go to the right, you goddamned stupid son of a bitch!' Then I'd get so mad and frustrated because I was so little and couldn't get them to do what I wanted that I'd jump right up and bite 'em on the side of their goddamn necks!"

In 1964, Harris moved into the Senate. He became a friend of Robert Kennedy and found himself visiting the Kennedy compound; he ran for the presidency in 1972; got national publicity as 1969 Democratic National Committee chairman, but Harris never forgot that he was once a five-year-old who drove the mules. He was often in awe of the people he hob-nobbed with as a Senator; too much so at times, he says, now that he is no longer in the Senate. For the past few years Harris has known the feeling of not having a power base, but he told friends it didn't bother him. He worked with LaDonna on her Americans for Indian Opportunity organization, wrote books and magazine articles, lectured. He was happy, he insisted, and he seemed so. He was more relaxed, enjoyed evenings with "just friends," who were no longer the big guns in politics. He seemed far less driven and ambitious than in the past, and a newspaperman remarked, "His not being a Senator makes it easier to like him." Like all people who either remove them-selves or are removed from office, Harris knew some people were talking about "poor ole Fred" but it genuinely didn't seem to bother him.

When the Harrises had their twenty-fifth wedding anniver-sary in 1974, the party was mostly Indian friends and old news-paper and lesser-level political pals. The evening ended with Harris sitting cross-legged on the floor, beating time on drums and leading Indian chants. One close Senator friend was hurt that he wasn't invited, but LaDonna said, "Fred just made up the list from those he was having fun with at the time."

Then one summer night in 1974 Harris, who has always hoped to galvanize his New Populism into a national force, was sitting in the kitchen, eating, and watching the televised im-peachment proceedings. "God *damn*," he said. "I'm going to run! Kennedy's not going to, I just feel that. [Kennedy with-drew from contention a few months later.] Mondale doesn't seem to be able to get things off the ground. [Mondale with-drew a few months later.] If things stay this way I'm going to consider it." I said, "Fred, you old hypocrite. You told me three

months ago you were content and liked being out of politics."
He said, "That's not hypocritical. I meant it at the time. I had
my two years of resting, now I'm interested again." By the fall
of 1974, he was, as they say "testing the waters" but very quietly.
He made trips to New Hampshire to test grass-roots sentiment
but he didn't want to get in too quickly. [His try in 1972 never
got as far as the New Hampshire primary.] But by spring of
1975, the Harrises were dividing their time between New
Hampshire and California—and a lot of points in between—
drumming up support and money. They were seldom home
and seemed exhilarated by the venture. One acquaintance said
cynically, "Hell, it gives Fred something to do." "I love Fred,"
said another former Hill colleague, "but he never understood
this town or how it works."

Harris's right-hand adviser, confidante, and "pusher" is La-
Donna. LaDonna wants Fred in a position of influence in order
to do more for the country and because she thinks he's qualified. Their oldest daughter is in law school, but their teenage
children, Byron and Laurie, live with them in McLean, Virginia, and are active in both their social life and their social causes.
When Laurie was twelve in 1974, she was for women's and Indians' rights, campaigning for her school to admit girls into
shop classes. She was an active participant in discussions in the
home and attended many of the Indian-dominated affairs of
her mother's.

LaDonna and Fred co-founded Oklahomans for Indian Op-
portunity in the sixties, and in 1970 she branched out to found
Americans for Indian Opportunity, with offices in Washington.
Angered at the paternalism of the Bureau of Indian Affairs,
LaDonna started this national organization to support Indian
Action Programs and self-help projects.

"There is no 'Indian problem' or 'black problem.' There is an
American problem, a human problem, a problem of making
clear that the right to be different and still be entitled to *full* citi-
zenship must be not only safeguarded but also encouraged."

LaDonna rattles off the statistics she knows too well, and recalls an expression of defeat and frustration that marks Indian
people "living in a society which denies them their basic rights."
The saying is "Today is a good day to die."

"One out of three Indians will be jailed. Every other Indian family will have a relative who dies in jail. In Minnesota, where Indians comprise six-tenths of one percent of the general population, they are from eight percent to twenty-eight percent of the prison population." These statistics were echoed when LaDonna and a group of Indians met with law-enforcement officers to determine why these conditions exist and to study the prison system's attitude toward Indians.

There are other statistics—high unemployment, a poverty life for most, a high suicide rate. Plagued by tuberculosis, viral infections, pneumonia, malnutrition, the Indian dies on the average at the age of forty-three, about twenty years earlier than the non-Indian. Infant mortality rate among Indians is twelve points above the national average.

The worst disease is the "hopelessness and demoralization of the Indian, which is the result of spirit-destroying prejudice," said LaDonna. "Indians don't want to 'melt' into the white man's society. They want the right to be different."

For many Indians, their lack of self-esteem begins in the American government boarding school. "We were told our language and culture were of no value," remembers LaDonna, who grew up in her grandparents' Oklahoma home where Comanche was the primary language. "We were made ashamed of our culture. To obtain our education we had to give up our Indianness.

"When I was twelve years old I was under the influence of the BIA mission. But I always felt something was wrong with what they were saying. I was as smart as they were, yet they were saying things that made me feel inferior. I have always been able to filter out t hat people are thinking and don't hold anyone in awe. Being a minority person, it's part of my survival kit. You evaluate people differently." LaDonna feels she was lucky that her mother, Liby Tabbytite, and her grandparents insightfully knew that if there was to be a future for their daughter she would have to understand both the white and nonwhite community. They fought against her being sent away to boarding school. "Generally BIA policy is to try to make white people out of Indians by placing them in schools so far from their homes that they have no chance of visiting their families or of being visited."

Largely through the encouragement of her grandmother, LaDonna made it through a nearby high school, where she met

Harris. A brilliant student, Fred was determined to get through law school; he had already decided on a career in politics. It meant hard work—nine exhausting summers following the wheat harvest all the way to North Dakota and scrambling for funds as a janitor while he learned the printing trade—a more solid means of getting through college. They dated whenever possible and LaDonna worked at a soda fountain. When they married, they lived in a two-room trailer house without inside toilet or bath while he attended the University of Oklahoma. Harris had just established a law firm when he was elected to the Oklahoma state senate at the age of twenty-five. He served from 1956 to 1964, when he was elected to fill the unexpired term of the late U.S. Senator Robert Kerr. In 1966 he was elected for the full six-year term.

In the early days, LaDonna was a "stoic," she said. "It was part of my protection as a minority person." It is a startling comment to those who know her today—dark-haired, handsome, very gregarious and fun-loving. Her credits are awesome: membership on a string of national human rights commissions, a convener of the National Women's Political Caucus, on the boards of national service associations. In 1973, Ms. Harris was selected as the Woman of the Year in the area of Human Rights in a national poll. But she is no humorless zealot. She laughs infectiously with her friends, loves to give impromptu dinners, and there is little trace of the quiet person she once was. Still, her habit of sizing people up served her well when she came to Washington. "Because of my background, I never put people on a pedestal the way Fred did. You the *person* is what counts."

Fred interjects, "I'm star-struck and she's not. I remember we were in Hyannis in 1965, staying with Bobby and Ethel and here comes Jackie in a bathing suit on a bicycle, two little kids running alongside. I recognized Caroline and I said, 'Hey! That's Jackie Kennedy!' LaDonna said, 'What did you expect in Hyannisport?' She can be sitting next to someone famous and not even care. I'm too much the other way." (Some in Washington have a different image of the Harrises and feel they were very much into the political social shuffle.)

LaDonna was not oblivious to the fact that in those days of the late sixties, when it was chic to invite minority members to your gatherings, there was a certain cachet in having a stunning

American Indian and her dynamic Senator husband as guests. Without bitterness or sorrow but with amused acceptance, she chuckled at the ones who no longer invite them. "I never played the game anyway. I just enjoyed it for what it was. And I *knew* what it was."

Unlike those who outgrow one another when they move from such struggling beginnings to national prominence, the Harrises remained "very very dependent on each other." La-Donna feels a lot of politicians "just want to marry the right image. It seems incredible that they don't confer with each other." Old-guard politicians objected to her close advisory position, the fact that she was always there. "Joan Kennedy's a good example of what it does to you when you're left outside of things," she said. Harris said, "Some of those poor wives might as well be a painted backdrop." LaDonna wanted to reform some of the Senate wives group to be more involved in today's issues but never got very far. Most were too timid about getting into anything controversial, she said.

Harris spoke easily of his life today outside the Senate, although he said it was a "six month adjustment." Does he worry about not having a power base? "I'm not worried, but I'm conscious of it. It dies that minute you leave office." So do the emoluments. "It took me a half year to change my *self* image. 1973 was the first year in 20 years I wasn't running for something. I never lost an election in my life. I'd had years of never traveling alone, going first class because I thought as a senator you *had* to. I drove one of those gas suckin' cars. I always had a staff person doing things for me. I never had to even call an airlines, someone always took you to the airport and picked you up. I never had to know how the world lives."

One thing Harris doesn't miss is the "necessary fakiness" of political office. "You live by it. You cannot survive without it. You get to posturin'. I can be just dead, *absolutely* dead, the damn ears stopped up from flyin', and then you go into a crowd and get this thing—it's kind of an adrenalin high." He is a spellbinding speaker and he said, "I hardly ever failed to get a standing ovation. You're *deeply* involved in the issues, but it's like performing. Anybody who's professional in politics hardly ever takes a bad picture. You never see 'em with their eyes halfclosed or chewing food or with their mouth gapped open. The first time I saw ole G. Mennen Williams, he was eating at a banquet, and every now and then he would freeze." Harris flashed his teeth in the best of political grins. "His eyes were always open, he wasn't blinkin'. He could tell when those cameras were comin' around. It's necessary fakiness, all right."

He gave a hearty laugh when I asked how he's been treated out of office. "Lots of people say, 'How're you doin'?' with their voices lowered, like you have a terminal disease. People wear me out askin' about why I decided not to run for the Senate again. It's hard to explain without sounding hokey. If I'd been defeated it might have hurt, but honest, I just wanted out. I was just wore out. If you get to where it's a drag; have to make yourself go to meetings, have to whip yourself around to make yourself go . . . well, I can't judge exactly my feelings. Bobby died, Johnson had left town. A lot of people fell out on the war. Hell, I didn't have that much clout in the Senate. Johnson and I fell out over the Kerner report. He thought I was disloyal. The Kerner Commission radicalized me and two things turned me off. One was Robert Kennedy's death. [LaDonna interjects, "He was one of the best people on Indian issues next to Fred."] The other was Humphrey's campaign. I had that Democratic chairmanship and I was trying to do something in the Senate and Humphrey wouldn't help me reform the Senate. I couldn't make the compromise and stay in. So we," he said, looking at LaDonna, "made a conscious decision. I had already decided not to run again when the presidential thing came along. It was just the thing to do. I thought the country was going to hell and I thought I might as well try as much as anyone." The effort seemed idealistic and unrealistic to politicians who saw in Harris an unwillingness to compromise enough to gain a broad base of support.

Not having the expenses he had as a Senator, Harris today said he comes out ahead with his lecturing, speeches, and writing. One reason Washington is still their base is because LaDonna's work is here. For an ex-Senator, Harris is remarkably at ease about taking a back seat to LaDonna's business and her friends. He is regarded as a co-partner in LaDonna's work and the fond dream of their Indian friends is to see him as Secretary of the Interior someday. Fred learned Comanche from LaDonna and her parents and is one of the few white men who is truly accepted into the Indian culture. He is glad his Senate seat gave LaDonna more visibility and clout at the time she launched AIO. As for her women's rights projects, Harris said, "I think I was terribly insensitive about women, except LaDonna. What changed first was the rhetoric. As I changed the words, I was forced to change my ideas."

For Harris, there seems not enough of a lasting contentment to remain out of politics. It's anybody's guess what will happen to his political future. Whatever it is, LaDonna and Fred Harris will do it together.

26

A Most Happy Team Couple

FRANK AND BETHINE CHURCH are consistently termed one of political Washington's most happy couples— even by those who work with them, often the most cynical examiners of the public happy-family mask worn by unhappy political families. An interview with them comes dangerously close to sounding like a parody of those *Modern Screen* stories about Hollywood's rare phenomenon, the long-standing happily wed duo. Gossip swirls around Washington couples like autumn leaves circling in the wind, but not around the Churches. When I mentioned to people that I was trying to find some political couples who had successfully worked out a balance between their public and private life, the first answer was always, "Have you talked to Frank and Bethine Church?"

And they do seem to have managed it. "Friends more than sweethearts" is how Bethine viewed their early fascination for one another, and yet she can remember all the letters he wrote her when he was in the service thirty years ago. He is both amused by and understanding of her chaotic approach to life and her worrisome nature, says she is the greatest influence in his life. They are both happiest in Idaho; after seventeen years in Washington they admit they can feel "lonely" here. When politics interfered with their private world and created a distance between Frank and their youngest son, Chase, they changed their public life around to be together more.

Church won national attention when he came to Washington

in 1956 as the youngest Senator, at the age of thirty-two, and then four years later was the keynote speaker at the Democratic National Convention; yet his pursuit of power seems more muted than that of many of his colleagues.

No, he wouldn't mind the presidency, but not enough to chase it. He'd take it "if someone served it up for breakfast . . ." He also says being a viable condidate is something that "circumstances control." As a liberal with little money and from a Western state, Church doesn't see the odds on his side. He recalled that he was "reasonably frightened" by the experience of his friend and colleague George McGovern. "You see the tremendous time and effort, when you're doing all the other things in the Senate as well. It's probably a tremendous ego trip to be involved in a race for the presidency—but it puts your marriage under the severest possible strain," Church said. "When Ed [Muskie] decided not to run with McGovern, it was because Jane really had had enough. There's a lot to that. McGovern's adjustment was difficult, but he has a lot of grit. He's come back to the Senate and is working just as before he ran—within two years. I think for people to want the presidency so badly that they will pursue it for years in the hustings requires not only elephant glands, which not all men possess, but also a terrible inner need for what they consider ultimate recognition in politics," he says.

After his 1974 election, however, Church began to listen to those people who said he should run for the presidency. He pulled back on his initial testing of support when he became chairman of the Senate committee investigating the CIA in the spring of 1975. Church said he couldn't possibly devote his time to both efforts, but rumors persisted that he would be in the running before the year was out.

And Church's tune changed somewhat. To run was not so bad after all. "Bethine and the boys have always been very political; they'd feel at home with it."

Church, a top-ranking member of the Senate Foreign Relations Committee, is a well-respected authority, who would like to be chairman. His major areas of legislative action are foreign policy and environmental protection. While describing himself as an unflagging liberal in the Borah tradition (Idaho's Senator Borah wanted in his day to recognize the Soviet Union), Church also prides himself on being able to work with conservatives. His views on world affairs have been in sharp and consistent contrast to U.S. policy in three areas—the Southeast Asian war, military spending, and foreign aid. His major contribution to the antiwar movement was his co-authorship of the Cooper-Church Amendment, which prohibited the return of U.S. ground combat forces to Cambodia without the consent of Congress. An anomaly in Idaho, Church was uncertain whether Idaho residents would accept him enough to send him back to the Senate in 1962. He had to fight all the user groups (i.e. loggers, miners, grocers) over his conservation stands and had the backing of only one daily newspaper, according to the 1972 Ralph Nader Congress Report. Church recalls that his father-in-law remarked, "You've got the cattlemen, the sheepmen, the lumbermen, and the miners against you. What I'd like to know, Frank, is how the hell you expect to be reelected? Even the dentists and doctors are against you!" (Church became the first Democrat in Idaho history to win a second term in the Senate.)

His voter appeal is in strong measure due to his abiding interest in social causes—the aged, conservation, fighting big oil monopolies—long before these were popular. He was calling senior citizens the forgotten Americans years before Medicare. "Western folks are independent thinkers," Church explains, and they allowed him his opposition to the Vietnamese war because it was consistent with the image that Church had projected. While some heralded Church's 1962 victory as the beginning of today's environmental movement, others viewed Idahoans as having only a surface interest in the more obvious ecological disasters such as wholesale destruction of the land by miners and loggers. Conservatism still runs high in Idaho—the Birchers tried to recall Church in 1967. His 1968 opponent, George Hansen, pictured Church as an appeaser of Communists and blacks.

Church lists his $42,500 Senate salary as his principal source of income, supplemented by relatively minimal earnings from lectures and articles ($5,000 annually). Unlike Lloyd Bentsen, who resents having to disclose his finances, Church has been for full financial disclosure for more than a decade.

Church, hardly the darling of the corporate world, has no backing from wealthy industrialists. (In 1968, a nationwide mailing on behalf of Church and McGovern returned an average contribution of $11.35. While some $200,000 was raised for him by the Church for Senate Committee, about $70,000 of the total came from peace groups outside of Idaho, and the average individual contribution was $14.) There are twelve government-paid trips a year. "It used to be much worse than it is now; when you were only allowed two trips a year," says Bethine. "But there is no expense money available when you travel from town to town within the state. Those expenses are out of pocket. And there is a very limited stationery and stamp allowance. Constituents who come here expect lunch at least, if not dinner. That's a $200 a month or more expense." To have more of a family life and to limit their expenses, the Churches try to split the month, going to Idaho only two weekends out of four. "We like to go together and we couldn't possibly afford to go back every weekend. We try to do five counties at a stretch. Those other two weekends we have as a family," says Bethine.

Since his low-budget campaigning relies on as much personal exposure as possible, the Senator goes to every possible courthouse session or local meeting where he can talk to people. By the end of a campaign, the callus in the wedge between his finger and thumb on his shaking hand is hard and brown. Ever the political wife, Bethine once visibly restrained her husband from the too firm political handshake, at a luncheon of senior citizens. "Bethine got to worrying that I was hurting some of these older people who had arthritic hands," recalls Church. "She whispered to me, 'You're pressing your thumb too hard.' Next thing I knew, I had forgotten and was shaking hands as usual. All of a sudden I felt this pressure on my thumb. I looked down and there was Bethine, calmly lifting my thumb up in the middle of a handshake!"

In Idaho Bethine is well known in her own right and comes from a strong political family. Her father was a U.S. I istrict Judge and former governor. Her husband said, "Bethine is absolutely perfect when it comes to politics." She says, "Maybe I'm pleased that many know me as Bethine, not just the Senator's wife, but I take the opposite view of some wives who don't like politics." The rewards of political life are as much hers as her husband's. "To be frank, I feel that I've got my cake and I get to eat it too. Because of Frank's job I have a chance to form my Child Eye Care Foundation; I am on the board of the Cerebral Palsy group and have clout, more than if I were an interested volunteer. Frank affords me something I appreciate having, and in return I afford him the help he likes." She can tour the hospitals and can relay information as well as an "emotional point of view" to her husband who, like many, gets too emotional to be effective in such situations. "I add a dimension; it gives Frank an ability to stretch himself. In the last six months I've visited twenty-eight nursing homes and senior citizens' centers in Idaho. You see these little old people—it's such a heart-rending thing in a country so big and so special—to see them so neglected."

While she sees the job as a joint career, Bethine Church laughs at the phrase. "I've tried to say, 'This is my career,' but it always comes out wrong. It just sounds so icky. I feel like Mrs. Goody Two Shoes for the next six hours when I say something like that."

Next to his wife, Church credits his father-in-law with having the strongest political influence on his life; Church's own father was more of a counterforce. A "staunch Republican" and owner of a sporting-goods store, Church's father never forgave himself for voting for Franklin Roosevelt in 1932, eight years after Frank was born. Politics was talked at home, but always from his father's viewpoint ("he hated Roosevelt with a joyous vengeance") so in self-defense Church went to the library to find out about Democrats and the other side of the argument. (By contrast, Church's father-in-law was one of the last federal judges appointed by Roosevelt.)

By the time Frank was in junior high he had decided on a career as a U.S. Senator. Although he credits Bethine's background in part for making her an understanding political wife, she says she had not looked for a political future. "Someone in my family was either running, winning, or losing elections all my life and I decided the last thing I wanted was to get married to a politician."

A factor not to be minimized in the Churches' relationship is their temperaments. They are well suited to the disjointed political life and do not fear upheaval. She said, "I live a little like I cook—adventurously. I really like to do a lot of things. Some want to make a nest, but if someone said, 'We're going to Timbuktu tomorrow,' I'd say, 'I've just got to get my toothbrush and the children.' I'm a seat-of-the-pants type of person." Her husband says, "I think in a political marriage, one basic is the attitude of both husband and wife toward public life.

Bethine is genuinely interested in it and the people she meets. For one thing, a lot of women just naturally dislike politics. I think the majority of wives are very much oriented toward the nest. Politics is an insecure profession. It takes you away from your roots, keeps you in Washington, it's a transient life, it's very demanding on a husband's time. It's difficult to make close friendships, everybody is so busy—just 'passing through,' so to speak. It's hard on a lot of women. The men who choose it are driven to it—that's not true of their wives."

Church, a handsome and likable man, said, "I've been here eighteen years and I have no feeling of belonging to this city." His wife agrees and finds about her only objection to a political life is that "you don't have time to cultivate close friends right in that middle part of your life—for your old age. I think almost all of your acquaintanceships in Washington are relatively surface."

Rather than seeking sustenance in a hectic social life, the Churches find it in time together. "Bethine's aware of all the pressures. She knows the Senate. She watches from the gallery and knows much of what goes on, feels the drama and tensions of issues on the floor. Probably one reason we have a happy marriage is that she understands all that. And home is peaceful. We have the best French restaurant in town." He looks at her and smiles. Bethine, plump and jolly, makes a crack about being the best sampler of her own cooking. "I'm always too fat." How do they cope with pressure? She jokes, "We cry a lot." For tension breakers the Churches play backgammon and solitaire, find that Scrabble is too much of an effort when both are exhausted from campaigning or politics.

Church has the enviable attitude that winning or losing isn't all that important. He came to this through a harrowing process. The Churches were young marrieds in their early twenties, with a six-month-old baby, when Church suddenly became ill. He had cancer. "They said he couldn't make it. It was a very rare type," Bethine said, absentmindedly knocking on a wood end table as she tells the story. "He had had terrible backaches, and then later there was a growth in the groin area. They took out a mass of lymph nodes all up the side. When they got to the kidney area, they decided they had cut so much out that they could not cut any more. After they did the pathology on him, they were just going to close him up; they said it was all over.

But they had misread the report. It was reread by a man who looked like God—the cancer was very receptive to X ray. It took us to the point of death, and Frank was nauseated for weeks from the treatment. The X rays just burned him up." Church's main meal was at noon to give him time to digest his food before the 4 P.M. treatments. "I read to him all the time. Sometimes if I could be very histrionic in my reading I could get him over the hump of nausea. I'd just read madly." She remembers, in particular, that *The Turn of the Screw* was enough of a thriller to absorb him. Frank took up the story. "One effect cancer did have on me—I don't know that it made that much difference to Bethine, she was always far less conservative as far as her inner core. I tend to be more cautious. But having so close a brush with death in my early twenties, I felt afterward that life itself was such a chancy proposition that the only way to live it is by taking great chances. I watched my maiden aunt, Eva, whom I loved dearly, carefully putting money aside, waiting for the day when she could retire on her very modest income—and then her dying three months before retirement. All her plans, those books she had on traveling, all those things she ever wanted to do, all snuffed out overnight . . ."

Although Church's Senate seat has been surprisingly secure, he and Bethine did not know that when they decided to "wing it" and go for the Senate in 1956 when he was all of thirty-two.

Bethine recalls, "We sold half a house to do it." The Churches were in the habit of referring to their home as "half a house" because they felt that was all they ever owned. The bank owned the rest.

While Frank and Bethine are both suited to the gypsy life of politics, they have different temperaments. She calls herself a "natural-born worrier." Her father gave her some advice on how to run a political life. "He told me, 'Now look, your mother traveled with me. You'll just have to go with Frank. Otherwise you'll never know what makes him sad or tired or happy.' That helped. I'm such a worrier that had I thought I was not doing the best by Chase and by Forrest, I'd just have been a wreck. As it is, I worried enough about all of them. Every woman is busy today. It's an era of terrific productivity for all women. With children, I found if there is a love, there is a sense of respect for you, too. Chase used to say, 'Just stay out of her way today, she's in one of her moods, but she'll be okay tomorrow.' And sometimes they really want you to be doing something important. Forrest, the older, was going through that cycle of "Mother didn't amount to very much'—it was during John Kennedy's campaign and they asked me to substitute for Ethel Kennedy as a speaker. He said, 'Mother, you've got to go!' Suddenly my stock went up."

Bethine is one team-player wife who does not avoid issues. She talks about them frequently. But she tries to stay clear of statistics, figures, and dates. "I'm always afraid I'm going to add or subtract a zero in my speeches."

Frank says they work as a team. So attuned are they to one another and what they want to say that one national reporter recalled a disconcertingly synchronized performance. "I had this chilling feeling that I was watching two actors, although I like them both. It was as if Frank would say his spiel and then Bethine would say hers. It all seemed rehearsed." Church describes their technique as "Bethine usually introduces me and then most of the time we answer questions. After, she circulates and I circulate through the crowd." While they are usually in agreement, Church said Bethine would normally defer to his views in public. Neither sees this as a copout but as a necessary expediency. "I think Bethine sensed from the beginning, knowing the state so well, that I, as a liberal Democrat, faced a stacked deck. She tried hard not to throw obstacles in my path. I feel she was less concerned about expressing any different view to display her own independence than in trying to help me overcome the odds at home."

We stopped talking long enough to go into a basement recreation room to watch a newscast in which Frank Church was starring. As Bethine and I talked, Church held up a warning hand, and we all watched him—attacking oil cartels and speaking out for the consumer. After, Bethine said, "That was great." Before, she had shouted up to son Chase, then eighteen, that if he wanted to he could see his father on TV. She tried to make it an effortless suggestion.

Sensitive to the problems of raising their children in a political life, the Churches recognized difficulties and did their best to change situations. Forrest was graduated a "scholar and a poet," from Harvard Divinity School. Recently married, he be-

came a minister in 1975. "How do you like that," jokes his
mother, "Reverend Church?" He is very close to the family and
is a "gung ho campaigner," his mother says.

But when younger, politics encroached on their private time.
Embassy dinners on weekends, receptions for the Idaho wheat
growers, staff phone calls at night. "The kids didn't complain
about the phone calls or us being away, but pretty soon we were
spending less and less time together," recalls Church. Their
younger son, Chase, was tuning out of his school work and,
Church said, "Luckily Bethine saw that we were going to have
to work things around to consider his needs." They got a cabin
in nearby mountains and whenever possible retreated there.
The boys rode Hondas and Church taught them how to skeet
shoot. But, mostly, said Bethine, "It was a place where they
could be together as a family—"before it gets to the point that
you forget what that's like."

Epilogue

Many slogans have sprung up since Watergate, dealing with a
change in politicians and politics. We hear of the "new face of
politics," the "new breed of politician," the "new approach to
politics." Many a 1974 candidate ran on a platform of "relentless honesty," and there is every indication that 1976 contest-
ants will continue this trend.

What all this actually means for government, for politicians
and their families, and for the public remains to be seen. After
all, hokum and façade have been with us since the beginning of
politics. Whether those in government can change or, more
important, *want* a change any deeper than cosmetically prudent
sloganeering is still a question mark.

The public people in this book raised more questions about
American politics than answers, but one point was clearly made
and repeated. A need to alter present-day political priorities
seems crucial to many public people if the quality of their personal lives is to be improved. Not only is it injurious and destructive to those individuals who felt the need to conform to

mythical models as political wives, children, and politicians, but it is also injurious to the political system that such hypocrisy was long the accepted, unquestioned, and "proper" behavior.

Today, in 1975, it seems that a disillusioned public, many of whom scarcely bother to vote, would be more than willing to allow politicians and their families to be themselves—to be as involved or uninvolved in the political folderol as they want to be—if politicians went about the business of doing what they are supposed to be doing, which is to govern.

However, this view is not shared by the bulk of our nationally elected officials who feel the need to give up their weekends and evenings, hustling from one bull roast to the next rubber-chicken banquet, from one fund raiser to the next speech, from one TV commercial to the next hand-pumping reception. For the sobering fact is the politician's time away from home and private life is spent, not so much in legislating as in all the "public relations" trappings of getting elected and staying there. And this public relations, ultimately, not only diminishes one's private life but takes away from the actual working of government. It is, all in all, a pretty silly process.

Even those who consider politics a rewarding life end on a note for change in this area. "I think this public relations business has gone too far," says Bethine Church, wife of Senator Frank Church and herself a self-styled politician. "I don't know how it gets undone, but I think people would have more confidence in us politicians if we could stop the treadmill. It isn't just terrible for a politician's personal life, it is terrible for our government. Eventually you're doing more PR than work."

This PR results in a cascade of pressures and problems—not enough time for the home and family, not enough sense of privacy, not enough sense of self, not enough time for the work these people were supposedly elected to do. It means that politics is not the best arena to attract quieter, dedicated people but draws, instead, the ones who are consummate limelight pursuers.

There are no quick answers for how, in this electronic world and highly personalized style of government, it all gets undone. But it would be nice if politicians made a start in that direction, so that the dehumanizing aspects of politics would be lessened and the "new face of politics" would be something more than just a neatly packaged public relations slogan.

Index

Nixon, Tricia, 130
Nixon administration, 107, 163, 217
Noble, Elaine, 324
Not for Women Only, 133, 141, 150
Novello, Angie, 197

O Congress (Riegle), 275
Olivetti, 44
Onassis, Jackie Kennedy. *See* Kennedy, Jackie
One Foot in Washington (Proxmire), 261
"Open marriage." *See* Marriage
Oswald, Lee Harvey, 372
"Other woman," 47, 274–75, 278–84. *See also* Sex and morals

Packwood, Robert, 197
Pan American Airways, 44
Parade magazine, 61
Party girls. *See* Groupies and teenyboppers
Peabody, Mrs. Endicott, 96
Pearson, Drew, 61, 187, 208
Pegler, Westbrook, 61, 76
Pension regulations bill, 401
Percy, Charles, 86, 223, 401
Percy, Lorraine, 86
Pink Elephant bar, 266
Platt, Thomas, 192
Playboy magazine, 113
Political aides, female, 172, 178–79, 194–99
Political aides, male, 149–71; conflicts with political wives, 109, 197; Teresa Heinz on, 112–13; relationship with politician, 192; and sex, 176–78
Political Education, A (McPherson), 145
Political families, 9–12; exploitation of, 27, 91, 248; and other families, 128–29; Sissy Farenthold on, 353, 360–61; and Fords, 35; masquerade and hypocrisy, 17–20, 30, 76–78, 85–86, 95, 123–24, 127, 432–33; political men and, 145–49, 168, 393; lack of privacy, 128–30, 410; public expectations of, 30, 79, 128–29. *See also* Campaigning and

campaigns; Separations and loneliness; individual politicians
Politicians (male): adulation and public expectations, 20, 58–59, 63–67, 75–76, 79–80, 103–4, 149, 152, 168, 223, 433; ego and insecurity of, 21, 27, 64, 161, 195, 250, 275, 283, 307, 309, 312, 313, 389, 401; family problems, 143–49, 168, 278, 304–5, 360; compared to political husbands, 327; and power, 22, 156, 199, 301, 313; psychological profile, 16–18, 20–23, 26–27; Pat Schroeder on, 346–49; star syndrome, 20, 48, 40–60, 63, 77–78. *See also* Congressmen; Emoluments of office; Narcissism; Political aides, female and male; Sex and morals; Women politicians
Politicians (female). *See* Women politicians
Powell, Adam Clayton, 172, 186, 293, 409
Presidential ambitions, 9, 28, 49, 172, 245; Bayh, 377; Bentsen, 399–400, 405; Chisholm, 333; Church, 425; Harris, 418–19; Kennedy, 67–70, 400; McCarthy, 246; McGovern, 257
Presidents, character of, 10–11
Press, 18, 59, 79; and Alioto affair, 87–89, 92; Chisholm presidential bid, 333; and Mandel affair, 232–36; and Carrie Lee Nelson, 107, 382; "news theater," 61; and Pat Nixon, 84–86; and politicians, 10, 11, 41; and political families, 76, 81–85, 95, 251; and reporting political sex stories, 181–83, 189; Margaret Trudeau on, 74–75
Privacy and publicity, 11, 40, 309, 315; and political children, 137; Congressmen and, 59–65; E. McCarthy on, 247, 249; in political life, 126, 128–30, 289, 409; and W. Proxmire, 256
Private Faces—Public Places (McCarthy), 244
Proxmire, Cici, 259

E
840.6   MacPherson, Myra.
M17   The power lovers : an intimate look at politics and marriage
        / Myra MacPherson. — New York : Putnam, c1975.
            446 p. ; 23 cm.
            ISBN 0-399-11495-5 : $10.00

            1. Statesmen's families—United States.   2. Statesmen's wives—United
        States.   I. Title. 3.United States-Politics and govern-
        ment,
308041 E840.6.M33   1975   329'.00973   75-18581
                                                                  MARC

            Library of Congress   75